Deleuze and the Problem of Affect

Plateaus – New Directions in Deleuze Studies

'It's not a matter of bringing all sorts of things together under a single concept but rather of relating each concept to variables that explain its mutations.'
Gilles Deleuze, *Negotiations*

Titles available in the series
Christian Kerslake, *Immanence and the Vertigo of Philosophy: From Kant to Deleuze*
Jean-Clet Martin, *Variations: The Philosophy of Gilles Deleuze*, translated by Constantin V. Boundas and Susan Dyrkton
Simone Bignall, *Postcolonial Agency: Critique and Constructivism*
Miguel de Beistegui, *Immanence – Deleuze and Philosophy*
Jean-Jacques Lecercle, *Badiou and Deleuze Read Literature*
Ronald Bogue, *Deleuzian Fabulation and the Scars of History*
Sean Bowden, *The Priority of Events: Deleuze's Logic of Sense*
Craig Lundy, *History and Becoming: Deleuze's Philosophy of Creativity*
Aidan Tynan, *Deleuze's Literary Clinic: Criticism and the Politics of Symptoms*
Thomas Nail, *Returning to Revolution: Deleuze, Guattari and Zapatismo*
François Zourabichvili, *Deleuze: A Philosophy of the Event* with *The Vocabulary of Deleuze*, edited by Gregg Lambert and Daniel W. Smith, translated by Kieran Aarons
Frida Beckman, *Between Desire and Pleasure: A Deleuzian Theory of Sexuality*
Nadine Boljkovac, *Untimely Affects: Gilles Deleuze and an Ethics of Cinema*
Daniela Voss, *Conditions of Thought: Deleuze and Transcendental Ideas*
Daniel Barber, *Deleuze and the Naming of God: Post-Secularism and the Future of Immanence*
F. LeRon Shults, *Iconoclastic Theology: Gilles Deleuze and the Secretion of Atheism*
Janae Sholtz, *The Invention of a People: Heidegger and Deleuze on Art and the Political*
Marco Altamirano, *Time, Technology and Environment: An Essay on the Philosophy of Nature*
Sean McQueen, *Deleuze and Baudrillard: From Cyberpunk to Biopunk*
Ridvan Askin, *Narrative and Becoming*
Marc Rölli, *Gilles Deleuze's Transcendental Empiricism: From Tradition to Difference*, translated by Peter Hertz-Ohmes
Guillaume Collett, *The Psychoanalysis of Sense: Deleuze and the Lacanian School*
Ryan J. Johnson, *The Deleuze-Lucretius Encounter*
Allan James Thomas, *Deleuze, Cinema and the Thought of the World*
Cheri Lynne Carr, *Deleuze's Kantian Ethos: Critique as a Way of Life*
Alex Tissandier, *Affirming Divergence: Deleuze's Reading of Leibniz*
Barbara Glowczewski, *Indigenising Anthropology with Guattari and Deleuze*
Koichiro Kokubun, *The Principles of Deleuzian Philosophy*, translated by Wren Nishina
Felice Cimatti, *Unbecoming Human: Philosophy of Animality After Deleuze*, translated by Fabio Gironi
Ryan J. Johnson, *Deleuze, A Stoic*
Jane Newland, *Deleuze in Children's Literature*
D. J. S. Cross, *Deleuze and the Problem of Affect*

Forthcoming volumes
Justin Litaker, *Deleuze and Guattari's Political Economy*
Nir Kedem, *A Deleuzian Critique of Queer Thought: Overcoming Sexuality*
Sean Bowden, *Expression, Action and Agency in Deleuze: Willing Events*
Andrew Jampol-Petzinger, *Deleuze, Kierkegaard and the Ethics of Selfhood*

Visit the Plateaus website at edinburghuniversitypress.com/series/plat

DELEUZE AND THE PROBLEM
OF AFFECT

D. J. S. Cross

EDINBURGH
University Press

Edinburgh University Press is one of the leading university presses in the UK. We publish academic books and journals in our selected subject areas across the humanities and social sciences, combining cutting-edge scholarship with high editorial and production values to produce academic works of lasting importance. For more information visit our website: edinburghuniversitypress.com

Edinburgh University Press Ltd
The Tun – Holyrood Road
12(2f) Jackson's Entry
Edinburgh EH8 8PJ

First published in hardback by Edinburgh University Press 2021

Typeset in 11/13 Sabon LT Std by
Servis Filmsetting Ltd, Stockport, Cheshire
and printed and bound by CPI Group (UK) Ltd, Croydon, CR0 4YY

A CIP record for this book is available from the British Library

ISBN 978 1 4744 8554 8 (hardback)
ISBN 978 1 4744 8555 5 (paperback)
ISBN 978 1 4744 8557 9 (webready PDF)
ISBN 978 1 4744 8556 2 (epub)

Contents

Acknowledgements

I thank first of all Chile's Fondo Nacional de Desarrollo Científico y Tecnológico (FONDECYT) for a generous postdoctoral fellowship (project #3170349), without which I couldn't have finished this project so soon.

This book passed through many generous hands at Edinburgh University Press. I greatly appreciate Ian Buchanan and Claire Colebrook's support for the manuscript throughout the review process that ultimately led to its inclusion in their series. Carol Macdonald's energy and responsiveness, from beginning to end, would have surpassed expectations of a commissioning editor even under normal circumstances. Tim Clark's careful attention to the manuscript proved that the dividing line between copy editor and reader is porous at best, and I appreciate his push on the question of Spinoza's anthropocentrism in Chapter 5.

With the title 'Deleuze and the Order of Faculties', I presented an early draft of Chapter 1 at the Segundas Jornadas Postdoctoral e Iniciación de Filosofía, held at the Pontifica Universidad Católica de Chile in Santiago (21–23 June 2017). I thank José Luis Liñán, José Antonio Gimenez and Sebastián Sanhueza Rodríguez for organising the event and encouraging me to participate even though I'd only recently arrived in Santiago. Their encouragement was only the earliest instance of their enduring hospitality.

An earlier and abridged version of Chapter 2 was published as 'Furtive Contemplations: Self, Time, and Affect in Deleuze' in a special issue of *CR: The New Centennial Review* on subjectivity (17.2). I thank Juan Manuel Garrido for his invitation to contribute and the *CR* for the right to republish a revised version here.

The first two sections of Chapter 3 were published in *Deleuze and Guattari Studies* as 'Euthanasia: Affect between Art and Opinion in What Is Philosophy?' (14.2). I thank Ian Buchanan and David Savat for publishing the piece and the journal for the right to republish it here.

I presented a small portion of Chapter 4 – with the same title – at

Acknowledgements

the first international conference organised by the Red de Estudios Latinoamericanos Deleuze & Guattari. The conference took place 12–13 November 2018 in Valparaíso, Chile. I thank Patricio Landaeta for the chance to participate. His efforts to rectify the discrepancy in Chile between the interest in Deleuze and Guattari's work and the institutional support for it have been invaluable.

I first presented part of Chapter 5 in Spanish as 'Ritmos del ser y la antinomia del afecto: sobre Spinoza y Deleuze' at *Cuerpos espacios movimientos. Entre arquitectura, filosofía y danza* on 13 December 2018 at the Pontificia Universidad Católica in Santiago, Chile. The subtitle for the day of my panel, to which I obliquely refer in the text, was *Cuerpos en movimiento* ('Bodies in Movement'). Along with other presentations from the conference, the text appeared in a special edition of the Chilean journal *Resonancias. Revista de Filosofía* (10). I thank Paula Cucurella for her *corrección del estilo* and, more generally, for her generous friendship over the years. I also thank Andrea Potestà not only for organising the conference and inviting me to participate but also, of course, for sponsoring my postdoctoral project in Chile. I minutely revised and immensely expanded the Spanish version of this chapter upon translating it into English for this book.

My debt to Rodolphe Gasché has many origins but no end. His seminar on 'geophilosophy' at the State University of New York at Buffalo in the spring of 2012 first exposed me systematically to Deleuze and Guattari. While *Geophilosophy: On Gilles Deleuze and Félix Guattari's* What Is Philosophy? (Northwestern 2014) has been formative for my relation to Deleuze and Guattari's work, my debt remains legible well beyond one work or even one corpus.

David E. Johnson's friendship and guidance are constants on which I've come to rely over the course of the past decade. In some of this book's arguments, Ajitpaul Mangat will no doubt recognise nodes from our many conversations about Deleuze; I'm grateful that he always insists upon greater clarity and relevance. I also thank Tyler Williams for his collaborations, if not on this project, on too many others to cram here.

I'm indebted to all the students in the Departamento de Filosofía at the Universidad Alberto Hurtado who attended my seminar on 'Deleuze y el afecto' in the Chilean spring of 2018. I generated a large part of the material for the second part of this book in the seminar, and it benefited greatly from their patience, questions and creative responses. I thank Samuel Yañez Artus for the invitation to teach the seminar.

ACKNOWLEDGEMENTS

In the spring of 2015, the Philosophical Reading Group at SUNY Buffalo read *Difference and Repetition*. In that context, I first worked out some of the basic problems presented in the first two chapters. I'm always grateful for the rigour and responsibility that a dedicated reading group demands.

Finally, I thank my parents, Donald A. and Susan E. Cross. Not only have they tolerated too many books in their basement for too many years now; my mother never hesitated to wade through boxes and foreign languages in search of a reference I didn't anticipate needing for this project or others. They've always made this uncontainable and untranslatable support their norm. 'Life just goes too fast sometimes and it's hard to keep.'

Abbreviations

Of Deleuze, Deleuze and Guattari, or any other author, all double citations refer to the original first and second, wherever available, to the English translation. For any text with standardised citations (for instance, Kant's *Critiques*), I don't give dual citations but include the relevant works in the bibliography. For German citations of Nietzsche (KSA: *Kritische Studienausgabe*), Freud (GW: *Gesammelte Werke*) and Heidegger (GA: *Gesamtausgabe*), I cite the collected works followed by the volume and either the page number or, when clear and relevant in the case of Nietzsche, the aphorism number. With respect to Spinoza, in particular, I cite the *Ethics* by part and proposition but every other work by volume and page number of the *Collected Works* (in which Curley gives marginal references to the Gebhardt edition). With the exception of the *Essays*, for which I give page numbers, I also follow convention when citing David Hume's works by book (in the case of *A Treatise of Human Nature*), part, section and paragraph. I regularly modify translations of Deleuze and Deleuze and Guattari and therefore don't draw attention to the modifications unless they bear directly upon my argument. In certain cases, this includes titles themselves. For instance, I don't see any justification for Martin Joughin's translation of *Spinoza et le problème de l'expression* as *Expressionism in Philosophy: Spinoza*. On the contrary, it eclipses expressionism as a *problem* and presents it as if it were a notion *in* philosophy rather than the culmination of philosophy itself (at least as Deleuze defines it). Similarly, the translation of *Critique et clinique* as *Essays Critical and Clinical* risks restricting the notions of the 'critical' and the 'clinical' to a textuality that Deleuze always takes for one gear in a much larger machine. Beyond citations of Deleuze with and without Guattari, I indicate whenever I modify the translation of any other work. I myself translate all works without a corresponding English reference.

AŒ   *Capitalisme et schizophrénie 1. L'Anti-Œdipe*. Paris: Minuit, 1972.

Capitalism and Schizophrenia: Anti-Oedipus. Trans. Robert Hurley, Mark Seem and Helen R. Lane. Minneapolis: University of Minnesota Press, 1983.

B   *Le bergsonisme*. Paris: Presses Universitaires de France, 1964.
      Bergsonism. Trans. Hugh Tomlinson and Barbara Habberjam. New York: Zone Books, 1991.

CC   *Critique et clinique*. Paris: Minuit, 1993.
      Essays Critical and Clinical. Trans. Daniel W. Smith and Michael A. Greco. Minneapolis: University of Minnesota Press, 1997.

CS   *Cours sur Spinoza*. Available online at *La voix de Deleuze*, http://www2.univ-paris8.fr/deleuze.

D   *Dialogues*. Paris: Flammarion, 1996.
      Dialogues II. Trans. Hugh Tomlinson and Barbara Habberjam. New York: Columbia University Press, 2007.

DR   *Différence et répétition*. Paris: Presses Universitaires de France, 1968.
      Difference and Repetition. Trans. Paul Patton. New York: Continuum, 1994.

DRF   *Deux régimes de fou. Textes et entretiens 1975–1995*. Ed. David Lapoujade. Paris: Minuit, 2003.
      Two Regimes of Madness: Texts and Interviews 1975–1995. Ed. David Lapoujade. Trans. Ames Hodges and Mike Taormina. New York: Semiotext(e), 2007.

ES   *Empirisme et subjectivité. Essai sur la nature humaine selon Hume*. Paris: Presses Universitaires de France, 1953.
      Empiricism and Subjectivity: An Essay on Hume's Theory of Human Nature. Trans. Constantin V. Boundas. New York: Columbia University Press, 1991.

FB   *Francis Bacon. Logique de la sensation*. Paris: Seuil, 2002.
      Francis Bacon: The Logic of Sensation. Trans. Daniel W. Smith. New York: Continuum, 2003.

ID   *L'île déserte. Textes et entretiens 1953–1974*. Ed. David Lapoujade. Paris: Minuit, 2002.
      Desert Islands and Other Texts: 1953–1974. Ed. David Lapoujade. Trans. Mike Taormina. New York: Semiotext(e), 2004.

K   *Kafka. Pour une littérature mineure*. Paris: Minuit, 1975.
      Kafka: Toward a Minor Literature. Trans. Dana Polan. Minneapolis: University of Minnesota Press, 1986.

L   *Lettres et autres textes*. Ed. David Lapoujade. Paris: Minuit, 2015.

Deleuze, Gilles. *Letters and Other Texts*. Ed. David Lapoujade. Trans. Ames Hodges. New York: Semiotext(e), 2020.

LS   *Logique du sens*. Paris: Minuit, 1969.

Logic of Sense. Trans. Mark Lester. London: Athlone Press, 1990.

MP   *Capitalisme et schizophrénie 2. Mille plateaux*. Paris: Minuit, 1980.

Capitalism and Schizophrenia 2: A Thousand Plateaus. Trans. Brian Massumi. Minneapolis: University of Minneapolis Press, 1987.

NP   *Nietzsche et la philosophie*. Paris: Presses Universitaires de France, 1962.

Nietzsche and Philosophy. Trans. Hugh Tomlinson. New York: Continuum, 1986.

P   *Pourparlers. 1972–1990*. Paris: Minuit, 1990.

Negotiations: 1972–1990. Trans. Martin Joughin. New York: Columbia University Press, 1995.

PCK   *La philosophie critique de Kant*. Paris: Presses Universitaires de France, 1963.

Kant's Critical Philosophy. Trans. Hugh Tomlinson and Barbara Habberjam. London: Athlone Press, 1984.

PS   *Proust et les signes*. Paris: Presses Universitaires de France, 1964.

Proust and Signs. Trans. Richard Howard. Minneapolis: University of Minnesota Press, 2000.

PSM   *Présentation de Sacher-Masoch. Le froid et le cruel*. Paris: Minuit, 1967.

Coldness and Cruelty. Trans. Jean McNeil. In *Masochism*. New York: Zone Books, 1991, pp. 7–138.

QP   *Qu'est-ce que la philosophie ?* Paris: Minuit, 1991.

What Is Philosophy? Trans. Hugh Tomlinson and Graham Burchell. New York: Columbia University Press, 1994.

R   *Rhizome. Introduction*. Paris: Minuit, 1976.

SPE   *Spinoza et le problème de l'expression*. Paris: Minuit, 1968.

Expressionism in Philosophy: Spinoza. Trans. Martin Joughin. New York: Zone Books, 1992.

SPP   *Spinoza. Philosophie pratique*. Paris: Minuit, 1981.

Spinoza: Practical Philosophy. Trans. Robert Hurley. San Francisco: City Lights Books, 1988.

Les philosophes apportent de nouveaux concepts, ils les exposent, mais ils ne disent pas, ou pas complètement les problèmes auxquels ces concepts répondent. [. . .] L'histoire de la philosophie doit, non pas redire ce que dit un philosophe, mais dire ce qu'il sous-entendait nécessairement, ce qu'il ne disait pas et qui est pourtant présent dans ce qu'il dit.

Deleuze, Interview with *Magazine littéraire* (September 1988)

Introduction

C'est l'humour, en tant qu'art des quantités intensives, qui joue de l'individu et des facteurs individuants.

Deleuze (DR 317|246)

Adermatoglyphia

Gilles Deleuze's friends never asked about his extraordinarily long fingernails. Secretly, anecdotally but not simply biographically, they perhaps bear the whole problem of affect.

Deleuze seemed to suffer from adermatoglyphia. Like the name suggests, the condition consists in an absence (*a*) of carvings (*glyphia*) on the skin (*derma*), that is, the whorls, loops and arches more commonly known as a fingerprint. Filled with nerve endings, these 'skin carvings' heighten sensitivity in fingertips because they increase friction when fingers glide over a surface. In 1943, in the first comprehensive treatise on dermatoglyphics, Harold Cummins and Charles Midlo write:

> Abundant nerve endings in the skin of the palmar and plantar surfaces serve the sense of touch. Their functioning is aided by corrugation of the skin. In testing the texture of a surface, the fingers or palm are rubbed back and forth over it. The drag against the ridges heightens the intensity of stimulation of the nerve endings. (Cummins and Midlo 23)

Fingers seem so well equipped to feel that, a century prior to Cummins and Midlo, Charles Bell argued that hands evidence an intelligent author in *The Hand, Its Mechanism and Vital Endowments as Evincing Design*. As if no one could touch anything without also touching upon the existence of God. Something of a heretical exception, however, the absence of ridges doesn't decrease Deleuze's sensitivity, as a dermato-glyphist might expect, but rather heightens it to an almost unbearable point. He kept his fingernails long so as to deaden the sensation:

> looking at the extremity of my fingers, I am missing the usually protective fingerprints [*empreintes digitales ordinairement protectrices*], such that

1

touching an object and above all a fabric with the tip of my fingers gives me a nervous pain that requires the protection of long fingernails. (P 13|5)

To say Deleuze's fingernails bear the whole problem of affect isn't to say affect in Deleuze's work can be traced back to the tips of his fingers. While the effort to exhaust an oeuvre in a biography is always reductive, it would be particularly violent in the case of an author whose oeuvre often criticises the biographical approach. Deleuze levels this critique most acutely in *Logic of Sense* because, while rejecting biography's explanatory force, he nevertheless incorporates anecdotes from an author's life as part of an author's work. Finding its beginnings in Diogenes Laertius and its systematisation in Nietzsche, Deleuze posits a method that seeks out the 'secret point' where anecdote and aphorism intermingle, where anecdote becomes an anecdote of thought, where aphorism becomes an aphorism of life: 'one must satisfy oneself with neither biography nor bibliography; one must reach a secret point where an anecdote of life and an aphorism of thought are the same thing' (LS 153|128). Deleuze would go on to apply the method not only to the Stoics, in dialogue with whom he broaches the method in *Logic of Sense*, but also to Nietzsche himself, as well as Spinoza, Kant and other interlocutors. I'll broach some of these 'vital anecdotes' in due time. For now, I only insist that, if the method applies to all philosophers, it also applies to Deleuze.

Michel Cressole studied with Deleuze at Vincennes. He wanted to write a book on Deleuze but turned bitter, so the story goes, when Deleuze refused to support the project. In a scathing letter appended (along with Deleuze's reply) to the book he wrote anyway, Cressole accuses Deleuze of chasing stardom, and he refers to Deleuze's extraordinarily long fingernails – twice – as a desperate ruse to stand out. Mocking the celebrity Deleuze won with *Anti-Oedipus* in particular, Cressole writes: 'Your black worker's coat is already the equivalent of Marilyn Monroe's pink dress with a pleated bodice and your long fingernails, Garbo's dark glasses' (Cressole 105; see also 104). Humouring him in reply, Deleuze accuses Cressole of choosing the basest or meanest interpretations possible and offers four alternatives. My reflections here about Deleuze's adermatoglyphia stem from the 'teratological and selectionist interpretation'.[1]

Neither Cressole nor Deleuze recalls that early philosophers had notoriously long fingernails, 'like the claws of wild animals', as Tatian says in his *Oratio ad Graecos* (Dobbin 53). If something nevertheless singularises Deleuze's fingernails, one must distinguish between types of singularity. More or less implicitly, indeed, Deleuze distinguishes the narcissistic singularity in Cressole's diatribe from the idea of constitutive singularity implemented in his own philosophy. The first singularity celebrates personality; the second enters into a multiplicity with other singularities that not only precede but also disrupt personality and personhood in general. In his impersonal multiplicity, in his 'Letter to a Harsh Critic', Deleuze includes his fingernails: 'One has become a set of loose singularities, last names, first names, fingernails, things, animals, little events: the opposite of a star [*vedette*]' (P 16|7). In a sense, however, even when he includes them in his more originary multiplicity, Deleuze doesn't do justice to his fingernails. More than *a* singularity in *a* multiplicity, Deleuze's fingernails in a sense touch upon the anonymity of all singularities. Because every fingerprint is unique and doesn't fundamentally change throughout an individual's life, for more than a century they have provided an official means of personal identification, catalogue and – above all – control. If, however, fingernails conceal a smooth space with no skin carvings and thus no personalisation, *every* depersonalising singularisation removes my prints, blurs my patterns, flattens the whorls, loops and arches that identify me as an individual person. This would perhaps be the place to juxtapose, on the one hand, Deleuze's association of multiplicity with schizophrenia and, on the other, the clinical research on decreased intensity in dermatoglyphic patterns in schizophrenic patients.[2]

If, however, Deleuze's universal because featureless fingertips mark a 'secret point' where anecdote and aphorism communicate, they do so at least twice. Not only because they mark – by erasure – a certain universalisation, as I just suggested, but also because this universalisation, this depersonalisation, is unbearable. The threshold of bearability obsesses Deleuze's work. Schizophrenic affect in the culminating synthesis of the unconscious in *Anti-Oedipus*, for instance, takes place 'at an almost unbearable point' (AŒ 27|18). Or again, in his *Presentation of Sacher-Masoch*, Deleuze paradigmatically shifts the super-sensible into the super-sensual (PSM 21|21). At a point more secret still, however, the almost unbearable pitch of sensation also leads Deleuze – this is why he grows his fingernails – to deaden his own super-sensuality. Deleuze suffered upon touching or touching upon any object (at this point I'm speaking about both his fingers and his philosophy) because the problem ultimately lies in an ineradicable sensibility. This dynamic between heightened sensitivity and the drive to reduce it, this secret point where the life and work of Gilles Deleuze touch excruciatingly, I call ambivalence.

The 'Problem' of 'Affect'

Both terms in this book's title – *problem* and *affect* – call for prefatory clarification.

Problem. The term requires particular attention because, albeit not entirely without precedents like – but not only – Kant's problematic approach to Ideas (DR 218 ff.|168 ff.), Deleuze fundamentally redefines it. His problem is no longer a moment of subjective, privative or provisional ignorance overcome on the path toward a greater body of knowledge with fewer problems to resolve in turn. Even in psychoanalysis, even where consciousness no longer reigns, even Freud doesn't hesitate to equate solution (*Lösung*) with dissolution (*Auflösung*) in the fundamental *Interpretation of Dreams* (GW II/III:104–5|125). So, it would already go against the grain to think that only a problem without a solution would merit the name. Deleuze, however, says something more paradoxical still: a problem has infinite possible solutions without ceasing to be problematic. For a problem, for Deleuze, refers to an ideal distribution of singularities that condition the genesis of 'solutions' in an actual state of affairs. So, far from a belated obstacle, a problem is an originary force. Now, solutions often retroactively veil problems, cloud and obscure them, hide their originary nature. This even explains the longstanding misconception of a problem as a resolvable and therefore provisional issue. Of a different order, however, solutions never dissolve a problem entirely, and signs of it persist even in the most resolute solution. One must remain sensitive, then, to a certain inversion in the relation between solution and problem: whereas solutions (not problems) hinder thought, problems (not solutions) force thought.[3]

To be sure, affect poses a problem *in* Deleuze's philosophy. For reasons at stake in Chapter 1 below, affect even poses the first problem, which gives it a role unthinkable in the ascetic tradition of philosophy. For the same reason, however, the 'problem' to which my title refers – the problem of affect – accounts for but differs from the problem as Deleuze redefines it: from its privileged position, affect also poses a problem *for* philosophy, and *this* problem problematises the process and even the possibility of *that* problem. In short, the problem that titles this book never entirely yields to the Deleuzian sense because, without relapsing into a pre-Deleuzian acceptation, the problem of affect poses the problem of problems (or even, at the risk of belabouring my syntax, the problem of the problem of problems insofar as Deleuze's 'problem' already problematises the 'problem' in the traditional sense).

Affect. As a referent, affect has many names and, as a name, 'affect' has many referents. Critics and theorists regularly preface any sort of totalising gesture by asserting that there is no single definition of 'affect' and, correlatively, no continuous contour surrounding a unified field of 'affect theory'. Understandably, the gesture is especially common at the beginning of special issues, edited volumes and genealogies.

- 'There is of course no single definition of affect theory' (Figlerowicz 3).

- 'There is no single, generalizable theory of affect: not yet, and (thankfully) there never will be' (Siegworth and Gregg 3).

- 'Affect theory, as scholars such as Sara Ahmed, Eugenie Brinkema, Mel Y. Chen, Ann Cvetkovich, Eve Sedgwick, Greg Seigworth, and Melissa Gregg have pointed out, tracks into divergent, and perhaps incommensurable, definitions' (Schaefer 1).

Which doesn't prevent critics and theorists from dividing the field into two: two lineages, two concepts. On the one hand, 'affect' as emotion, lived experience, subjective feeling accessible to consciousness. On the other, 'affect' as an often physiological but always pre-psychological, impersonal, non- or never fully intentional event. Emotion and affect, Brian Massumi announces in a text considered a cornerstone of contemporary affect theory, 'follow different logics and pertain to different orders' (Massumi, *Parables* 27). The terms and their interrelations vary, of course, but the impersonal understanding of affect traces back to Deleuze, if at times only implicitly through what Donovan Schaefer calls the 'Deleuzian dialect'.[4] Even when critics or theorists reclaim Spinoza, Deleuze creates the Spinoza they reclaim in ways at which I'll hint in this introduction and, in Part II below, address in painstaking detail.

Hence, however variegated the field may be and although he himself never speaks of it as such, Deleuze supports an immeasurable half of 'affect theory'. But this schematic division between 'affect' (as emotional experience) and 'affect' (as intense event) often ignores Deleuze's own thought and lexicon in at least three ways.

First, far from opposing them, Deleuze uses the terms 'affect' and 'emotion' synonymously in, for instance, *Anti-Oedipus* (AŒ 27|18 and 104|84) and *Logic of Sensation* (FB 44|39 and 48|45). Nor is the synonymy reserved for 'affect' and 'emotion'. In fact, Deleuze often refers to the same affective apparatus with an array of interchangeable terms that vary according to both the work and the argument at hand: 'sentiendum', 'intensity', 'sensation', 'feeling' and so on. While Deleuze always conceives the apparatus of 'contemplation' in association with the production of an originary or primordial sensation, for instance, in *Difference and Repetition* he calls 'primary sensibilities' that which – still as a function of contemplation – he and Guattari call 'affect' in *What Is Philosophy?* (see Chapter 2 below for the full progression). The tendency to restrict this terminological variety to 'affect', accordingly, will call for justification.

A wider lexicon, at the same time, doesn't necessarily homogenise all levels of affect according to Deleuze. On the contrary, the schematic division between subjective emotion and Deleuzian affect – this is its second limit – suggests that there's no correlate of 'emotion', 'feeling' or 'lived experience' in Deleuze. Or at least none to speak of. A proponent of 'purity' in general and 'pure' intensity in particular, Deleuze isn't entirely innocent with regard to propagating this presumption. Nevertheless, he consistently distinguishes between tiers or dimensions of affect and, while the relation between tiers might vary from one work to the next, his theory consistently takes into account both divides of a division that would relegate him to only one side. In *What Is Philosophy?*, for instance, Deleuze and Guattari distinguish between 'affect' and 'affection' and, while they clearly privilege the former over the latter, affects must be drawn or extracted from affections, which therefore have a fundamental place in their theory. Analogous arguments also hold for the distinction between the empirical exercise of sensibility and the paradoxical exercise in *Difference and Repetition*, feeling and affect in *Logic of Sensation*, so on and so forth. More than mere figure, in this literal synecdoche, part of the field contains it all.

Third, 'affect' itself isn't a stable or univocal term throughout Deleuze. Homonymy, put simply, is not synonymy. Continuities traverse Deleuze's work, as I'll establish already in the first chapter below, but one can outline these continuities only by remaining sensitive to shifts in lexicon that don't necessarily correspond to a shift in terms. While 'affect' consummates the materialist psychiatry of *Anti-Oedipus* (see my Conclusion below), for instance, 'affect' in *What Is Philosophy?* operates one of the most brutal disembodiments in the history of philosophy (see Chapter 5 below). Such variations would even seem to paralyse any project in advance that would speak with self-assurance of 'affect according to Deleuze', in praise or in scorn, as if it were one term in his work from beginning to end.

Clearly, then, I won't proceed indexically, literally, by following every instance of the word 'affect' in Deleuze's work. Literality doesn't guarantee conceptuality. At times, the word 'affect' isn't thematically relevant (which, of course, can prove symptomatic in its own right and thus relevant in its very irrelevance). At times, Deleuze gives 'affect' another name. At times, 'affect' goes unnamed but remains operative in the logic of the argument. Only by loosening the name, without neglecting it, can one do justice to what it tries to name. But, then, why privilege 'affect' to the detriment of every other possible term?

Apart from a brief reference to intensity as the perversion of *le bon sens* (Foucault 898), affect doesn't constitute one of the 'access roads' that Michel Foucault takes to reach the heart of Deleuze's oeuvre. Nevertheless, if a Deleuzian century is still in the air, it hovers in no small part thanks to the field of affect theory in which, perhaps, Deleuze's has had his greatest impact.[5] Accordingly, I speak of 'affect' strategically. The term keeps my chapters generally conversant with affect theory even when, immersed in Deleuze, they don't address 'affect theory' or 'theorists' in a strict sense (if, indeed, there is one). Consequently, if I were to argue that the champion of affect treats affect with ambivalence, not only Deleuze's theory of affect would be at stake. Not even only his whole philosophy. The ambivalence would also send a seism through every proposition, every work, every theory of affect more or less securely, openly or willingly stratified upon it. To have situated the analyses comprising this book under the heading of 'sensibility' or 'emotion' or 'intensity' would have risked obscuring, if not altogether losing, the affective stratigraphy in which they intervene.

As such or in itself, however, affect theory isn't my primary concern. Not interested in the theory so much as what it can explain culturally, socially and politically, an affect theorist might say the same. But I'm not interested in 'applying' Deleuze either. Still less in assessing and comparing applications. On occasion I'll point out uses and abuses, insights and oversights, but my interests lie elsewhere. Before Deleuze and Guattari's work can be applied to, identified with or in any way affirmed in any issue anywhere, before we begin deterritorialising or stuttering, we ought to know – to whatever extent possible – what we're applying, identifying or affirming. The most astute and useful work on Deleuze today bears witness to the fact that this preliminary task is far from achieved. At the risk of appearing inapplicable, contingent and perhaps irrelevant, 'scholarly' in a pejorative sense, I focus first and foremost on the role of affect in Deleuze's work. Only this perspective allows me to gauge, in turn, any novelty or complicity of Deleuze's affect with regard to the ascetic tradition.

Ambivalence

I borrow this term – 'ascetic' – from Nietzsche, who often uses it, for instance in *Twilight of the Idols,* to describe the effort to eradicate the senses, the paradigmatic moment of which Nietzsche finds in the Sermon on the Mount: 'if your eye offends you, pluck it out' (cited in Nietzsche, KSA 6:82|*Twilight* 172). To priestly asceticism, to be sure, Nietzsche opposes another asceticism, *his* asceticism, an *immoralist* asceticism that – in this context – spiritualises the senses rather than eradicates them. From a wider perspective, however, the triumph represented by the passage from one asceticism to the other isn't as great or decisive as Nietzsche's praise suggests. His seamless transition and implicit analogy between *love* (*Liebe*: the spiritualisation rather than the Christian eradication of the senses) and *hostility* (*Feindschaft*: the appreciation rather than the Christian destruction of enemies) suggests that sensibility remains, if not the enemy, at least inimical (6:84|173). Eradicate or spiritualise the senses, repress or deify them, both ultimately aim *to desensitise.* A more sensitive perspective doesn't require purifying feeling of all reference to spirituality, intelligibility or mentality but rather asks why, at the very moment Nietzsche reasserts sensibility (in this respect, recalling lessons from Heidegger, not one example among others in the history of philosophy), he should also debase and abandon it. The inseparability of positive and negative valences with regard to sensibility, in its most general formulation, I call *ambivalence.*

Not merely affect, then, but Deleuze's ambivalent treatment of affect constitutes this book's most general object. With all the caveats I've already rehearsed, more precisely, this ambivalence is the problem of affect. At work and at stake throughout Deleuze's writings, with and without Guattari, its contours and scope will only become clear cumulatively in the chapters that follow, but a few opening remarks here can serve to orient the six chapters in which it unfolds. Far from exhaustive, I'll outline four basic traits of ambivalence that conjugate and combine, contract and expand, but always in some measure operate.

(1) PURE

In *Francis Bacon: Logic of Sensation*, Deleuze himself outright rejects ambivalence. Bacon creates affects on canvas, but affects are never simple. Each affect or, as Deleuze most often says in this context, each sensation engages multiple levels, and this 'irreducibly synthetic character' (FB 42|37) might lead one to think ambivalence a suitable concept with which to define or at least a relevant concept with which to discuss sensation. Drawing on Bacon's own refusal to blend 'love' and 'hostility' in paint (Bacon and Sylvester 43), Deleuze cites two problems with the hypothesis of ambivalence, which he attributes to psychoanalysis. Two problems or, more keenly, two versions of one and the same problem. Ambivalence locates the sensation, namely, *either* in the spectator with regard to the figure in the painting *or* in the figure with regard to something else in the painting. Either I feel ambivalence regarding *Two Figures Lying on a Bed with Attendants*, or the 'attendants' on the periphery panels of the triptych feel ambivalence regarding the two figures lying on the bed in the centre panel. Whether in the spectator or in the painting, however, both cases rely upon the representation of an object. Ambivalence, then, seems to complicate the mechanism of feeling by sustaining incompatible feelings toward one and the same object, but it still functions within the regime of representation, figuration and narrative that Bacon's work disrupts precisely by creating sensations. Here, as if to punctuate his opposition to ambivalence and the facile feelings that comprise it, Deleuze uses the noun 'affect' for the first and only time in the *Logic of Sensation*: 'Yet, there are no feelings [*sentiments*] in Bacon: nothing but affects [*affects*]' (FB 44|39).

So, as he so often does, Deleuze distinguishes between *sensation* and *sensation*. Whereas sensation *as feeling* refers to the effects of an object on my mind or body, even if at times multiple, sensation *as affect* runs deeper because it pertains to cosmic and otherwise imperceptible forces like time and gravity bearing upon the body immediately, that is, without mediation through representation or the idea of an object. These cosmic forces give Bacon's affect its synthetic – but not ambivalent – character insofar as they exceed the sensation of any given domain but, by traversing all domains at once, relate each to every other. When a synthetic and synesthetic force invests the visual domain in particular, Deleuze says, it appears as painting (FB 46|42). A decade later, in *What Is Philosophy?*, Deleuze once again rejects the psychoanalytic notion of ambivalence in the name of more fundamental affects. This time, however, the rejection holds not only for Bacon's paintings, not only for painting in general, but also for art as the discipline that creates affects (QP 175|174). I'll return to this definition often in the chapters that follow.

So, contrary to the very nature of affect, contrary to Deleuze and to Bacon, contrary to painting, art and the nonrepresentational nature of creation in general, by what right do I still speak of ambivalence and, more audaciously still, invoke it to consolidate Deleuze's entire oeuvre? The point, first of all, isn't to defend psychoanalysis. Not simply in any case. The psychoanalytical hypothesis of ambivalence is much more complex than Deleuze grants but, when the time comes (in Chapter 6 below), I'll mark the limit that Freud's notion of ambivalence shares with the history of philosophy. Far from denying the limit that Deleuze attributes to ambivalence psychoanalytic or otherwise, I harden it, add other limits and argue that these also limit the tradition at large. And yet, I still speak of 'ambivalence' because neither psychoanalysis nor philosophy exhausts its resources. Rather than 'mixed feelings' toward this or that object, even if one takes 'object' in the widest possible sense, a deeper and more problematic ambivalence bears upon affect itself. A Kantian inspiration but not strictly formal, I call this ambivalence *pure*, accordingly, because it has no object other than affect.[6] Because it unfolds before anything feels *either* ambivalent *or* univalent, there's ambivalence wherever there's feeling. Affect is ambivalent, in short, even when it isn't. This ambivalence, pure and prior, Deleuze neither escapes nor embraces.

Indeed, it even operates Deleuze's very rejection of ambivalence in the *Logic of Sensation*. Deleuze distinguishes between sensation and sensation, between the 'feeling' he rejects and the 'affect' he affirms, and counts ambivalence strictly among the former. If one takes a general affectability as the conglomerate of both sensations, however, a pure ambivalence appears precisely insofar as Deleuze *negates* one to *posit* the other. This general perspective raises a whole series of questions. Why must the logic of sensation include a sensation that it opposes? Are these two affective regimes ever in fact separate or in principle separable? Why else would they merit the same name? When Deleuze does give them different names, like *le sentiment* and *l'affect*, why do both names cleave to the same semantic spectrum? Why else, indeed, would Deleuze at times slip from one to the other? If each is truly independent of the other, a more direct question, then why does representational sensation 'threaten' and 'endanger' cosmic sensation throughout the *Logic of Sensation*? What, finally, separates Deleuze's rejection of feeling – at least feeling in one sense – from the long tradition of philosophical asceticism running from Plato through Descartes to Husserl and even Heidegger?

These questions hold for works well beyond Deleuze's book on Bacon and, in each instance, demand different formulations and different answers. To remain with *Logic of Sensation*, since I've given it a general value here by way of introduction, Deleuze recognises that even in a strict sense, even in the sense he affirms, 'sensation' still needs some form of representation or figuration. If Bacon still paints figures, whether Pope Innocent X or himself, he does so for the sake of sensation: whereas abstract art loses all sensation to geometric forms, abstract expressionism confuses all sensation in pure chaos (FB 102|109). The scandal, of course, is that Deleuze rejects 'sensation' as *sentiment* – along with ambivalence – precisely because it relies upon representation, which is to say, figuration. So, in his attempt to negotiate the prescription and the proscription of figuration, which is also his attempt to divide sensation from sensation, Deleuze distinguishes the *figural* from the *figurative*, *primary* figuration from *secondary* figuration, the *Figure* from *figuration* (FB 92|97–8). Only a patient analysis beyond the scope of an introduction could do justice to this distinction and Deleuze's reliance upon Bacon's practice of 'manual marks' to ratify it. I'll limit myself to noting that, according to Deleuze himself, the distinction between the figural and the figurative is 'interior' and thus always already compromised (FB 91|97). Yet, since the distinction between the figural and the figurative supports the distinction between affect and feeling, between *figural* sensation and *figurative* sensation, the compromise of one distinction also compromises the other. This contagion, in turn, invites a general perspective from which 'affect' and 'feeling' no longer oppose, as critics assume (e.g., Bertelson and Murphie 148), but rather mutually implicate each other, each passing into the other in a passion of passions. In light of this more general perspective, a matrix charged with both positive and negative valences, Deleuze's treatment of sensation appears ambivalent in a new sense.

(II) IRREDUCIBLE

The stakes thus begin to focus. For Deleuze has reason to treat affect with ambivalence. It both *promises* and *threatens* his system, philosophy and art, thought – in short – as Deleuze defines it.

Not without a certain calculation, my formulation seems to detract from any novelty I might attribute to ambivalence. In their introduction to *The Affect Theory Reader*, Melissa Gregg and Gregory Seigworth proclaim that the question concerning whether affect is a promise or a threat constitutes 'one of the most pressing' in affect theory (Gregg and Seigworth 10). Gregg and Seigworth refer to Lauren Berlant in particular, since her work, an extract of which they include in their *Reader*, shows that affect often entangles promises and threats. The explanatory force of her concept 'cruel optimism', indeed, shouldn't be underestimated. It explains how I might remain attached to a fantasy of the good life that not only prevents me from flourishing but also, more cruelly still, prevents me flourishing in precisely the way that my fantasy promises. Compiling its name from this simultaneously *promising* and *threatening* attachment, Berlant's 'cruel optimism' appears to anticipate fundaments of what I call 'ambivalence'. At times, not coincidentally, Berlant even describes optimism that becomes cruel as 'ambivalent' (Berlant 14).[7]

At least one fundamental fact, however, separates cruel optimism from ambivalence. 'These kinds of optimistic relation are not inherently cruel', Berlant says at the outset of *Cruel Optimism*. 'They become cruel only when the object that draws your attachment actively impedes the aim that brought you to it initially' (Berlant 1). Even though Berlant speaks of 'conditions of possibility' (24), her transcendental language proves misleading insofar as not all experience is always *both* optimistic *and* cruel. Beyond any object relation, any fantasy or cluster of promises, the greatest optimism of *Cruel Optimism* – the optimum optimism – holds onto the promise that optimism was not always or will not always be cruel, that optimism only becomes cruel at a given moment in a psychic or social history, that one can therefore protect, recuperate or cultivate a relation without ambivalence. 'I have indeed wondered whether all optimism is cruel [. . .] But some scenes of optimism are clearly crueler than others' (Berlant 24–5).

While it would be naive to deny the relation types Berlant describes or the gradations of cruelty that lead her to believe that not all relations are cruel (but what minor premise mediates her deduction of *non-cruelty* from *degrees* of cruelty?), the ambivalence at stake in Deleuze's work is more fundamental. It doesn't consist in a list of positive and negative valences according to which the object – in this case affect itself – would prove 'good' in one respect and 'bad' in another or benevolent at one time and malevolent at another. Taken seriously, no doubt, this would already raise questions for the widespread portrayal of Deleuze as an unambiguous champion of affect, but it doesn't go far enough. Deleuze remains ambivalent toward affect *for one and the same reason*. Not *although* but rather precisely

- *because* affect is the 'royal faculty', it jeopardises the doctrine of faculties (see Chapter 1);
- *because* it dissolves the self, it regenerates the self (Chapter 2);
- *because* it leads the charge against opinion, it collaborates with opinion (Chapter 3);
- *because* it eternalises the body, it destroys the body time and again (Chapter 5);
- *because* it springboards the percept, it blinds the percept (Chapter 6);
- *because* it generates the surface, it collapses the surface (Conclusion).

The common ground of apparently opposing valences, the positive and the negative, makes the ambivalence rigorously irreducible. Any attempt to isolate the positive from the negative, the optimism from the cruelty, the promise from the threat also inevitably replicates the negative, the cruelty, the threat. The privileged position of affect in Deleuze's thought, in this light, positions affect to ruin it.

The irreducibility that distinguishes ambivalence from cruel optimism also, more generally, distinguishes it from the analytical concept of ambivalence dominated by the principle of noncontradiction in the tradition. Even the relatively recent tradition. Freud, for instance, presumes that ambivalence is only sustainable insofar as a psychic topology insulates mutually exclusive valences in distinct regions since, otherwise, they would cancel each other out (Freud, GW 9:40|*Totem* 29–30). How could it be otherwise? If ambivalence were irreducible, if two valences were inseparable without being equivalent, then it would be both necessary and impossible *to analyse* ambivalence in the critical, clinical or etymological sense. In Chapter 6 and in the Conclusion, respectively, I'll argue that this analytical limit desensitises both psycho-analysis and schizo-analysis to its own irreducible ambivalence.

(III) INTENSIFYING

Even within affect theory, the 'affective turn' is not without contro-versy. Massumi, although often cited as one of the turn's leading voices, rejects the idea of a turn to affect because it implies that affect is an isolatable 'thing' (Massumi, *Politics* 150). Taking Massumi as a representative of the very 'turn' Massumi denies, without reference to his denial and thus a bit insensitively, Timothy Bewes makes a similar argument. The phantom disagreement, then, only underscores a still more general agreement concerning the turn. 'On its own terms – as an entity that is inimical to conceptualisation, subjective intention or linguistic transcription – affect cannot be made the object of a critical "turn"'. Bewes concludes: 'The so-called "turn to affect" is, in fact, nothing other than a turning *away* from affect' (Bewes 317).

One could argue against a turn 'away' from affect on the same grounds on which a turn 'to' affect proves problematic; everything depends on how one approaches the 'turn'. Although one could say of *being* what Bewes says of *affect*, for instance, Heidegger describes his transition from the openness of Dasein to being in *Being and Time* toward the openness of 'being as being' in later texts as a turn (*Kehre*).[8] Earlier still, in arguably the first 'turn' not *in* but *into* philosophy itself, in the *Republic* Plato teaches the soul to turn from the shadows of the cave and toward what is:

> just as an eye cannot be turned around from darkness to light except by turning the whole body, so this instrument must be turned around from what-comes-to-be together with the whole soul, until it is able to bear to look at what is and at the brightest thing that is – the one we call the good. (Plato, *Republic* 518c)

Plato's turn, in other words, turns to no 'object', no 'thing', no 'being'. In fact, to the extent that Plato places the good *beyond* being (*Republic* 509b), this turn doesn't even turn to being 'itself'. These are far from the only references in the history of philosophy that should make one hesitate before a blanket rejection that, in response to an unjust turn to affect, risks an injustice in turn.

Justified or not, this scepticism with regard to an 'affective turn' offers an inadvertent lesson. Even when they criticise the possibility of 'turning' to affect, namely, critics do so in the name of affect. They deny a turn to affect, not because affect remains minimally complicit with the tradition from which it therefore never entirely turns, but on the contrary because affect – whatever it is and if it 'is' at all – remains too radical for the metaphysical kinetics of a turn. A conservative Deleuze, especially with regard to affect, never crosses our minds. Even at the other end of the critical spectrum, when Slavoj Žižek sets out to overturn Deleuze's philosophy by reversing the 'body without organs' into 'organs without bodies', he does so to make the concept 'all the more subversive' (Žižek xii). Not *subversive* but *all the more* subversive, which is to say, Deleuze's philosophy is *already* subversive, and the reversal won't be entirely revolutionary since it reverses what was already revolting, already revolving, already revolutionary. As if one could question Deleuze but not his subversiveness.

In the current critical landscape, accordingly, the controversy should be clear if I argue that Deleuze remains fundamentally complicit with the tradition that both critics and acolytes take him to revolutionise. The reference to Plato is felicitous in this regard. In *Logic of Sense*, the turn away from the cavernous shadows and toward the Idea leads Deleuze to associate the Platonic 'heights' with a movement of *conversion*. The rerouting of libidinal energy for the purposes of constructing a metaphysical surface beyond Plato, Deleuze calls *perversion*. The corporeal affects in the depths of which it all begins, however, Deleuze calls *subversion*.[9] It's not clear if Žižek has this schema in mind when he sets out to supplement Deleuze's 'subversiveness'. In the lexicon of *Logic of Sense*, regardless, subversion isn't the aim or the end. On the contrary, the subversive depths of affect are only the first step toward the construction of a metaphysical surface at which the entire enterprise aims. In light of which the subversiveness of affect, constantly threatening to collapse the surface grounded upon it, becomes a problem with which Deleuze struggles throughout *Logic of Sense*. This isn't the first or the last time affect creates a genetic impasse and *ambivalates* Deleuze's work. I'll address other cases in the chapters that follow and this one in particular, in *Logic of Sense*, in the Conclusion. I anticipate the impasse here only to point out that the threat posed by affect – not the affect of threat, even if it too involves ambivalence (Massumi, 'Future Birth' 69 note 11), but rather the threat of affect – leads Deleuze to join the ascetic tradition: *conjurer l'affect*, he says, dispel affect, avoid and avert it (LS 108|88). Perhaps no work more clearly than *Logic of Sense*, but still only for instance, reveals the 'affective turn' motorised by Deleuze to be an at most partial reading.

If I insist upon neglected complicities with the tradition, I don't, of course, thereby deny all ruptures in either Deleuze's work or in affect theory more generally. Beginning her argument with more sensitivity than most to the relation of affect theory with the history of philosophy, Rei Terada argues that 'emotion', to use her lexicon, has always constituted a problem for philosophers because it wedges 'self-difference' into cognition (Terada 3). Emotion comes into its own only today, it follows, when contemporary thought comes to prioritise difference: 'theories of emotion are always poststructuralist theories' (Terada 3). Although she never says so explicitly, consecrating relatively little topographical space to him in comparison with her discussions of Jacques Derrida and Paul de Man, Deleuze culminates Terada's analyses of emotion's incompatibility with the traditional notion of subjectivity for which self-difference is intolerable (Terada 91–2, 110). It doesn't figure in her bibliography, but *Difference and Repetition* would confirm Terada's argument most clearly since there, reconceiving philosophy as a philosophy of difference toward which every philosopher has implicitly strived but so far failed to achieve, Deleuze celebrates sensibility as the first faculty to grasp difference 'in itself'. And yet, even when difference takes priority, even when sensibility becomes the 'royal faculty', even then sensibility doesn't take the reins reliably, leading Deleuze to reduce the sensibility he privileges. Whence the ambivalent matrix of my opening chapter below: sensibility threatens to annul the pure and originary difference it alone grasps, in the very gesture of grasping it, and in the same stroke ruin philosophy before it ever rigorously begins. Even 'poststructuralist' philosophy. That 'emotion' (to recycle Terada's lexicon) troubles traditional philosophy with premonitions of difference, in short, doesn't prevent it from troubling contemporary philosophy with atavisms of identity.

Rather than vacillating between *Deleuze the subversive* and *Deleuze the conservative* or deciding once and for all for one or the other, the challenge is to think them together. Any theory that doesn't respect the genetic force, the irreducible multiplicity, the radical singularity of affect doesn't reach the profound level at which it consistently operates throughout Deleuze's work. To be sure. Far from excluding complicity, however, the very radicality of affect intensifies Deleuze's asceticism. For if indeed Deleuze seeks to reduce affect, as I have already indicated and will argue more acutely in the chapters that follow, he doesn't seek to reduce 'affect' as the tradition understands it. Whereas the tradition most often reduces affect because – rightly or wrongly – it has already posited affect as inessential or in any case reducible, Deleuze reduces affect even after he himself argues for its irreducibility. So, not despite or in addition to but in light of his break with the tradition, the Deleuzian reduction of affect would prove more reductive than any of which the most ascetic tradition could even attempt because it reduces the irreducible. Consequently, Deleuze's thought *intensifies* the ascetic tradition. My use of the word 'intensifying' here doesn't correspond to – or exclude – Manuel DeLanda's individuating use of the term or to the three senses in the glossary he appends to *Intensive Science and Virtual Philosophy* in an attempt to restore the fluidity of Deleuze's lexicon (DeLanda xvii and 199). It consolidates two irreducible but inseparable senses: in one sense, Deleuze's thought 'intensifies' the ascetic tradition precisely by rendering it intense, by embodying and sensitising it, by reasserting the affect it seeks to reduce and avoid; in another sense, however, Deleuze's thought 'intensifies' the tradition by not merely continuing but also even heightening its project, by reducing irreducible affect, by thereby becoming more traditional than the tradition itself. I use other terms to describe this double logic, like 'hyperbolic' (since *hyper-* means both beyond and excessively) and 'extra-traditional' (since 'extra' means both outside and more), but 'intensifying' has the added advantage of keeping the affective stakes in view. All nevertheless point toward the same conclusion: Deleuze's thought becomes *both* more subversive *and* more conservative than *both* acolytes *and* critics tend to think.

(IV) Systemic

I've been speaking of 'Deleuze's ambivalence'. I even introduced the problem of affect with an anecdote that at a 'secret point', following Deleuze's description and deployment of the anecdotal method, becomes indistinguishable from his work. But the ambivalence isn't simply attributable to Gilles Deleuze, to any individual, to any psyche in general. Rather, it bears upon a system of thought.

On multiple occasions in her campaign to reclaim form as an irreducible component for affect study (in film theory in particular), Eugenie Brinkema expresses her reserve with respect to the widespread use of 'affect' as a catchphrase for resistance to systematicity (Brinkema 3, 4, 7, 30, and so on).[10] Rather than simply endorsing or rejecting it in principle, and without denying its often superficial deployment in the field, one should stop to appreciate the necessity (to say nothing of the difficulty) of this resistance. It is, of course, nothing new to philosophy. Plato himself struggled to bridle his black steed in the upward ascent toward the Ideas at the very beginning of philosophy (*Phaedrus* 246a ff.). But 'system' is a modern notion.

Surging in seventeenth-century philosophy in reaction to empirical successes in the sciences, systematisation begins with a point of apodictic certainty like, in what historians often credit as the first system, the Cartesian cogito from which one then deduces a series of rigorous consequences in the effort to explain all phenomena in the world and the world itself.[11] If affect – to advance a Deleuzian refrain I'll address at length in Chapter 2 below – 'dissolves the self' or in any way breaks the deductive chain, then affect resists the system at its very foundation. Reprioritising affect would be one way, perhaps the most prominent today, to unanchor the stable certainty with which a system seeks to fix and exhaust the world in the most general sense.

Affect can be systematic, nevertheless, without being systematic. The apparently categorical opposition between 'system' and 'affect' still leaves room for more fundamental reconciliations insofar as the traditional basis of the system on certainty and its correlate concepts doesn't preclude a more contemporary use. Deleuze makes this particularly clear in a profession of faith that has the added advantage of contrasting the two approaches: 'I believe in philosophy as a system. The notion of system upsets me when one relates it to coordinates of the Identical, the Similar, and the Analogical' (DRF 338|361). As the first of the three temporal syntheses in *Difference and Repetition* (taken up in Chapter 2) or the third of the three unconscious syntheses in *Anti-Oedipus* (taken up in the Conclusion),[12] affect always intervenes at specific moments and with specific functions in what Deleuze never hesitates to call a 'system'. Even though the Deleuzian system would unleash chaos for the Cartesian.

Commentators thus do an unwitting but great disservice to the affect they celebrate when, without a careful discourse preparing the abstraction, they tear it from the system in which it operates. In so doing, they obscure the ways in which the entire system hangs upon affect, and they numb themselves to the very force they seek to wield. *A fortiori*, they also overlook any ways in which affect might threaten not only the modern system but also, as I argue in some fashion in every chapter that follows, even the Deleuzian. The asystematicity of affect thus extends even further than the asystematic acolyte would wish to extend it. But the systematicity of affect doesn't *oppose* its asystematicity. On the contrary, the privileged position that affect enjoys in the Deleuzian system positions it to threaten the system that depends upon it. So, I refrain from labelling affect *either* 'systematic' *or* 'asystematic' once and for all because, even in the widest sense, it is *both* and therefore *neither*.

18

I call this dilemma between the systematic and asystematic *ambivalence* and this ambivalence, in turn, I call *systemic*. For 'systemic' is not 'systematic'. Not only can the asystematic have systemic effects; the asystematic only registers its force through the system it allegedly resists. In which case the asystematic is asystematic only insofar as it remains systemic, if not systematic.

The Deleuzian 'system', of course, takes different shapes in different works, responds to different problems, speaks different languages. One could even say of Deleuze's oeuvre what Deleuze himself says of the 'pure game' in the ninth series of *Logic of Sense*: each throw of the dice, each work, effects a virtual system that changes not only the configuration of singular points but also the rules by which they operate. In the chapters that follow, as occasion arises, I'll take pains to argue for continuities across what Deleuze calls variously 'affect', 'sentiendum', 'sensibility', 'sensation' and so on. My earlier reference to the first synthesis of time in *Difference and Repetition* is particularly pertinent in this regard since it fabricates an originary sensibility through a mechanism of 'contemplation' that runs uninterrupted from Deleuze's first book in 1953 (*Empiricism and Subjectivity*) to his last in 1993 (*Critical and Clinical*). Across all systems, however, the greatest invariant is ambivalence. I aim to show the forms and contours of ambivalence not only in a given system but also across Deleuze's various systems and even the systems between which he himself locates a rupture. At stake in systemic ambivalence, in short, are *not only* continuities across Deleuze's oeuvre, *not only* eventual ruptures from one work to the next, but also the continuity of the *continuities* and the *ruptures*.

Clearly, then, neither affect nor ambivalence constitutes an object of study like others. Because they operate the very systematicity of the system, they warp a sensitive analysis in specific ways. Of which, still by way of introduction, I'll index only two under apparently contradictory headings so as to cover as much ground as economically possible.

Distraction. Because affect has its place in the system, especially because its place in the system is foundational, it cannot be the only factor in question. It remains solidary with other concepts, at the limit, with every other concept the philosopher would create. The systematic scope of affect appears, accordingly, only if one also takes into account the concepts it commands or obeys at a greater or lesser distance. This holds especially for a thinker like Deleuze who tries to chase all transcendence from his system in order to let every element reverberate freely with every other. Another reason for which an indexical approach to 'affect' could never clarify its scope, paradoxically, the very centrality of affect requires bracketing affect in order to address problems that – at least at first glance – have little to do with it. One must lose focus to keep it. Chapter 3 is exemplary in this regard. At stake is a general affectability that leads art to collaborate with the opinion it also combats (§1), but the consequences quickly spread to vitalism (§2), the major-minor distinction (§3) and style (§4).

Concentration. I don't pretend to exhaust the problem of affect. I situate important works, passages and problematics only in passing and leave others – like Deleuze's *Cinema* books – nearly or entirely unaddressed.[13] This isn't simply an oversight or underperformance. The systematicity of affect and ambivalence makes an exhaustive treatment impossible. At the same time, however, this ubiquity doesn't preclude key moments in which the ambivalence operates with particular force and clarity. On the contrary, precisely because ambivalence operates everywhere, one must choose strategic moments at which to engage it. A justification of the moments I choose, however, requires more general reflections on Deleuze's corpus.

Deleuze's bibliography divides roughly into three categories corresponding roughly to three stages. First, his work begins with the history of philosophy in *Empiricism and Subjectivity* (1953). Second, no longer *on* but now *in* the history of philosophy, Deleuze does his own philosophy for the first time in *Difference and Repetition* (1968). 'There's a great difference between writing the history of philosophy and writing philosophy', Deleuze says in the preface to the American edition of *Difference and Repetition*. '*Difference and Repetition* was the first book in which I tried "to do philosophy"' (DRF 280|300). In *What Is Philosophy?*, the third type with only one token, Deleuze no longer merely 'does' philosophy but also, with Guattari, defines the philosophy he did. Obviously, these categories seep.[14] Deleuze's historical work already has philosophical originality. 'I loved authors', he tells Claire Parnet in *Dialogues*, 'that seemed to be part of the history of philosophy but escaped from it in one respect or everywhere' (D 21|14–15). Inversely, Deleuze's philosophical work still engages the history of philosophy, just as he defines philosophy as the creation of concepts long before *What Is Philosophy?*

I would have to continue multiplying caveats, each more specific than the last, but this provisional schema suffices to indicate why, quantitatively at least, the following chapters so often cite *Difference and Repetition* and *What Is Philosophy?* As the work in which he first does philosophy and the work in which he finally defines the philosophy he does, they effectively frame Deleuze's oeuvre. Back in the American preface to *Difference and Repetition*, a text dated 1986 and published in 1994, Deleuze writes that everything he would write – even what he wrote with Guattari – 'is connected to this book' (DRF 280|300). Just as *Difference and Repetition* anticipates later works, moreover, *What Is Philosophy?* recollects earlier ones. While the title asks about the nature of philosophy in general, *What Is Philosophy?* opens in much more personal terms: 'What have I done my whole life?' (QP 7|1). So, on the one hand, *Difference and Repetition* and *What Is Philosophy?* provide pressure points for the problem of affect. On the other hand, the very centrality of these books necessitates recourse to other works. In Chapter 4, for instance, I can only argue that Deleuze's Spinozism reaches its purest pitch in *What Is Philosophy?* by showing the subtle but decisive ways it falters in earlier texts like *Spinoza and the Problem of Expression* and *Spinoza: Practical Philosophy*. Although based upon one book, even one passage of one book, my argument would remain systematically inaccessible to the sort of fragmentary reading that Quentin Meillassoux proposes.[15]

Itinerary

Each chapter identifies and analyses a configuration of Deleuze's system, affect's fundamental role within it and the ambivalence that troubles it. While each stands alone and offers a holistic view of the ambivalence inhabiting and inhibiting the deepest and earliest strata of Deleuze's thought, each also builds upon the others in specific ways that establish both the profundity and the longevity of the ambivalence such that, in short, there is no univalent stratum or moment.

    1. The Royal Faculty. Under the heading of 'Ambivalence', the first part includes three chapters that establish Deleuze's ambivalence, for the strategic reasons elaborated above, from the moment he first does philosophy in *Difference and Repetition* to the moment he defines the philosophy he did in *What Is Philosophy?* Chapter 1 thus begins with *Difference and Repetition*. This beginning is, in itself, somewhat controversial. Nearly everyone speaks of affect in Deleuze; hardly anyone speaks of sensibility in *Difference and Repetition*. Even the entire doctrine of faculties that Deleuze elaborates in the

latter is regularly neglected, underappreciated or outright discarded as insignificant and tangential. But there's no better, indeed, no other place to begin an inquiry into affect according to Deleuze. If Deleuze first 'does' philosophy in *Difference and Repetition*, then the doctrine of faculties effectively contains his first theory of affect, and it establishes that affect is not merely fundamental to his philosophy from the beginning but, more vitally still, fundamental to the very beginning of his philosophy.

More specifically, the faculties are indispensable to philosophy as Deleuze first does it, as a philosophy of difference, because they grasp difference, and Deleuze privileges sensibility as the first faculty to grasp difference. From imagination to thinking, any other faculty only ever grasps difference after and thanks to sensibility. Deleuze thus stakes his entire philosophy on the 'sensibility' that, in his later work, he comes to call 'affect'. In the very gesture of grasping difference, however, sensibility also already annuls it. Because philosophy only rigorously begins when difference reaches thought, sensibility jeopardises philosophy as a whole before it ever even begins. I call the sensible a 'hitch', then, because it both anchors and hobbles the chain of faculties and thus philosophy at large, which leads Deleuze to treat sensibility with ambivalence from the very moment he sets out 'to do' philosophy. The remaining chapters show that, uniquely each time but always, affect continues to hitch Deleuze's philosophy until the end.

2. Furtive Contemplations. Chapter 2 focuses upon Deleuze's complex inheritance of David Hume's concept of 'contemplation'. The concept gives Deleuze the resources to argue that affect precedes the self, the ego, *le moi*. He mobilises the originary affect operative in contemplation, accordingly, as the first step toward 'dissolving' the self and, in the same stroke, not only Cartesian philosophy in the broadest sense but also the regime of representation solidary with it. Only a first step, however, because contemplation still traffics in the idea of the self that hinders philosophy as Deleuze would redefine it. The result, once again, is a systemic ambivalence according to which Deleuze both praises and scorns sensibility for one and the same reason.

In addition to relocating the ambivalence outlined in Chapter 1, however, Chapter 2 also provides a strategic pivot in the progression of my argument. As the most enduring in Deleuze's arsenal, the concept of contemplation provides economic resources for arguing that ambivalence spreads across Deleuze's entire oeuvre.

After elaborating 'contemplation' as it pertains to the problem of the self in Hume's *Treatise* in the first section, I spend the remaining three showing how the unresolved impasse constitutes a source of ambivalence in *Empiricism and Subjectivity* (1953), *Difference and Repetition* (1968) and *What Is Philosophy?* (1991). Respectively, that is, in Deleuze's first intervention in the history of philosophy, in his first attempt to do philosophy and in his retrospective reflection upon the philosophy he did.

3. Between Art and Opinion. Having established the continuity of Deleuze's ambivalence from *Empiricism and Subjectivity* to *What Is Philosophy?* in Chapter 2, in Chapter 3 I delve deeper into the ambivalence of the latter work. According to *What Is Philosophy?*, all disciplines think in a strict sense and, in so doing, combat opinion. Because art and opinion both originate in sensibility, however, art has both a privileged and a precarious position in the struggle against opinion: *privileged* because it alone fights opinion at its source; *precarious* because the provenance art shares with opinion constantly tempts art to collaborate with opinion. Three propositions, each drawn from *What Is Philosophy?*, allow me to develop the resulting ambivalence and show how far its scope reaches by relating it to multiple works and contexts.

i. Percepts and affects constitute 'Life in the living or the Living in the lived' (QP 172|172).
ii. Opinion is 'in its essence' majoritarian (QP 147|146).
iii. Art needs 'style' to raise perceptions to percepts and affections to affects (QP 170|170).

A rigorous development of each proposition reveals that the root of both art and opinion in sensibility renders their distinction porous. Since, however, art is the last line of defence against opinion, the consequences of this sensible porosity exceed art. They reach all three disciplines of what Deleuze and Guattari call 'thinking' in general.

4. Spinoza, Socrates of Deleuze. Holding chapters four through six, the second part shifts gears. Michael Hardt calls Spinoza 'the philosopher who has advanced farthest the theory of the affects and whose thought is the source, either directly or indirectly, of most of the contemporary work in this field' ('What Affects Are Good For' xi). Hardt adds an endnote describing Deleuze's *Spinoza and the Problem of Expression* as 'the most complete and innovative reading of the affects in Spinoza' (xiii note 2), but this generous epithet is still

too modest. Much like Kafka rigorously creates his own precursor, as Borges says, Deleuze creates the Spinoza at the source of contemporary affect theory. For Deleuze, however, Spinoza's importance goes beyond affect. According to what Deleuze calls the 'paradox of Spinoza', from which I borrow the title for the second part, Spinoza is *the least philosophical* because his 'affects' appeal to non-philosophers like artists, but he is also *the most philosophical*. Before addressing affect in Chapter 5, accordingly, I address the importance of Spinoza for Deleuze's philosophy in Chapter 4.

I do so from an unexpected perspective. To criticise or to celebrate it, commentators tend to stress Deleuze's definition of philosophy as 'the creation of concepts', but the invention of 'conceptual characters' is equally indispensable to philosophy as Deleuze defines it. Hence, although he never says so, Deleuze needs a conceptual character, as well. Spinoza, I argue, constitutes not only the conceptual character of *What Is Philosophy?* in particular but also, in general, the conceptual archetype of philosophy as Deleuze defines it. The conceptual character, however, is always distinct from its namesake and, by emphasising evolutions in his reading, I argue that Deleuze too *characterises* Spinoza. In his early work, in fact, Deleuze critiques Spinoza for failing to achieve the very immanence for which he celebrates Spinoza in his later work. By insisting upon this earlier critique, which Deleuze never redresses, one begins to suspect that he and Guattari *invent* the Spinoza of *What Is Philosophy?* to operate philosophy as they define it there.

5. *Affectus* Becoming *l'Affect*. In Chapter 5, now in the second leg of Deleuze's paradox, I address Spinoza as the non-philosophical creator of affects. I say *Deleuze's paradox* because, just as Chapter 4 argues that Deleuze invents Spinoza as a conceptual character, Chapter 5 inhabits the space of a certain betrayal. For Spinoza, *affectus* refers to an individual's passage or (in Deleuze's terms) 'becoming' between two states of the same individual. Deleuze, however, radicalises this idea of becoming such that, rather than two states of a single individual, it now takes place between heterogeneous individuals. On the one hand, affect receives an autonomy rarely known, if ever, in the history of philosophy; no longer the sensation of a being, from which it derives and to which it remains subordinate, affect becomes a 'being of sensation'. On the other hand, the ontology or autonomy of sensation operates a reduction of the body and materiality in general that seems to reintroduce and ratify the ascetic tradition. *Seems*, however, because the consequences are in

fact more severe. Severe or, in the sense I outline above, hyperbolic: because affect reduces the body Deleuze himself holds to be irreducible, because the irreducible never reduces once and for all, because affect therefore reduces the body again and again, every creation of affect prolongs an endless cycle of brutality.

6. Deleuze and the First 'Ethics'. Chapter 6 focuses upon 'Spinoza and the Three "Ethics"'. This relatively brief but dense text not only holds Deleuze's final and most refined encounter with Spinoza's system; as the last text of his last book, *Critical and Clinical*,[16] it also in a sense culminates Deleuze's own oeuvre. In it, Deleuze associates 'affects' with what Spinoza calls the first genre of knowledge in the *Ethics*, 'concepts' with the second and 'percepts' with the third. By envisaging the three genres as a genetic progression, Deleuze privileges affect as an irreducible origin. Much like his treatment of the 'royal faculty' in *Difference and Repetition*, however, this privilege is not univalent. Not only because the philosopher's ultimate aim – the percept – marginalises affects but also and more decisively because the same affects that offer the first and, at first, the only springboard toward percepts can also, for the same reason, halt the entire movement. While Chapters 4 and 5 develop each leg of the 'paradox of Spinoza' independently, in short, my sixth chapter hardens the paradox – both with and against Deleuze – by arguing that Spinoza's 'non-philosophical' affects promise and threaten his 'philosophical' percepts on the same grounds. In the same stroke, my final chapter comes full circle by demonstrating that what I call 'the sensible hitch' in my first chapter on Deleuze's early philosophy still structures and jeopardises philosophy in his last reading of Spinoza.

Notes

1. 'One can always say that my mother cut them for me and that it is related to Oedipus and castration (grotesque but psychoanalytical interpretation). One can also remark, looking at the extremity of my fingers, that I am missing the usually protective fingerprint, such that touching an object and above all a fabric with the tip of my fingers gives me a nervous pain that requires the protection of long fingernails (teratological and selectionist interpretation). One can also say, and it is true, that my dream is to be not invisible but, rather, imperceptible and that I compensate for this dream by possessing nails that I can put in my pocket such that nothing seems more shocking to me than someone looking at them (psycho-sociological interpretation). One can finally say: "You must not bite your nails because they are yours; if you

like nails, bite those of others, if you wish and if you can" (political, Darien interpretation). You, however, you choose the ugliest interpretation: he wants to stand out [*se singulariser*], to be Greta Garbo' (Deleuze, P 13–14|5; in Cressole 109–10). For Cressole's letter, see Cressole 99–105. Originally appended to Cressole's book as 'Lettre à Michel Cressole' (Cressole 107–18), Deleuze republished his reply in *Pourparlers* (*Negotiations*) as 'Lettre à un critique sévère' ('Letter to a Harsh Critic'). On the situation surrounding this exchange, see François Dosse's biography (*Biographie* 260–1|*Intersecting* 215–17). That Deleuze not only republishes his reply in his own oeuvre but also republishes it as the first text of *Pourparlers* – even though it isn't the earliest text chronologically – reflects the sincerity with which he nevertheless took some of Cressole's criticisms or, at least, the replies they occasion.

2. L. Fañanás, P. Moral and J. Bertranpetit conclude that ridge count is predictably lower on the fingers of schizophrenics (424) and lower still in subgroups without a family history of schizophrenia (426). On how their study compares with earlier studies on dermatoglyphics and schizophrenia, see 424.

3. See especially DR 89|63–4, 182–3|140 and 190|146; LS series nine, 127|104 and 145–6|120–1.

4. Schaefer, *The Evolution of Affect Theory*, '1. The Deleuzian Dialect of Affect Theory' (6–22).

5. Deleuze always took Foucault's comment about a 'Deleuzian century' as a joke (P 12|4 and 122|88). Not without reason. Foucault says the century will perhaps be Deleuzian one day because, today, Deleuze's oeuvre hovers 'above our heads' (Foucault 885). The joke being that the 'incorporeal' rises above the body (and hence our heads) metaphysically – if not literally – like a 'mist' or 'vapor' (LS 15|5, 20|10, etc.). A little later, Foucault winks with a variant of the same expression to describe the incorporeal rather than, at least ostensibly, Deleuze's legacy: 'not at all in the hearts of men, but above their heads' (Foucault 893).

6. Compare Kant's resolution to the problem of pure intuition in advance of any object of cognition by way of the '*the form of sensibility*' in §9 of the *Prolegomena* (4:282). I'll address Deleuze's recourse to and critique of Kant in Chapter 1 below.

7. Berlant isn't the first to identify this affective predicament. Although she does not cite it, Ronald de Sousa's *The Rationality of Emotion* culminates in analyses of '*basic tragedies of life*' (de Sousa 328) in which the condition for a good also undermines it. What Berlant calls 'cruel optimism', what de Sousa calls 'basic tragedies', both call 'ambivalence': 'Each of these sources of the deepest level of ambivalence presents us with a necessary condition of a fundamental good, where that condition itself conflicts directly with the enjoyment or the perpetuation of

26

that good' (de Sousa 329). For similar formulations, see also de Sousa 302 and xviii.

8. See 'The Turn' (GA 11:113–24|*Technology* 36–49), of course, but Heidegger also offers useful reflections on his progression in the third of his *Four Seminars* (especially GA 15:345|47).

9. For this schema, see especially series eighteen; for subversion in particular, see LS 229–31|197–9 and 283|243.

10. Brinkema, for her part, doesn't entirely reject the asystematicity of affect or Deleuze. She takes Deleuze's liberation of affect from the subject as her point of departure (Brinkema 23), and she herself eventually situates at least one affect – grief – beyond systematicity (71, 94). Nevertheless, when Schaefer cites Brinkema's comments on the synonymy of affect and asystematicity as if she herself endorsed them (Schaefer 50), he represents the reinvasion of the very tendency that he and – this is the point – Brinkema both attempt to resituate.

11. For an overview of modern philosophy and the rise of the system within it, see the fourth volume of Frederick Copleston's *History of Philosophy* (especially 17 and 29–33).

12. For a reading of the three syntheses of time in *Difference and Repetition* as the philosophical foundation of the three syntheses of the unconscious in *Anti-Oedipus*, see Ian Buchanan's *Deleuze and Guattari's* Anti-Oedipus: *A Reader's Guide* (50 ff.). One would have to add the three serial syntheses of sense in *Logic of Sense* (LS 62|47, 203–4|174–5, 267|229, 273|234 and Appendix II.1).

13. For a recent take, see Nadine Boljkovac's *Untimely Affects: Gilles Deleuze and an Ethics of Cinema*.

14. Deleuze himself divides his oeuvre into more numerous categories (L 11–14|11–14). It would take time but not much effort, however, to merge several of them. He classifies the *Capitalism and Schizophrenia* volumes under 'critical and clinical', for instance, but the schizophrenic is a 'conceptual character' *in* philosophy (QP 72|70).

15. In an effort to make a passage from *What Is Philosophy?* the '*instrument*' rather than the '*object*' of his elucidation, Meillassoux reads Deleuze 'like a Pre-Socratic from whom we would no longer have but a few sparse fragments' (68). Of course, Meillassoux doesn't respect the rules of his own game but, even before he begins citing the rest of Deleuze's oeuvre, he already in a sense cites everything else in the very 'fragment' he imagines inheriting. It includes a crowning moment: 'The one who knew full well [*pleinement*] that immanence was only immanent to itself . . . was Spinoza. Thus, he is the prince of philosophers' (QP 51–2|48). In context, this passage culminates the account of philosophy's history that Deleuze offers in the only work in which he defines philosophy itself at systematic length. Which is to say, Meillassoux not only chooses his inheritance; he not only chooses wisely; he reads the

work he does *not* inherit before he ever begins to read the fragment he *does* inherit as either the 'object' or the 'instrument' of an elucidation.

At the same time, incidentally, does Meillassoux's imagination not instantiate the ambivalent structure of all inheritance? Do we not always in some sense *choose* our philosophical inheritance? Not only insofar as we choose to read one book or passage or word rather than another but also, provided we read rigorously, insofar as we leave a mark on what we choose to read. In which case Meillassoux's Pre-Socratic fiction doesn't go far enough. Inheritance sets fire not only to nearly everything from Deleuze the Pre-Socratic, as Meillassoux would have it, but also to the fragments that survive. Both the rest and the remainder. At which point the division between 'object' and 'instrument' no longer holds. No one, perhaps, blurs this limit more royally than Deleuze, inheritor of Spinoza, but his inheritance only becomes manifest when one reads more than its crowning moment.

16. 'The Exhausted' was added to the English translation. In French, Deleuze published *L'épuisé* a year earlier in Samuel Beckett's *Quad* (1993).

PART I

Ambivalence

The Royal Faculty

What if Deleuze's work embodied a more profound ambivalence than any in the history of philosophy? An ambivalence that bore more profoundly not upon this or that object or action, thing or idea, but rather upon sensibility itself and even the very being of the sensible. What if, in the very act of rehabilitating sensibility, Deleuze condemned it more brutally than Plato at his most Platonic or Descartes at his most Cartesian? What if everything in the philosophy that Deleuze first does and never abandons, the philosophy of difference in *Difference and Repetition*, began by double-crossing sensibility? What if sensibility jeopardised – even already ruined – philosophy on its eve? Even after an 'affective turn' that turns so much upon Deleuze, have we read Deleuze yet? Is 'affect' – not only but even and especially in Deleuze – ever entirely pure of a return to the ascetic tradition from which it would turn?

These questions might surprise, even antagonise, because everything points to the contrary. There's reason to credit Deleuze as the first philosopher to treat sensibility *as* sensibility, in its own right, as a singular and irreducible faculty. That which can *only* be felt, the purely sensible being of the sensible, what Deleuze calls the *sentiendum* in *Difference and Repetition* – *affect* in *What Is Philosophy?* – breaks palpably from previous conceptions of sensibility. Although they don't exhaust the history of philosophy or even the philosophers (or the works) from which I draw them, two classical conceptions in particular give an initial feel for the Deleuzian rupture. I'll invoke them only schematically here.

1) *Platonic.* To call Plato's aversion to the body well known is an understatement; it grounds the very tradition of philosophy in a sense. At times, to be sure, Plato seems to soften his austerity. The *Phaedrus*, for instance, seems far from an utter denial of the body since, as Martha Nussbaum has shown, the body plays an epistemic function by giving us '*information*' – her stress – '*information*' on the whereabouts of the good and the beautiful (Nussbaum 215). Even then, however, any epistemic advances instigated or oriented

by the body come only after it weighs us down and sets us back; Plato revalorises the body, to whatever extent he does, only as a means to anamnesis, that is, only as a means to remember something from another plane off-limits to our 'dull sense-organs' (*Phaedrus* 250a–b). Still a 'living tomb' (250c), the body plays a leading role in the *Phaedrus* because it ultimately leads to its own reduction. Not merely submissive, not merely informative, the most reliable body disembodies.

2) *Cartesian*. Notoriously, in his search for certainty, Descartes attacks (*aggredior, s'attaquer*) the senses first of all in the first *Meditation*. As the foundation of his former beliefs, the senses spare Descartes the task of enumerating his opinions, one by one, so as to cast a doubt upon each individually. Without in the least disturbing Descartes' thought, however, I could easily reformulate as *sentio* the *cogito* to which his attack on the senses leads: no longer *I* think *therefore I am*, now *I* feel *therefore I am*. This sensible displacement would seem to grant the senses an ontological status that Plato, for instance, denies them. The body would no longer entomb my being but, on the contrary, certify it beyond all doubt. In which case, without simply lapsing into a naive empiricism, the senses would ground not unsound opinion but progressive knowledge; I could survive madness, dreams and the most malicious demon, I could survive the methodological end of the world itself in the certainty of my own existence, because *I feel*. And yet, the Cartesian system authorises me to translate *cogito* into *sentio* only insofar as feeling is nothing but a modification of thinking. 'Lastly, it is also the same "I" who has sensory perceptions' (*who has sensory perceptions* translates *qui sentio* in Descartes' original Latin, *qui sens* in the 1647 French translation that Descartes authorised),

> or is aware of bodily things as it were through the senses. For example, I am now seeing light, hearing a noise, feeling heat. But I am asleep, so all this is false. Yet I certainly seem to see, to hear, and to be warmed. This cannot be false; what is called 'having a sensory perception' [*sentire; sentir*] is strictly just this, and in this restricted sense of the term it is simply thinking [*nihil aliud ... quàm cogitare; rien autre chose que penser*]. (Descartes, *Œuvres* VII:29, IX: 23|*Writings* II:19)

I feel therefore I am only because *I feel therefore I think*. Descartes recuperates sensibility, to the extent that he does, only by reducing it to thinking.

The Platonist reduces affect to think, in sum, while the Cartesian reduces affect to thinking. The antiquity of names like 'Plato' and 'Descartes' shouldn't lead one to assume that these treatments of sensibility belong to the distant past and have long been overcome. When Heidegger, for instance, rehabilitates anxiety (*Angst*) as the fundamental attunement (*Grundbefindlichkeit*) and assigns it a pivotal role in the analysis of that exemplary being 'Dasein' that, in turn, grounds the whole ontological enterprise of *Being and Time*, he does so ultimately only by submitting the affect to conceptual understanding. To Dasein's *Sichverstehen* more specifically: 'Because the anticipation [of death] absolutely individualizes Dasein and lets it, in this individualizing of itself, become certain of the wholeness of its potentiality-of-being, the fundamental attunement of anxiety belongs to this self-understanding [*Sichverstehen*] of Dasein in terms of its ground' (Heidegger, *Sein* 266|*Being* 254, translation modified).[1] So, I could have chosen other names to speak of what I'm calling the 'Platonic' and 'Cartesian' treatments of sensibility, but I haven't chosen Plato and Descartes at random. They occupy critical places with regard to sensibility in *Difference and Repetition*, and I'll return to both in due time. For now, by way of introduction, I invoke them only to indicate Deleuze's rupture with the classical ambit within which the tradition thinks sensibility: Deleuze *neither* rejects sensibility as a prison (Plato) *nor* recuperates sensibility in terms of thought (Descartes) but, rather, seeks the absolutely ignorant, immemorial and unimaginable specificity of sensibility, what can only be felt, the being of the sensible, what Deleuze calls the *sentiendum*. But he doesn't stop there. Deleuze goes so far as to privilege sensibility as the very origin of philosophy, of his philosophy, of the philosophy he first claims to do in *Difference and Repetition* (1968) and will continue doing until he finally defines philosophy as such in *What Is Philosophy?* (1991). For this reason alone, the recuperation of sensibility makes philosophy something philosophers since Plato would struggle to recognise and understand.

As I'll have many other occasions to confirm in this chapter and those that follow, there should therefore be little or no controversy in suggesting that Gilles Deleuze contributes, perhaps more than any other philosopher, not merely to the rehabilitation and popularisation of affect today but also, more fundamentally, to the very determination of what we grasp as 'affect'. Which might be the first time anyone has ever grasped affect if, indeed, we grasp it for the first time – thanks to Deleuze – in its irreducible specificity and originality. An audacious consequence: the philosopher has no body until 1968.

More audaciously still: if sensibility is indeed irreducible and even the first irreducible faculty, if there can therefore be no philosophy without sensibility first of all, then 'philosophy' itself doesn't properly begin until Deleuze embodies it in *Difference and Repetition*.

One thus gets a sense of the seism that convulses not only affect theory but also philosophy at large if, as I'll argue here, sensibility nevertheless occupies a radically ambivalent place from the very beginning of Deleuze's philosophy. Deleuze's sensibility has perhaps been both under- and over-appreciated: at stake are *both* a rehabilitation of sensibility without precedent in the history of philosophy *and* the greatest reduction of sensibility that philosophy has and will have known. The stakes are hyperbolic but only apparently contradictory. The reduction of sensibility is greater than any in philosophy *because* it reduces a sensibility rehabilitated without philosophical precedent, *because* it reduces sensibility in its irreducible singularity, *because* it reduces the very being of the sensible. And because, at the same time, Deleuze privileges sensibility as the origin of philosophy in *Difference and Repetition*, sensibility both *founds* and *founders* philosophy before it ever even starts. This double movement of founding and foundering, both anchoring and hobbling the chain of faculties from sensibility to thinking, is one of the reasons why I speak of sensibility as a *hitch*.

The hitch isn't limited to Deleuze. Whether presented as a guide to *Difference and Repetition* (Joe Hughes: *A Reader's Guide*), a general elaboration of transcendental empiricism (Levi Bryant: *Difference and Givenness*), an exposition of Deleuze's theory of sensation (Daniel Smith: *Essays on Deleuze*) or a relatively free attempt to rethink body and affect after Deleuze (Brian Massumi: *Parables for the Virtual*), any work with a ground, end or impetus in Deleuze that doesn't take this profound ambivalence into account from the beginning – as the beginning – hasn't entirely read Deleuze. The structure of ambivalence is uncompromising; to see it only in part is not to see it at all.[2]

A Doctrine of Faculties

A doctrine of faculties, Deleuze holds, is 'absolutely necessary' for the philosophical system today (DR 186|143). *Tout à fait nécessaire.* Today, in Deleuze's day that's still our own, philosophy means philosophy of difference. And a doctrine of faculties is *tout à fait* necessary today for philosophy as philosophy of difference because the faculties grasp difference 'in itself'. Far from strange or marginal, then, the facultative doctrine operates the entire enterprise of *Difference and Repetition*. Without it, difference would be inconceivable, beyond reach, and there would be no philosophy. Whence the necessity.

Where the 'object' is difference, however, Deleuze can't rely on the faculties as they already exist in the history of philosophy since, to his mind, philosophy so far has failed to grasp difference. Which is why, in chapter 3 of *Difference and Repetition*, Deleuze overhauls the very notion of 'faculty' while, at the same time, thematising and critiquing the dogmatic presuppositions that have so far prevented philosophy from becoming a proper philosophy of difference (the notorious 'image of thought'). The gestures are systematically solidary, and their solidarity suffices to reveal the superficiality of any commentator who thinks that 'creation' in Deleuze isn't also critically engaged with the history of philosophy, with the past, with 'tradition'. Among whom, perhaps, even Jacques Derrida would figure.[3]

Deleuze tends to call the traditional exercise of the faculties 'empirical'. In this acceptation, which of course isn't the only in Deleuze's transcendental empiricism, 'empirical' refers to the determination of the faculties on the basis of everyday recognition. But difference doesn't yield to recognition. On the contrary, the model of recognition ruins any chance for philosophy as a philosophy of difference insofar as it operates upon the principle of identity both subjectively and objectively, that is, with respect to both the self-identical subject that grasps an object and the self-identical object that a subject grasps. The two are systematic: the identity of an object guarantees that a subject can grasp the same object with different faculties, and this facultative harmony or concordance constitutes the identity of the subject in turn. 'Recognition is defined by the concordant exercise of all the faculties on an object supposedly the same' (DR 174|133). As a result, recognisant faculties can only ever grasp difference as a modification of identity; to the extent that they do, they don't grasp difference 'in itself', in its own right, but rather as the 'difference' between two or more self-same objects from which it presumably derives. X is X and Y is Y before X differs from Y. From Aristotle to Hegel, this is for Deleuze the fundamental error that has limited philosophy to a merely *conceptual difference* to the detriment of a proper *concept of difference* (especially DR 41|27).

But a facultative doctrine based on identity and recognition not only fails to grasp difference 'in itself'. It also fails to account for the specificity of the faculties that allegedly comprise it. Sensibility, memory and thinking might have particular data (*données*) and particular acts through which they invest or interpret their particular data but, because they seize the same object, the empirical exercise of any faculty never exercises that faculty alone. Sensibility, for instance: because other faculties can also and therefore in principle already seize their object, the senses always feel both *too much* (they feel what surpasses them) and *too little* (they feel nothing that properly belongs to them). Even when ostensibly overwhelmed, the work of the senses is delegated to other faculties, and this unanimity distends any intensity across insensate faculties in advance. In this sense, harmony is violence; the very harmony of the faculties robs sensibility of everything sensible, memory of the memorable, thinking of the thinkable and so on. The 'empirical' doctrine thus disintegrates the very faculties that compose it. This facultative dilution or dilation is then aggravated *ad infinitum* insofar as the form of identity that surrenders a recognisable object to all faculties of the same subject also surrenders it to every faculty of every other subject. Everyone, Deleuze says. 'Simultaneously, recognition thus demands a subjective principle of the collaboration of the faculties for "everyone", that is to say, a common sense as *concordia facultatum*' (DR 174|133). Insofar as he exercises his faculties in the harmonious recognition of an object (apart from a brief sublime moment), even the pioneer of the transcendental – even Kant – remains too 'empirical'.[4]

Wherever Deleuze speaks of the insensible, the immemorial, the unthinkable, wherever he appeals to the inability or *l'impuissance* to feel, to remember, to think, he does so to break the faculty's empirical exercise. That 'pure' difference can't be felt, remembered or thought empirically, however, doesn't mean difference can't be grasped in a *different* exercise that Deleuze describes variously as 'differential', 'superior', 'disjunctive', 'paradoxical', 'transcendent', 'transcendental' and 'empirico-transcendental'. One proposition in particular consolidates two principal aspects of this other exercise: 'Transcendent does not at all mean that the faculty addresses objects beyond the world but, on the contrary, that it seizes what in the world concerns it exclusively and bears it [*la fait naître*] into the world' (DR 186|143). A faculty is exercised otherwise, 'transcendently', when it grasps what both concerns it exclusively and midwives it. Of the two – exclusivity and nativity – I'll begin with exclusivity, with what's exclusively felt, exclusively remembered or exclusively thought, with what concerns a faculty exclusively. In reality, there are two exclusions: one *inter* and the other *intra*.

36

The first, the inter-exclusion concerns one faculty's exclusion of every other. If the harmony of empirical faculties hinges upon a self-identical object that precludes all chances for grasping veritable difference, then exclusivity becomes an indispensable tenet for a doctrine of transcendent faculties meant to grasp difference. The exclusively sensible object, for instance, the difference meant purely for sensibility, difference as it can only be felt, Deleuze calls the *sentiendum*. By exercising sensibility exclusively, by excising as much as exercising the faculty, the *sentiendum* escapes the grasp of every other faculty and, at the same time, breaks the unity of common sense as *concordia facultatum*. Insofar as the transcendent exercise of sensibility concentrates in sensibility alone, intensely, unmediated and unmitigated by any other faculty, it breaks a fundamental postulate of the dogmatic image of thought. Transcendent, here, means iconoclastic.

I call the second exclusivity involved in sensibility's transcendent exercise 'intra-exclusion' because, in a sense, it excludes a faculty from itself. On the model of recognition, the faculty of sensibility is supposed to be uniform, and the object it senses self-identical, so any encounter with difference underived from and untraceable to a prior identity confronts sensibility with a limit, that is, with what sensibility can't sense. At the same time, precisely because sensibility confronts its limit, because precisely sensibility confronts its limit, precisely because precisely sensibility confronts a limit proper to it, 'a proper limit' (DR 182|140), what can't be felt can only be felt. So, sensibility (transcendently exercised) excludes sensibility (empirically exercised), but the higher sensibility sensitised to difference emerges at the limit of the empirical senses and thus only by traversing them, which is why Deleuze proclaims that this higher sensibility is born '*in* the senses' (DR 182|140, my emphasis).

The strategic recourse to exclusivity, however, runs its own risk of dogmatism in turn. To disrupt the dogmatism of 'common sense', each faculty must have its own object and its own exercise, but Deleuze's prescription of what can only be felt, only remembered, only thought inevitably valorises *propriety* and *purity*: proper to sensibility, proper to memory, proper to thinking; pure feeling, pure memory, pure thinking. A 'proper limit' (DR 182|140, 189|145), 'proper element' (DR 184|141), 'pure thinking' (DR 185|142), 'the passion proper to it' (DR 186|143). Because Deleuze makes recourse to propriety and purity in numerous contexts throughout his writings, insistently enough to call Deleuze a *puritan*, it's worth briefly lingering on the problem here in the tenets of his first philosophy. For the idea of the proper, even when – even especially when – the axis shifts from identity to difference, remains dogmatic. With difference at stake, what can belong? What can remain pure? Deleuze himself proclaims that the nomadic distribution of being elaborated in *Difference and Repetition* blurs all properties, all proprieties, all *propriétés* (DR 54|36). How, then, can any of the faculties indoctrinated to grasp being as difference retain any sense of propriety? And yet, insofar as a properly transcendent exercise of a faculty demands a doctrine *more appropriate* for the singularity of each faculty than its empirical determination can allow, insofar as the transcendent exercise proper to a faculty also jealously guards it from a more recognisable exercise open to anyone and anything and therefore ultimately proper to no one and nothing, Deleuze's properly transcendent exercise critiques the dogmatic doctrine precisely for its lack of propriety. For not being proper enough. At its most critical, without simply losing its critical force, Deleuze's doctrine risks becoming even more dogmatic than the dogma it critiques insofar as it revalorises propriety even after it blurs all propriety.

Deleuze won't always avoid the dogmatism risked by his regular recourse to propriety and purity. Far from it. But, in this case, the second of the two inextricable aspects of a faculty's 'transcendent' exercise (nativity) offset the potentially conservative values operative in the first (exclusivity). With renewed emphasis: 'Transcendent does not at all mean that the faculty addresses objects beyond the world but, on the contrary, that it seizes what in the world concerns it exclusively and *bears it into the world*.' What concerns a faculty exclusively in the world also bears it into the world. One shouldn't be misled by Deleuze's regular use of the term *éveiller*, 'to wake', to describe the way in which an empirical faculty reaches its transcendent exercise; the Kantian atavism[5] has limited bearing on Deleuze's doctrine since, while Kant takes his faculties for granted, for Deleuze each is born in the encounter with its limit and thus doesn't pre-exist it. Similarly, Deleuze can speak of 'raising', *élever*, an empirical faculty to its transcendent exercise only loosely because the transcendent exercise isn't simply a new use for the old faculty. 'The object of the encounter' – difference, in this case, is the *sentiendum* – 'really midwives [*fait naître*] sensibility in the senses. [. . .] This is not a sensible being, but rather the being *of* the sensible' (DR 182|139–40). So, even if sensibility grasps what only sensibility can grasp, sensibility doesn't precede the encounter with 'its' object. This object might be proper to that faculty, the *sentiendum* to sensibility, the *memorandum* to memory, the *cogitandum* to thinking, but the appropriation of 'faculty' to 'object' can't be programmed in advance if the faculty itself is born in the encounter. The object will have been proper to the faculty, but the entire encounter and thus the faculty itself might not have been. And therefore might not be. Between faculty and object, Deleuze says, there's 'no affinity and no predestination' (DR 189|145).

Perhaps only this fragile fortuity, at bottom, separates Deleuze's *rencontre* from Heidegger's *Er-eignis*. For Deleuze's encounter appropriates being (as difference) to a being (a faculty) but, while Heidegger generously describes the event of being's appropriation to a particular being in terms of a 'gift' (*es gibt Sein*), Deleuze's appropriation is never programmed to this or that faculty in advance, never to any one being, for instance, to 'Dasein'.[6] Of the two events, both appropriative and both in a sense proto-ontological, one establishes rank among beings in a *Rangsetzung* (Heidegger, GA 65:66|*Contributions* 53), while the other anarchises the distribution of being (Deleuze, DR 55|37).

Transcendence

At this juncture, having developed the idea of a transcendent exercise of sensibility and before coming to the problems it entails, two perspectives upon Deleuze's work as a whole become accessible. The stakes of the *sentiendum* go well beyond the third chapter of *Difference and Repetition* beyond which, however, the word literally never occurs.

The first perspective bears upon a remarkable but largely overlooked or ignored continuity in Deleuze's work with respect to sensibility. Between 1968 and 1991, between *Difference and Repetition* and *What Is Philosophy?*, between the first book in which Deleuze attempts 'to do' philosophy and the book in which, with Guattari, he thinks back on what he did in doing philosophy throughout his life, terms and emphases shift, but nothing fundamental changes with respect to sensibility. Deleuze establishes at least two structural invariants for his future work.

First, when Deleuze and Guattari distinguish percept from perception and affect from affection in *What Is Philosophy?*, when they claim that the percept and the affect exceed all lived experience, *tout vécu*, all affection and all perception as lived experience (QP 164|164), they rearticulate the paradox of the *sentiendum*: what can't be felt can only be felt. Affection is to the empirical exercise of sensibility, in other words, as affect is to the transcendent. This chapter, then, only begins to address the more general question as to why Deleuze would consistently divide sensibility and purify it of itself, how hermetically he might do so and with what consequences. Nevertheless, although the transcendent exercise of sensibility traverses Deleuze's oeuvre in various forms with various names, *Difference and Repetition* remains a privileged point of reference because, by placing sensibility in a doctrine in which it relates to other faculties, its privilege and its peril – and the inseparability of the two – come clearly into view.

Second, if the *sentiendum* does indeed midwife sensibility, if sensibility is always born anew and different in the encounter with its object, then the transcendent exercise of sensibility pertains not to sensations, not even the most novel, but rather to new sensibilities. This definition extends to the other end of his oeuvre; rather than this or that sensation, even if unprecedented and unrepeatable, affects as Deleuze defines them in his later work constitute 'new ways of feeling' (P 224|165). When the transcendent exercise of the faculty of sensibility that, we'll soon see, begins philosophy in *Difference and Repetition* becomes the task of art in *What Is Philosophy?*, the artist effectively creates *sentienda* that midwife new sensibilities into the world. It makes no difference if Deleuze and Guattari don't say 'sentiendum' or refer to *Difference and Repetition* by name. The chapters that follow will substantiate this continuity.

The second perspective bears more generally upon the word 'transcendence'. The exercise that Deleuze calls 'transcendent', as I've already pointed out, he also calls 'paradoxical' and 'disjunctive', among other names, but I've insisted upon 'transcendence' for a reason. It's true that the same year, in *Spinoza and the Problem of Expression* (1968), Deleuze already announces immanence as 'philosophical vertigo' (SPE 163|180); it's also true that, more than two decades later in *What Is Philosophy?*, 'the vertigo of immanence' (QP 52|48) – a formulation that has entitled more than one reading of Deleuze – wins Spinoza the twin title of 'prince' and 'Christ' of philosophers (QP 51|52; 62|60), epithets I'll take up in detail in Part II below. But 'transcendence' isn't, to say the least, 'a term strictly prohibited by Deleuze' (Žižek 10). Deleuze's recourse to the term in the doctrine of faculties in *Difference and Repetition* demands a massive redistribution rarely, if ever, taken into account by readers of all calibres and agendas. If the transcendent exercise of a faculty brings it into the world, then 'transcendence' doesn't oppose 'immanence' but, on the contrary, conditions it. Indeed, beyond anything Deleuze explicitly says, it would be possible to show – counter-intuitively – that the 'empirical' recognition of an object removes it from the world: because it can be reached by all faculties and all subjects, anywhere and any time, a faculty's 'empirical' exercise doesn't merely grasp the object but also tears it – and the faculty – from all spatiotemporality. From the world. Every 'empirical' sensation would be catastrophic; the very sensation that should open a subject to the world would destroy it. So, for Deleuze, 'transcendence' doesn't oppose 'immanence' and never has. Not simply, not entirely. By the time of *What Is Philosophy?*, 'transcendence' will have become a pejorative word but, respecting the exercise of the indispensable faculties in *Difference and Repetition*, *immanence* can oppose *transcendence* only if and after *transcendence* opposes *transcendence*. Even in *What Is Philosophy?* Deleuze and Guattari speak of 'the non-exterior outside or the non-interior inside [*le dehors non-extérieur ou le dedans non-intérieur*]' (QP 62|60). One would have to resituate and recalibrate every categorical distinction between immanence and transcendence, like the one with which Agamben proposes to structure a genealogy that culminates in Deleuze,[7] in light of the fundaments it ignores in Deleuze's work.

The Royal Faculty

While the faculties don't harmonise with themselves or with each other, while they even mutually exclude one another, while they're fortuitously born and reborn, they don't transcend each other or themselves without a certain relation, a 'communication' and even a strict order. Deleuze calls this tenet of his doctrine 'the most important'. It's also one of the most enigmatic and, for reasons I'll slowly show, the most problematic. The doctrine stipulates a certain sequence among the faculties *even though* and *because*, in their superior exercise, they no longer grasp a self-identical object accessible to all faculties at once or in any order.

> And this is the most important: from sensibility to the imagination, from the imagination to memory, from memory to thinking – when each disjointed faculty communicates to the other the violence that carries it to its proper limit – it is each time a free figure of difference that wakes the faculty and wakes it as the different of this difference [*le différent de cette différence*]. (DR 189|145)

The facultative chain is *broken* and *violent* but *orderly* and *communicative*. Sensibility begins by sensing what cannot (empirically) and can only (transcendently) be sensed, namely, the *sentiendum*; when sensibility forces the imagination to imagine what it has (not) sensed, sentiendum becomes *imaginandum*, which cannot and can only be imagined; when the imagination forces memory to remember what it has (not) imagined, imaginandum becomes *memorandum*, which cannot and can only be remembered; when memory, finally, forces thinking to think what it has (not) remembered, memorandum becomes *cogitandum*, which cannot and can only be thought. Sensibility-sentiendum – imagination-imaginandum – memory-memorandum – thinking-cogitandum. This order links the faculties into a rigorous chain. Because the object is 'pure' difference, because difference differs each time, because each faculty grasps difference differently, the chain is broken. Because each faculty is forced from its empirical exercise into its transcendent exercise, forced to remember (for instance) what can't be remembered, the chain is violent.

Without reference to Deleuze's primary source for this facultative order, it might seem arbitrary and declarative. Deleuze, for his part, never hides his inspiration. He draws upon Book VII of Plato's *Republic* for his discussion of faculties not only in *Difference and Repetition* but also in earlier texts like *Nietzsche and Philosophy* and *Proust and Signs*.[8] Certain structural features drawn from Plato's text recur in each of these instances. Only in *Difference and Repetition*, however, does Deleuze harden the order, indoctrinate it and sign it as a 'philosopher' and not simply, according to his own distinction, as a 'historian' of philosophy.[9] The most important structural recurrent, a constant in both the historical and the philosophical work, places the *origin* of all higher exercise in sensibility and its *end* in thinking.

'There is something in the world that forces thought' (DR 182|139). According to Plato, certain objects in the world force us to think because, rather than immediately yielding to the unity of recognition, they cause opposing sensations and thereby pose veritable 'problems' (Plato, *Republic* 523b–c). To take Plato's example, which Deleuze relays, a finger is recognisably a finger whether it's large or small, hard or soft, so on or so forth; no finger poses the question of what a digit is in itself. But it becomes a 'problem' when the senses report opposing characteristics to the soul; when one finger appears large and at the same time another small, one hard and another soft, the senses summon the intellect to ask what 'large' and 'small', 'hard' and 'soft' are in themselves such that they can characterise the same thing at the same time. Rather than a discord between interlocutors that measurement can resolve before it generates hostilities, as in the *Euthyphro* (7c), in this case the object itself seems to disagree with itself. Sensibility thus inaugurates a movement of anamnesis toward the intelligible realm. We sense, we remember, we think; sensibility forces memory forces thought.[10]

Now, Plato isn't Platonism. On multiple occasions, Deleuze indicates pivotal moments when Plato wavers at the edge of what will have been the dogmatic image of thought. Moments when Plato becomes Platonic. One of the most decisive moments, for Deleuze's inheritance of Plato, concerns the movement of the proto-faculties in confrontation with what ultimately forces thought in the *Republic*. Because something summons thinking, because it begins with the force of a contingent event, because thinking thinks as the result of an unforeseeable encounter, Plato isn't simply Platonic; his thought already follows a radical empiricism in the superior sense that Deleuze recuperates. Thinking is an event and, to that extent, Plato already 'reverses' what will have been Platonism or, at least, already winds the revolutionary torque. Yet, because the immutable identity of Ideas never ceases to orient every facultative operation in the movement, Plato also at the same time prepares the world of representation. Prepares but doesn't yet establish because, for Deleuze, only Aristotle truly immerses philosophy in representation.[11]

> Discovering the superior or transcendent exercise of the faculties, Plato subordinates it to the forms of opposition in the sensible, similitude in reminiscence, identity in essence, analogy in the Good; he thereby prepares the world of representation; he operates a first distribution of its elements and already covers the exercise of thought with a dogmatic image of thought that presupposes and betrays it. (DR 185–6|142–3)

The fate of sensibility best reveals the severity of Plato's betrayal. For Plato, the force of thought begins in sensibility, a priority that Deleuze aggressively endorses: there's something in the world that forces thought and 'in its first character', Deleuze affirms, it can only be felt (DR 182|139). But Plato's sensible moment is short-lived, provisional and ultimately anaesthetised. By calling upon thought, by qualifying the same thing (a finger) with impossible because opposing qualities (big and small, hard and soft), the senses become an index of their own insufficiency and thus the catalyst of their own extinction. Everything within the confused limits of the senses must be removed in order to think, for instance, Large and Small as such and through argument alone (Plato, *Republic* 532a). At the end of the dialectic journey that Plato's epistemic prestidigitation only begins, the sun sets its phantom light on all sensation, for it too is still too sensible, leaving thought alone in dark contemplation of the Good.[12]

While for Plato, however, the unintelligibility of certain sensations (big and small, hard and soft) is a sign that we must disembody, a sign of the weakness and even vileness in our nature that we must overcome (*Republic* 602c–603a), the same encounter for Deleuze is a sign of the positive force proper to sensibility. This, then, is the precise moment to mark Deleuze's unprecedented recuperation of sensibility in the history of philosophy since Plato. Unprecedented because Deleuze insists not only on the irreducibility of sensibility, on the properly sensible, on what can only be felt and therefore can't be absolved in Platonic anamnesis or classified as Cartesian thinking. Deleuze insists not only on the *sentiendum*. He insists upon sensibility as the first and irreducible link in a facultative chain that remains, nearly two and a half millennia after Plato's *Republic*, *tout à fait* necessary for philosophy today. On the eve of imagination, memory and thinking, while every other faculty sleeps, sensibility wakes to difference, and philosophy takes its first violent steps:

> on the path that leads to that which is to be thought, everything launches from [*tout part de*] sensibility. From the intensive to thought, thought always happens to us [*nous advient*] through an intensity. The privilege of sensibility as origin appears in that what forces sensing [*ce qui force à sentir*] and what can only be sensed [*ce qui ne peut être que senti*] are one and the same thing in the encounter, whereas the two instances are distinct in the other cases [i.e., for the other faculties]. Indeed, the intensive, difference in intensity, is at once the object of the encounter and the object to which the encounter raises sensibility. (DR 188|144–5)

Like all faculties in their transcendent exercise, sensibility apprehends what it alone can apprehend (inclusive exclusivity), but sensibility alone apprehends *what it alone can apprehend* as *what forces it to apprehend* (exclusive exclusivity). Sensibility, in other words, is the only faculty to grasp difference directly and on its own. Other faculties seize difference, and they seize difference as they alone can seize it, but each is forced into a confrontation with difference by another faculty. The imagination in its transcendent exercise apprehends difference as it can only be imagined (*imaginandum*), difference as it therefore can't be sensed, but the imagination is forced to imagine difference, albeit *its* difference, by a prior sensible exercise that first grasps difference and then 'communicates' or 'transmits' it to the imagination. Imagination, memory and thought never encounter difference, their own difference, on their own. Every other faculty depends upon sensibility to midwife its superior exercise by delivering 'pure' difference. Consequently, insofar as the transcendent exercise of every faculty grasps what's proper to it, insofar as a faculty doesn't properly exist – as *that* faculty and no other – until it grasps what it alone can grasp, insofar as no faculty can grasp its difference until sensibility grasps the *sentiendum* and transmits it down the chain, sensibility hitches Deleuze's entire doctrine of faculties.

But not only the doctrine of faculties. For a time, the most critical time before any other faculty properly exists, sensibility is the only link to difference, the only access, the only opening. The only chance. Everything may very well spring from originary difference but, without the sensible encounter, there'd be no way of ever even suspecting difference as the origin, much less grasping it. It's not even enough to say that sensibility remains 'closest' to originary difference. Sensibility's the only faculty even in the vicinity. Because sensibility holds this 'privilege as origin', because it anchors the facultative chain and thus secures the doctrine that remains entirely necessary for philosophy even today, because sensibility holds vigil over every other lethargic faculty, over difference in itself, over the world itself, philosophy stands and falls with sensibility's inaugural encounter with difference. There is philosophy, if at all, only because there is sensibility. Only because there is sensibility first. Which is why Deleuze calls sensibility – but even this epithet seems to understate its importance – 'the royal faculty' (DR 198|152).

The Original Origin

And yet, sensibility isn't the only origin. There's another, more 'radical' still. Here, Deleuze begins to turn on sensibility upon which everything turns. It's not yet a question of outright antipathy countervailing 'the privilege of sensibility as origin', but the displacement is seismic in its own right insofar as Deleuze displaces sensibility in its irreducibility and even after having privileged it as the origin of all transcendent faculties and, *a fortiori*, of philosophy itself.

Deleuze also calls 'pure' difference 'in itself' the Idea, and he repeatedly denies that it belongs to any one faculty. The point naturally follows if indeed each transcendently exercised faculty grasps as it alone can grasp. Certain Ideas traverse all four faculties, but sensibility grasps each as the strictly sensible *sentiendum*, the imagination as the strictly imaginary *imaginandum* and so on down the chain. Unthinkable for a dogmatic tradition that tends to reduce all faculties to mere modifications of thinking.

> Thinking is supposed to be naturally upright [*droite*], because it is not a faculty like the others but rather, related to a subject, the unity of all other faculties that are only its modes, which it orients according to the form of the Same in the model of recognition. (DR 175|134)

Descartes is representative in this respect, which is why my opening remarks thematised Cartesian sensibility as a reference point for gauging the Deleuzian rupture. For Descartes, sensing (*sentire, sentir*) is nothing but thinking (*cogitare, penser*) whereas, for Deleuze, thinking becomes one more link in a broken chain of faculties.

> It also seems [*On dirait*] that there are Ideas that traverse all the faculties without being the object of any one in particular. Indeed, as we will see, it is perhaps necessary to reserve the name Ideas not for pure *cogitanda* but, rather, for instances that go from sensibility to thinking and from thinking to sensibility capable of engendering in each case, according to an order that belongs to them, the transcendent or limit-object of each faculty. (DR 190|146)

And later:

> Ideas, however, thus correspond to all the faculties in turn [*tour à tour*] and are not the exclusive object of any one in particular, not even thought. (DR 250|193)

Not even thought. I'd venture to say *especially not thought*: if thinking comes last in Deleuze's broken chain, it's the youngest faculty, the most languid and somnolent, the last to stir, the last to have an Idea, the faculty the birth of which thus demands the most violence.

And yet, despite his own declarations, despite his critique of the Cartesian privilege of thinking, despite the Idea's essential impropriety or impertinence, Deleuze doesn't hesitate to associate Ideas with thinking in particular.

> Ideas are not the object of a particular faculty, but they singularly concern one particular faculty to the point that one can say: they come from it (in order to constitute the *para-sens* of all the faculties). (DR 251|194)

One must understand the specific originality of thinking, first, in order to understand how a faculty can originate Ideas without ceasing to be one faculty among others and, second, in order to set the cogitative privilege next to 'the privilege of sensibility as origin' and thereby measure the sensible displacement. Everything hinges upon the so-called *para-sens*. Ideas come from thinking in order to constitute the *para-sens* of all the faculties. What, then, is the 'para-sense'?

Deleuze privileges sensibility as 'the origin' because it grasps the Idea first. After it 'communicates' the Idea to other faculties, when other faculties grasp the Idea for themselves, the Idea 'metamorphoses'. Because the faculties grasp a metamorphic Idea and not a self-identical object, the facultative chain doesn't harmonise into what Deleuze calls common sense. At the same time, however, because 'something' leaps from faculty to faculty, the faculties 'communicate' in a certain sense. 'There is therefore something communicated from one faculty to another, but it metamorphoses and does not form a common sense' (DR 190|146). This communiqué is the para-sense. A formulation meant to oppose *le sens commun* and *le bon sens* (in Chapter 2 I'll clarify why at times I hesitate to translate these terms), *le para-sens* refers to the Idea in its progression from *sentiendum* to *cogitandum*, beyond or beside (*para-*) the 'sense' in which the faculties normally, empirically, harmoniously grasp their object. It constitutes 'the only communication', the only connection, in an otherwise entirely broken chain: 'In this regard the Ideas, far from having a *bon sens* or a *sens commun* for their milieu, refer to a *para-sens* that determines the only communication between disjointed faculties' (DR 190|146). Thinking comes at the end of the chain, but it will have been the aim and the origin insofar as it alone grasps the 'para-sense' of the movement as a whole. In short, Deleuze claims that in grasping *its* difference, the *cogitandum*, thinking grasps the difference of differences and thus gathers together – without simply repairing them – the broken pieces of the facultative chain. Which is why Deleuze can hold not only that Ideas concern thinking in particular but also that thinking is 'the radical origin of Ideas' (DR 251|194).

Contrary to what readers often presume, Deleuze never relinquishes the demand for unity or totality. He critiques totality, to be sure, but he critiques totality when it *precedes* or *exceeds* what it totalises, when the unity reduces the singularity of the components and their encounter. The displacement of thinking to the end of the facultative chain is a fundamental feature of Deleuze's critique of the ultimately Platonic tenet according to which, to borrow a refrain from an earlier elaboration of the problem of totality in *Proust and Signs*, 'Intelligence comes before'. If the para-sense totalises the facultative chain, the totality comes at the end and therefore doesn't infringe upon the singularity of any other exercise but, on the contrary, affirms it.

> There is therefore a point where thinking, speaking, imagining, feeling, etc., are one and the same thing, but this *thing* only affirms the divergence of the faculties in their transcendent exercise. In question, then, is not a common sense [*sens commun*] but, rather, a 'para-sense' (in the sense in which paradox is also the opposite of good sense [*le bon sens*]). (DR 250|194)

From *Bergsonism* to *What Is Philosophy?*, one would have to engage Deleuze's longstanding commitment to the notion of multiplicity in this connection.[13] I won't do so here, however, because granting the para-sensical totality of the facultative chain as a multiplicity still doesn't prevent the radically original place assigned to thinking from producing at least two other dogmatic effects between the lines of Deleuze's doctrine.

1) Why should this totalisation be reserved for *thinking* alone? Why should thinking be idealised above all other faculties? Why should no other faculty be capable of constituting the so-called *para-sens* of a facultative series? Deleuze himself authorises and even presupposes these questions, without posing them, by insisting that thinking is one faculty among others and that Ideas concern all faculties.

Thinking is the radical origin of Ideas but, when difference is original, 'radical origin' doesn't mean what the tradition would lead one to expect. Which, of course, Deleuze recognises. 'But in what sense should we understand "radical origin"? [. . .] what does it mean to come out of [*sortir*] or to find one's origin? Where do Ideas come from [*d'où viennent*] . . . ?' (DR 251|194–5). Curiously, the last question amounts to asking where Ideas come from that come from thinking. What's the origin of Ideas that originate in thinking? To designate thinking as the radical origin of Ideas, then, doesn't explain the origin of Ideas but itself calls for explanation. Why does Deleuze place such inordinate trust in thinking as the origin of Ideas? In the ten pages that follow these questions, Deleuze weaves a tortuous response with recourse to questions and problems, imperatives and games of absolute chance, but the radical origin of Ideas is never grounded in the specificity of thinking. On the contrary, thinking continues to figure as only one faculty among others, one example of ideation, which Deleuze's conclusion only ratifies: 'an origin is assigned only in a world that contests the original as much as the copy' (DR 261|202).

The conclusion in itself should surprise no one. As a conclusion to his development of the three syntheses of time much earlier in chapter 2, in very similar terms, Deleuze excludes 'the assignation of an originary and a derivative' (DR 163|125). As a result, however, the brutality of thinking's para-originality only redoubles. For Deleuze privileges thinking as the radical origin of Ideas not only where he insists that Ideas concern all faculties singularly, not only where he insists upon thinking as one faculty among others, but also both *after* and *before* he concludes that no origin can be 'assigned'. At which point a ponderous atavism of the dogmatic image that Deleuze seeks to abolish comes to faint but unmistakable light. However qualified, whatever violence and fortuity thinking might entail, wherever Deleuze resituates thinking, the privilege of thinking retains an essential continuity with the tradition that begins when Parmenides posits being and thinking in a relation so peculiar that they're the 'same'.[14] Earlier, I marked a certain rupture between Deleuze's *rencontre* and Heidegger's *Er-eignis*, but a more profound continuity persists here. However harshly Deleuze criticises Heidegger's recourse to the 'same' in discussions of difference, however harshly he criticises the generosity with which Heidegger gives being (*es gibt Sein*) to a being that thinks, to Dasein, Deleuze himself can promise para-sense to thinking alone only through the 'same' recourse to an affinity between thinking and being. A *tryst* if not outright *philia* (φιλία).

> It is true that Heidegger conserves the theme of a φιλία, of an analogy or, better, of a homology between thought and what is to be thought. This is because he keeps the primacy of the Same, even if the latter is meant to gather difference and to comprehend difference as such. Whence the metaphors of the gift, which substitute for those of violence. (DR 188 note 1|321 note 11; see also DR 89–91|64–6)

Elsewhere, when Deleuze traces the origin of the 'gift' in the relation between 'participated' and 'participator' to Plotinus (SPE 154|170), he indirectly but essentially associates Heidegger with Neo-Platonism. Nothing guarantees, however, that substituting 'violence' for 'generosity' makes any essential difference. How violent, contingent, fortuitous or broken is a chain of encounters – how aberrant is the movement[15] – when we know by doctrine where it ends? End and beginning of faculties, the last that will have been first, Deleuze's thinking remains more *archaic* than *anarchic* in this sense. I'll return to this finality below.

2) While no faculty should enjoy any privilege over any other with

respect to their superior exercises, while the question of hierarchy shouldn't even arise on the transcendent plane insofar as each faculty – in contrast to their harmonious exercise in common sense – seizes the differential Idea that and as it alone can, while for that reason Deleuze concludes that Ideas belong to no faculty in particular, the Ideas nevertheless concern one faculty more 'singularly' than any other. 'At the same time, the Ideas are not the object of one particular faculty, but they singularly concern one particular faculty' – *elles concernent singulièrement une faculté particulière* – 'to the point that one can say: they come from it' (DR 251|194). Seizing what it alone can seize, every faculty might be singular in its transcendent exercise, but thinking is singular twice. Thinking is *singularly singular* because, in what relates to the Idea, it has priority over all other faculties that therefore, in the end, will have been an at best infinitely distant second. *Difference and Repetition* therefore doesn't contain a doctrine of faculties; there is at most one faculty, the faculty of faculties (thinking) that alone grasps the Idea of Ideas (parasense). It's more symptomatic than coincidental or convenient that, even though Deleuze criticises Descartes for reducing all faculties to modes of thinking in an effort to preserve the singularity of every single faculty, as if without thinking he at times refers to the faculties as if they belonged to thinking: 'Thinking and all *its* faculties . . .' (DR 181|138, my italics).

If thinking secondarises every other faculty, however, it secondarises sensibility first of all, for sensibility is in fact the first to grasp difference. In which case Deleuze's attempt to recuperate the irreducible singularity of sensibility against the Platonic turn not only ends up reducing sensibility after all. If also incidental, the reduction is even more brutal than any in any era of philosophy's history. Plato reduces the sensible for the sake of purely intelligible Ideas. Descartes reduces sensibility because it merely modifies thinking. *Deleuze reduces sensibility in its very irreducibility*. At the very moment Deleuze vindicates sensibility, at the very moment he seeks to appreciate and name – for the first time – the purely sensible aspect of being, the very being *of* the sensible, the purely sensible being of the sensible, at the very moment he privileges sensibility as the 'origin' of a facultative chain without which there would be no philosophy, no thinking, no difference to speak of, he anesthetises being through thinking's more singular and original grasp of it. This won't be the last time.

I stress sensibility, but the reduction isn't limited to that faculty. In principle, it isn't limited at all. As the 'radical origin' of Ideas, as their singular warden, as the factory of differential Ideas meta-morphosing from faculty to faculty, from encounter to encounter, thinking monopolises the Idea at the expense not only of the faculties addressed within the pages of *Difference and Repetition*. Not only sensibility, imagination and memory. Deleuze never claims to estab-lish the faculties comprising the doctrine once and for all; he only reclaims the necessity of the doctrine and expounds its requisites. Even if certain formulations regarding a 'complete doctrine' suggest that Deleuze believes in the possibility of an exhaustive catalogue, the doctrine in principle has no last page if faculties are indeed born from fortuitous encounters. Once the identity of the object grasped and that of the subject grasping it cease to set parameters, once objects are encountered and faculties born, the doctrine opens to faculties never before suspected in the history of philosophy. 'For we can say nothing in advance; we cannot judge the search in advance' (DR 187|143). And yet, even though Deleuze opens the doctrine to unprecedented and unsuspected faculties, even though the very idea of 'doctrine' has perhaps never been less dogmatic, an unbridled trust already assigns the origin of every faculty that the doctrine might contain. 'Our subject here is not the establishment of such a doctrine of the faculties. We seek only to determine the nature of its requirements [*exigences*]' (DR 187|144). The doctrine itself thus requires that, come what faculties may, thinking be the radical origin of the Idea they grasp. For thinking is the 'radical origin' of Ideas for all faculties known or suspected, discovered or unsuspected, past or future. Which is to say, in incalculable sum, Deleuze's thought reduces infinite faculties.

The Sensible Hitch

If, of course, one manages to think.

Thinking, the radical origin of Ideas, never comes first. In fact, it doesn't come first twice. First, like all faculties, thinking must be forced into its transcendent exercise; second, it isn't the first faculty forced into its transcendent exercise. The last to grasp the Idea, think-ing is even the most dependent, and it depends most upon sensibility because sensibility always grasps difference first. Such that, if think-ing will have been the radical origin of Ideas, sensibility's privilege as origin might be provisional, perhaps even only methodological, in any case less radical than the radical origin, but for that very reason everything hinges precariously upon it. If thinking ultimately monopolises the Idea, if its singular concern for Ideas secondarises all other faculties even in their singular exercise, if thinking displaces even faculties so far undiscovered and even unsuspected, thinking itself never happens if sensibility doesn't happen first. Affective anachronism, sensibility is both pre-primary and secondary, both the origin and the afterthought of a more original origin. Sensibility constitutes the origin's origin, the radical's root, insofar as it – *its* difference, *its* violence, the *sentiendum* – must force thinking toward its transcendent exercise and thus, enigmatically, toward its own origin. I've cited the passage already:

> on the path that leads to that which is to be thought, everything launches from sensibility. From the intensive to thought, thought always happens to us through an intensity. The privilege of sensibility as origin . . .

Thinking depends upon every link in the chain because every link in the chain precedes it, to be sure, but it depends upon the sensible hitch first of all. Sensibility's the first and, for a time, the only sign of difference in the world and therefore the only hope for thinking and for philosophy. Hence, should the sensible encounter prove unreliable or in any way ambivalent, the entire doctrine could collapse before it ever reaches its origin, its other origin, its 'radical' origin in thinking. The entire doctrine and, with it, philosophy at large could collapse before it ever radically begins. Whence *the sensible hitch* – anchor *and* obstacle – of Deleuze's doctrine and philosophy. By which I mean not only the philosophy of *Deleuze* but also philosophy in general if, as Deleuze suggests, there had been no philosophy until he does it as a philosophy of difference in 1968.

How, then, does sensibility grasp its difference? How does sensibility's grasp on its object jeopardise the origin before it originates? Whence the ambivalence? When it claims its privilege, its private law, when it alone stirs on the evening before everything as the only inkling of difference, sensibility grasps a *sign*. 'Sensibility, in the presence of what can only be felt [*senti*] (the insensible at the same time), finds itself before a proper limit – the sign – and is raised to a transcendent exercise' (DR 182|140). In the Platonic turn, the conflicting reports offered by the senses about one and the same object constitute a sign of the higher realm of Ideas wherein the intellect resolves the conflict. Deleuze recycles the sensible pivot in his doctrine but re-determines the Idea of which the sensible is a sign in terms of difference. Sensibility grasps a sign of difference. Already in the 'Introduction' of *Difference and Repetition*, Deleuze systematises his definition of the sign in terms of difference and dissymmetry.

> We call 'signal' a system endowed with elements of dissymmetry, provided with orders of disparate size; we call 'sign' what happens within such a system, what flashes in the interval, like a communication established between disparates [*disparates*]. (DR 31|20)

The sign flashes between dissymmetrical, disparate, differential elements. To that extent, it seems to remain continuous with the Saussurean principle, still paradigmatic today even when unacknowledged, according to which differential relations constitute the sign (both signifier and signified). I invoke Saussure in order to place Deleuze's idiosyncratic definition of the sign on more familiar terrain, but the invocation has essential limits. Deleuze criticises Saussure, namely, for concluding that the differential relations comprising the sign make it purely negative.

Saussure: 'All of the preceding amounts to saying that *in language there are only differences*. Moreover: a difference presupposes in general positive terms between which it is established, but in language there are only differences *without positive terms*' (*Cours* 166|*Course* 120, translation modified).

Deleuze: 'Let us return to the linguistic Idea: why does Saussure, at the moment he discovers that "in language there are only differences", add that these differences are "without positive terms", "eternally negative"?' (DR 264|204).

For Deleuze, contra Saussure, the negative constitutes a transcendental illusion the mechanism of which, in more general terms, I won't engage at length until Chapter 4 below. More importantly here, Deleuze's sign results from a positive concept of difference he calls the Idea. Far from limited to language, moreover, in *Logic of Sense* Deleuze suggests that all phenomena are signs insofar as they find their reason in difference (LS 301|261).

If, then, we first approach difference through a sign, we have no direct access to the productive difference that it signals. Despite the potential obscurity of his idiosyncratic terms, Deleuze speaks clearly in this regard: 'In short, we know of intensity only when already developed in an extensity [*étendue*], and covered over by qualities' (DR 288|223). When Deleuze nevertheless claims that the transcendent exercise of sensibility grasps difference *immediately* in the encounter (DR 188|144), the 'immediacy' only means sensibility doesn't depend upon another faculty for its difference. Sensible difference might be 'the noumenon closest to the phenomenon' (DR 286|222), but even the 'closest' never coincides. Immediate access to difference only means the least mediate.

This crucial hermeneutics would already suffice to rattle the entire facultative chain.[16] If sensibility grasps signs of difference, it might misinterpret the sign, fail to trace it back to difference, and thus have nothing to pass along to the rest of the faculties that – along with philosophy itself – depend upon it. In fact, however, sensibility risks much more than misinterpretation. A misinterpretation doesn't necessarily affect what it misinterprets, which one can therefore in principle revisit and reinterpret. The Deleuzian sign, by contrast, annihilates what it signals.

> We call 'signal' a system endowed with elements of dissymmetry, provided with orders of disparate size; we call 'sign' what happens within such a system, what flashes in the interval, like a communication established between disparates. The sign is indeed an effect, but the effect has two aspects: one by which, as a sign, it expresses the productive dissymmetry; the other by which it [the sign] tends to annul it [the dissymmetry]. (DR 31|20)

In which case the sign doesn't signal the coming annihilation or annulment of difference. The sign itself annuls difference; the sign signals difference *by* annulling it. Rather than the otherwise more accurate or at least more fluent 'to cancel', I prefer to translate *annuler* more literally as 'annul' or 'nullify' in order to keep these disastrous stakes clear through the etymological reference to *nullity*, *null*, *nil*, not (*ne-*) any (*ullus*). In this case, not any difference.

Whatever the novelty in its formation, formulation and deployment, Deleuze's sign remains equivocal, like all signs, but this equivocity is unlike any other. The sign can be grasped as the expressive effect and thus the effective expression of a positive and productive difference, or it can be grasped with reference to its tendency to annul difference, that is, grasped as a 'quality' attributable to some self-same 'thing' through the mechanisms of recognition presupposed in the merely 'empirical' exercise of sensibility. One grasp strangles the difference that the other would pass along to the other faculties. Hence, the stakes of this hermeneutical crossroads can't be exaggerated. The entire doctrine depends upon it, including and most of all the archaic link, the extremity, the 'radical origin' that Deleuze calls 'thinking'. There is, in short, an absolute and inadmissible jeopardy in the first link of the facultative chain without which philosophy today can't become a philosophy of difference. An *absolute* jeopardy because the movement toward thinking and the radical origin of Ideas always begins in a sensible encounter with signs that, by definition, never signal difference without also, at the same time, already annulling it. An *inadmissible* jeopardy because Deleuze never allows himself to doubt that the chain will reach its final link, that difference will be thought, that there will be philosophy.

To be sure, Deleuze constantly recalls the difficulty and scarcity of thinking. With admiration and approval he cites from the opening of Heidegger's *What Is Called Thinking?*: 'Man can think in the sense that he possesses the possibility [*die Möglichkeit*] to do so. This possibility alone, however, is no guarantee to us that we are capable of thinking [*daß wir es vermögen*]' (Heidegger, GA 8:5|*Thinking* 3). In the same sentence in which he cites it, Deleuze commandeers Heidegger's thought and finishes it in his own paradoxical terms: 'what is to be thought is also the unthinkable or the unthought, that is to say, the perpetual *fact* that "we do not yet think"' (DR 188).[17] Deleuze stresses the fact. As a matter of *fact* we do not think, this fact is *perpetual*, but it's *only* a fact. On another level, thinking remains possible. This is the paradoxicality of the paradoxical exercise of the faculties in Deleuze's doctrine: the *cogitandum* can't be thought on the factual plane and must be thought on the transcendent plane. With the possibility of thinking on transcendent reserve, whether the path is generous or violent matters little in the end. Deleuze insists that the chain running from sensibility to thinking is 'forced and broken' (DR 190|145), but how 'broken' is a chain if Deleuze can nevertheless warp thinking to sensibility with it? How 'broken' is a chain that always has the same beginning and the same end? How 'violent' is a series of encounters when the outcome is certain, indeed, forced? When it always ends in thinking perforce? When we end up thinking according to doctrine?

Deleuze, then, limits his break to a fracture. The profound ambivalence of the sensible sign, however, threatens to break the broken chain beyond repair, threatens to finish what Deleuze started, threatens to unhinge the chain and end philosophy before it ever starts to think. If the first link is the weakest because ambiguous and insecure, it is also the strongest because its very weakness could unhinge the whole facultative chain and, in the same semiotic flash, the philosophy for which it remains *tout à fait* necessary today. The most violent encounter of all is thus the sensible. The sensible is even the only truly violent encounter because it's the only one that really jeopardises the superior exercise of thinking. While every other violence secures thinking, forces it, sensibility threatens it with the violence of another force. The symbolic violence of sensibility goes unnamed in Deleuze's doctrine since this violence isn't done *in* the doctrine but rather *to* the doctrine itself. This violence doesn't submit to thinking and therefore commits, perhaps, the only real violence to thinking. Sensibility might never wake, which is to say (both transitively and intransitively), might never wake itself and might never wake thinking.

Implications

When Deleuze returns to the sensible in depth in chapter 5 of *Difference and Repetition*, 'Asymmetrical Synthesis of the Sensible', he recognises the sensible hitch indirectly but precisely by taking out insurance against it.

We first meet difference as 'intensity', as sensible difference, but we first meet intensity, first know or rather know of it, only when it's already covered over (*recouverte*) by 'qualities' (DR 288|223). This is another way of saying we first encounter difference through an 'empirical' sensibility unequipped to grasp it. Empirical sensibility grasps a mere 'quality', which isn't difference itself, in itself, but can 'signal' difference. Large or small, for instance, soft or hard are qualitative signs. Insofar as it relates these qualities to a supposedly self-same object like, say, a finger, sensibility continues to operate empirically, dogmatically, with no sign of difference. Insofar as these qualities qualify the same object at the same time, however, insofar as they create a conflict that defies thought based upon identity, for Deleuze – if not for Plato – these qualities signal a more original difference as their cause. 'Whence the double aspect of the quality as sign: to refer to an implicated order of constituting differences, to tend to annul these differences in the extended order that explicates them' (DR 294|228). I've already thematised the stakes of this herme-neutical crossroads, but crucial elaborations here in the last chapter of *Difference and Repetition* harden the *jeopardisation* of difference into an irrecoverable *loss*.

One of the two roads in this crossroads leads to the end of difference. In fact, because we first know of difference through the qualities that tend to annul it, we extrapolate the movement from difference toward homogenisation as an incontrovertible principle. As if by default, we not only take this road but even accelerate upon it. This 'we' is wide. More than any given individual, it includes philosophy, science and even – beyond any specific discipline – all 'good sense' (*le bon sens*) from the end of the nineteenth century to the mid-twentieth when, as Deleuze says in the preface to *Difference and Repetition*, difference was finally in the air. 'We know how, at the end of the nineteenth century, these themes of a reduction of difference, of a uniformisation [*uniformisation*] of the diverse, of an equalisation of the unequal formed for the last time the strangest alliance: between science, *le bon sens* and philosophy' (DR 288|223). Deleuze's eclectic terms are often hard to follow in Chapter 5 precisely because this inter- and extra-disciplinary tendency to reduce and homogenise difference authorises him, if not even obligates him, to draw upon a number of theories and discourses to describe it (economics, thermodynamics, embryology, philosophy and so on).[18]

Deleuze's doctrine of faculties paves the other crossroad. Given the same quality or qualities, the transcendent exercise of sensibility doesn't rush 'forward' to annul difference but, rather, grasps quality as a sign of difference and then turns 'back' (wakes memory) to the difference that made those qualities possible in the first place. Rather than this or that sensible being (*le divers*), sensibility's transcendent exercise seeks the being of the sensible (*la différence*).

Yet, because they tend to annul difference, qualities don't offer a stable platform for interpretation; they don't last long as signs of difference.

> It is true that qualities are signs and fulgurate in the hiatus [*l'écart*] of a difference, but, precisely, they measure the time of an equalisation, that is to say, the time taken by difference to be annulled [*s'annuler*] in the extensity [*étendue*] in which it is distributed. (DR 288|223)

Difference is time sensitive. At least at first, in its sensible aspect, it must be grasped now – or never. '*Signs* . . . always belong to the present' (DR 106|77). The sensible hitch grows more urgent: only sensibility grasps signs and begins the movement back toward difference but, if sensibility doesn't grasp the glimmer of difference in time, if it altogether loses intensity to quality, if it loses the being of the sensible to a sensible being, it will have nothing to communicate to the other faculties, and philosophy as a whole stalls before it begins. 'Even if' – this two-word qualification (*même si*) is one of precious few indications that Deleuze is aware of the problem that sensibility poses for (his) philosophy, although he avoids formalising the problem, insofar as it indicates that sensibility's privilege as the first ligament is also at bottom a liability – 'even if difference tends to distribute [*répartir*] into the diverse in such a way that it disappears and to uniformise [*uniformiser*] this diverse that it creates, it must first be felt, as that which gives the diverse to be felt' (DR 292|226–7). Even if qualities destroy the difference they signal, even if sensibility has no guarantee of grasping difference in time, even if sensibility remains complacent with the annihilation of difference, difference must first be felt.

This is the context in which Deleuze attempts to take out insurance against the sensible annihilation of difference. Deleuze never denies that difference is annulled, nullified, *annulée*.[19] It's 'really' annulled, he insists, in reality, *réellement*. But difference is annulled only 'outside itself', in another regime or on another plane, in the realm of what Deleuze calls 'extensity' (*l'étendue*), the realm in which dynamic intensity becomes stationary quality, the realm of sensible beings and the merely empirical exercise that grasps them (DR 309|240). In itself, difference is never abolished; it remains 'implicated in itself' (DR 294|228). By 'implication', then, Deleuze doesn't mean that the intensity of differential being is 'implicated' in the qualities of sensible beings. At least not primarily. This implication is secondary (DR 305|237) and, since quality also tends to annul the difference implicated in it, doesn't last long. More primordially, more importantly, difference remains implicated in itself, folded upon itself, self-involved. A patient reading would have to coordinate *Difference and Repetition* with the systematic and genealogical presentation of 'implication', 'complication' and 'explication' in *Spinoza and the Problem of Expression*.[20] To the point, Deleuze doesn't inaugurate the idea that the source, the primordial cause, the origin withdraws from what it produces. Whether Plato's Idea, Plotinus's 'One' or Spinoza's God,[21] whether an emanative cause that remains exterior to what it produces or the immanent cause to which Deleuze opposes it, Deleuze himself remarks that these responses to the problem of participation all commonly posit, despite all other 'profound' oppositions, that the origin 'remains in itself' (SPE 155|171). No longer commenting upon Plato, Neo-Platonists or Spinoza, when Deleuze affirms in his own philosophy that originary difference remains in itself, auto-implicated, he too accepts this feature of self-preservation that therefore survives and localises all shifts, seisms and ruptures in the history of philosophy from Plato to Deleuze. In a certain sense, Deleuze has no choice. Difference can survive its annihilation only if it remains insulated in itself from the qualities that it creates but that nevertheless annul it. Even when it seems long gone, dissipated into qualities, difference remains folded upon itself and thus not only *unannulled* but even *unannullable, proprement inannulable*, 'properly unannullable' (DR 299|232).

Which means, for Deleuze, there is still and always hope for philosophy. This, then, might be Deleuze's response to what I've called the sensible hitch: even if, despite all the force of the most forceful encounter, you never manage to exercise sensibility properly, even if you never make it beyond a merely empirical exercise inadequate to difference, even if your sensibility grasps *qualities* rather than *sentienda* and thus has no difference to pass on to your memory, your imagination, your thought, even if none of your faculties wake, even if there's no sign of difference in the world, difference remains unaffected in itself. Unaffected by your torpidity, by your transcendent anaesthesia. No number of failures to feel difference could ever really jeopardise philosophy *even if* difference must first be felt for philosophy to begin. *Even if* no one ever actually feels difference before it's covered over by qualities. *Even if* sensibility hitches the chain. Implication keeps difference and therefore thinking and therefore philosophy in reserve.

And yet, even if I keep Deleuze's faith in the perpetual promise of philosophy, the concept of implication has a tenuous but essential limit that he never seems to realise. While I'll limit myself to the second, this limit holds *a fortiori* for the entire tradition that Deleuze thematises in *Spinoza and the Problem of Expression* and reclaims in *Difference and Repetition*. Namely, even if the auto-implication of difference guarantees sensibility all the time in the world to wake up and grasp it, even if one day sensibility has its moment, even if it comes to difference before difference comes to nothing, it won't grasp pure difference in itself. For the tendency to annul difference isn't limited to philosophy or science or to *le bon sens* to which philosophy and science cater. There's another, more originary, more problematic tendency: 'the tendency of differences of intensity themselves *à s'annuler* in the qualified extended systems' (DR 289|224). At stake is no longer an epistemological tendency, a tendency in philosophy or in science, but rather an ontological (*being of the sensible*), a pathological (*sensibility of the senses*), a logical (*reason of the sensible*), an ontopathological tendency of difference itself. So far, I've translated the reflexive *s'annuler* passively as 'is annulled', but I now have reason to translate it as 'annuls itself': difference itself tends to annul itself. Or, more simply, drawing upon an English resource that allows a verb to linger between an open transitive and an implicit reflexive: *difference annuls*. There is, in short, a tendency to annul in the very auto-implication that insulates difference from its annulment.

On the one hand, this other tendency – not simply that of qualities but, rather, that of intensive difference itself – follows a strict necessity. If indeed difference alone is originary in the system (for instance, DR 163–4|125), then only difference can account for its own annulment in the final analysis. Difference might annul in another regime, in 'extensity' and as 'quality', but Deleuze constantly recalls that difference itself 'creates' the extensity and qualities in and as which it annuls. Which is why, although the majority of his analyses give difference an alibi by placing the end in another realm, Deleuze nevertheless admits that difference operates its own annulment: 'it seems to rush to suicide' (DR 289|224). Deleuze can preserve the originarity of difference only if, insofar as difference ends, difference ends itself. Only if difference has suicidal tendencies.

On the other hand, the implication can't be contained. I've spoken of jeopardy: sensibility might not grasp its difference, it might not transmit difference to thinking, it might ruin philosophy. No longer a jeopardy, the suicidal tendencies of difference end the game in advance. Or at least radically change it. Raising the faculty to a higher, paradoxical, transcendent or transcendental exercise now makes no difference. Even at its summit, sensibility will never grasp difference 'purely' or 'in itself'. Not because identity is more originary after all or because difference is already in itself absolutely null. My point here is more tenuous but no less decisive: if difference tends toward the qualities in which it annuls, then it already opens onto the realm that will ruin it and the qualities that will 'cover' it before it ever submits to them, indeed, before they even exist, before difference ever creates them and therefore even if difference never actually annuls. As a result, difference never remains entirely 'implicated in itself'. How can it if, however self-involved, it already tends toward the extended plane of qualities that, in the attempt to shelter difference, Deleuze describes on more than one occasion as its 'outside' (DR 294|228 and 309|240)? This tendency brings the annihilistic outside tenuously but tenaciously into the most intimate folds of difference itself, which is therefore never entirely 'itself'.

For the same reason, sensibility will never grasp difference as pure intensity, never as Deleuze prescribes, never 'independently of extensity or before the quality in which it is developed' (DR 305|237). Never entirely. Again, I don't mean to suggest that 'extensity' and 'quality' are already fully developed in the folds of difference. Deleuze no doubt taps the notion of 'tendency' precisely in order to relate intensity to qualities while keeping them at a distance, but even the most tenuous opening onto quality suffices to withdraw difference as intensity, surreptitiously, from a facultative exercise indoctrinated to grasp it 'in itself' and 'purely'. If intensity already tends toward extensity, toward qualities, toward the regime in which it will cease to differ, then extensity, quality and the end of intensity already pertain to the most primordial difference. Pure difference will never be imagined, remembered or thought, because it will never be felt first of all. What can't be felt, perhaps, can't be felt after all.

Once sensitised to it, one finds symptoms of this facultative failure at the transcendent level throughout *Difference and Repetition*. As if indecisive about where the tendency should originate, for instance, Deleuze attributes a 'tendency' to annul difference to difference itself, to philosophy and the sciences (DR 288|223), to *le bon sens* (DR 289|223), to extension and quality (DR 303|235) and to the sign (DR 31|20). Similarly, even after assuring philosophers of difference that there's no need 'to save' or 'restore' difference since it remains implicated in itself (DR 294|228), he nevertheless recognises the need 'to restore difference in [*dans*] intensity' (DR 342|266). Along the same lines, since 'explication' pertains to the qualitative realm outside (*ex*) the folds (*plies*) of implication in Deleuze's idiosyncratic terms,[22] his rule 'not to explicate (too much)' (DR 314|244, 335|261) – in itself symptomatic – softens his call to grasp difference independently of extensity and qualities (DR 305|237). All of these symptoms and others unnamed would require separate developments, at times separate discourses, but they all point to the same issue: philosophy can recreate its faculties, it must recreate its faculties, but it can never grasp difference. Not 'purely', not 'in itself', not without a tenacious trace of identity.

Notes

1. On this point, see also the section on 'Euthanasia' in Chapter 3 below.
2. Not only does Hughes miss the profound ambivalence of sensibility in *Difference and Repetition*. When he questions the necessity of including

the facultative doctrine in a 'comprehensive account' of *Difference and Repetition* ('strange and marginal', he calls it [73]), he also *a fortiori* remains insensitive to the importance of the doctrine in general and sensibility in particular for the rest of Deleuze's writings.

Bryant takes Deleuze's comments on the faculties seriously, systematically, and even respects sensibility's privilege as the original faculty, but he too remains insensitive to its ambivalent place in Deleuze's system. At times, he unwittingly inherits the ambivalence; at other times, his reading contorts and multiplies distinctions (e.g., with respect to 'signs' [Bryant 100 and 132]) in an attempt to protect sensibility from the negative propositions bearing upon it in *Difference and Repetition*.

In 'Deleuze's Theory of Sensation: Overcoming the Kantian Duality', the sixth of Smith's *Essays on Deleuze*, the systemic factors that catalyse what I call the sensible hitch are present and developed to various degrees (sensibility is irreducibly singular; everything begins in sensibility but ends in thought; sensibility forces thinking; the sensible sign cancels difference; and so on), but Smith never configures them in such a way that would allow him to draw the ambivalent consequences that result for Deleuze's philosophy in general and theory of sensation in particular.

A bit arbitrarily, as he himself admits, Massumi generalises the term 'affect' in *Parables for the Virtual* to name the co-implication of the virtual and the actual at work in any actual thing (*Parables* 35). While Deleuze often figures as only one name among others in his analyses, on occasion Massumi nevertheless calls attention to the centrality of Deleuze for his re-elaboration of affect, which one could confirm by tracing many of the book's basic problems, concepts and arguments to precedents in Deleuze's work. Only one precedent matters here. Namely, Massumi's description of 'affect' rehearses – without acknowledging it – Deleuze's paradoxical formulation of the *sentiendum*: that which *cannot be felt* (in a traditionally empirical exercise of sensibility) *can only be felt* (in the superior exercise of sensibility). Massumi adopts and varies the paradox on several occasions throughout the influential opening of his *Parables*, 'The Autonomy of Affect' (30, 32, 33, 36, 42; see also 133, 136, etc.), which 'sets the stage' for the rest of the book (17). To the extent that Massumi thus more or less openly grounds his *Parables* in Deleuze's paradoxical exercise of the faculty of sensibility, they inherit its pure ambivalence.

3. But only perhaps: 'I never felt the slightest objection, even virtual, against any of his discourses, *even if* I happened to murmur . . . *perhaps* against the idea that philosophy consists in "creating" concepts' (Derrida, *Chaque fois unique* 236|*Work of Mourning* 193, my italics, translation modified). For a more nuanced discussion, see my article, 'Apocrypha: Derrida's Writing in *Anti-Oedipus*'.

4. Kant: 'there would be no reason why other judgments necessarily would have to agree with mine, if there were not the unity of the object – an object to which they all refer, with which they all agree, and, for that reason, also must all harmonize [*zustimmen*] among themselves' (*Prolegomena* 4:298). Deleuze: 'It is clear that Kant thus traces [*décalque*] the so-called transcendental structures on empirical acts of a psychological consciousness' (DR 176–7|135). For Deleuze's passing note on the Kantian sublime, see DR 187 note 1|320–1 note 10. See also PCK, especially 73|50 ff. Deleuze, of course, isn't the first to accuse Kant of empiricism. 'Kant, though he attacks empiricism, still remains dependent upon this very empiricism in his conception of the soul and the range of tasks of a psychology' (Husserl, HUA 6:117|*Crisis* 115; see also §30). While Husserl credits Kant with the first transcendental philosophy (§27), he accuses Kant of limiting transcendental subjectivity to empirical subjectivity (what Husserl calls the 'soul') and, more specifically, determining consciousness's constitutive work in terms of the mathematical objectification for which transcendental subjectivity should account (cf. especially 97|94). See also Emmanuel Housset's comments in *Husserl et l'énigme du monde* (87–9 and 121) on the supplementary texts of Husserl's *First Philosophy* and on the sixth of his *Logical Investigations*. In *Logic of Sense*, without ever acknowledging his Husserlian precedent in this regard, Deleuze accuses Husserl himself of the same empiricism of which he accuses Kant (LS 119). Much later and more decisively in *What Is Philosophy?*, Deleuze critiques the phenomenological sense of 'transcendental', which Husserl proclaims the widest and most radical, as one more moment on the path toward pure immanence no longer immanent *to* subjectivity. In Chapter 6, however, I'll argue that immanence and transcendentalism in the Husserlian sense amount to two extremes of the same auto-affection.

5. 'There is no doubt whatever that all our cognition begins with experience; for how else should the cognitive faculty be awakened [*erweckt*] into exercise . . . ?' (Kant, *Critique of Pure Reason* B1). Despite Deleuze's longstanding admiration for Hume and the empiricism he represents, to which I'll turn in detail in the next chapter, Hume also takes the faculties for granted or, as he says, 'endowed' (*Enquiry* 1.14).

6. For instance, see 'the other peculiar property [*Eigentümliche*]' of *Ereignis* at the end of Heidegger's 'Time and Being' (GA 14:28|23).

7. Agamben 238–9. For an attempt to elaborate and mobilise Agamben's schema in a reading of the relation of Deleuze to Derrida, see the sixteenth essay of Daniel Smith's *Essays on Deleuze* ('Deleuze and Derrida, Immanence and Transcendence: Two Directions in Recent French Thought'). Modifications notwithstanding, Leonard Lawlor either adopts or reaches Agamben's genealogical schema – without

naming him – in the opening pages of *Derrida and Husserl*. I'll return to this genealogy on occasion in other chapters.

8. See DR 181 note 1|320 note 8; NP 169 note 1|210 note 33 (see also 78|50, where Deleuze already speaks of a 'superior empiricism'); PS 121–2|99–100.

9. From Deleuze's preface to the English translation of *Difference and Repetition* (xv), reprinted in *Deux régimes de fou* (280): 'There's a great difference between writing the history of philosophy and writing philosophy. [. . .] *Difference and Repetition* was the first book in which I tried "to do philosophy".'

10. Plato, *Republic* 523c–524a. Notably, Plato's sequence lacks imagination. Following suit, Deleuze initially omits the imagination from his own recuperation of the Platonic chain. The *imaginandum* is only a question at first: 'is there an *imaginandum* . . . that is indeed also the limit, the impossible to imagine?' (DR 186|143). In the next paragraph, Deleuze suddenly inserts the imagination as one of the necessary links in the facultative chain. His source for the imagination, at least here, is the Kantian sublime (DR 187 note 1|320–1 note 10), and it would be worth speculating, first, on why he inserts the imagination in the chain as its second link and, second, on why he hesitates to do so.

11. For more on Aristotle's completion (and Leibniz's and Hegel's Christian expansion) of the representational regime that Plato prepared, see LS 298–300|259–60. Deleuze isn't the only or the first person to accuse Plato and Aristotle of installing representational thinking. Heidegger, however, is more considerate. Representation eclipses being, to be sure, insofar as beings lend themselves to representation only after being has already been interpreted in a certain light, but it remains creative in the case of Plato and Aristotle because, as the first to represent, they create the very realm in which being – and the forgetting of being – would be forgotten throughout the history of metaphysics. See Heidegger GA 65:64|*Contributions* 51. Deleuze will have a similar inspiration in *What Is Philosophy?* when he argues that, although Plato calls for contemplating Ideas, he first had to create the concept of Idea (QP 11|6). Deleuze never says so but, analogously to Heidegger's claim, this creation eclipses creativity itself.

12. Compare Plato's metaphorical recourse to the sun in the cave allegory with his disdain for the 'vulgar praise of astronomy' (Plato, *Republic* 528e). Due to its political agenda, however, the *Republic* can't uproot the soul from the sensible altogether. The city obliges the philosopher to descend and reign (520e), against his or her rational will, because argument alone commands nothing. In light of which, the sensible preserves the irreducible realm of politics.

13. See DR 236 ff.|182 ff. (ideal multiplicities) and 247–51|191–5 (facultative multiplicities).

14. See Heidegger, GA 11:36|*Identity* 27. When the faculties grasp the Idea, difference 'in itself', they grasp Being (DR 297–8|228; see also QP 42|38).

15. The notion of 'aberrant movements' has undeniable explanatory force with respect to Deleuze's oeuvre with and without Guattari. David Lapoujade establishes as much already in the introduction to the work to which the notion lends its name. In the space of relatively few pages, he broaches texts, problems and concepts from every era, ambit and genre of Deleuze's work, a diversity that only the notion of 'aberrant movement' seems to traverse and unify. As if *Aberrant Movements* were itself an aberrant movement through all the aberrant movements in Deleuze's work. Necessarily among these movements, then, is the doctrine of faculties in *Difference and Repetition*, which Lapoujade invokes by name (Lapoujade 18–19|32–3). All the aberrations, however, only strengthen the question: how aberrant will the movement of and between faculties have been if, doctrinally, it always ends in thinking? Perhaps incidental, perhaps symptomatic, Lapoujade speaks of the 'immemorial in memory' and the 'unthinkable in thought' but – twice in the same passage listing the doctrine's faculties – omits sensibility (Lapoujade 18–19|33), the royal faculty, the original faculty from which everything launches and that therefore, we'll soon see, jeopardises everything. Although Lapoujade by no means takes the transcendent exercise for granted (see also 63|80–1), the greatest aberration in this preordained movement would be precisely what arrests it.

16. Of course, I recognise the controversy risked by speaking of 'hermeneutics', let alone a 'crucial' hermeneutics, in a philosopher notorious for rejecting interpretation. A twohanded remark holds not only for *Difference and Repetition* but also for works like *Logic of Sense* and *Anti-Oedipus* in which the same hermeneutical crossroads takes other forms. On the one hand, I don't simply contradict Deleuze's allergy to interpretation since at stake here is a decision, not between this or that interpretation, but rather between interpretation and non-interpretation. The same decision, on the other hand, shows that Deleuze isn't immune to all interpretation whatsoever. On the contrary, no interpretation proves more significant than the interpretation meant to eliminate interpretation itself.

17. I cite only the French in this instance because, no doubt accidentally, Paul Patton omits this entire clause in his English translation, which would fall on page 144. On the difficulty and scarcity of thinking, see also DR 173|132, 198|152–3 and 353|275.

18. Although he only occasionally follows Deleuze's sources and even his arguments, see Manuel DeLanda's *Intensive Science and Virtual Philosophy* for a reconstruction of Deleuze's thought as it bears upon mathematics and sciences. On DeLanda's reconstructive strategy, see

xii–xiii; on the scientific backdrop of 'tendency', see especially 7 ff.; on the cancellation of difference, which DeLanda calls 'one of Deleuze's most important theses regarding the intensive' and the 'key to Deleuze's philosophy' (62), see 68 ff. As I'll soon show, however, much more than an 'illusion' – albeit an 'objective' illusion – is at stake, let alone one that can be overcome (69).

19. Not even three decades later in *What Is Philosophy?* (QP 26|21). See also AŒ 192|160, where unconscious intensity is annulled in its movement toward historico-social extension. I treat the ambivalence that operates *Anti-Oedipus* in the conclusion to this book.

20. Deleuze broaches these terms by the third page of the 'Introduction', but see also SPE 159|175. In *Difference and Repetition*, see especially 359–60|280–1.

21. One could also add Heidegger here. Cautiously, however, since he would undoubtedly dispute the causal conceptuality as a metaphysical determination of being. He speaks, rather, of sending: 'A giving [*Geben*] which gives only its gift [*Gabe*], but in the giving holds back [*sich selbst . . . zurückhält*] and withdraws [*entzieht*], such a giving we call sending [*das Schicken*]' (Heidegger, GA 14:12|*On* Time 8).

22. 'There is no room for surprise concerning the fact that difference *à la lettre* is "inexplicable". Difference explicates [*s'explique*], but, precisely, it tends to be cancelled in the system in which it explicates. Which only indicates that difference is essentially implicated, that the being of difference is implication. For difference, to explicate is to annul [*s'annuler*], to dispel the inequality that constitutes it. The formulation according to which "to explicate is to identify" is a tautology' (DR 293–4|228).

2

Furtive Contemplations

What more useful than all the passions of the mind, ambition, vanity, love, anger? But how oft do they break their bounds, and cause the greatest convulsions in society?

Hume, *Dialogues* 11.11

Il y a moi dès que s'établit quelque part une contemplation furtive . . .

Deleuze, DR 107|78

In Chapter 1, I focused upon sensibility in the doctrine of faculties in the third chapter of *Difference and Repetition*. As the first work in which Deleuze 'does' philosophy, it constitutes Deleuze's first theory of affect. Deleuze speaks of 'sensibility' rather than 'affect', to be sure, but he establishes fundamental features that go unaltered in his later work where the term 'affect' prevails.[1] The facultative doctrine, however, isn't the only moment in *Difference and Repetition* in which sensibility plays a fundamental role. Sensibility also operates the first of the three syntheses of time in the second chapter. I'll eventually pinpoint coordinates to suggest that sensibility in the doctrine of faculties *is* sensibility in the first synthesis of time since, not without reason, there has been confusion on this issue, but the systematic solidarity between the syntheses of time and the doctrine of faculties doesn't prevent Deleuze from drawing upon other sources to elaborate sensibility in terms of time. He draws the concept of contemplation, namely, from David Hume.

The paleonym might mislead. This 'contemplation' isn't the 'contemplation' most readily recognised in or, indeed, inaugural of the philosophical tradition. It isn't Plato's contemplation of Ideas. Because the Platonic Idea prepares the regime of representation detrimental to what it really means to think, Deleuze and Guattari don't hesitate to deny that, along with more modern and contemporary inflections like 'reflection' and 'communication', philosophy isn't contemplation.[2] But Deleuze doesn't thereby reject contemplation in every form. The very soul that would 'contemplate' a Platonic Idea stems from a prior and more profound 'contemplation' that

67

Deleuze inherits from Hume and, far from being a never really but always ideally disembodied contemplation of an immutable Idea, this other contemplation operates through what Deleuze calls a 'primary sensibility'.

While often cited and celebrated by sensitive readers like Agamben (to whom I'll return at the end of this chapter), this sensible contemplation nevertheless doesn't escape scrutiny in turn. Hume himself already signals a fundamental impasse in the work of contemplation with regard to the idea of the self. Upon inheriting the concept, Deleuze also inherits its impasse. He displaces and redistributes but never entirely overcomes it. This impasse ultimately establishes in Deleuze's system and discourse an ambivalence at once primary (insofar as it bears upon the first temporal synthesis), profound (insofar as the first synthesis founds the system) and pure (insofar as it has no object other than sensibility itself).

The point isn't simply, however, to rehash the ambivalence I outline in Chapter 1 in other terms here in Chapter 2. Contemplation is the longest running concept in Deleuze's oeuvre. With unparalleled longevity, it operates in some capacity from the first chapter of *Empiricism and Subjectivity* (1953) to *Critical and Clinical* (1993). From Deleuze's first book to his last. To address contemplation, then, I can no longer limit my purview to *Difference and Repetition*. In what follows, accordingly, after renewing and hardening the impasse in Hume (§1), I'll show that and how Deleuze displaces but doesn't resolve the impasse in *Empiricism and Subjectivity* (§2), that and how he imports it into his own philosophy in *Difference and Repetition* (§3) and that and how it continues to ambivalate his philosophy when he defines it in *What Is Philosophy?* (§4). Precisely because it traverses Deleuze's work as a historian of philosophy, as a philosopher and as a historian of his own philosophy, no concept bears greater witness to the indefatigable scope and subterranean consistency of the ambivalence across Deleuze's work.

Extra Interiority

At its most poignant, the impasse of contemplation will concern the unity of the mind, but it unfolds from the most original point of Hume's philosophy. At the end of the Abstract, published anonymously in 1740 and meant to clarify the basic argument of *A Treatise of Human Nature*, Hume anticipates his contribution to philosophy and its history.

> Thro' this whole book, there are great pretensions to new discoveries in philosophy; but if anything can entitle the author to so glorious a name as that of an *inventor*, 'tis the use he makes of the principle of the association of ideas, which enters into most of his philosophy. (*Treatise*, Abstract 35)

Hume doesn't invent the association of ideas, even by his own account, but his use of it is so original, he says, that he nevertheless deserves the glorious name 'inventor'. Most inventive, among the principles of association, is no doubt the use Hume makes of causality. Its ground is contemplation.

According to the fundamental maxim that Hume proposes in the opening section of the *Treatise*, all ideas derive from impressions, that is, from perceptions or sensations as they first appear in the mind; ideas are nothing but fainter images of impressions that we deploy in thinking (*Treatise* 1.1.1.1). But the idea of causality troubles the maxim and despite appearances, although Hume never articulates the problem in this way, shows that the fundamental maxim of empiricism isn't entirely empirical. Because Hume also holds that perceptions always remain atomic, discrete, a causal relation *between* terms as such never gives itself to perception. Perceiving B follow A in what we habitually take as a causal relation, the mind observes the succession of B immediately after A, but it never observes the causation itself. 'When we consider these objects with the utmost attention', Hume says, 'we find only that the one body approaches the other; and that the motion of it precedes that of the other, but without any sensible interval' (1.3.2.9). Defying Hume's fundamental maxim, then, there seems to be no prior impression – no 'sensible interval' – from which to derive the idea of causality as a necessary connection between terms.

The search for this sensible interval propels Hume's analyses until, after 'beat[ing] about all the neighbouring fields' (1.3.2.13), it leads him to shift the very ground of causality. Ideas derive from impressions, but ideas can impress the mind again in turn, and from this secondary impression, from this 'impression of reflection' (1.3.14.22), Hume attempts to derive the idea of causality. The mind receives an impression of object A and then, contiguous and in succession, an impression of object B. When the sequence repeats, the repetition neither discovers nor produces anything new in the objects themselves (1.3.14.17–18). Yet, by *contemplating* the constant contiguity and succession of the same two objects or other pairs resembling them, by reflecting upon a multiplicity of instances of one object or type of object immediately following another, the mind begins to feel their connection; it feels compelled to think of B whenever A (1.3.14.20). From this feeling arises the new idea that B always follows A, that B necessarily follows A, that A thus causes B. Hume, of course, recognises the scandal.

> What! the efficacy of causes lie in the determination of the mind! As if causes did not operate entirely independent of the mind, and wou'd not continue their operation, even tho' there was no mind existent to contemplate them, or reason concerning them. Thought may well depend on causes for its operation, but not causes on thought. (1.3.14.26)

The decisive role of feeling in contemplation explains why Deleuze, for his part, will relate contemplation to sensibility throughout his writings.

For the same reason, one should appreciate the unique status of this contemplative feeling. Because it surges *between* impressions or ideas, this 'feeling' is neither a primary nor, even though Hume himself classifies it as such, a secondary 'impression' in the proper sense. It is not a passion, desire or emotion that arises when the soul is affected by the idea of a primary emotion. I am hungry (primary impression), which produces the idea of pain (primary idea), and the idea of hunger pains affects me in turn with aversion or fear that, Hume says, 'may properly be call'd impressions of reflection' (1.1.2.1). To be sure, Hume might leave room in the category of secondary impressions for the feeling of necessary connection when he says that impressions of reflection derive 'in a great measure' and 'mostly' from ideas (1.1.2.1). For 'mostly' means not entirely. Yet, the feeling of necessary connection nevertheless remains unique in its kind because – unlike passions, desires and emotions – it cannot be retraced to a primary idea (like pain) or, through the idea, to a primary impression (like hunger). It arises only through the repetition of primary impressions and primary ideas that, in themselves, never produce the feeling of necessary connection.

Though it therefore seems to have no proper place in the '*Division of the subject*' (1.1.3), life itself depends upon this feeling insofar as experimental or experiential reasoning, all reasoning concerning matters of fact, depends upon it.[3] One can't rigorously think without first feeling or, rather, without having felt twice: once through the isolated impressions and, once again, through the contemplation of those impressions in their contiguous and sequential repetition. This latter feeling, the feeling of feelings that at the same time feels nothing strictly speaking, frees thought from present impressions insofar as it allows the mind to extrapolate a causal relation and mobilise it to reason concerning past and future events. At the limit, I am not utterly disoriented by everything that happened, happens or will happen – I am not traumatised all the time – thanks only to this utopic feeling of contemplation.

If, then, 'contemplation' is one term among others that Hume uses to describe the mind's relation to a set of recurring perceptions that give rise to the idea of necessary connection defining causality ('reflection', 'observation' and 'consideration' are others), its function can't be overestimated. Coeval with life itself, Hume praises nature for making the operation instinctual, mechanical, rather than leaving it to our own unreliable faculties. 'It is more conformable to the ordinary wisdom of nature to secure so necessary an act of the mind, by some instinct or mechanical tendency' (*Enquiry* 5.22). Contemplation is too important, too vital, to operate ourselves. In fact, it's not exactly an 'act of the mind' because, in enigmatic ways I'll progressively clarify, the mechanics of contemplation must unify the mind before the mind can either 'act' or 'suffer'. Hume eventually specifies that contemplation 'acts in us unknown to ourselves' (9.6), which is more precise but still misleading if, indeed, contemplation also constitutes the 'us' within which it acts.

For the same reason, however, because contemplation is both *mechanical* and *genetic*, when the feeling of contemplation begins to seduce the mind, to lead it astray, the error is both *automatic* and *ineradicable*. Strictly speaking, there's no error at all if one understands 'error' as an avoidable misstep or miscalculation. This errancy, rather, has two tiers, and it will haunt the fate of contemplation in Deleuze from *Empiricism and Subjectivity* to *What Is Philosophy?*

First tier. Hume calls the self a fiction, but he never simply denies the self. He denies only the predominant conception of it, namely, 'perfect identity and simplicity' (*Treatise* 1.4.6.1). Any idea of perfect identity or simplicity must be based on a prior impression that, according to Hume, we never have. 'For from what impression cou'd this idea be deriv'd' (1.4.6.2)? We nevertheless have a *great* and *natural* propensity toward this misconception (1.4.6.4 and 5). Before we know what human nature really is, in the course of *A Treatise of Human Nature*, we know not only what it isn't; without knowing *what it is*, we know that *whatever it is* cannot entirely escape *what it isn't*. There's therefore truth in fiction without the fiction being true, and whatever idea of self that Hume might posit in our fiction's stead will never entirely replace or eradicate it. Not when truth itself generates the fiction that obscures it. This transcendental illusion constitutes an essential continuity between Spinoza, Hume, Kant and Deleuze that their greatest differences only drive deeper still.[4]

Why exactly, in the case of Hume, do I so naturally tend to mis-recognise my own nature, my identity, my self? Hume argues by analogy. He begins with the misperception of identity in objects before applying the same reasoning to the misperception of personal identity. This methodological choice will have considerable conse-quences, so it's important to follow the terms of the analogy in the order that Hume develops them.

Suppose two perceptual series, one of the same object over time (identity), the other of distinct but closely related objects in succes-sion (diversity). While diverse objects themselves should entertain no interrelation 'close' or otherwise, feeling makes possible the confu-sion of diversity with identity. We tend to confound identity with diversity because the feeling that arises from contemplating a succes-sion of closely related objects resembles the feeling that arises from contemplating the persistence of one and the same object. They are, Hume says, 'almost the same to the feeling' (*Treatise* 1.4.6.6). We can correct our error upon closer scrutiny, but the tendency proves so natural, so great, that we grow tired of correcting ourselves and eventually accept the idea that the closely related objects really are the self-same object. We then hypostatise a fiction of perfect identity to absorb any perceivable variation that might otherwise indicate that the 'object' perceived at one time and then another isn't one and the same. 'Thus', Hume concludes, 'we feign the continu'd existence of the perceptions of our senses, to remove the interruption; and run into the notion of a *soul*, and *self*, and *substance*, to disguise the variation' (1.4.6.6).

Such is the origin of the fictional idea of identity as it pertains to animals, plants and objects in general, and Hume submits our equally fictional idea of personal identity to 'the same method of reasoning' (1.4.6.14). Every perception remains different, distinguishable and separable from every other, and Hume denies the idea of a primor-dial and immutable self in which perceptions would inhere. He calls upon causality, rather, to unify perceptions and thereby constitute a self. Whence the sense in which, earlier, I anticipated contemplation as the mechanism that unifies the mind: 'the true idea of the human mind', according to Hume, 'is to consider it as a system of different perceptions or different existences, which are link'd together by the relation of cause and effect' (1.4.6.19). Albeit not one idea among others, the self pertains to a rather late stratum of consciousness. To Hume's mind, it isn't an impression; it isn't even an idea or a secondary impression. The idea of the self is a *secondary idea* that derives from a *secondary impression*, which arises only after we contemplate *primary ideas* that result from *primary impressions*. If, however, the mechanism that leads us to fictionalise identity in the outer world also operates by analogy in the inner, in the psyche, then we tend to confuse the diversity of our perceptions with identity. The fiction of personal identity arises because, although all our perceptions remain diverse and discrete, the causal link between them becomes so close, so strong, so habitual that we *feel* they're nothing but one continuous and lifelong stream of perception. Confounding perceptions with apperception, we then fabricate the idea of personal identity, of self-identity, to repave any perceptual alterity that might irrupt to suggest otherwise.

The contemplative machinery with which Nature so wisely secures our reason, in short, runs too well. Causality, too effectively. In the case of identity, not a case of mistaken identity but the very mistake of identity, contemplation associates perceptions so closely that we confound them into a single perception. The fiction of identity is a limit case, perhaps, but it isn't an exception. On the contrary, it only brings the industry of contemplation more clearly to light. Even in the legitimate constitution of a causal relation, the mind doesn't simply contemplate terms that already exist as 'cause' and as 'effect'. Previously an abyss, the channel from A to B affectively forged in contemplation constitutes A as the cause of B and B as the effect of A, hence, A and B as we know them, as cause and effect, as A and B. Neither cause nor effect is cause or effect without contemplation. In which case, the feeling that leads us to believe in fictions of identity may very well be illegitimate, 'errant' and 'arrant', but it only aggravates the basic mechanics on which causality, reasoning and life depend. In both cases, contemplation fabricates the object it contemplates.

Second tier. When Hume claims that the contemplation of diversity and the contemplation of identity are 'almost the same to the feeling' (cited above), the word 'almost' reserves the right to distinguish the diverse from the identical. If we can't eradicate the propensity to error, we can perhaps correct the error itself. On another order, however, contemplation becomes outright impassive. Hume himself is the first to admit it. Referring to the section *Of personal identity* (1.4.6), from which I have been citing, he formulates the impasse in the Appendix to the *Treatise*.

> In short there are two principles, which I cannot render consistent; nor is it in my power to renounce either of them, viz. *that all our distinct perceptions are distinct existences*, and *that the mind never perceives any real connexion among distinct existences*. (*Treatise*, Appendix 21)[5]

Which is to say, *the mind never perceives any real connection among all our distinct perceptions*. Such that the mind, which is nothing but the necessary connection of the perceptions that comprise it, never perceives itself and, consequently, the provenance of my idea of my 'self' becomes empirically inexplicable. To be clear, what Hume finds unsatisfactory in his own account is not the derivative status of the self, which he took to be generally accepted in his day.[6] More insatiable still, his dissatisfaction concerns the very viability of his principles of association for connecting the different perceptions of the mind and thereby constituting an idea of the self that, while neither identical nor simple nor original, he never doubts.

Hume's description of the mind in its native state is famous: 'a bundle or collection of different perceptions, which succeed each other with an inconceivable rapidity, and are in a perpetual flux and movement' (*Treatise* 1.4.6.4). As Deleuze poses it, Hume's fundamental question will be: '*how does the mind become a human nature?*' (ES 2|22). The short answer is causality, a brief rehearsal of which reveals the impasse to which it leads. For Hume, again, the true idea of the human mind is a causally regulated system of perceptions (*Treatise* 1.4.6.19). Like all ideas, however, the idea of causality must stem from a prior impression, which Hume traces to an impression of reflection. First, I receive an impression; this impression then becomes an idea and, upon reflection, this idea impresses me anew as an impression of reflection. Hume also calls impressions of reflection 'internal' impressions because, insofar as they result from ideas, they take place entirely within the mind. Impression, idea, internal impression and then, finally, the idea of causality meant to unify the mind. In view of which Hume comes to hesitate over his recourse to causality in order to unify the mind, not because the self should have some sort of substantial priority, but rather because the idea of causality originates *within* the mind the *within* of which it constitutes.

While Hume notoriously and often by his own admission mean-
ders in his search for the impressive origin of the idea of necessary
connection in the first book of the *Treatise* (1.3.2.13), he nevertheless
follows a direct path from *outer* to *inner* that both sets his course and
limits its horizon. His intractable principles pose no obvious problem
with respect to the external world because, while discrete, diverse
objects or diverse moments of the same object synthesise by way of
a detour through a feeling in the mind that contemplates their recurrence. Indeed, the fiction of identity originates because, in my mind,
the diverse synthesises so well that I mistake it for identity. When it
comes to connecting my own perceptions, however, this detour is no
longer or, rather, not yet available since precisely the circumscrip-
tion of my interiority is now in question. Unlike the inner feeling
that connects outer objects, the feeling that would unite my distinct
perceptions must unite the very mind within which those perceptions
take place. Because Hume begins in the exterior and reasons on the
basis of a feeling that he places within the mind, he finds his self
an exile when, by analogy, he turns inward to explain the unity of
consciousness that until then he takes for granted.

Having dispersed the mind into its several perceptions, in other
words, Hume doesn't manage to reunite them. Which is why, symp-
tomatically, whenever he imagines a mind without habit, without
knowledge of this or that cause or *a fortiori* of causality in general,
he imagines it already fully constituted. He imagines a person and, at
times, a very particular person. Deleuze can no doubt praise Hume
for secularising the concept of belief,[7] but Hume's philosophy is
never entirely laic since the man he conceives without custom and
without cause, without a past and without expectation, already has
a religious formation. 'Adam, though his rational faculties be sup-
posed, at the very first, entirely perfect . . .' (*Enquiry* 4.6). Whether
Hume names Adam in passing, in jest or in all sincerity is beside
the point. Hume presupposes the self that he can't explain, and this
presupposition is theological before it's empirical.

If one insists upon the topological and analogical work of contemplation without simply rejecting or confounding the strata of Hume's
system, the contemplative feeling shows the extent of its uncanniness.
On the one hand, just as relations between outer objects don't inhere
in the objects themselves, the relations between inner perceptions
also need a distinct ground on which to relate. The feeling that
links the mind's distinct perceptions into a self must be external to
them, hence, external to the self. In which case the unity of the mind

always comes from elsewhere and remains a stranger. On the other hand, just as relations between outer objects develop only within the mind, the link between distinct perceptions must also come from within. Since it now binds the mind within which exterior objects connect, however, the link between distinct perceptions must come from a more intimate interiority still. The feeling that associates the mind's several perceptions is thus foreign to the mind on the one hand but, on the other, comes from nowhere else. At once exterior and interior, the affective site of the self demands an *extra interiority*, that is, a 'second' and 'greater' interiority that is also at the same time – drawing upon both senses of the word 'extra' – 'outside' interiority. Essentially unsettling, the contemplative feeling can't be situated in the mind-object or inner-outer divides that it crosses from both sides.[8] Its potential to disrupt these confines is precisely what Deleuze will find so appealing for his own philosophy. Appealing enough, in any case, to adopt contemplation as the origin and ground of philosophy when he attempts to do it, for the first time, in *Difference and Repetition*.

Dénouement

But only after addressing Hume as a 'historian' of philosophy in *Empiricism and Subjectivity*.

In the same Appendix in which he formulates the impasse, Hume refuses to admit that it's 'absolutely insuperable' (*Treatise*, Appendix 21), but he himself won't manage to overcome it. He recasts the arguments of the *Treatise* in the *Enquiry* without his prior speculations about self-identity. In his 1957–58 course on Hume, Deleuze confirms the more modest scope of Hume's later work. 'What will disappear in the works that followed the *Treatise*: the identity of things and of the self' (L 122|120). But this doesn't stop Deleuze in turn from attempting to resolve the problem of the self in *Empiricism and Subjectivity*. The latter being his first book, Deleuze's oeuvre in a sense begins in response to this problem. His complex schema composes many moving parts, many over- and under-determinations, many intervals after which a seemingly abandoned theme reappears to carry the moment. I inevitably oversimplify, then, by isolating three moments here in order to outline Deleuze's response to Hume's impasse and, more importantly, to mark its limit. My argument that the problem of the self ultimately goes unresolved in Deleuze's first and only frontal encounter with it will begin the larger argument in turn that, although it metamorphoses with very different effects, the problem of the self continues to haunt Deleuze's recourse to contemplation in subsequent works and leads him to treat the feeling that operates it with profound ambivalence. *Profound* because, without entirely subscribing to it, Deleuze will found his philosophy upon contemplation as the first synthesis of time in *Difference and Repetition*.

These three moments of Deleuze's response to Hume's impasse comprise a progression. Each corresponds to a distinct idea of the self or, rather, to the idea of the self from three distinct perspectives that, in turn, correspond to the three books of the *Treatise*: understanding, passions and morals. Only the moral self, according to Deleuze, overcomes the impasse.

1) *Of the Understanding*. As the title of *Empiricism and Subjectivity* suggests, Deleuze poses the problem of the mind's unity in terms of subjectivity. If the mind is a bundle of discrete and unrelated perceptions, how does the bundle unify into a 'subject'? According to the first moment in what Deleuze articulates as the empirical progression toward subjectivity, epistemological principles of association unify the mind: resemblance, contiguity and especially causality. Yet, for all the reasons I rehearse above, the application of these principles to unify the mind within which they operate leads precisely to the impasse in question.

Rather than *analysing* personal identity into perceptions in the vain and anachronistic attempt to pinpoint the origin of the principle that would unify it, Deleuze seeks *to synthesise*. But he doesn't simply synthesise the mind's discrete perceptions via epistemic principles of association that remain foreign to them. He also seeks to synthesise the mind's discrete perceptions *and* the principles themselves. Which implies three basic elements: (i) the mind as a bundle of perceptions; (ii) the principles that unify the mind into a subject; (iii) the self as the synthesis of mind and principles. Depending on the context, Deleuze coins and redefines a number of terms to describe these elements, but I won't dwell on the somewhat idiosyncratic lexicon or his justifications of it.

> How can the subject [*le sujet*] and the mind [*l'esprit*], at the limit, become only one in the self [*le moi*]? The self must be at the same time collection of ideas and tendency, mind and subject. It is synthesis, but incomprehensible, and it unifies in its notion, without reconciling them, the origin and the qualification. (ES 15|31)

The synthesis, then, is at least double: not merely the synthesis of the mind through principles but also and more importantly the synthesis of the mind and the principles that synthesise it. This reformulation of Hume's impasse is important since it sets the parameters for what Deleuze will eventually recognise as a resolution to the problem of the self. Deleuze will proclaim the impasse surmounted, namely, when the principles that unite the mind are no longer foreign to the mind they unite. Now a question of synthesis rather than analysis, Deleuze is no longer constrained to retrace the idea of the self to an originary perception of mental unity or of a unifying principle. Perceptions and principles share a fate – the self – without sharing an origin.

2) *Of the Passions.* Early in the section on personal identity in the first book of the *Treatise*, Hume distinguishes between the self as it regards thinking and the self as it regards the passions or, as he puts it, 'the concern we take in ourselves' (*Treatise* 1.4.6.5). Although Deleuze calls these two perspectives two selves (ES 20|35), the self as it regards the passions is presumably the same self the constitution of which Hume seeks in Book 1. For he regularly supposes the self as the object of the passions in Book 2. For instance, Hume's very first passions – the 'simple', 'uniform' and most common passions *pride* and *humility* – have the idea of the self as their ultimate object.

> The first idea, that is presented to the mind, is that of the cause or productive principle. This excites the passion, connected with it; and that passion, when excited, turns our view to another idea, which is that of the self. Here then is a passion plac'd betwixt two ideas, of which the one produces it, and the other is produc'd by it. The first idea, therefore, represents the *cause*, the second the *object* of the passion. (*Treatise* 2.1.2.4)

The idea of my beautiful house causes pride, for example, only in relation to my idea of myself. If the idea of the self already results from a certain 'passion', insofar as causation unifies the mind (1.4.6.19) and insofar as causation itself stems from an impression of reflection (1.3.14.22), then the passion of the self is in a way the passion of passions, a pre-primary passion, an impassionate passion.

Nevertheless, Deleuze no doubt has reason to stress that, in Hume, the self as it concerns the passions orients the mind in a way that epistemological principles cannot. Hume calls the influence of the associative principles upon the imagination 'a gentle force' (*Treatise* 1.1.4.1). They facilitate the transition between ideas, in other words, but they don't provide any orientation according to which one idea would prevail over another. More disorienting still, precisely because ideas are discrete or atomic, their relations are volatile. 'If we reason *a priori*', Hume says, 'anything may appear able to produce anything' (*Enquiry* 12.29; see also 4.10). Or as Philo says in the *Dialogues concerning Natural Religion*, reiterating Cleanthes' 'argument *a posteriori*' for Demea:

> Were a man to abstract from everything which he knows or has seen, he would be altogether incapable, merely from his own ideas, to determine what kind of scene the universe must be, or to give the preference to one state or situation of things above another. [. . .] He might set his fancy a-rambling; and she might bring him in an infinite variety of reports and representations. (*Dialogues* 2.11–13)

In principle, we might imagine anything as the cause of anything else because there is no necessary connection until contemplation creates it by way of experience. Even in experience, however, the orientation is not complete, and we rely upon passion to provide the orientation that knowledge cannot. Both in *Empiricism and Subjectivity* (ES 58|63) and a few years later in his 'Course on Hume' (L 147|145), Deleuze borrows Hume's example of fraternity. Because my relation to my brother is reciprocal, the thought of one – regardless of which – should in principle lead to the thought of the other. Yet, while I always think of myself when I think of my brother (how else could I recognise him as *my* brother?), I don't necessarily think of my brother whenever I think of myself because my idea of myself orients my mind and regulates its direction at all times.

> The passage is smooth and open from the consideration of any person related to us to that of ourself, of whom we are every moment conscious. But when the affections are once directed to ourself, the fancy passes not with the same facility from that object to any other person, how closely so ever connected with us. (*Treatise* 2.2.2.16)

This self-orientation constitutes the second moment in the mind's progression toward subjectivity and Deleuze's dénouement to the problem of the self. While the mind is fixed *into* a self on the epistemological plane, it is fixed *by* the self on the plane of passion, and the passions thus bring the mind and its unifying principles into a greater synthesis. 'We see how the two species of affection, relation and passion, are situated with respect to each other', Deleuze says; 'the association connects ideas in the imagination; passion gives a sense and direction [*un sens*] to these relations, thus a penchant to the imagination' (ES 58|63).

3) *Of Morals*. If, however, everyone were everywhere oriented

only by self-involved passion, society would become inexplicable at best, perpetually violent at worst. The problem of morality will be to mitigate, if not eradicate, this violence at its source. Sympathy operates this mitigation. While human nature entails a certain amount of sympathy, however, the self limits our natural sympathy. I sympathise with family and friends but less so, if at all, with a stranger. Precisely insofar as I remain the reference point of my sympathy, moreover, my sympathies conflict with those of others. As a result, to the extent that I don't sympathise with everyone, sympathy is itself a source of violence. 'No one has the same sympathies as another; the plurality of partialities thus defined is contradiction; it is violence' (ES 25|38).

Deleuze, however, insists on the distinction between sympathy and selfishness or egoism. Whereas society would require a negation or limitation of egoism, it requires a positive extension of the ego's connatural sympathy. Nearly a decade before proactively condemning reactivity and negation in *Nietzsche and Philosophy*, Deleuze finds in Hume the valorisation of a pure positivity to which he'll attempt to remain faithful in all his writings, through whatever author he channels, in response to every problem he addresses.

> In fact, if society finds *as many* obstacles in sympathy as in the purest egoism, the very structure of society changes according to whether one considers it on the basis of egoism or on the basis of sympathy. Egoisms, indeed, would simply have to be limited. For sympathy, it is something else: one must integrate them, integrate them in a positive totality. (ES 26|39)

If I'm naturally sympathetic, even if my natural sympathy is limited to my neighbours, there's a slight but decisive space between my self and my selfishness, which the whole problem of morality consists in amplifying without, therefore, simply restraining the self. Deleuze will submit this schematic extension of sympathy to further refinement, reflection and even correction. My main interest here only concerns how this idea of a moral whole sets the unexpected stage for his dénouement to the problem of the self.

The problem, again, consists in the heterogeneity of discrete perceptions and the principles that unify them, between what Deleuze calls variously ideas and tendency, mind or imagination and subject, origin and qualification. Epistemologically, principles of association bind the mind into a self; passionately, the idea of the self affects the mind and orients it. Although the mind is already affected twice over, into and by the self, Deleuze calls the sequence so far a 'simple effect'. The 'complex effect' occurs when the mind in turn reflects a passion affecting it. This reflection extends the idea of the self beyond its determined circumstance and, in the case of sympathy, toward the invention of a moral whole, that is, an inclusive or integrative society. From the reflective extension of the mind's affection or passion, its sympathy, a new idea of the self emerges: no longer an epistemic self, no longer a passionate self, but now a moral self. 'What constitutes the self, in fact and now, is the synthesis of affection itself and its reflection, the synthesis of an affection that fixes the imagination and of an imagination that reflects the affection' (ES 59|64). Because this self – the now moral self – merely reflects and redeploys its own affection or passion, because the unifying principles are therefore no longer alien to it, the self synthesises the mind and its regulation and, in the same stroke, seems to overcome the impasse. 'Thus', Deleuze announces, 'the problem of the self, without solution on the plane of the understanding, finds only [*uniquement*] a moral and political dénouement in culture' (ES 59|64).[9]

There are, no doubt, several points on several levels to appreciate and to pressure in Deleuze's account. For instance, one might hesitate over the unspoken *telos* of autonomy and autochthony driving Deleuze's effort to ground the principles synthesising the self in the self, which even seems to obey classical demands of a *causa sui* or pure auto-affection.[10] The extension of sympathy, that is, of my self insofar as it is minimally sympathetic, might even make society a society without love, without singularity, without alterity. Perhaps there is no other. I won't press the tenability of society or the accuracy of Deleuze's reading of Hume in general, however, because my primary concern here remains the fate of Hume's impasse in *Empiricism and Subjectivity*.

Before reaching what will have been an impasse, when Hume distinguishes between the self as it regards thinking and the self as it regards the passions, he clearly claims his subject to be the self as it regards thinking: 'we must distinguish betwixt personal identity, as it regards our thought or imagination, and as it regards our passions or the concern we take in ourselves. The first is our present subject' (*Treatise* 1.4.6.5). Hence, if one insists on the epistemological site of Hume's impasse, then Deleuze not only leaves it unresolved. By attempting to respond to it on the moral plane, he doesn't respond at all. He displaces and circumvents without surmounting the impasse. In which case Hume's fundamental question – '[*h*]*ow does the mind become a human nature?*'; 'how does a collection become a system?';

'[h]ow does the mind become a subject?' (ES 2–3|22–3) – goes unanswered and the impasse unresolved in Deleuze's first and only frontal encounter with it.

Dénouement, in short, isn't *solution* or *resolution*. As a result, the problem is buried, sedimented, but continues to emit disruptive seisms each time Deleuze makes recourse to the notion of contemplation or the feeling by which it operates. Already in *Empiricism and Subjectivity*, for instance, Deleuze admits a 'double implication' – a co-implication, a complication – of passion and epistemology that would undermine his attempt to quarantine the epistemic plane and resolve the problem of the self solely (*uniquement*) on the moral plane (ES 58|63). Beyond *Empiricism and Subjectivity*, when Deleuze returns to 'contemplation' in *Difference and Repetition*, he'll recognise that the impasse is ultimately insurmountable by the very fact that, albeit first and foundational, he attempts not only to limit his recourse to contemplation but also even to destroy it. But he perhaps underestimates it. For even a limited, provisional and self-destructive recourse to 'contemplation' suffices to problematise what Deleuze calls 'thinking' from *Difference and Repetition* to *What Is Philosophy?*

Organic Extension

In *Difference and Repetition*, in comparison with *Empiricism and Subjectivity*, Deleuze extends contemplation in a very different direction. In what seems, indeed, the very opposite direction. While it unfurls on the moral and cultural plane in *Empiricism and Subjectivity*, he extends contemplation to the very threshold of the organic, of the living, of animation in *Difference and Repetition*. It remains there until the end.

Difference and Repetition is the first book in which Deleuze attempts 'to do' philosophy, to speak in his own name, to write as a philosopher (DRF 280|300). He's no longer doing the history of philosophy he did, for instance, in *Empiricism and Subjectivity*. His objects and his objectives are no longer, if they ever were, simply those of Hume. When Deleuze begins chapter 2 of *Difference and Repetition*, 'Repetition for Itself', by reformulating Hume's 'famous thesis' concerning contemplation, it becomes a platform from which he launches his search for a notion of repetition that, because it no longer derives from identity, no longer opposes difference. Contemplation continues to bear upon sensibility and the self but, now following his own agenda, Deleuze no longer seeks to address or redress the problem that it poses in and for Hume's philosophy. He seeks neither a *dénouement* nor a *solution* but, on the contrary, a *dissolution* of the self because, as a function of identity, the self precludes the creation of a proper concept of difference, which constitutes the whole agenda of *Difference and Repetition*. His extension of contemplation to the organic takes the first step toward that end. But only the first. Even in its redeployment, contemplation remains profoundly ambivalent in ways that Deleuze himself both thematises and overlooks – and therefore underestimates. The ambivalence becomes so consuming that, through recourse to it not merely *on* but rather *as* the foundation – *la fondation* as opposed to *le fondement* (DR 108|79) – in the form of the first of three syntheses of time, the philosophy that Deleuze attempts to do for the first time stalls the moment he begins to do it.

Neither chance nor lack of imagination leads me to anticipate the problem of the first synthesis of time in the same terms in which, in Chapter 1, I develop the problem of the facultative chain. Each of the three temporal syntheses synthesises time on the basis of one of its three components (1 – present, 2 – past, 3 – future), and Deleuze draws upon a philosopher or philosophers to develop each synthesis (1 – Hume, 2 – Bergson, 3 – initially Kant and ultimately Nietzsche). But each temporal moment also narrates the genesis of a faculty to which it corresponds: sensibility and the present, memory and the past, thought and the future. Which is why the same order recurs in the doctrine of time and the doctrine of faculties: both syntheses and faculties begin in sensibility and end in thinking. Present – past – future :: sensibility – memory – thinking. The temporal and facultative series together comprise what Deleuze calls the dissolved self (*le moi dissous*). The self that alleges self-identity and self-control in the tradition of philosophy, in the end, dissolves into a series of passive temporal syntheses, that is, a broken chain of faculties.

Time: 'The selves [*moi*] are larval subjects; the world of passive syntheses constitutes the system of the self, in conditions to be determined, but the system of the dissolved self' (DR 107|78).

Faculties: 'It is a forced and broken chain, which traverses [*parcourt*] the pieces of a dissolved self [*moi*] and the borders of a fractured I' (DR 190|145).

The doctrine of faculties thus reprises the sensibility operative in contemplation. Yet, neither coincidence nor negligence leads a systematic reader like Levi Bryant not only to separate but also even to oppose the sensibility in the originary synthesis of time from the sensibility in the transcendent doctrine of faculties.[11] For sensibility plays a role so profoundly ambivalent in the temporal syntheses that one would all too naturally suppose that it simply cannot be the same sensibility that Deleuze elsewhere openly praises as 'the royal faculty' in the doctrine of faculties (DR 198|152). While this section formalises this ambivalence and sounds its depths in *Difference and Repetition*, the next section – the last – shows that and how the ambivalence survives even in Deleuze's later work.

Hume flatly denies the reality and positivity of difference. Part of the history of philosophy that fails to achieve a philosophy of difference or even feel its necessity, he considers difference 'rather as a negation of relation, than as any thing real or positive' (*Treatise* 1.1.5.10). This negation, however, doesn't prevent Deleuze from finding the resources in Hume, despite Hume, for posing at its heart the problem of difference in its relation to repetition.

'*Repetition changes nothing in the object that repeats, but it changes something in the mind that contemplates it*: Hume's famous thesis carries us to the heart of a problem' (DR 96|70).[12] What Deleuze calls the 'state of matter' entails a perfect independence of its constituents, which leaves repetition unthinkable. In a series of repeating elements or cases, whether A A A or AB AB AB,[13] the absolute disappearance of one element or case before the appearance of the next prevents one from properly speaking of the 'same' element or the 'same' case in multiple instances. Rigorously, then, nothing repeats. While the so-called state of matter obliterates repetition, however, repetition remains possible for the mind. Perhaps only for the mind. Case after case changes nothing in the objects themselves, but the pseudo-repetition brings about a palpable difference in the mind contemplating it. The contemplative mind, namely, begins to feel itself determined to think of B whenever A appears. Out of habit, we anticipate B whenever A.

A double current thus flows from contemplation. On the one hand, the retention of A in anticipation of B pertains contemplation to time, to what Deleuze will initially privilege as the first of three temporal syntheses, and the retention of A in anticipation of B through a feeling pertains the time of contemplation to sensibility.

On the other hand, contemplation draws a difference from repetition and thereby seems to reconcile the two. Whence the problem to the heart of which Hume's famous thesis carries us:

> Is this the for-itself of repetition, an originary subjectivity that must necessarily enter into its constitution? Is it not the paradox of repetition that one can speak of repetition only through the difference or the change that it introduces in the mind that contemplates it? Through a difference that the mind *draws* from repetition? (DR 96|70)

These questions aren't rhetorical; they bear upon the entire enterprise of *Difference and Repetition*. Deleuze's response often appears ambiguous for a precise reason: while an 'originary subjectivity' would make possible repetition and even reconcile it with difference, the necessary passage through subjectivity would make impossible a repetition rigorously 'for itself'. Repetition would repeat only for a subjective mind, which remains problematic even if the subjectivity in question is originary. This matrix informs all the ambivalence with which Deleuze's system invests the notion of contemplation.

In developing the originarity of this 'originary subjectivity', Deleuze's recourse to Hume quickly reaches a limit. Hume, he says, goes no further than 'sensible and perceptual syntheses' (DR 99|72). In Hume, to be sure, contemplation is already in a sense originary. If Hume still speaks of contemplation as an 'act', it isn't a conscious act; it isn't an act I can perform with the understanding. It conditions not only active thought, not only all experimental reason, but also life in general. 'It is more conformable to the ordinary wisdom of nature to secure so necessary an act of the mind, by some instinct or mechanical tendency' – I cited the beginning of this passage above – 'which may be infallible in its operations, may discover itself at the first appearance of life and thought, and may be independent of all the laboured deductions of the understanding' (*Enquiry* 5.22). Yet, perception remains the unit, unity and therefore limit of Hume's biology. Even when Hume imagines the most basic form of life of which any self is capable, he imagines it as a single perception. Hume's oyster problematises the idea of a substantial identity or self, but its perception remains whole. 'Suppose the mind to be reduc'd even below the life of an oyster. Suppose it to have only one perception, as of thirst or hunger. [. . .] Do you conceive any thing but merely that perception?' (*Treatise*, Appendix 16).

Deleuze doesn't simply abandon contemplation as a result. On the contrary, he extends contemplation to a micro-organic level below or before perception. 'Every organism in its receptive and perceptive elements, *but also in its viscera*, is a sum of contractions, of retentions and expectations' (DR 99|73, my italics). At which point, it seems, everything that is – whatever it is – is a function of contemplation: perception, the visceral apparatuses of perception, even the object perceived. For the same reason, perception loses relevance or at least the reign it enjoyed in Hume's system. While Deleuze doesn't seem to doubt a discernible threshold between the 'organic' and the 'material', he nevertheless extends the category of the organic immensely. Examples of contemplation accumulate from what one would regularly take to be a state of matter: not merely the heart, muscles, nerves and cells but even water, earth, light and air. Anything that endures, Deleuze suggests, endures by contemplating (*tout est contemplation !*).[14]

The extension of contemplation, however, also extends its ambivalence. Because an organic synthesis synthesises through contemplation, a micro-contemplation, it still synthesises through a sort of self. Deleuze treats these organic selves, which respond to his question concerning an 'originary subjectivity', from two irreducible but inseparable perspectives. This, in short, is the profound ambivalence that structures Deleuze's treatment of contemplation, of even the most primary sensibility, which I've been preparing for some time now.

On the one hand, Deleuze celebrates contemplation as a first step toward a dissolution of the self that he anticipates, prescribes or proclaims in every chapter of *Difference and Repetition* and still pursues in subsequent works like *Logic of Sense*, *Anti-Oedipus* and *Critical and Clinical*. If contemplation still operates through a self, the contemplative selves at the organic level aren't yet the self that philosophy dogmatically postulates in tandem with common sense. The magnanimous and unanimous Self scaffolds upon these *petits moi* that Deleuze describes variously as sub-representational souls, silent witnesses and larval subjects. These selves undermine the self they also make possible. 'Beneath the self [*le moi*] that acts, there are little selves [*petits moi*] that contemplate and make possible action and the active subject' (DR 103|75). The unification of little contemplative selves into a unanimous organism might very well be an 'achievement' (Protevi 38), but it doesn't achieve that for which Deleuze strives: 'domains of an other nature where there is no longer either self or I' (DR 332|258).

The organic extension of contemplation, however, isn't limited to multiplying, relativising and belittling *le moi*. Deleuze recognises that these gestures alone would leave the self largely unaffected. He finds in contemplation a first step toward a more rigorous dissolution, a more fundamental challenge to unanimity, because the soul itself surges in the contemplation of elements or cases that remain heterogeneous both to it and, at the material limit, to each other. An organic self, a *petit moi*, contemplates itself only in contemplating something entirely other from which it proceeds and remains forever estranged. The soul, in other words, doesn't 'contemplate' at all if the transitive syntax of this formulation – 'the soul contemplates A and B' – suggests that there is *first* a soul and *then* its contemplation of diverse elements; rather, the soul is both born in and ruptured by the very contemplation of what it contemplates. Only to that extent does contemplation really begin to dissolve the self.

> The self [*le moi*] thus has no character of simplicity: it does not even suffice to relativise, to pluralise the self, all while keeping each time an attenuated simple form. The selves are larval subjects; the world of passive syntheses constitutes the system of the self, in conditions to be determined, but the system of the dissolved self. (DR 107|78)

Beyond the eccentric system developed in *Difference and Repetition*, from *Empiricism and Subjectivity* (ES 109|99) to *Critical and Clinical* (CC 78|58), from his first book to his last, only this contemplative dissolution of the self into the heterogeneity it contemplates allows Deleuze to claim, in the name of empiricism in general and Hume in particular, that relations are external to their terms and not also, not simply, internal to the mind.

On the other hand, insofar as elements still require some sort of self for their synthesis even at the organic level, insofar as even these organic syntheses still suppose – if not simply presuppose – a self (however *petit*), Deleuze condemns the contemplation he praises and the first synthesis of time that it operates. Dismissing the psychological tenor of the first synthesis of time as 'simply a matter of convenience of presentation' (DeLanda 104) misses not only the extension of the psychological beyond its restricted sense but also, more importantly, the limit that even this extended sense of the psychological imposes upon the first synthesis.[15] Which is why, already in the 'Introduction' and long before the second chapter's discussion and detail, Deleuze limits contemplation in advance to the merely 'psychological' movement of a *petit Moi* (DR 15|7). By recalling the supposition of the self as a limit to the first synthesis of time throughout *Difference and*

Repetition, Deleuze effectively concentrates the value of contemplation entirely within its inaugural force. Contemplation is never enough, in other words, because it is already too much.

> We have nevertheless seen the extent to which it was necessary to suppose some self [*de moi*] as a condition of passive organic syntheses, already playing the role of mute witnesses. Yet, precisely the synthesis of time effected in them refers to other syntheses as well as other witnesses and leads us to domains of an other nature where there is no longer either self or I [*ni moi ni Je*] . . . (DR 332|258)

This is perhaps the most visible sense in which Deleuze's recourse to contemplation begins to resurrect or re-erect the basic contours of the impasse to which it leads in Hume. Hume seeks to unite the self and Deleuze to dissolve it, but the contemplative genesis of the self remains a problem for both.

While Deleuze readily thematises the limit of contemplation, he perhaps underestimates its effect when he calls the first synthesis 'insufficient' (DR 291|226). For *a* might not suffice to reach *z* without impeding progress toward it. Contemplation, however, not only fails to achieve the movement toward the dissolution of the self that it initiates; it jeopardises the whole movement. By contemplating the recurrence of elements or cases, the mind or soul contracts a habit of expectation, feels carried to one whenever the other occurs, but thus creates an essential asymmetry in its synthesis of time. 'The passive synthesis, or contraction, is essentially asymmetric: it goes from the past to the future in the present, thus from the particular to the general, and thereby orients the arrow of time' (DR 97|71). From the past to the future, from the particular to the general, an untold threat to Deleuze's whole programme lies in these two qualifications of a single orientation. Although they constitute one and the same threat, the negative valence of the same systemic ambivalence, I'll present them separately so as to present the threat more clearly.

Generality. Elements don't change upon repeating, but something changes in the mind. The mind draws a difference from repetition, and the difference drawn, Deleuze says, is 'generality itself' (DR 97|71). A case in isolation would hold only for the particular moment in which it occurs, but the contemplation of resembling cases leads to a generalisation of the sequence that makes possible the anticipation and recognition of others in the future. I anticipate tomorrow in light of yesterday, but I don't therefore anticipate yesterday's sunrise tomorrow. Not in particular. I don't even anticipate tomorrow's sunrise in its unforeseeable particularity. Drawn from the contemplation of past dawns, only the general idea of a sunrise after sunset allows me to anticipate the sun tomorrow at all. Largely pedagogical, this everyday example no doubt supposes someone – call him Adam – contemplating the sun rise and set with fully formed faculties, but the movement of generalisation it describes also extends to organic contemplation. When Deleuze speaks of the thousand contemplations that we are in our most basic composition, when he says 'we are contemplations', he also says 'we are generalities' (DR 101|74).

But Deleuze seems to be of two minds with respect to generality. On the one hand, he clearly asserts that contemplation yields repetition for itself and genuinely reconciles difference and repetition. On more than one occasion (DR 98|71, 103|76 and 366|286). On the other hand, however, he leaves no doubts about his stance on generality, which he sides with identity in the regime of representation in which repetition 'for itself', difference 'in itself' and the reconciliation of repetition and difference remain impossible. Obviously, the generality of the general concept 'sunrise' reduces the singularity of each sunrise to which it applies day after day. Which is no doubt why, in the very first sentence of the 'Introduction', Deleuze proclaims: 'Repetition is not generality' (DR 7|1). Deleuze goes on to specify that contemplation, in particular, is neither repetition nor difference. Once again on more than one occasion (DR 12|5, 13|6 and 15|7–8). As a syllogism, the conclusion appears inscrutable.

> Repetition for itself is not generality.
> Contemplation produces generality itself.
> Contemplation is repetition for itself.

Contemplation's generally double status never surfaces with such acuity in *Difference and Repetition*, however, because Deleuze presumes a subtle redistribution. Distributing generality into types or tiers ostensibly allows him to condone it in the organic syntheses of contemplation and, at the same time, to condemn it as a function of the active faculties of the unanimous self. The formulation occurs only once, at the end of the most sustained discussion of contemplation in *Difference and Repetition*, but proves decisive in this respect: 'it is always a question of drawing a little difference, *poor generality*, from the repetition of elements or from the organisation of cases' (DR 108|79, my italics).

Poor generality, *pauvre généralité*, appears to receive its impoverished character in contrast to the magnanimous self layered upon the purely passive syntheses of our more primordial souls. A feeling binds discrete elements together. Deleuze, following Hume, insists that memory or the understanding can subsequently reconstitute the particularity of the coagulated elements without, however, returning to the atomism of the state of matter. I can recall or conceive A independently of B, for instance, even after their affective synthesis into a causal relation. This retroactive reflection of particulars constitutes a higher and more proactive consciousness. 'The past is then no longer the immediate past of retention', Deleuze writes, 'but rather the reflexive past of representation, particularity reflected and reproduced. In correlation, the future also ceases to be the immediate future of anticipation to become the reflexive future or prevision, reflected generality of the understanding' (DR 98|71). If the difference that a contemplative soul draws from repetition is 'generality itself', generality in general divides between 'poor' generality and 'reflected' generality, between poor generality and a richer generality, between a pre-reflexive generality and a reflected generality. Over against a generous generality, a poor generality would generalise enough to synthesise an immediate past and an immediate future but not the distant past or the distant future. It would come *beyond* the atomistic 'state of matter' but *before* an active subject constituted by the manoeuvrability of a past and a future gained by reflecting the immediate past and the immediate future, by rendering them applicable to the distant past and the distant future, by enriching their generality. No longer absolutely particular and not yet fully general, no longer the inanimate matter that negotiates no generality and not yet the unanimous faculty that manipulates generality, poor generality would be a limited general, a little general, barely enough to afford a few moments, to claim and have them, to endure, to be.[16]

Only thus would a *pauvre généralité* remain 'sub-representational', as Deleuze suggests (DR 114|84, 366|286, etc.), closer to the dissolution of the self than to its security. But to what extent can the impoverishment of generality redeem it and, in turn, the mechanism of contemplation that draws it? A year earlier in *Voice and Phenomenon* (1967), Derrida warps the same distinction as it structures Husserlian phenomenology by demonstrating that, if there is indeed a difference between the retention-protention of internal time-consciousness (what Deleuze calls 'poor generality') and the memory-anticipation of representational thought (a more generous generality), it can only be a difference of degree. Deleuze eventually draws attention to the Husserlian terminology he taps in the first synthesis of time (DR 109|80) – the 'immediate past of retention' over against the 'reflexive past of representation'; the 'immediate future of anticipation' over against the 'reflexive future or prevision' – and one could easily import the upshot of Derrida's critique: insofar as both terms are made possible by a wider and more primordial structure of repeatability, the distinction is derivative and porous.[17]

The consequences, of course, differ for Husserl and for Deleuze. While Husserl seeks to protect the immediacy of the present as the ground of evidence for a transcendental ego, Deleuze seeks to dissolve the ego altogether, but both rely upon the ultimately untenable distinction between immediate retention and general memory, between immediate protention and general anticipation, between 'poor' generality and 'reflexive' generality. No doubt, there are degrees of generality. No doubt, the general can be degraded or enriched to this or that end. No doubt, generality at the organic level of contemplation wouldn't be as general as the generality at work in an actively animated self. But however impoverished, however *ungeneral the general*, it remains general and thus essentially continuous with the categories of identity and the regime of representation anathema to the reconciliation Deleuze seeks of difference and repetition.

Of course, the distinction between 'poor' and 'reflected' generalities isn't final. The decisive division is never simply displaced from the general over against repetition-difference to one generality over against another. The programme of philosophy traverses the first synthesis of time as a first but mere stage in its movement toward a third synthesis that, based on the future, will fight against both the present and the past, the first synthesis of time and the second, Habitus and Mnemosyne, sensibility and memory. But the future of philosophy becomes uncertain to the extent that it *first* relies upon and finds its ground in the contemplations – the generalities – that never dissolve the self as reliably as Deleuze often suggests. A thousand mute witnesses testify to this false start.

Futurity. The second problem – or second aspect of the problem – of contemplation concerns the orientation of time from past to future. Because the contemplation of past elements or cases generates a feeling of anticipation (of B whenever A), the movement from the particular to the general is also a movement from the past to the future. The more these and other resembling cases repeat, the more cases contemplated, the more likely it becomes, we feel, that one element will follow the other. Fletched in contemplation, the arrow of time thus points toward the future as a function of probability. If never entirely certain, the future becomes more probable, more predictable, more calculable in proportion to the cases contemplated. For Hume, the belief that the future will resemble the past constitutes the very possibility of reasoning in all matters of fact, action and life. 'Custom', another word for the habits created in contemplation,

> is the great guide of human life. It is that principle alone, which renders our experience useful to us, and makes us expect, for the future, a similar train of events with those which have appeared in the past. (Hume, *Enquiry* 5.6)[18]

For Deleuze, however, the consequences are disastrous.

While Deleuze concludes that contemplation orients 'the arrow of time' early in chapter 2, he doesn't broach its devastating consequences for another 200 pages. So, if one stops reading too soon,[19] one neglects that contemplation grounds *le bon sens* (DR 290|225). At the outset of his *Discourse on the Method*, Descartes uses *le bon sens* as a synonym for 'reason' and describes it as 'the power of judging well and distinguishing the true from the false', a power which is 'equal in all men' (*Œuvres* VI:1–2|*Writings* I:111). Deleuze, for his part, places *le bon sens* together with common sense among the first postulates of the dogmatic image of thought in chapter 3 of *Difference and Repetition*, where it receives – so often the case in Deleuze – an at once systematic and idiosyncratic treatment.[20] For the moment, I retain only what bears upon the problem of contemplation. Namely, the double sense of *sens* upon which Deleuze's formulation draws: *le bon sens* means 'the right direction', in this context, because it consists in the orientation of time from the past to the future; *le bon sens* means 'good sense', in the same stroke, because this orientation toward the future allows us to prepare, to plan, to calculate tomorrow. By orienting time according to the presupposition that the future will resemble the past, however, contemplation inaugurates a movement that annuls or annihilates all difference. For a world conditioned by difference grasped only in contingent encounters, accordingly, *le bon sens* is 'by nature eschatological' (DR 289|224).

To be clear, the prevision or presentiment provisioned by the first synthesis of time doesn't *become* eschatological; 'eschatological' doesn't modify *le bon sens* as an adjective that might or might not describe it in other circumstances; 'eschatological' isn't eventual or accidental if this direction of time is eschatological *by nature*. By orienting time around the familiarity of a general past, contemplation eclipses the event, the new, which is to say, any real future. Which is why this eschatology doesn't anticipate the world's end; anticipation itself, rather, ends the world. Anticipation ends the world no matter what one anticipates and whether or not it ever comes. Unlike any other, this eschatology concerns the end of the world precisely insofar as it has a foreseeable future; the world has no future *because* it has a future. Regardless of the future it has. Not an impending catastrophe, not an event on or just beyond the horizon opened by a range of calculation, the world's end can't be predicted or calculated because it inhabits the very structure of prediction and calculation. The end comes quietly, perniciously, without troubling good or common sense, and it happens all the time.

Contemplation, in short, isn't only 'insufficient'. It not only complies with the dogma that Deleuze seeks to destroy. Contemplation constitutes *dogmaticity* itself. The problem of the first synthesis of time, of contemplation, of habit thus runs much deeper than 'a dull continuum of routine' (O'Keefe 85). It founds the very foundation of the tradition – *le bon sens* – with which Deleuze must break, the dogmatic image he must destroy, the everyday apocalypse he has to avert in order to do philosophy, for the first time, as a philosophy of difference.

In response, Deleuze will pit another future against the future that opens in contemplation. He calls it 'the final goal of time' (DR 125|94). This other future, the third synthesis of time, reaches regions where there is no self, no generality and no prevision, none of the regressive effects of contemplation. The bellicose language that Deleuze mobilises to describe the relation between syntheses reflects the charges against contemplation. This imagery alone demands one resituate all of Deleuze's celebrations of sensibility as one valence in a more general ambivalence. Each term pitting the third synthesis against the first is a testament to the threat that contemplation – sensibility – poses to the philosophy that it also inaugurates: *expulser, renier, défaire, briser; corriger, contredire, éliminer, destituer, subordonner, lutter contre, laisser sur chemin; détruire* (DR 122–3|90–1, 125–6|94 and 151|159). Philosophy only begins, at this point, if contemplation has no future. Only if thought – and here Deleuze risks intensifying the ascetic tradition of philosophy at least since Plato – will have had no sensibility.[21]

But the odds are against Deleuze. For my purposes here, I need not engage the inner workings of the third synthesis of time, Deleuze's association of it with Nietzsche's eternal return or his formal mobilisation of Kant's transcendental aesthetic to reach it. Nor, for that matter, need I engage the second synthesis based on memory in Bergson, which intervenes after the first only to be destroyed along with it by the third. However absolute the destruction is *in the end*, *from the beginning* it will have been conditioned by what it seeks to expel, to eliminate, to destroy. And this according to the very 'programme' of Deleuze's philosophy: 'to make use of the repetition of habit and that of memory, but to make use of them as stages and leave them on the way – to struggle against Habitus with one hand, against Mnemosyne with the other' (DR 125|94). By that time, however, all that Deleuze laments of contemplation will have already found footing. For contemplation simultaneously grounds *both* the passive syntheses of time that lead to the dissolution of the self without which repetition can't be grasped 'for itself' or difference 'in itself' *and* the good sense that sustains the calculating, the probable, the magnanimous self. It thus generates – and therefore exceeds as their common matrix – *both* the dogmatic image of thought *and* the iconoclastic philosophy of difference and repetition meant to break it. Deleuze sees the passage through the first two syntheses as a means for insuring – this is his word: *assurer* – the programme of his philosophy, but contemplation draws the starting line of a race that the future has no assurance of winning.

'The selves are larval subjects; the world of passive syntheses constitutes the system of the self, in conditions to be determined, but the system of the dissolved self' (DR 107|78).

'*Le bon sens* is grounded in a synthesis of time, precisely the synthesis that we have determined as the first synthesis, the synthesis of habit' (DR 290|225).

Contemplation is a double ground, a double genesis and thus a double cross. Because it grounds movements toward a selfless future and toward *le bon sens*, both in accordance with and against the programme of Deleuze's philosophy, it both launches the programme and commandeers it. This is the ambivalent sense in which, once again, Deleuze's philosophy would always also stall as soon as it begins, before it begins, because it begins in sensibility.

Contemplating Chaos

In a brief interview in 1969, Deleuze claims to go further in *Logic of Sense* than in *Difference and Repetition* (ID 198|144). In a note written for the Italian translation of *Logic of Sense* seven years later, he clarifies that his dissatisfaction with *Difference and Repetition* pertains to its still traditional topology, its recourse to a 'classical height' and an 'archaic depth' with which he claims to break in his work on surfaces in *Logic of Sense* (DRF 59–60|65). By way of conclusion to this book, I'll argue that this transition between works never takes place as smoothly as Deleuze suggests, here and elsewhere, since affect in 'archaic depth' both inaugurates and threatens the superficial enterprise of *Logic of Sense* in the same way that – with the same ambivalence with which – sensibility both inaugurates and threatens the differential and repetitional enterprise of *Difference and Repetition*. For the time being, I only stress that, whatever the distance between the two books and whether or not Deleuze himself defaults to its best judge, he doesn't simply renounce contemplation. Any shortcomings he finds in *Difference and Repetition* only emphasise his preference for the pages on contemplation: 'it is nevertheless not the case that I do not like certain pages of [*Difference and Repetition*], in particular those on fatigue and contemplation' (DRF 59|65). In his 1973 'Letter to a Harsh Critique', Deleuze more severely denounces the 'university apparatus' that overburdens both *Difference and Repetition* and *Logic of Sense* but, even there, contemplation survives: 'there are pages that I like in *Difference and Repetition*, those on fatigue and contemplation for instance, because despite appearances they come from a living lived experience [*vécu vivant*]' (P 16|7). His fondness for those pages will last a lifetime, but more than personal preference is at stake. Over two decades later, contemplation resurfaces in *What Is Philosophy?*, in his defining work, in the work in which he and Guattari set out to define the disciplines that comprise thinking. It resurfaces twice, in fact, once in philosophy and once in art. To conclude this chapter, I'll accelerate a few remarks concerning the way in which, surreptitiously, ambivalence returns as well.

I began this chapter by recalling that the philosopher, on Deleuze and Guattari's account, doesn't contemplate Ideas. Before Plato could contemplate an Idea, he had to create the concept of Idea (QP 11|6). But contemplation isn't always contemplation. Over against Platonic contemplation, there's also a radically empirical contemplation that, for Deleuze and Guattari, does indeed exemplify philosophy

(Examples III and IV). If Deleuze intuits philosophy as the creation of concepts early on in his work, long before he hardens his intuition into a definition with Guattari in *What Is Philosophy?*, he praises empiricism for its conceptual creativity just as early.

'Such is the secret of empiricism. Empiricism is neither a reaction against concepts nor a simple appeal to lived experience. On the contrary, it undertakes the maddest creation of concepts that has ever been seen or heard' (DR 3|xx).

'Empiricism knows nothing but events and others; thus, it is a great creator of concepts. Its force begins the moment it defines the subject: a habitus, a habit, nothing other than a habit in a field of immanence' (QP 51|48).

In the preface to the English translation of *Empiricism and Subjectivity*, published the same year as *What Is Philosophy?* (1991), Deleuze reiterates habit as an 'answer' to the problem of the self (*Moi*), even perhaps 'the most striking answer' (DRF 342|365). In both *What Is Philosophy?* and the preface to *Empiricism and Subjectivity*, however, he seems to forget or chooses to ignore that this answer also raises questions. Has Hume's impasse been overcome? Was *le bon sens* eradicated from contemplation? Did generality finally go bankrupt? When was the future saved from the eschatological arrow of time? What, in short, of the programme to destroy Habitus? If an exemplary concept from an exemplary creator of concepts also augurs the dogma of identity and the regime of representation, might it not also expose a limit of all conceptual creativity and thus philosophy itself as the creation of concepts?

Deleuze and Guattari seem to sidestep these questions. They invoke empiricism in *What Is Philosophy?*, after all, as one example among others and not even the most paradigmatic. If unresolved and unspoken problems continue to reverberate in Deleuze and Guattari's brief allusion to empirical habit, even if one would expect them to resurface here – if nowhere else – in Deleuze's reflection on the philosophy he did throughout his life, the problems will not run as deeply as they did in *Difference and Repetition* because habit, contemplation, feeling no longer operates an originary synthesis founding philosophy as a whole. In another discipline, however, contemplation isn't simply an example. While philosophy creates concepts, art creates sensation, and contemplation constitutes the sensation that art creates. 'Sensation', Deleuze and Guattari say, 'is pure contemplation' (QP 212|212). Side-lined by philosophy, if not abandoned, contemplation comes to define the disciplinarity of the artistic discipline.

As one should already suspect, what Deleuze and Guattari call 'sensation' isn't a given sensation in the daily course of life. Art creates percepts and affects, and percepts and affects differ in nature from the perceptions and affections that compose everyday lived experience (*vécu*). Perception and affection not only presuppose a readymade sensibility overtaken by everyday data; they presuppose a more or less uniform sensibility for everyone. In 1968, Deleuze would have called this dogmatic presupposition common sense. Art, however, extracts a percept or affect from the perception or affection of lived experience and, in so doing, creates an entirely new and other sensibility. In a 1989 letter, roughly contemporary to *What Is Philosophy?*, Deleuze describes percepts as 'new ways of seeing and hearing', affects as 'new ways of feeling' (P 224|165). Not *a* sight, *an* audition or *a* feeling but new *ways* of seeing, hearing and feeling. Bringing together the two senses of 'aesthetic' that Deleuze had a long and active interest in reconciling, the artistic sense and the sensible, art as the creation of affects reconditions experience itself.[22] Rather than a new experience, it alters what can be experienced in the first place. By contrast, even the newest perception or affection – even if previously unseen, unheard or unfelt – remains banal because it never reaches this genetic level of sensible creation.

'Sensation is pure contemplation', to continue the citation, 'for it is by contemplation that one contracts, contemplating oneself to the extent that [*à mesure que*] one contemplates the elements from which one proceeds' (QP 212|212). At this point, Deleuze and Guattari footnote a reference to the pivotal section from Hume's *Treatise*, *Of the idea of necessary connexion* (1.3.14), but the reference is hardly necessary for readers of *Difference and Repetition*. The mechanism and its formulation are immediately recognisable. Matter, passivity, sensibility, soul and subject, fatigue, pleasure, narcissism: numerous themes from *Difference and Repetition* – some of which I've developed and others economically excluded – resurface with an artistic valence in *What Is Philosophy?* One must, of course, remain sensitive to contemplation's disciplinary displacement from philosophy to art. Nevertheless, from its organic extension into a philosophy of difference 'in itself' and repetition 'for itself' to its artistic deployment two and a half decades later, as a temporal synthesis or as artistic creation, contemplation pertains in each instance to genetic sensibilities.

In Hume, the contemplation of repeating elements or cases in the mind generates a feeling that binds them but, when he applies the same logic to the mind itself, he effectively places this feeling *before* the self and gives it an uncanny autonomy that Deleuze exploits. Which is why, in those pages of *Difference and Repetition* still dear to him, Deleuze calls this primordial feeling of contemplation 'a primary sensibility' (DR 99|73).

Between *Difference and Repetition* and *What Is Philosophy?*, however, Deleuze's confidence in contemplation changes. As the first synthesis of time in *Difference and Repetition*, a thousand contemplative souls inaugurate the dissolution but cannot entirely dissolve the self or, therefore, reach repetition for itself. They lead *either* to a later temporal synthesis where there is no self *or* to a magnanimous self with more active faculties *but*, in either case, to their own destruction. In *What Is Philosophy?*, Deleuze and Guattari no longer speak of *petits moi*, they now speak of a 'brain-subject', but they still attribute a soul to the contemplation of matter, and one would expect to find at least traces of the ambivalence with which Deleuze systematically treated contemplation years earlier in *Difference and Repetition*. 'This is why the brain-subject is here called *soul* or *force*, since only the soul conserves by contracting what matter dissipates' (QP 212|211). The soul even implicates an interiority – 'a pure internal Feeling', *un pur Sentir interne* (QP 214|213) – that Deleuze attacks in numerous contexts in and beyond *Difference and Repetition*. Effects and all, however, contemplation appears to operate the being of sensation in art without any explicit problematisation.

I say without any *explicit* problematisation, however, because the basic problem of contemplation returns through a backchannel. The mind's native state is chaotic. Deleuze and Guattari's description of this mental chaos bears a remarkable but far from circumstantial resemblance to Hume's description of the mind before perceptions are causally linked into the system that he calls a self.

'[The mind is] a bundle or collection of different perceptions, which succeed each other with an inconceivable rapidity, and are in a perpetual flux and movement. [. . .] The mind is a kind of theatre, where several perceptions successively

'We ask only for a little order to protect us from chaos. Nothing is more painful, more anguishing than a thought that escapes itself [*s'échappe à elle-même*], ideas that flee, that disappear having barely been sketched [*à peine ébauchées*], make their appearance; pass, re-pass, glide away, and mingle in an infinite variety of postures and situations' (Hume, *Treatise* 1.4.6.4). already eaten away [*rongées*] by oblivion and precipitated into other ideas that we master no more [than the previous ideas]' (QP 201|201).

Despite the shared premise, however, Deleuze and Guattari quickly dismiss the entire history of associationism – to which Hume and his concept of contemplation ostensibly belong – as an insufficient response to the threat of chaos and the demand for order.

> We demand only that our ideas link together [*s'enchaînent*] according to a minimum of constant rules, and the association of ideas has never had any other sense, to furnish us those protective rules – resemblance, contiguity, causality – that allow us to put a little order in ideas ... (QP 201|201)

Deleuze and Guattari criticise the association of ideas because it attempts to typify and fix the possible relations between ideas in advance and, in so doing, stifles thinking. Attempting to protect the mind from its native chaos, associationism overreaches and risks arresting thought completely. It posits a fundamental conformity of the future to the past and thereby precludes the new, the event, an affect, for instance, a being of sensation. In which case, even if Deleuze no longer uses these terms, contemplation still orients the arrow of time, still grounds *le bon sens*, still announces the end of the world at the beginning of thought.

Now, Deleuze and Guattari don't name Hume, let alone contemplation, when they object to the association of ideas in *What Is Philosophy?* But the reference is clear. While he never claims to invent the association of ideas, Hume does for the first time reduce the principles of association to three types. The three types, namely, that Deleuze and Guattari single out to condemn. 'Though it be too obvious to escape observation, that different ideas are connected together,' Hume says,

> I do not find that any philosopher has attempted to enumerate or class all the principles of association; a subject, however, that seems worthy of curiosity. To me, there appear to be only three principles of connexion among ideas, namely, *Resemblance*, *Contiguity* in time or place, and *Cause* or *Effect*. (*Enquiry* 3.2; see also 5.14)

Not only does Hume claim to be the first philosopher to reduce all associations to three, which thus makes Deleuze and Guattari's enumeration of the 'protective rules' an anonymous but unmistakeable reference to Hume. Hume also in the same stroke claims to account for all thought – both *a priori* ('relations of ideas') and *a posteriori* ('matters of fact') – with these three categories or classes. So, when Deleuze and Guattari proclaim these three categories to miss and even inhibit thought, to avoid thinking, they make a nearly wholesale critique of Hume's philosophy at its most original. Deleuze knows these categories come from Hume, of course, even if he doesn't draw the consequence of his critique.[23]

So, insofar as it operates the foremost of these relations, Deleuze returns to contemplation with a variant of the same ambivalence that has accompanied the concept since Hume created it. On the one hand, contemplation creates new sensibilities, new beings of sensation; it defines aesthetic creativity in every sense. On the other hand, contemplation associates ideas, fixes the mind and engrains opinions against which the artist, the philosopher and the scientist must struggle in their respective disciplines. The artist in particular engages in an endless struggle if for no other reason than he or she must struggle *against* contemplation *with* contemplation. Even the most sensitive discussions of contemplation in Deleuze have overlooked this ambivalence and, *a fortiori*, its consequences. Agamben, for instance, recognises the passage on 'pure contemplation' in *What Is Philosophy?* as 'one of the most important' in Deleuze's late philosophy but ignores its root in Hume and, for that matter, its determination as an artistic endeavour (Agamben 233). The oversight merits stress not because source work is in itself indispensable or because Agamben himself resorts to a number of genealogies in *Potentialities*, not even because the notion of contemplation happens to be one of Deleuze's oldest, but rather because it also neglects the longstanding impasse that accompanies even the purest contemplation. If opinion and art, perception and percept, affection and affect, philosophy and dogma all divide *within* contemplation, can contemplation ever be pure enough? Can contemplation purify itself – of itself, of the associations it forges, of its catastrophic effects? Like philosophy, even any 'coming philosophy' (Agamben 220 and 238), art would reach its ruin as soon as the writer reaches for the page, the painter for the canvas, the musician for the measure. I'll address these artistic stakes in more detail in the following chapter.

Notes

1. See especially the section on 'Transcendence' in Chapter 1 above.
2. 'We see at least what philosophy is not: it is neither contemplation, nor reflection, nor communication' (QP 11|6; see also P 186–7|136–7). On the Platonic preparation of the regime of representation, see DR 185–6|142–3 and my commentary in Chapter 1 above.
3. See 1.3.2.2 in the *Treatise* and Sections IV and VII in the first *Enquiry*.
4. I'll address transcendental illusion in Chapters 4 and 6 below.
5. Here are the formulations as they occur in the course of the *Treatise*: (1) 'every distinct perception, which enters into the composition of the mind, is a distinct existence'; (2) 'the understanding never observes any real connexion among objects' (1.4.6.16).
6. 'Most philosophers seem inclin'd to think, that personal identity *arises*' – Hume's emphasis – 'from consciousness; and consciousness is nothing but a reflected thought or perception' (*Treatise*, Appendix 20).
7. 'Hume discovers *belief* as the ground of knowing. [. . .] Because the notion of faith is universalized, secularized, religious belief becomes susceptible to a radical critique' (L 186|184). See also Deleuze's preface to the English translation of *Empiricism and Subjectivity*. For the irruption of this secular belief, although Hume doesn't pose the problem in these terms, see especially *Enquiry* 5.8 ff.
8. For an account of the self in Hume that stresses the imagination, see chapter 2 of David E. Johnson's *Kant's Dog*, especially 57–62.
9. In this light, Jeffrey A. Bell stops a self too short when, in *Deleuze's Hume* (48), he attributes priority to the passionate self.
10. On Deleuze's auto-affection, see 'The Phenomenologist and the Pantheist' in Chapter 6 below.
11. See chapter 3 ('Transcendental Empiricism: The Image of Thought and the "Phenomenology" of the Encounter') and chapter 4 ('First Moment of the Encounter: The *Sentiendum*') of *Difference and Givenness* (especially 76–7, 87–92 and 99–100). One could also confirm the systematic simultaneity of the first synthesis and the first faculty through the sign. Compare DR 182|140, 106|77 and 100|73, along with Bryant 93 and 99–100.
12. Hume: 'But 'tis evident, in the *first* place, that the repetition of like objects in like relations of succession and contiguity *discovers* nothing new in any one of them [. . .] *Secondly*, 'Tis certain that this repetition of similar objects in similar situations *produces* nothing new either in these objects, or in any external body' (Hume, *Treatise* 1.3.14.17–18).
13. Deleuze associates 'cases' with Hume (AB AB) and 'elements' with Bergson (A A), but he engages Bergson only insofar as Bergson engages Hume: 'There is no surprise that Bergson rediscovers Hume's analyses . . .' (DR 98|71). Bergson has his moment in the second synthesis of

time – memory – in *Difference and Repetition*. While he doesn't cite it, the first synthesis of time in *Difference and Repetition* would thus support Bell's argument that, despite what Bergson's own critique of associationism might lead one to think, Deleuze's recourse to Bergson remains consistent with his recourse to Hume. See §3 ('Creative Evolution and Pragmatics') of chapter 2 ('Becoming Who We Are') of *Deleuze's Hume*.

14. Deleuze refers to the *Enneads* for his generalisation of contemplation in both *Difference and Repetition* and *What Is Philosophy?*

> 'Organisms wake with the sublime words of the third *Ennead*: everything is contemplation!' (DR 102|75).

> 'Plotinus managed to define all things as contemplations, not only men and animals, but also plants, earth, and rocks' (QP 212–13|212).

15. While DeLanda doesn't limit his analyses to temporality based upon the present (DeLanda 121), he considers the first synthesis to be 'the core of Deleuze's theory of time' (202) and thus ignores Deleuze's call to destroy the first synthesis with a third, even though this destruction constitutes the very 'programme' of Deleuze's philosophy. I am working toward this destructive programme and its ambivalent undertow in this subsection.

16. Patton's translation of *pauvre généralité* as 'weak generality' obscures the essential relation of possession to being: 'Finally, one is only what one *has*; it is by a having that being forms here, or that a passive self *is*' (DR 107|79).

17. 'Without reducing the abyss that can in fact separate retention from re-presentation, without concealing that the problem of their relations is nothing other than the history of "life" and of life's becoming-conscious, we must be able to say *a priori* that their common root, the possibility of re-petition in its most general form, the trace in the most universal sense, is a possibility that not only must inhabit the pure actuality of the now, but also constitute it by means of the very movement of the différance that the possibility inserts into the pure actuality of the now' (Derrida, *La voix* 79|*Voice* 58). A mistake symptomatic in ways that exceed my scope here, the latest French editions of *La voix et le phénomène* replace 'la différance' in this passage with 'la différence'.

18. See also *Enquiry* 4.16, 4.19, 4.21, 4.23, 6.4, 8.16 and 10.4.

19. For instance, Posteraro 96.

20. See DR 173–5|132–4, along with my commentary on the faculties and the annulment of difference in Chapter 1 above. Deleuze gives his clearest explanation of *le bon sens*, however, in *Logic of Sense*. I'll quote only the 'systematic characteristics' with which he concludes:

The systematic characteristics of *le bon sens* are thus: the affirmation of only one direction; the determination of this direction as going from the most differentiated to the least differentiated, from the singular to the regular, from the remarkable to the ordinary; the orientation of the arrow of time, from the past to the future, according to this determination; the guiding role of the present in this orientation; the function of prevision thus made possible; the type of sedentary distribution in which all the preceding characteristics unite. (LS 94|76)

21. Hume, too, has a place in this ascetic tradition. After having asserted a certain admixture of evil with all good as a 'uniform law of nature' in *The Natural History of Religion*, he writes: 'And, in general, no course of life has such safety (for happiness is not to be dreamed of) as the temperate and moderate, which maintain, as far as possible, a mediocrity, and *a kind of insensibility*, in everything' (Hume, *Natural* 15.3, my italics).

22. On the two senses, their problematic hiatus and possible reunification, see LS 300–7|260–6. See also Daniel Smith's 'Deleuze's Theory of Sensation: Overcoming the Kantian Duality' in his *Essays on Deleuze*.

23. See L 121–3|119–21, where Deleuze attributes these three principles of association to Hume but holds him apart from the 'associationists' due to his love of paradox and his refusal of all reductionism. Compare also QP 56|53 where, referring to Hume by name, Deleuze and Guattari name 'association' as one of 'the great empirical concepts'.

3

Between Art and Opinion

There is philosophy, there is art, there is thinking neither with nor without affect. Never *without affect* because it occupies a fundamental place in Deleuze's system. Never *with affect* because it always also undermines the system it supports. I call Deleuze's double recourse to affect 'ambivalence' in a sense that one shouldn't rush to confound with the sense that psychoanalysis, affect theory or Deleuze himself gives to the term.

Chapter 1 addresses Deleuze's first theory of affect in *Difference and Repetition*. His first theory of *affect* because, although he speaks of 'sensibility' rather than 'affect', he already establishes fundamental features of what he would come to call 'affect' in later works. His *first* theory of affect because, although he already speaks of 'sensibility' in earlier works, he attempts to do his 'own' philosophy – by his own account – for the first time in *Difference in Repetition*.

Chapter 2 shifts to a problematic of which, traversing Deleuze's work from beginning to end, *Difference and Repetition* is itself only a moment. Haunted by the same systemic ambivalence as the doctrine of faculties, namely, 'contemplation' spreads the ambivalence from *Difference and Repetition* back to his first book on *Empiricism and Subjectivity* and forward to his defining work of *What Is Philosophy?*

Delving deeper into the ambivalence underlying affect in *What Is Philosophy?*, this chapter picks up where the previous leaves off. Because *What Is Philosophy?* aims to define thinking, not only philosophy but also its relation to the other disciplines, it in a way opens the most systematic view on the problem of affect in Deleuze's oeuvre. So, if Chapter 1 above launches the problem of ambivalence with the doctrine of faculties in *Difference and Repetition*, while Chapter 2 measures its longevity through the problem of contemplation, Chapter 3 will establish its systematicity with regard to thinking in *What Is Philosophy?* After reformulating and formalising the ambivalence in terms of *What Is Philosophy?* (§1), I show how wide it spreads by following its impact on three issues that, at first sight, might seem entirely unrelated to the problem of affect: death (§2), the minor (§3) and style (§4).

Avant-Garde

The writer, Deleuze and Guattari say in *What Is Philosophy?*, never faces a blank page. The painter, never a blank canvas; the musician, never a blank measure. The artist's materials are always plagued in advance by opinion, by cliché, by what art *as* art defies. 'It is even because the canvas is first of all covered with clichés that the painter must confront chaos and hasten destructions, in order to produce a sensation that defies every opinion, every cliché (how many times?)' (QP 204|204).

There are two temptations here. On the one hand, one could easily accuse Deleuze and Guattari of a rather banal conception of art; hardly anyone, from a historical or a theoretical perspective, would deny that art defies opinion. On the other hand, one could just as easily accuse Deleuze and Guattari of the 'reactionary' thinking that they themselves thematise and condemn elsewhere; if the painter paints *because*, as Deleuze and Guattari say, the canvas is covered with opinions, his or her work would merely react to the opinion upon which it therefore depends and even structurally affirms before destroying. In which case, indeed, the destruction would never really be destructive and art, perhaps, never really artistic.

If, however, these temptations are only temptations, if Deleuze and Guattari's conception of art in defiance of opinion isn't as banal or reactionary as it might at first seem, it's because art doesn't defy just any opinion. It doesn't defy an opinion about this or that work or even any opinion about art in general. Art, Deleuze and Guattari say, defies all opinion (*toute opinion*), all cliché (*tout cliché*). At stake in what Deleuze and Guattari call 'art' is the very horizon of *doxa*.

There'll be no struggle greater than the struggle with opinion but, even so, it isn't the first struggle. The original struggle is against chaos. This holds for all disciplines, for art, science and philosophy, for 'thinking' as Deleuze and Guattari define it. 'What defines thought, the three great forms of thought, art, science, and philosophy, is always the confrontation with chaos [*affronter le chaos*]' (QP 198|197). But the confrontation with chaos is more than most can bear. We're neither all nor always artists, scientists or philosophers. Faced with ideas that vanish, flee or redistribute at infinite and therefore unmasterable speeds, 'opinion' seems to provide a means for stabilising thoughts.

> Nothing is more painful, more anguishing than a thought that escapes itself [*s'échappe à elle-même*], ideas that flee, that disappear having barely been sketched [*à peine ébauchées*], already eaten away [*rongées*] by oblivion or precipitated into others that we master no more [than the previous ideas]. [. . .] This is why we want to cling to fixed opinions so much. (QP 201|201)

Yet, precisely because opinions are fixed or immobilised, *arrêtées*, they threaten thinking as much as they promise to relieve it. They threaten thought even more than the chaos from which they promise to relieve it.[1] The philosopher, artist and scientist thus redirect their efforts; no longer merely confronting it, they ally with chaos in the struggle against opinion. 'It seems [*On dirait*] that the struggle *against chaos* is not without an affinity with the enemy, because another struggle develops and takes on more importance, *against opinion*' (QP 203|203).

So, the artist struggles against opinion, but the artist doesn't struggle alone. The artist has comrades in the other disciplines, in philosophy and science. All three disciplines of thought struggle against opinion since, as forms of thinking, opinion threatens all three. And yet, even if art, philosophy and science lock arms to form a common front against opinion, the thickest fighting breaks out in one discipline in particular. Not the discipline that one might with good reason expect: even though opinion names one of three traits that lead Deleuze and Guattari to assert that philosophy is originally Greek,[2] even though opinion still haunts 'the popular, democratic, and occidental conception of philosophy' (QP 145|144), even though the fate of philosophy since the Pre-Socratics has been bound up with opinion, the struggle against opinion is most confrontational and most intimate in art. For art and opinion, according to Deleuze and Guattari, have a common provenance. They both pertain to sensibility.

When Deleuze and Guattari formalise the process by which opinion forms in relation to sensibility, they propose more than a sociological survey. At stake is the very disposition toward indoctrination. In relating to an object, I perceive this or that quality, and each quality affects me in a certain way. 'Opinion', for Deleuze and Guattari, names any rule drawn from the correspondence between a perception and an affection (QP 145|144); opinion doesn't name this or that more or less informed, more or less personal belief about a given object or phenomenon but rather, more profoundly, the regulation and regularisation of the relation between perception and affection. As a given correspondence, as a rule and regularity between a given perception and a given affection, an opinion in turn gives rise to a group of subjects that follow the same rule. Subjects become subjects and group together, in other words, according to the opinions they share; they're affected in the same way by the same perceptions as a rule. While it might seem commonsensical when formulated in this way, the mass mechanism of opinion can't be overestimated: not only because it presupposes that, while perceptions and affections may vary, the faculties of perception and affection themselves are predetermined; not only because it presupposes that the preformed and predetermined faculties of perception and affection are, beyond any difference of opinion, the same for everyone; but also and above all because, if we share the same faculties of perception and affection determined in advance, these faculties determine in turn – still in advance – the very horizon of experience. Experience would be limited to experiences that these predetermined faculties can yield. Another name for death, all *doxa* is always already *orthodox*.[3]

If sensibility thus constitutes the problematic source of opinion, Deleuze and Guattari would have reason to condemn or at least restrain it like so many philosophers before them. Instead, they make a novel distinction. The artist, Deleuze and Guattari say, creates *percepts* and *affects* but, if the writer (for instance) never faces a blank page, it's because the artist creates percepts and affects by wresting them from the *perceptions* and *affections* of everyday lived experience.[4] Art thus bears directly upon the components of opinion. Yet, while percepts and affects engage perceptions and affections from the very beginning, while no page (canvas or measure) is ever blank, percepts and affects nevertheless differ essentially from the perceptions and affections from which the artist draws them. Percepts and affects exceed the lived experience that opinion regulates and regularises. *All lived experience*, they say, *tout vécu* (QP 164|164). Percepts and affects thus aren't sensations if, traditionally speaking, 'sensation' means a receptivity to stimuli homogeneously presupposed in every subject. By contrast, a percept or affect cannot be attributed to every (if any) subject but, it's important to emphasise, not because of some artistic or decadent elitism; rather, each percept and each affect constitutes *a new sensibility*, that is, not a new sensation but a new way of seeing and hearing, a new way of feeling, of experiencing (P 224|165). Deleuze's investment in the creation of new sensibilities, as I argue in Chapter 1 and verify in Chapter 2, dates at least from *Difference and Repetition*. With Guattari in *What Is Philosophy?*, however, Deleuze gives this genetic investment one of its purest expressions: 'The goal [*but*] of art, by means of the material' (I'll return to this pivotal reference to material means in the last section of this chapter),

> is to wrest [*arracher*] the percept from perceptions of an object and from the states of a perceiving subject, to wrest the affect from affections as a passage from one state to another. To extract [*extraire*] a block of sensations, a pure being of sensation. (QP 167|167)

The 'purity' of a pure being of sensation, *un pur être de sensation*, in the first instance means pure *of* perception, *of* affection, *of* lived experience, hence, pure of the horizon of opinion.

Now, insofar as opinion regulates perception and affection, and insofar as art seeks to extract percepts and affects from perceptions and affections, the 'goal' of art gives it both a *privileged* and a *precarious* place in the interdisciplinary struggle against opinion.

A privileged place because only art combats opinion at its very source. The extraction of percepts and affects from perceptions and affections doesn't leave the latter intact. While opinion hypostasises perceptions and affections and, in so doing, stabilises experience and promotes conformity to it, art wrests from perceptions and affections new sensibilities that trespass the bounds and binds of all opinionated experience. The other disciplines attack opinion, they have their tactics and execute them valiantly, but 'one does not fight against perceptive and affective clichés', Deleuze and Guattari say, 'if one does not also fight against the machine that produces them' (QP 150|150). Art thus becomes the measure of all resistance; it alone attacks opinion at its source in perception, in affection, in a word, in sensibility. Deleuze regularly draws attention to his status as a philosopher; even when speaking of art, science or cinema, he never claims to be anything else. Here, however, it seems art must save philosophy; art must save all disciplines; art must save thinking. Neither *pour l'art* nor *nur für Künstler*, much more than art's at stake in art.

A precarious place, however, because the pertinence of both art and opinion to 'sensibility' makes possible their confusion. Deleuze and Guattari thematise this confusion in relation to the novel in particular, but their comments hold for all forms of art insofar as they engage from the beginning – even if only to rupture them – perceptions and affections. Insofar as, that is, there's no blank page.

> We insist on the art of the novel because it is the source of a misunderstanding: many people think that one can make a novel with one's perceptions and affections [. . .] One may very well have a great sense of observation and a lot of imagination: is it possible to write with perceptions, affections, and opinions? (QP 170–1|170)

Deleuze and Guattari treat this confusion as a matter of fact, but the confusion of art and opinion wouldn't in fact be possible, certainly not widespread, if art didn't entertain a certain affinity with opinion in principle. Nevertheless, while Deleuze and Guattari speak readily of art's affinity with chaos, they deny all affinity with opinion; indeed, they admit art's affinity with chaos in order to deny art's affinity with opinion. 'It seems that the struggle *against chaos* is not without an affinity with the enemy, because another struggle develops and takes on more importance, *against opinion*' (cited above).

Because opinion is so fundamental, cliché so engrained, because it ultimately involves the very mechanism of representation with which we normally figure the world itself, in his book on the *Logic of Sensation* Deleuze gives the painterly destruction of clichés prevailing upon the unpainted canvas its most consequential name: *catastrophe* (FB 94|100 *et passim*). Yet, one can amplify this catastrophe into an anthem, a 'motto for critical theory' (Clough, 'Introduction' 28), only by overlooking art's *collaboration* with the opinion against which it struggles. For when one insists on art's genetic engagement with perceptions and affections, when one insists not only on percepts and affects but also on the movement by which the percept and affect in a sense derive from perceptions and affections, when one insists that perceptions and affections are in this sense at least provisionally 'essential' to the very existence of art that nevertheless remains irreducible to them and, indeed, destroys them, the front line in the struggle against opinion begins to show certain pores. These pores signal the possible impossibility of *purifying* not only percept of perception, not only affect of affection, but also art of opinion. The consequences are subtle but profound if, for the reasons I've just rehearsed, art is the first and last line of defence in the interdisciplinary struggle against opinion. Not only critical theory, certainly not only its motto, thinking itself is at stake.

This elaboration of the mechanism that – for better and for worse – binds art and opinion to sensibility forms the warp of what follows. Affect fortifies art against opinion and in the same stroke leaves it vulnerable to opinion. Not two analytically separable processes, affect fortifies art in the same stroke that vulnerabilises it. At least three positions or propositions from *What Is Philosophy?* not only manifest and confirm but also extend in various directions art's at once disruptive and conservative force that, at the limit, constitutes both the promise and the compromise of Deleuze and Guattari's thinking. At stake, once again, is a systemic ambivalence.

1) Percepts and affects constitute 'Life in the living or the Living in the lived' (QP 172|172).
2) Opinion is 'in its essence' majoritarian (QP 147|146).
3) Art needs 'style' to raise perceptions to percepts and affections to affects (QP 170|170).

In the three sections that follow, I address each of these propositions at length. While each section takes its point of departure in propositions from *What Is Philosophy?*, none are limited – none can be limited – to the immediate horizon of the latter. On the contrary, the decisive role and systematic scope of affect as Deleuze and Guattari define it in *What Is Philosophy?* become evident in relation to problematics that appear to exceed its purview.

Euthanasia

> To fear death, gentlemen, is no other than to think oneself wise when one is not [. . .] No one knows whether death may not be the greatest of all blessings for a man, yet men fear it as if they knew that it is the greatest of evils. And surely it is the most blameworthy ignorance to believe that one knows what one does not know.
>
> Plato (*Apology* 29a–b)

The vitalist streak, of course, isn't limited to art or to *What Is Philosophy?* Deleuze famously describes all his writings as 'vitalistic' (P 196|143). But, for two reasons that ultimately amount to variations of a single reason, *vitalism* isn't always *vitalism*.

First, one must distinguish between *life* and *life*. Deleuze and Guattari call the perceptions and affections of everyday experience *le vécu*, 'lived experience' or more literally 'the lived'. But what Deleuze and Guattari call 'chaos', that which art renders sensible in order to rupture the affections and perceptions ossified by opinion, they also call 'life'. More specifically, because the percept renders visible the chaos subtending what we understand as 'life' in the more restricted sense of 'lived experience', they call it 'Life in the living or the Living in the lived [*la Vie dans le vivant ou le Vivant dans le vécu*]' (QP 172|172).

Second, one cannot distinguish between *life* and *death*. Not entirely. As Alain Badiou recognises, what Deleuze recuperates as 'life' for his own philosophy ('Life in the living', for instance, 'Living in the lived') would more traditionally be called 'death' (*Clameur* 23–4|*Clamor* 12). To underwrite Badiou's general observation and, eventually, to mark its limit, I turn to Bergson. Bergson in general – *Matter and Memory* in particular – has a lasting influence on Deleuze and, for the same reason, readers regularly assimilate Deleuze and Bergson in a single 'vitalist' movement that, whether praised or condemned, overlooks the incommensurability between the two at the most vital moment.[5] The moment Deleuze seems to inherit Bergson's vitalism most naively therefore proves opportune for marking the precise way in which Deleuze's 'vitalism' remains not only irreducible to but also even mortifying for 'vitalism' in a more traditional sense.

I'm invoking Bergson as a foil to the heterodoxy of Deleuze's understanding of 'life' but, in its own right, Bergson's basic schema in *Matter and Memory* complicates the traditional horizon before ultimately submitting to it. According to Bergson, I encounter a stimulus in the present, and this stimulus launches a call to the virtual depths of memory in order to supplement, to clarify and even to determine my perception of it. A 'perception', in other words, poses a question answered in more or less depth by a more or less capable memory. Perception thus conceived – as a question – has the potential to unsettle all epistemological certainty based upon the present, which is to say, the entire tradition of epistemology.[6] Bergson's notion of an interrogative perception even has the potential to unsettle metaphysics at large if indeed, after Heidegger, metaphysics names the determination of being in terms of the present.[7] The present can't answer the question of *what is*, it can't provide an answer to the meaning of being, because it, too, is a question. 'Every such question is what is termed a perception' (Bergson, *Matière* 43|*Matter* 45).

However, in saying Bergson's perception has the potential to unsettle the horizon of metaphysics as the determination of being in terms of the present, I say 'potential' for a reason. For the question of perception ultimately only reveals the extent to which Bergson nevertheless regulates consciousness and its nonconscious resources on the basis of the present, the actual, the stimulus. The present isn't

DELEUZE AND THE PROBLEM OF AFFECT

complete, the present isn't itself, the present isn't present until the more or less distant past intervenes to determine it, depending upon the memorial resources available to a consciousness, but the present situation filters all memories that don't coordinate or concur with it. For systematic reasons I won't engage here, Bergson posits that the entirety of memory is repeated in reaction to every stimulus, at every moment, in every present, and as a result irrelevant memory-images inevitably overflow (*déborder*) whatever parameters the present might set, but they comprise a fringe (*frange*) or an obscure zone (Bergson, *Matière* 90|*Matter* 85). Insofar as this fringe remains *in the present* but *beyond perception*, it constitutes an irremediable imperceptibility in every present perception and a risk to all science based upon it, but its marginalisation bespeaks the centrality of the present and perception in Bergson's account. Any memory that manages to present itself in perception without in some way resembling or serving it, any irrelevant memory that migrates from margin to centre, from fringe to perception, from virtual to actual, Bergson relegates to the status of an 'accident', a 'dream' or 'madness'. Or even *death* if, as Bergson holds throughout *Matter and Memory*, the equilibrium between the present and the past is 'the fundamental law of life' (167|150, 200|180).

To be sure, Bergson constantly critiques the errors that stem from overextending the practical attitude, but he doesn't offend common sense when he considers the irruption of irrelevant memories deadly. If a present stimulus is a danger to which I can't react because I'm distracted by the sudden and involuntary surge of the long-forgotten memory of, say, the taste of madeleine before mass on Sunday mornings in Combray, then the danger becomes more dangerous still. There is indeed a menacing undertone, even a catastrophic indifference to life, in Proust's exquisite pleasure: 'And at once the vicissitudes of life had become indifferent to me, its disasters innocuous, its brevity illusory . . .' (Proust, *Du côté de chez Swann* 58|*Swann's Way* 48). The very mechanism through which I supplement my grasp of the present with memories in order to survive it, in this case, will have inhibited my survival of it.

A malfunction for Bergson, to be sure. Nevertheless, Leonard Lawlor quite rightly points out that, for Bergson, the unexpected irruption of the past in the present is a sign of our freedom (*The Challenge of Bergsonism* 35 *et passim*). While dreams, for instance, name a potentially fatal detachment from the present, they also mark a certain freedom from the present that allows us to call upon the past in order to supplement a present perception in the first place. Which is why, in a decisive passage, Bergson writes: 'we must be able to withdraw ourselves from the action of the moment [*l'action présente*], we must have the power to value the useless, we must have the will to dream [*il faut vouloir rêver*]' (*Matière* 87|*Matter* 83). Dreams, then, constitute a double detachment: *both* a vital freedom from the present *and* a fatal diversion from it. If, however, the difference between one dream and another lies in the *will*, the *vouloir*, the ability to mobilise the oneiric past for the purpose of the present, then Bergson's lucid dreaming would reinstate intentionality and the present precisely where they should no longer reign. Only because the present continues to reign even in its absence, even in the past that has never been entirely present, can Bergson continue to conceive the oneiric irruption of the past as madness, as an accident, as a threat to life.[8]

The regulation of the past in terms of the present, memory in terms of perception and the virtual in terms of the actual thus has theoretical limits and axiological consequences that, otherwise so affirmative, Deleuze criticises. In *Bergsonism*, Deleuze recognises that Bergson links the 'law of life' to the present and, consequently, regulates the virtual with the actual. 'In question, in all of this' (*tout ceci* refers to the whole movement through which the virtual actualises), 'is the adaptation of the past to the present, of the use of the past as a function of the present – of what Bergson calls "attention to life"' (B 68|70). Deleuze doesn't take issue with this adaptation until *Difference and Repetition*, however, where a rare and often overlooked but not entirely unique passage critiques Bergson's model of memory as a whole for its basis in recognition. If my engagement with the virtual past consists essentially in understanding the perception of a given stimulus, then the virtual is effectively nothing but an auxiliary meant to make *recognition* more efficient, more exhaustive, more accurate and more domineering. Even if a stimulus forces an 'animal' to react immediately, even if a 'human' can delay a reaction long enough to reflect, to call upon memory, to re-determine the present perception to his or her advantage, both cases hinge upon recognising the stimulus. 'One can, like Bergson, distinguish two types of recognition, the cow's recognition before the grass and man's recognition calling upon his memories, but neither can be a model for what it means to think' (DR 176|135).[9]

Like the human in *Matter and Memory*, the artist in *What Is Philosophy?* calls upon the virtual. But everything changes when

Deleuze and Guattari reprioritise the relation between the virtual and the actual. The artist no longer calls upon the virtual in order to elaborate the present, to strengthen recognition, to shape or sharpen the perception of this or that stimulus. On the contrary, the artist taps the virtual precisely in order to disrupt the mechanism of recognition upon which perception depends. The point is not to supplement but to rupture the actual with the virtual, which is in part why Deleuze and Guattari speak of *percepts* and *affects* rather than *perceptions* and *affections*. Although it ventriloquises D. H. Lawrence and many of the terms are his (the umbrella, the firmament, the slit, the vision of windy chaos), one passage in particular consolidates Deleuze and Guattari's theory of art concerning this point:

> In a violently poetic text, Lawrence describes what makes poetry: men ceaselessly fabricate an umbrella that shelters them, under which they trace a firmament and write their conventions, their opinions; the poet, however, the artist practices a slit in the umbrella; he tears the very firmament to make a bit of free and windy chaos pass through and to frame in a brusque light a vision that appears though the slit . . . (QP 203|203)

This vision of chaos, for Deleuze and Guattari as for Lawrence, is a vision of life: 'A glimpse of the living, untamed chaos. For the grand chaos is all alive, and everlasting. From it we draw our breath of life' (Lawrence 237–8). The point is no longer to submit the virtual to the actual or even to balance the two; the point is no longer to render an actual perception more comprehensible, more practical, more malleable; the point is to sensitise or sensibilise chaos itself. Embodied here by the artist, Deleuze's self-proclaimed 'vitalism' could for Bergson only be a dream, an accident, madness – death. Only death, indeed, for most of the history of philosophy. Deleuze and Guattari don't draw the consequences with respect to Bergson, but they're well aware that artistic life is fatal: upon slitting the umbrella and letting a bit of free and windy chaos pass through, upon seeing 'Life in the living' or 'the Living in the lived', the artist seems to return from 'the land of the dead' (QP 202|202).[10] From the perspective of everyday perceptions, of lived experience, of opinion in general, Life in the living *is* the land of the dead. Insofar as chaos is death and affect the sensibilisation of chaos, what Deleuze and Guattari say of unconscious intensity in *Anti-Oedipus* also holds for artistic creation in *What Is Philosophy?*: 'death is what is felt [*ressenti*] in all feeling [*sentiment*]' (ACE 399|330).

Badiou's recognition of Deleuze's philosophy of life as a philosophy of death is thus irreproachable. But it's nevertheless incomplete. For in reality, according to Deleuze, there are two deaths. There's death, to be sure, in 'the fracturing of my actuality and the dissipation of my limit' (*Clameur* 24|*Clamor* 12), in the unregulated and unfiltered eruption of the virtual in the present, in the dissolution of the ego or self (*moi*) in all its ossified forms. There's death, in short, in 'the land of the dead'. But there's also death in too much actual, in any determination of the horizon of experience in advance, in being cut off from virtuality. 'It would be a mistake', Deleuze says in *Difference and Repetition*, 'to confuse the two faces of death' (DR 333|259). *What Is Philosophy?* names these two faces 'chaos' and 'opinion'.

Opinion, for its part, is always fixed, always fixed opinion, always *arrêtée* (QP 201|201). Before drawing out its relation to death, the fixity of opinion offers occasion to reconfirm the general horizon within which – or even as which – Deleuze and Guattari understand opinion. Long before Deleuze and Guattari's artist, Descartes too sought to rid himself of all his opinions, and we know how much hope he placed in even only one fixed point.

'I am here quite alone, and at last I will devote myself sincerely and without reservation to the general demolition [*eversioni*; *détruire*] of my opinions' (Descartes, *Œuvres* VII:18, IX:13|*Writings* II:12).

'Archimedes used to demand just one firm and immovable point in order to shift the entire earth; so I too can hope for great things if I manage to find just one thing, however slight, that is certain and unshakeable' (VII:24, IX:19|II:16).

Descartes destroys his opinions in search of a certain and unshakeable fulcrum (*firmum & immobile* in Descartes' Latin, *fixe et assuré* in the French translation he authorised). If, however, opinion itself means fixity, as Deleuze and Guattari suggest, then the Archimedean point that Descartes locates in the cogito (and *a fortiori* everything based upon it or discovered through it: God, body, world, science) would be one more opinion that the painter hastens to destroy on canvas. The certainty of the Archimedean point doesn't remove the deductive chain from the horizon of *doxa*, as Descartes hoped, but only ingrains it more insidiously within opinion since it no longer appears as opinion, indeed, since it appears only after all opinions appear to have been destroyed. Descartes destroys every opinion except one: knowledge.

More generally, we tend to think of opinions as relative and at least potentially shifting, it's true, but opinion wavers only within rigidly fixed limits according to Deleuze and Guattari. Behind this or that opinion, *doxa* always presupposes a more or less stable experience (for which 'cogito' is only one name), a more or less homogeneous reality experienced by subjects with a more or less homogeneous sensibility. Any variability with respect to an experience ultimately only confirms this more general limit. A given object or episode might affect you and me differently, we might be at variance with respect to the affection that a perception occasions, but I can compare my affection to yours only if I presuppose that we have the same faculty of sensibility and that what our sensibility senses is the same. An era of 'alternative facts' changes nothing fundamental in this regard. We can disagree only after already having implicitly agreed that the horizon of experience, if not this or that experience, remains fixed for everyone. As a result, wherever there's opinion, understood from this more general (and more limiting) perspective, *nothing rigorously happens*, which is why opinion constitutes a form of death. One need only compare Deleuze's constant relation of life to movement with the insistence that opinion is always fixed, arrested, *arrêtée*.

Unlike Descartes, whose Archimedean project appears naiver than ever after Deleuze and Guattari's redistribution of opinion and fixity, the artist doesn't destroy opinions for the sake of finding or founding an archaic point of certainty. Certainty no longer opposes opinion; certainty modifies opinion as the ultimate mode of fixity. The artist, rather, destroys opinion to render chaos sensible. And yet, whatever the extent to which chaos opposes opinion (opposes fixity, opposes certainty, opposes cogitation), chaos too is a form of death. I've already suggested that, when they epithet chaos as 'the land of the dead', Deleuze and Guattari implicitly recognise chaos as death, but they draw the consequences less readily. They hesitate to admit that at the limit, like opinion, chaos constitutes a certain immobility. Indeed, they describe chaos as precisely the opposite. Chaos, they say, is the infinite speed of ideas. In absolute chaos, however, in chaos pure and simple, the infinite speed at which ideas appear and disappear becomes indistinguishable from 'the immobility of silent and colorless nothingness' (QP 201|201).[11] The very speed of chaos immobilises it; it trades one immobility for another. Which is why, once again, the 'Living in life' is also the 'land of the dead'.

So, when it comes to death, absolute chaos would appear no different from absolute opinion, which Deleuze and Guattari obliquely confirm when they admit that *une œuvre de chaos* is no better than *une œuvre d'opinion*. And yet, not all deaths are equal. Deleuze and Guattari initially define philosophy, art and science by their particular styles of engaging chaos. For the non-artist, the non-philosopher and the non-scientist who can't bear to engage chaos, opinion seems to offer harbour. Since, however, opinion protects thinking from chaos by fixing a relation between ideas that allows them to resist the chaotic speed at which they'd otherwise disappear, opinion ends up immobilising thought. In the fragile balance between the threat of chaos and the temptation of opinion, opinion tends to eclipse chaos and run rampant. As a result, the thick of the struggle shifts from chaos to opinion.

But Deleuze and Guattari don't stop there.

Because the struggle with opinion becomes more important, the thinker forges an alliance with one adversary in order to fight the other. I've already cited parts of the relevant passages but, now in terms of death, they start to tell another story.

'It seems that the struggle *against chaos* is not without an affinity with the enemy, because another struggle develops and takes on more importance, *against opinion* that nevertheless claimed to protect us from chaos itself' (QP 203|203).

'A work of chaos is certainly not better than a work of opinion; art is made no more of chaos than of opinion but, if art fights against chaos, it is in order to borrow from chaos the weapons that it turns against opinion, in order to conquer opinion better with proven weapons [*des armes éprouvées*]' (QP 204|204).

Thinking doesn't struggle as a matter of life and death; it's a matter of death and death. Elsewhere, Deleuze and Guattari critique the Freudian death drive, the instinct that drives all life to return to a prior state of matter, and scathingly label it 'psychoanalytic euthanasia' (AŒ 477).[12] By pitting one death against another, however, a good death against one worse, the system of thinking in *What Is Philosophy?* also promotes a *euthanasia* of its own (*eu*: good + *thanatos*: death). To confirm chaos as the better death in *What Is Philosophy?*, despite any reserve in its regard ('a work of chaos is certainly not better . . .'), one need only compare the way in which Deleuze and Guattari watch the philosopher flee in horror before the prospect of an opinionated discussion, while praising the 'affective athleticism' of the artist engaged in chaos.

'Every philosopher flees when he or she hears the sentence: let's have a discussion' (QP 33|28).

'An Athleticism that is not organic or muscular but, rather, an "affective athleticism" . . .' (QP 173|172).[13]

By emphasising the axiomatic and axiological imbalance between death and death, which is by no means limited to opinion and chaos or to *What Is Philosophy?*,[14] the point isn't simply to recuperate opinion or reassert its value or rights. Not, in any case, without radically recalibrating each of these notions. For the stance taken toward death(s) in *What Is Philosophy?* has consequences for the range and originality of what Deleuze and Guattari call 'affect' in particular and 'thinking' in general. Despite the overhauled machinery and the idiomatic language in which they assemble it, the struggle *with* chaos *against* opinion is, in the final analysis, fundamentally familiar to the western tradition of thought. To be sure, it recalls Plato's many attacks on opinion on the one hand and, on the other, his determination of philosophy as practice for dying and death (*Phaedo* 64a). I'll make my way back to the dying Socrates below. More recently and more intimately still, when Deleuze and Guattari send the artist to face chaos, they repeat a pivotal gesture from Heidegger's *Being and Time*. Because even Agamben – *just after* he reads Deleuze's elaboration of life in the context of art in *What Is Philosophy?* as one of the most important moments of Deleuze's late philosophy and *just when* he situates Deleuze after Heidegger genealogically – still believes that Deleuze ultimately sought 'a life that does not consist only in its confrontation with death' (*Potentialities* 238), I'll make my point patiently.

In *Being and Time*, Heidegger seeks to pose the question of the meaning of being, that is, not of this or that being (*Seiende*) but of being itself (*Sein*). Nevertheless, without the privilege he grants one being in particular, the question of being would never arise. 'Is the starting point arbitrary, or does a certain being have priority [*Vorrang*] in the elaboration of the question of being?' (Heidegger, *Sein* 6|*Being* 7). This privileged or prioritised being, this being with a salient rank – a *Vorrang* – among all beings, Heidegger names *Dasein*. For an understanding of being (*Seinsverständnis*), Heidegger stresses (*Sein* 12|*Being* 11), determines the very being of Dasein (*Seinsbestimmtheit*). The first division of the first part of *Being and Time*, accordingly, offers a fundamental analysis of Dasein in order to prepare the ontological question. The second division then analyses temporality as the horizon within which Dasein always understands being.

Upon transitioning to the second division, however, Heidegger announces an essential lack (*einen wesentlichen Mangel*) in the first. Namely, by limiting the interpretation of Dasein to its everyday existence, the first division of *Being and Time* doesn't interpret Dasein as a whole and, as a result, its interpretations aren't primordial or originary (*ursprünglich*). To fill this lack, to totalise Dasein, Heidegger turns to death. As an absolute limit, death completes Dasein's existence and thereby secures the originarity of Heidegger's interpretation, which in turn secures the possibility of an interpretation of the meaning of being. 'The "end [*Ende*]" of being-in-the-world is death. This end, belonging to the potentiality-of-being [*Seinkönnen*], that is, to existence, limits and defines the possible totality [*Ganzheit*] of Dasein' (*Sein* 234|*Being* 224).

I'm not suggesting that death is ever the 'same' for Deleuze, Guattari and Heidegger. At times, on the contrary, their deaths have remarkably different contours and consequences. In the first synthesis of time in *Difference and Repetition*, for instance, Deleuze speaks of our temporal constitution as a thousand little selves (*petits moi*) that quite literally die all the time. While Heidegger mobilises death in the effort to totalise Dasein's existence, Deleuze's little mortal souls constitute a first step toward an absolute dissolution of the self.[15] Heidegger seeks to interpret being by totalising Dasein; Deleuze, to nomadise being by fracturing the self. These tensions perhaps reach their greatest pitch when, in *Anti-Oedipus*, Deleuze and Guattari outright reject being-toward-death in an effort 'to schizophrenize' death (AŒ 398|330).

I could qualify and fortify these divides or wedge others between Heidegger and Deleuze in and beyond *Being and Time* and *Difference and Repetition*. They can't be overestimated. But none would detract from the more profound continuity of *Being and Time* and *What Is Philosophy?* in relation to death, which I've been preparing for some time now. Heidegger and Deleuze and Guattari, namely, seek to appropriate that which by all accounts – their own included – should exceed all appropriation.

Heidegger, for his part, appropriates death on two tiers.

First, as is well known, death for Heidegger constitutes the most proper, *die eigenste*, Dasein's ownmost possibility. Reflecting that one Dasein can never die in another's stead, that I might sacrifice myself for another but thereby at most delay the other's death only for a time, Heidegger approaches death in terms of a certain 'mine-ness' (*Jemeinigkeit*). 'No one can take the other's dying away from him [*abnehmen*]. [. . .] Every Dasein itself must take dying upon itself [*auf sich nehmen*] in every instance. Insofar as it "is," death is always essentially my own' (Heidegger, *Sein* 240|*Being* 231). From Sartre through Levinas to Derrida, this death of mine launches a politico-ethical polemic that engages some of the most prominent philosophers in a century that was one of human history's bloodiest.[16]

The second appropriation of death or, rather, the second tier of the same appropriation is more general and analytically prior although less known or at least less debated. Heidegger can only posit *Jemeinigkeit* as the principal aspect of a concept of death if he has *already* appropriated death at least structurally by presupposing that it can be conceptually grasped in the first place. It's true that the concept of death isn't taken for granted but must be won (*gewonnen*), true that Heidegger moves carefully through the first chapter of the second division in *Being and Time* in order to win it, true that it's won from everyday preconceptions of death and various types of 'ends' that don't pertain to Dasein (*Verenden, Exitus, Ableben*), but in the end and on the whole Heidegger doesn't doubt conceptuality's grip on death. Dasein as a whole and thus ontology as a field ride upon it. 'The being-at-an-end of Dasein in death, and thus its being a whole, can, however, be included in our discussion of the possible *being* whole in a phenomenally appropriate way *only if*' – my emphasis – 'an ontologically adequate, that is, an *existential* concept of death [*Begriff des Todes*] has been attained [*gewonnen*]' (*Sein* 234|*Being* 224). Heidegger, of course, critiques the sciences insofar as they limit the determination of being to an objective presence that, although legitimate, tends to occlude more primordial presencings of being.[17] But Heidegger himself remains 'scientific' in an even broader sense insofar as he submits even death to a certain scrutiny. Nietzsche first signals this scientific drive in *the dying Socrates*.

> Taking this thought to light our way, let us now look at Socrates: he then appears to us as the first man who was capable, not just of living by the instinct of science, but also, and this is much more, of dying by it. This is why the image of the *dying Socrates*, of a man liberated from fear of death by reasons and knowledge [*durch Wissen und Gründe der Todesfurcht enthobenen Menschen*], is the heraldic shield over the portals of science, reminding everyone of its purpose, which is to make existence [*Dasein*] appear comprehensible [*begreiflich*] and thus justified . . . (Nietzsche, KSA 1:99|*Birth* 73)

Sure, Heidegger insists upon an anxiety before death (§50) that a recently condemned Socrates would proclaim irrational and blameworthy, but Heidegger too pacifies himself with an even greater 'scientific' comfort – or, as Nietzsche would say, 'optimism' – insofar as that same anxiety makes possible the totalisation of Dasein and, in turn, anchors access to the 'meaning' of being at the most primordial level. The most profound anxiety is also functional and only provisional.

Deleuze and Guattari, for their part, don't speak of a 'concept' of death in *What Is Philosophy?* and, when they speak of death, they certainly don't speak of it in terms of the mineness with which Heidegger jealously grasps it. One can recall 'the splendor' of the impersonal 'one' when 'one dies' in *Logic of Sense* (LS 178|152). One can insist that Deleuze and Guattari introduce 'schizoanalysis' in *Anti-Oedipus* by rejecting hermeneutics (AŒ 378|314).[18] They still follow in Heidegger's wake when, in *What Is Philosophy?*, they write: 'if art fights against chaos, it is in order to borrow from chaos the weapons that it turns against opinion, in order to conquer opinion better with proven weapons' (cited above). What 'chaos', what 'silent nothing', what 'land of the dead', what *death* can yield any sort of ally to any extent whatsoever? What death can be wielded or aimed and still be death? What death can be recruited, enlisted, drafted? What can be 'borrowed' from death? What can death 'lend' except that which revokes all capacity to lend and borrow, that which ends all lending, all exchange, all economy? One can count on death only, to borrow a line from Emily Dickinson, '[i]n broken mathematics' (*Poems* 47). Not because I know what death is, but because I don't, I know that whoever returns from the land of the dead never landed among the dead.

In their rush to combat opinion, in short, Deleuze and Guattari end up domesticating chaos and vitalising death. While this is not the only instance in which they do so, not even the only instance in which they do so as a function of affect,[19] for the sake of concluding here I limit myself to outlining two possible responses to the appropriation in *What Is Philosophy?* While neither path turns entirely from Deleuze and Guattari, both stray from the system they call 'thinking'.

The first path would insist upon the unappropriatability of death. Deleuze and Guattari quietly admit as much when, for instance, they speak of chaos as 'the immobility of silent and colorless nothingness' (cited above). What happens to Deleuze and Guattari's creativity, to thinking, to philosophy, science and especially art if death has no allies? It would be a mistake merely to think that opinion would spread and stifle all creativity. Not because this wouldn't happen; it would be a mistake because the loss of an ally, of *the* ally, of the *only* ally of art, philosophy and science isn't *only* the loss of an ally but also, to stay on Deleuze and Guattari's bellicose register, the acquisition of an enemy. *Both* opinion *and* chaos – both *death* and *death* – run rampant and ravage all creation, all disciplinarity, all sisterhood of thought. Deleuze and Guattari's entire system of thought is troubled here in its ready reliance on a complex but still naive distinction between ally and enemy.

A second path might accept Deleuze and Guattari's enlistment of death as an ally. As a result, however, opinion would become *deadlier than death* if, indeed, the struggle with opinion eclipses the struggle with chaos. We'd have to reread Deleuze from the beginning on the basis of the essential and therefore originary possibility of being absolutely 'cut off' – I don't borrow this expression haphazardly from *Difference and Repetition* (DR 267|207) – from the virtual, from affects and percepts, from chaos, from the Living in the lived. One name for this essential possibility now becomes 'opinion', which neither art in particular nor thinking in general can either avoid or destroy.[20]

The same seism registers in Heidegger. Just as chaos is euthanasia and opinion the worst death for Deleuze and Guattari, Heidegger extrapolates 'inauthentic' being-toward-death from chatter or patter, 'idle talk', the *Gerede* of the so-called they. Inauthentic being-toward-death expresses itself in opinion: 'the self of everydayness is the they [*das Man*] that is constituted in the public interpretedness which expresses itself in idle talk [*Gerede*]. Thus, idle talk must make manifest in what way everyday Dasein interprets its being-toward-death' (*Sein* 252|*Being* 242). What do they say of death? They say, Heidegger says, 'one also dies in the end, but for now one is not oneself affected [*unbetroffen*]' (253|243, translation modified). Heidegger might argue that this banal idea of death is neither Dasein's only nor its most authentic; the everyday notion of death might even hinder Dasein from relating to death more authentically. Perhaps one does need *courage* to feel *anxiety*. Nevertheless, since an authentic being-toward-death totalises Dasein's existence and thereby enables the entire ontological enterprise, the deadlier death becomes the death that totalises nothing. In fact, if all genuine speech (*Rede*) must draw (*schöpfen*) that which it says from that about which it speaks so as to make it manifest (*offenbar*) and accessible (*zugänglich*) to others, as Heidegger insists in the opening remarks on his phenomenological method (32|31), then perhaps all *Rede* is *Gerede* when it comes to death. This more mundane death, in short, constitutes a greater threat for ontology than any 'authentic' or 'proper' (*eigentliches*) being-toward-death because, at bottom, an authentic being-toward-death isn't a threat at all in the end but, rather, a promise – of totality, of hermeneutics, of the meaning of being.

Major Minor Warp

> . . . vivre et écrire, l'art et la vie, ne s'opposent que du point de vue d'une littérature majeure.
>
> Deleuze and Guattari (K 74|41)

'Opinion is in its essence the will of the majority and already speaks in the name of a majority' (QP 147|146). If it ruptures all opinion, inversely, then art 'in its essence' should speak – in a sense to be determined – in the name of a minority. As that by which art ruptures opinion, furthermore, all affect should be minoritarian, and all affection majoritarian. The distinction between the minor and the major, in short, refigures the struggle between art and opinion.

Accordingly, if the front line between art and opinion is porous because of their common provenance in sensibility – the hypothesis guiding my discussion in this chapter – then the same porosity will blur the distinction between the minor and the major, just as it blurred the distinction between life and death in the previous section. The space between the minor and the major, in other words, would constitute another region to which a systemic ambivalence spreads. Not one region among others, however, the minor-major distinction also activates the political valences of words like 'subversive' or 'conservative' that describe the ambivalence troubling Deleuze's theory of affect. This major moment, in other words, indicates the political stakes always – if also at times implicitly – operative here and in other sections of this and other chapters.

Why, then, is opinion always an opinion of the majority? One might think, on the contrary, that nothing is more subjective, more personal, more individual and therefore less 'majoritarian' than opinion. But the sensible genesis of opinion matters precisely in this regard. On the basis of the correspondence between a given perception and a given affection, according to Deleuze and Guattari, a group of subjects with the same opinion forms. As an opinion triumphs, the perception-affection correspondence no longer unites only the likeminded; it becomes a model – a 'perceptive and affective model' – that demands conformity (QP 147|146). But one shouldn't be misled by the sequence. If certain opinions take time to spread while others never prevail, a prevalent opinion's demand for conformity on a mass scale only makes the essence of opinion more apparent: every opinion strives to set the parameters of experience itself. Opinion doesn't *become* majoritarian; it's already 'in its essence' the will of the majority. My opinion proves majoritarian from the beginning and even if, paradoxically, I alone have it. Even if no one has it, before anyone even adopts it, opinion is majoritarian.

Beyond this brief invocation, the major doesn't resurface in *What Is Philosophy?* Although the claim relating opinion and majority thus comes and goes quickly, Deleuze and Guattari prepare it over the course of at least a decade and a half. The essentiality of the relation between opinion and majority both authorises and demands returning to and lingering on Deleuze and Guattari's earlier reflections upon the distinction between the major and the minor. 'The three characteristics of minor literature are deterritorialization of language, insertion of the individual into the immediate-political, collective assemblage [*agencement*] of enunciation' (K 33|18). Of these three traits, thematised in chapter 3 of *Kafka: Towards a Minor Literature* ('What Is a Minor Literature?'), I'll focus largely on the first for the sake of economy, but my comments hold for all three because, from the beginning, they are inseparable.

Deleuze and Guattari draw the distinction between the major and the minor from an entry in Kafka's diaries from 25 December 1911. In the entry, remarkably, the formulation 'minor literature' never occurs. Not exactly. In fact, one could argue that the rise of what, after Deleuze and Guattari, we so readily call 'minor' in the critical landscape results from a loose and loaded translation – if not simply a mistranslation – of Kafka. In *Kafka*, Deleuze and Guattari quote from Marthe Robert's translation of Kafka's diaries (Grasset 1954) and, while they criticise her interpretation of Kafka on more than one occasion,[21] they implicitly agree with her in at least one fundamental respect. What Robert translates as *des littératures mineures*, what Deleuze and Guattari repeat and independently develop as *la littérature mineure*, what anglophones have come to call *minor literature* with more or less insouciance, Kafka calls *kleine Literaturen*, literally, 'small literatures'. In the 1948 English translation (Schocken), not without a certain justification since Kafka also mentions a *kleine Nation* and a *kleines Volk*, Joseph Kresh apparently takes the formulation as a hypallage and elaborates his translation into 'the literature of small peoples'.

'*Schema zur Charakteristik kleiner Literaturen*' (*Tagebücher* 132).	'Schéma pour établir les caractéristiques des littératures mineures' (*Journal* 183).	'A character sketch of the literature of small peoples' (*Diaries* 150).

Kleiner, mineures, small: the formulaic variations are important for more than merely terminological reasons. For the moment, I'll stress only one of the characteristics in Kafka's notes that will have the most general significance for Deleuze and Guattari's adoption and adaptation of the distinction between the 'major' and the 'minor': so-called minor literature, namely, lacks 'irresistible national models' (Kafka, *Tagebücher* 130|*Diaries* 149). Initially, Kafka invokes this lack as an advantage since, without a model, nothing inspires those who have no talent whatsoever (the *völlig Unfähige*) to write and overburden literature, but it soon becomes apparent that the models themselves place an even greater burden on literature. Kafka's concern finds a perhaps unexpected precursor in David Hume who, centuries prior, recognised that too many 'models of eloquence' in any nation discourage young and aspiring authors from 'rivalship' with the models they admire (Hume, *Essays* 135). Beyond this or that epigone, Hume – like Kafka – even recognises that a few great writers 'fix the tongue' for posterity (*Essays* 209). Yet, whereas 'the want of perfect models' produces 'a false taste' for Hume (*Essays* 107), for Kafka – for Deleuze and Guattari's Kafka – there is no standard of taste. On the contrary, the destruction of models becomes an end in itself.

> Goethe probably retards the development of the German language by the force [*Macht*] of his writing. Even though prose style has often travelled away from him in the interim, still, in the end, as at present, it returns to him with strengthened yearning [*Sehnsucht*] and even adopts obsolete idioms found in Goethe but otherwise without any particular connexion with him, in order to rejoice in the completeness [*vervollständigten Anblick*] of its unlimited dependence. (Kafka, *Tagebücher* 133|*Diaries* 152)

Now, Goethe might be paradigmatic, but 'great' (*große*) literature isn't limited to such obvious 'father-symbols', as Freud calls him (GW II/III:358–9|*Interpretation* 367). Part of the originality of Deleuze and

Guattari's reading lies in universalising Kafka's observation concerning a lack of national models. Taking this lack to its extreme, they harden the consequences into a theory that will accompany them until, for instance, the artist creates affects to combat the 'perceptive and affective models' of opinion in the last book that bears both their names.

In this regard, the translative slip from *klein* through *mineur* to *minor* becomes pivotal. It's arguably the source of the most facile confusion in Deleuze and Guattari's analyses. For the translation of *klein* as 'minor' authorises reference to 'major' by implicit opposition to it, and this opposition in turn opens a spectrum of formulations and divisions pertaining to the more familiar concepts of 'majority' and 'minority'. But *major* is no longer *major*, and *minor* no longer *minor*. 'Majority' no longer means 'common' or 'consensus', and 'minority' no longer means 'less than half'. Neither refers to any sort of determined population, even though Deleuze and Guattari constantly draw examples from very precise demographics, beginning with Kafka's own sociolinguistic situation between German, Czech and Yiddish in Prague at the turn of the twentieth century. Number no longer counts. 'Majority is defined by a model to which one must conform', whereas 'minority has no model' (P 235|173). The division doesn't fall between a major model and a minor model but, rather, between any model and no model. Accordingly, a minority can remain minor even when more numerous than the majority, and a majority can remain major even where its model has only one adherent. Even if no one adheres to the model, indeed, the major remains major insofar as there remains a model to which one might adhere. This should hold whether the literature in question is a *model for* or *modelled on*.

In distinguishing the major and the minor, of course, Deleuze and Guattari more immediately aim to problematise traditional interpretations of Kafka, especially the facile psychoanalytic readings that reduce Kafka's work to a father complex unfolding as an inner drama. But the distinction raises a series of questions. Is it ever possible to shed all models whatsoever? Even if I manage to convince myself that I've written a line or two without recurring to Goethe or any of the greats, can I be sure that no one will ever draw a model in turn from what I myself have written? Even if no one else ever sees what I've written, could a model not be drawn from it still in principle? Inversely, is it even ever possible to conform to a model entirely?

These are, in any case, the terms of Deleuze and Guattari's wager when they harden the absence of national models in *kleinen Literaturen* into an absence of all models whatsoever in *la littérature mineure*. At the limit, to be sure, only an absolute absence of any transcendent principle fixing literary parameters in advance could create the conditions for a rigorous event and its non-hierarchical horizon, to which Deleuze and Guattari give various names like 'anarchy', 'nomadism', 'immanence' and 'rhizome'. Only absolute immoderation could jam the mechanisms of opinion beyond repair. But Deleuze and Guattari give greater weight to the theoretical *value* of the distinction than to its rigorous *possibility*. For they, too, recognise that the minor not only needs the major but even needs the major twice. Without mitigating the theoretical demand for a veritable minor, this double implication of the major in the minor symptomises the possible impossibility – in fact and in principle – of 'minor literature' as Deleuze and Guattari read it. To be sure, other signs could be adduced to develop the disruptive implication of the minor in the major in order to show that the major is never purely major, which Deleuze and Guattari and proponents of their major-minor distinction most often stress. This gesture is partial, however, because it leaves unproblematised not only the minor itself but also, more generally, the category of 'purity' upon which depends any isolation of the minor from the major and vice versa. The irreducible implication of the major in the minor is more consequential than the minor in the major, in short, precisely because Deleuze and Guattari stake literature, politics and life itself in the minor rather than the major.

1) First, the minor needs the major precisely in order to flee it, to direct the so-called line of flight, *la ligne de fuite*. In their reading of Kafka, for instance, Deleuze and Guattari search for elements of expression that 'deterritorialise' language from its referential function. Like Josephine's piping that passes into song or Gregor's shrill accompaniment to his sister's violin, these elements operate 'an active neutralization of sense [*sens*]' (K 38|21). This 'active neutralization' is no doubt novel. Whereas phenomenology neutralises – another name for 'reduces' or 'suspends' – for the sake of accessing sense, Deleuze and Guattari neutralise sense itself. Rather than neutralising a sensible sign and even the object to which it refers for the sake of regressing to the mental processes that bestow sense in the first place, rather than regressing toward a deeper terrain of consciousness, Deleuze and Guattari neutralise sense by fleeing – by a line of flight – toward an absolute deterritorialisation.[22] Not a regression but a flight, not a new terrain but deterritorialisation.

And yet, all novelty notwithstanding, an unneutralised and even unneutralisable vestige of sense or meaning will subsist in even the most neutralised and deterritorialised writing. Somewhat against his Marxist professions, Deleuze mobilises 'the line of flight' to avoid the contradictions and negations of the dialectic model of historical analysis (P 232|172), but the line of flight will nevertheless never be a pure flight because, whatever positivity with which Deleuze and Guattari expressly determine the line of flight, the *flight* is always also a flight *from*. The preposition 'from' is also in a sense a presupposition; that from which the line flees will always leave a trace in the flight itself. Otherwise, if some sort of pure minor were ever achieved or even imaginable, all flight would stop. Which Deleuze and Guattari acknowledge in a passage that, for obvious reasons, rarely gets cited: 'Of sense there subsists only enough to direct [*seulement de quoi diriger*] the lines of flight' (K 39|21). Only enough. Sense might cease to exhaust or dominate language, but neither Josephine's song nor Gregor's shrill can ever neutralise sense entirely because they still need enough – *seulement de quoi* – to direct the flight. To be clear, I'm not suggesting that the neutralisation has no effect on sense or that the line of flight remains immobile. For anyone seeking absolute non-referentiality or a pure deformation of sense, however, for anyone seeking the absolute deterritorialisation of language, 'only enough' is still too much because infinitely more than none. Even if the flight's vector can't be predicted on the basis of the sense it flees, a residuum of sense retains something of a managerial status. The subsistence of sense, however minimal, remains enough *to direct* the line of flight (diriger *la ligne de fuite*).

The more one insists upon this directive, the more difficult it becomes to distinguish the neutralisation of sense from its greatest extension. For sense still manages to direct the literary line, however minor, even after it has been actively neutralised and abandoned. Sense thus directs its own deterritorialisation, which one could read as a limit of either sense or deterritorialisation. To reformulate this fundamental collaboration in terms of *What Is Philosophy?* and the problem of affect that concerns me here, if opinion is 'in its essence' majoritarian and if art destroys opinion, then a minimal opinion will still and always direct art. An affection will always direct the affect extracted from it. Which not only means the artist never faces a blank page or an empty measure. No artist will ever absolutely purify any affect of every affection. This is the first sign that one needs a greater matrix – a warp – from which to think the major and the minor (sense and flight, opinion and art, affection and affect).

2) While the first complication or co-implication of minor and major concerns the struggle *to deterritorialise*, to take flight from a territory, the second concerns the temptation *to reterritorialise*. In the last paragraphs of *Kafka*, albeit parenthetically, Deleuze and Guattari thematise 'dangers' to a minor struggle that don't come from the majority, which is to say, dangers internal to the minor itself: 'to reterritorialise, . . . to remake power and law, also to remake "great literature"' (K 154|86). The danger doesn't lie in the majority's reaction to minor opposition or protest; internal to the minor, rather, the danger lies in making the minor major in turn. Because the minor endangers itself with the major, this danger is ineradicable.

This inner threat would already suffice to demand one rethink any essential opposition between the major and the minor. While a 'danger' might be avoided and more or less insured, however, Deleuze and Guattari elsewhere and on more than one occasion admit that reterritorialisation and remodelling – remajoring – is in fact inevitable. In a 1990 interview, Toni Negri asks Deleuze point-blank how a minoritarian becoming can become powerful (*puissant*), how 'resistance' can become 'insurrection', how the minor can have any real impact in the world without ceasing to be minor. Deleuze responds:

> When a minority creates models for itself, it is because it wants to become a majority, and it is no doubt [*sans doute*] inevitable for its survival [*survie*] and its wellbeing [*salut*] (to have a state, be recognized, establish its rights, for example). (P 235|173)

Deleuze himself provides a telling example when, eleven years prior to the interview with Negri, he writes an 'Open Letter to Negri's Judges', citing above all 'a certain principle of identity' on the part of the accused and the accusation without which a defendant – in this case Negri himself – cannot defend himself (DRF 156|169).

Deleuze, then, doesn't simply improvise his reply. It receives more systematic treatment in *A Thousand Plateaus*, however, when he and Guattari write:

> Even and especially politically, it is difficult to see how those upholding a minor language can operate if not by giving it, if only in writing, a constancy and homogeneity that make it a locally major language capable of forcing official recognition. (MP 129|102)

As if trying to save the value and validity of categories that find themselves more and more problematic, compromised and impure,

Deleuze and Guattari make almost incidental recourse to the idea of a 'locally major language' (*une langue localemente majeure*). As if a 'minor language' could remain 'minor' if it becomes major only locally, only within certain topographical limits, only to a certain extent; as if a limited degree of majority might give the minor the political recognition it needs to survive while protecting it from becoming an outright model. A major minor over against a major major (not unlike, returning to a theme from Chapter 2 above, a general generality over against an impoverished generality). Not only does the redistribution perforate the distinction between the minor and the major. How tenable is the idea of a 'locally major' minor language when the major isn't – this was the point of departure in Kafka – a numerical or demographic notion? Where the major concerns the presence of any model whatsoever, possible or actual, the distinction between 'local' and 'global' has no bearing. As a result, if indeed the major holds the secret of the minor's survival and wellbeing, *sa survie* as well as *son salut*, then the minor can't survive apart from its own death. No flight from the major ever gets very far if, in the end, it must nevertheless remain 'locally major'. Once again, oppositions like major and minor, model and flight, wellbeing and infirmity, survival and death begin to lose their explanatory power.

Deleuze and Guattari know this. In the fourth plateau of *A Thousand Plateaus*, when they bring the major-minor question to bear patently and patiently on the fundamental postulates of linguistics as a field, they explicitly thematise the co-implication of the major and the minor, and the effect at first sight seems even-handed. Just as the minor remains essentially susceptible to a major treatment, the major is vulnerable to a minor becoming. On the one hand, 'a minor language does not escape the conditions for a treatment that extricates [*dégage*] a homogeneous system and extracts [*extrait*] constants from it'; on the other hand, 'the more a language has or acquires the characteristics of a major language, the more it is worked over [*travaillé*] by continuous variations that transpose it into a "minor" language' (MP 129–30|102). But Deleuze and Guattari quickly introduce a dissymmetry in the formulations by hardening their claim concerning the variations that undermine the major language: '*You will not achieve a homogeneous system that is not still or already worked over by an immanent, continuous, and regulated variation*' (MP 130|103). If the major, understood as a homogeneous system of language that Saussure first named *la langue*,[23] is always either *still* or *already* traversed by minorisations, then it's always *too early* or *too late* for the mother tongue. The major never has its moment. By contrast, while Deleuze and Guattari admit that the minor can't escape the *conditions* for a major treatment, they leave intact the possibility of a purely minor use of language, if only for a moment, before the majority overtakes the minor with its models, constants and standards that would allow one to study it in the name of linguistics as a hard science. While the major is still or already and therefore never not minorised, the minor might at one point, under certain conditions, lend itself to a major treatment that therefore only belatedly befalls it.

This asymmetry, even if one grants it, still fails to secure the minor as a pure category. Even if the minor is always only susceptible to a major treatment that therefore might come after the event or in fact never at all, the minor still bears a major streak. Before the minor ever actually receives or resists a major treatment, if it never entirely escapes the conditions for a major treatment, if a linguist could extract models from it in principle and even if no one ever does so in fact, then the minor always already in a way hosts the major. In other words, in Deleuze and Guattari's words otherwise, *you will not achieve a minor language that is not still or already compromised by a major treatment*. Although Deleuze and Guattari carefully avoid this conclusion in *A Thousand Plateaus*, it must be taken into any rigorous account of the minor because, insofar as it never escapes the conditions for a major treatment, the major in a sense conditions the minor. The extraction of models from minor writers might indeed be 'the worst' (MP 469|378). Insofar as the major already inhabits the minor as an essential possibility, insofar as the minor therefore cannot be understood without the major it might become, the worst is analytic to the best.

In both of these complications or co-implications of the major and minor, both the struggle to deterritorialise and the danger of reterritorialisation, the greater question doesn't concern the minor or the major but rather their common matrix, that is, the difference between the major and the minor prior to the major and the minor in the purity that Deleuze and Guattari readily deny in one case (the becoming-minor of the major) but piously protect in the other (the major extraction of the minor). One name for this matrix might be 'style'.

On the one hand, Deleuze and Guattari constantly turn to style as a minor force. Among many possible, I limit myself to telescoping a few references in some of the texts within which I've been working here:

- 'it is through style that one becomes animal' (K 15|7).
- 'What we call a style ... is precisely the process of continuous variation' (MP 123|97).
- 'Each time one needs a style ... to raise lived perception to the percept, lived affection to the affect' (QP 170|170).

I'll resist the temptation to say more here about these invocations of style, which unite a number of apparently unrelated notions from Deleuze and Guattari's work (becoming-animal, continuous variation, percept and affect). For my immediate purposes, the general mobilisation of style as a minorising apparatus is in each case more important than the details of its operation in the context in which it intervenes.

On the other hand, Deleuze and Guattari invoke 'style' to name the major. In fact, it names more than the major; it names ineradicable aspirations toward the major that not even a lack of national models can curb or deflate. This is even the closing thought of the chapter in which Deleuze and Guattari read the literature of small peoples according to Kafka. 'How many styles, or genres, or literary movements, even very small ones, have only one single dream: to assume a major function in language, to offer their services as a State language, an official language' (K 49|27).

A question of style thus interposes itself in the major-minor divide and prior to it. How can 'style' sustain a reference, in neither case coincidental, to both the major and the minor, to the 'State' and the 'animal', to an official language and stuttering, to the system and its outside, that is, to the constant and the *sous-système* or *hors-système*? 'A determination other than the constant would thus be considered minoritarian [*minoritaire*], by nature and no matter the number, that is to say, a sub-system [*sous-système*] or an outside-system [*hors-système*]' (MP 133|105). What complicity and co-implication between the major and the minor allow both to operate in terms of 'style'? What abyss does the word 'style' hide that allows it to name both? Style, in any case, goes unopposed. For all division, opposition and contamination between the major and the minor take place *within* style, which thus engulfs both sides of the opposition that Deleuze and Guattari summon it to describe. Even what Deleuze and Guattari call 'nonstyle' turns out to be the greatest style of all (e.g., P 224|165).[24]

I broached style as a possible 'matrix' of the minor and the major, but 'warp' is a more fitting name. For style not only *founds* the distinction between the minor and the major. It not only *weaves* the minor and the major together. In the same stroke it *distorts*, *deforms* and *denatures* the distinction as it structures Deleuze and Guattari's discourse. Style warps the distinction not only between the minor and the major but also, as I now turn to show in the last section of this chapter, between affect and affection, between percept and perception, between art and opinion.

Style Each Time

Le style, chez un grand écrivain, c'est toujours aussi un style de vie, non pas du tout quelque chose de personnel, mais l'invention d'une possibilité de vie, d'un mode d'existence.

Deleuze (P 138|100)

'Style is necessary each time – a writer's syntax, a musician's modes and rhythms, a painter's strokes and colors – in order to raise lived perceptions to the percept, lived affections to the affect' (QP 170|170). I announced this proposition at the outset of this chapter, but I also invoked it at the end of the last section to propose style as what I call the major-minor warp. More specifically, I invoked it in support of the minor force of style, but the proposition in itself is much more difficult to locate on the major-minor scale than the formulation might suggest. I would oversimplify if I said style is indispensable to art and thinking as Deleuze and Guattari define them. If indeed style raises perception to the percept, affection to the affect, then style constitutes the very difference between percept and perception, affect and affection. No difference between percept and perception or affect and affection would exist without style, such that art's disciplinary specificity and possibility both depend upon it. Because art differs from opinion as percept from perception and affect from affection, furthermore, art's struggle with opinion – the most intimate among all the disciplines – becomes a question of style. For the same reason, none of these distinctions charting the creative topology and process of *What Is Philosophy?* suffices to situate the therefore elusive notion of style that, rather, marks their limit.

At times, Deleuze and Guattari claim that each artist's style of, 'method' for, extracting percept from perception and affect from affection constitutes an essential part of the work.

The goal [*but*] of art, by means of the material, is to wrest [*arracher*] the percept from perceptions of an object and from the states of a perceiving subject, to wrest the affect from affections as a passage from one state to another. To extract [*extraire*] a block of sensations, a pure being of sensation. To this end, one needs a method that varies according to each author and that constitutes part of the work [*fait partie de l'œuvre*] . . . (QP 167|167)

To be sure, even or perhaps especially in art, method isn't simply style. The idea of a 'method' bears a number of epistemic presuppositions that, when not entirely redefined in texts like 'The Method of Dramatization', leads Deleuze to reject the term outright (for instance, DR 215|165). The principle of clarity and distinction, the division of each difficulty into ultimate parts, the progression from the simplest to the most complex, the totalising review and enumeration: one could find a Deleuzian inspiration to break each of the four rules comprising the Cartesian method (Descartes, *Œuvres* VI:18–19|*Writings* I:120). Here in *What Is Philosophy?*, by contrast, both 'method' and 'style' describe unique procedures to which artists submit their material in order to extract a being of sensation, a block of sensations, a composition of percepts and/or affects. 'The particular material of writers are words and syntax, a created syntax that rises irresistibly in their work [*œuvre*] and passes into sensation' (QP 167|167). Accordingly, while it would be rash – if not simply wrong – to think artists are always friendlier to style than philosophers, it's not difficult to understand why style becomes an essential part of the artwork as Deleuze and Guattari understand it: insofar as style wrests from perception and affection the percept and affect that define an artwork, art wouldn't work without style.

At the same time, Deleuze and Guattari posit a distinction that implicitly expels style from art in a strict sense. While 'aesthetic composition' refers to the collection of percepts and affects that constitutes art proper, 'technical composition' pertains to the materiality that, although a necessary component for the aesthetic composition of a work of art, Deleuze and Guattari refuse to call art in a strict sense. Properly speaking, art (affect – percept) is *immaterial* and, by situating style on the plane of technique, Deleuze and Guattari remove it from art altogether.

> Composition, composition, this is the only definition of art. Composition is aesthetic and what is not composed is not art. One nevertheless will not confound technical composition, the work of the material [*travail du matériau*] that often calls upon science to intervene (mathematics, physics, chemistry, anatomy), and aesthetic composition, which is the work of sensation [*travail de la sensation*]. (QP 192–3|191–2)

True, here again, Deleuze and Guattari don't name style in association with the material. But the expulsion of style from art proper necessarily follows when they include within the horizon of technique – not to be confused with art – elements that they elsewhere attribute to style. 'To be sure, technique comprehends many things that are individualized according to each artist and each work: words and syntax in literature . . .' (QP 193|192). Syntax is the first element Deleuze and Guattari name when they assert the necessity of style in raising perception to percept and affection to affect. 'Style is necessary each time – a writer's syntax . . .' (cited above). Indeed, Deleuze regularly relates style to syntax throughout his writings; the literary notion marks Deleuze so profoundly that he goes so far as to posit philosophy's creation of concepts as a 'syntax' and, hence, the syntax of concepts as a question of style (P 179|131, 192|140, 223|164). Technically, nevertheless, syntax and therefore style don't belong to art proper. Scandalously if also silently, as a result, Deleuze and Guattari exclude style from the art that nevertheless needs it *à chaque fois*.

There's therefore no art with or without style. Style constitutes part of the work but works on a technical plane outside artistic composition in a strict sense. Style is both within and without art, essential and extraneous, a part and apart, necessary and superfluous, so on and so forth. Not even art, not even the discipline traditionally most open to and invested in questions of style, can properly circumscribe style. Artistic and technically inartistic, however, the double status of style doesn't leave the artistic process intact. It signals a problem for thought in general by contaminating affect with affection and percept with perceptions, 'aesthetic composition' with 'technical composition', art with opinion.

Idea with matter.

Because Deleuze and Guattari regularly vindicate a certain materialism, no doubt, readers regularly overlook or understress (perhaps Deleuze and Guattari first of all) that the entire theory of art and affect in *What Is Philosophy?* hinges upon the relentless reduction of matter.[25] Deleuze and Guattari's opening claim concerning art implicitly hinges upon the success of this reduction: 'Art conserves, and it is the only thing in the world that conserves itself' (QP 163|163). The self-conservation of art, its autonomy as its eternity, hinges upon the reduction in principle (*en droit*) of its material support because only on this condition does the defining percept or affect reach a level of rarefaction that enables it to hover beyond all determined perceptions and affections, all lived experience, all 'human' experience. Only upon its disembodiment does affect or percept achieve an ideality freed from the time and place of its creation; only upon its demateri-alisation does sensation precede and exceed whoever suffers it; only then do Deleuze and Guattari speak of a 'pure' being of sensation. No matter the difficulty of *actually* or *factually* paring sensation of the material that conditions it:

> the sensation is not the same thing as the material, at least in principle. That which in principle conserves itself in itself is not material, which constitutes only the condition in fact, but, as long as this condition is fulfilled ... , that which conserves itself in itself is the percept or the affect. (QP 166|166)

Deleuze and Guattari never draw the conclusion so bluntly, but it necessarily follows that, in the end and 'at least in principle', neither percept nor affect will have depended upon the material in which 'in fact' they originate. Art is art *because* it reduces its material. Because it's purely ideal or spiritual.

This artistic reduction of matter doesn't take place for the first time in *What Is Philosophy?* An important precedent, *Proust and Signs* sheds somewhat unexpected light on this artistic reduction of matter by relating it explicitly to style. Style thus becomes not merely ideal (part of the artwork), not merely material (part of the technical plane), but above all the idealisation that moves between them.

Deleuze claims that Proust's account of art doesn't end with the mechanism of involuntary memory. In fact, since involuntary memory isn't the end, it will not have mattered at all. In a letter to Joseph Voeffray dated 1983, Deleuze says that, whenever he writes, he begins with a simple idea that's been largely overlooked: 'for example, in my Proust [book], the simple idea was that memory had no importance' (L 92|91). In the case of *Proust and Signs*, however, he also recognises that this simple idea was ultimately ineffective: 'people still speak of memory' (L 92|91). Nearly thirty years after his letter and more than fifty after the original publication of *Proust and Signs*, rightly or wrongly, people still speak of memory.[26] But memory in Proust is insignificant, according to Deleuze, precisely because it's involuntary. That involuntary memory takes place 'naturally' in the course of life, according to Deleuze, leads Proust to doubt the specificity of art at the end of his *Search*. Proust's doubt concerns the old distinction between art and nature and, given the horizon within which the question arises, Deleuze responds via Proust somewhat unexpectedly.

On the one hand, for *Proust and Signs* and for his own philosophy beginning with *Difference and Repetition*, Deleuze retains from Proust the prioritisation of what *forces* thought – the *Signs* in *Proust and Signs*. This violent force promises to disrupt and disorder the 'rationalist' sequence that posits a primordial Idea that everything after merely develops and confirms. Whence the rationalist mantra: 'Intelligence comes before'.

On the other hand, despite the necessarily violent encounter with which he would assure the event and authenticity of thinking, Deleuze nevertheless posits art's supremacy over nature – in Proust – on the basis of a certain mastery or manoeuvrability of what occurs only involuntarily in the natural course of life. The artist wields what nature imposes. And the artist achieves mastery, more specifically, through the *dematerialisation* and *spiritualisation* of signs. It's no longer the unassuming taste of a madeleine that resonates with the past to produce the Image or Idea of 'Combray' in its essence; it's now words and syntax. It's now, in a word, a question of style. Deleuze emphasises:

> At the end, however, we see what art is capable of adding to nature: it produces resonances themselves, because *style* makes any two objects resonate and from them dislodges a "precious image," *substituting the free conditions of an artistic production for the determined conditions of a natural unconscious product.* (PS 186|155)

The conditions of art are free, *libres*, only when freed from an intractable material that the artist cannot control. In literature, in contrast to nature's mechanical caprice, style can make *any two objects* resonate. 'Still too heavy, Nature and life have found in art their spiritual equivalent' (PS 186|155).

The spiritual resonance of objects in literature still forces readers to think, it still constitutes an 'encounter' unprogrammed by a prior Intelligence, but it resounds most because it's free, because autonomous, because independent of the materiality on which nature depends for the production of the same effect in the ordinary course of life. *Œuvre* becomes *manœuvre* at the very moment art supposedly breaks from the dogmatic categories of mastery and manipulation by forcing thought wilfully. While things force thought in nature, thought forces itself in art. One would have to distinguish two forces here – the force of nature and the force of thought – and problematise the distinction for the same reason. Keeping focus, I'll limit myself to pointing out that style operates this entire process of artistic rarefaction so intimately that Deleuze merges it with the Image, the Idea, the immaterial Essence produced in the resonance between any two objects in a work of art. The implicit reference to Buffon,[27] important in its own right, only intensifies the essentialisation of style.

'Style is not the man; style is essence itself' (PS 62|48).	'But style is never the man; it is always of the essence (nonstyle)' (PS 200–1|167).

What, then, is style? The question becomes preposterous. The propositions that emerge between *What Is Philosophy?* and *Proust and Signs* don't exhaust the possible positions of style in art or in Deleuze's work, let alone in general, but they suffice to problematise – in the spirit of Deleuze and as a counterweight to him – what we collectively and collectedly call 'style'.

– Style raises perceptions and affections to percepts and affects and therefore is an essential part of the work of art.
– Technically, style pertains to the materiality it works and therefore is not an essential part of the work of art.
– Neither material nor ideal, style dematerialises and spiritualises and, because it does so freely, is the very Essence of art.

Both material and immaterial, technical and aesthetic, voluntary and involuntary *and* the passage between them, style intractably crosses all the oppositions with which Deleuze structures art and therefore, given the privileged place of art in thinking in general, thinking in general.

In order to establish this impossible confluence of propositions on style, I've gathered texts written some thirty years apart and, in so doing, I've done a certain violence to each. In response to which, I might problematise the threshold meant to divide a 'violent' reading from a 'nonviolent' reading. I might add justifications throughout Deleuze's oeuvre, which works and reworks its materials from one book to the next, from one context to the next, at times from one proposition to the next. I might also recall the very premise of *What Is Philosophy?*, which opens as a reflection not only on the nature of philosophy but also, more specifically, on Deleuze and Guattari's own oeuvre: 'what was it that *I* did my whole life?' (QP 7|2, my emphasis). I might underscore the hyperlink to *Proust and Signs* in

Deleuze and Guattari's parenthetical claim in *What Is Philosophy?* that memory intervenes little '(even and especially in Proust)' (QP 167|167). To show that Proust still informs Deleuze's understanding of style until the end, I might juxtapose the epigraph of *Critical and Clinical* –

> Beautiful books are written in a sort of foreign language
> Proust, *Contre Sainte-Beuve*

– with related passages from *What Is Philosophy?*:

> The writer makes use of words but by creating a syntax that makes them pass into sensation and that makes everyday language [*la langue courante*] stutter or tremble or cry or sing: this is style, the "tone," the language of sensations, or the foreign language in language . . . (QP 176|176)

Although indispensable, this scholarship would only prepare the essential question. How does *style* accommodate, invite and even generate such shifting and even opposing determinations? Why does it do so, moreover, without thematisation or reflection on the part of Deleuze who, indeed, constitutes only one example in this regard? One of the greatest champions of style[28] – the very height of art, its material burden and the gravity between them – wasn't always quite sure how to champion it.

That style both inhabits and exceeds each term in the distinctions that distinguish the artistic discipline (technique and composition, matter and idea, perception and percept, affection and affect, so on and so forth), that style operates both major and minor tendencies and thus warps their distinction, that style always creates a style of life together with a transcendent principle that stifles it: that doesn't simply mean there is no art or, for that matter, only opinion. It does mean there is no purity, no univalence, because – in style – every affection and every perception still and already infect every affect and every percept that originate in them as a matter of fact. This infection will remain a mainstay when, in Part II below, I trace the distinction between affect and affection back to its source in Spinoza.

Notes

1. Opinion thus converges and conspires with the association of ideas: both arrest thinking. Opinion poses here in Chapter 3 the same problem contemplation poses in the final section of Chapter 2 above. Deleuze and Guattari go on: 'This is why we want to cling to fixed opinions so much.

We demand only that our ideas link together according to a minimum of constant rules, and the association of ideas has never had any other sense, to furnish us those protective rules – resemblance, contiguity, causality – that allow us to put a little order in ideas' (QP 201|201).

2. On these three traits (*autochthony, philia, doxa*), see chapter 1 of Rodolphe Gasché's *Geophilosophy*.

3. In his earlier work, Deleuze regularly pits orthodoxy against paradox. In *Difference and Repetition*, over against the traditional doctrine of the faculties that only hypostatises and 'philosophises' everyday recognition, Deleuze posits a differential doctrine that consists in a facultative exercise that he defiantly calls 'paradoxical' (see Chapter 1 above). *What Is Philosophy?*, however, appears more demanding. If paradox isn't simply orthodox, it's nonetheless determined in terms of *doxa* and, to that extent, doesn't break with opinion sufficiently. 'Even the man of "paradox" expresses himself with so many winks and so much self-assured foolishness [*sottise*] only because he claims to express everyone's secret opinion and to be the spokesman for what others do not dare to say' (QP 147|146). Hence, the artist defies opinion, not because he or she has a different or uncommon opinion about art, life or anything whatsoever but, rather, because he or she has no opinion. Neither orthodox nor paradoxical, the artist is artistic only by destroying doxicality itself.

4. I call the distinction between 'affect' and 'affection' novel even though it translates Spinoza's distinction between *affectus* and *affectio*. In Chapter 5 below, I'll show the *betrayal* that makes possible, if not necessary, the omission of any reference to Spinoza in Deleuze's most systematic adoption of affect (chapter 7 of *What Is Philosophy?*). These reflections already inhabit the hiatus.

5. In certain ways, of course, Deleuze himself promoted this insensitive classification. For instance, the volume containing his selected passages from Bergson's work bears the title *Mémoire et vie* ('memory and life').

6. Compare, for instance, Husserl's '*principle of all principles*' in §24 of *Ideas* 1: '*every originary presentive intuition* [originär gebende Anschauung] *is a legitimizing source of cognition* [Erkenntnis]' (Husserl HUA III/1:51|*Ideas* 44). See also §28 of the later *Crisis*: 'Perception is the primal mode of *intuition* [Urmodus der Anschauung]; *it* exhibits with primal originality [*Uroriginalität*], that is, in the mode of the self-present [*Selbstgegenwart*]' (Husserl, HUA 6:107|*Crisis* 105, Husserl's emphases).

7. See especially Heidegger, *Sein* 25|*Being* 24.

8. For the same problematic twenty years after *Matter and Memory* (1899), see 'La conscience et la vie', a text delivered in English in 1911 but translated into French and heavily revised in 1919 for *L'énergie*

spirituelle (*Mind Energy*). For the role of dreaming in the exploration of the virtual in Deleuze, see DR 281–4|218–20.

9. In *Bergsonism*, Deleuze addresses these two forms of recognition uncritically (B 66 note 2|127 note 35). Incidentally, this double rejection of the animal's *reaction* and the human's *reflection* in the name of *thinking* could provide one means for responding to Derrida's critiques of Deleuze in (primarily) sessions five and six of the first volume of *The Beast and Sovereign*.

10. Not only the artist, of course, but also the philosopher and especially *the* philosopher Spinoza: 'That frugal life without property, eroded [*minée*] by disease, that thin and puny body, that oval and brown face with flashing black eyes, how to explain the impression that they gave of being traversed by Life itself, of having a power identical to Life?' (SPP 19–20|12; see also P 196|143).

11. To relate this problem telescopically to Part II on 'The Paradox of Spinoza' below, see Deleuze and Guattari's 'Memories of a Spinozist' in *A Thousand Plateaus* (plateau 10), where they speak of immanence as a plane of 'absolute immobility *or* absolute movement' (MP 312|255, Deleuze and Guattari's emphasis).

12. This formulation comes from 'Bilan-programme pour machines désirantes', a text appended to the second edition of *L'Anti-Œdipe* but omitted in the English translation. For an English translation, see Guattari, *Chaosophy* 90–115 (105 for the formulation in question).

13. Both the interlocutor and the athlete nevertheless trace to the same *agonistic* aftermath of the crisis of sovereignty in ancient Greece. See Jean-Pierre Vernant's *The Origins of Greek Thought* (especially 41–2|45–7). For more on artistic athleticism, see rubric three of FB and P 179–81|131–2. Although Deleuze doesn't refer to Artaud in his discussion of 'affective athleticism' in either the *Logic of Sensation* or *What Is Philosophy?*, the formulation clearly stems from the twelfth section of *The Theatre and its Double*. While Artaud attributes the affective sphere to the actor, however, all artists are affective athletes according to Deleuze.

14. The shifting topology would also factor in each instance, but see also the two deaths in *Logic of Sense* (LS 177–9|151–3, 182|156, 244|209 and 258–60|222–3) and in *Anti-Oedipus* (AŒ 399|330 and 477). Maurice Blanchot's *The Space of Literature*, of course, is an indispensable reference in each case.

15. See DR 96–108|70–9 (especially 103|75 and 107|78) and Chapter 2 above.

16. On this polemic and its historical context in the century of two world wars, see Marc Crépon's *Vivre avec*, translated into English by its subtitle as *The Thought of Death and the Memory of War*.

17. See especially 'Science and Reflection' in *The Question Concerning Technology* ('Wissenschaft und Besinnung' in GA 7).

18. On the ways in which a certain hermeneutics nevertheless conditions their project, see Chapters 1 above and 6 below.

19. See also ACE 398|330 and FB 62|62.

20. Reconstructing a Deleuzian system based upon Bergson's *Matter and Memory*, guided by a single comment from *What Is Philosophy?*, Meillassoux not only reaches the same distinction in deaths as the 'principal interest' of his model (Meillassoux 90). Remarkably, he seems to draw the same consequence: 'The terror of the philosopher faced with philosophies of communication, or at least certain avatars of it – the philosopher's way of grovelling [*ramper*], invoked by Deleuze, as soon as one proposes a discussion – would be a terror before his own possible death' (Meillassoux 92). Yet, rather than hardening discussion into a death deadlier than chaos, he recuperates discussion for chaos: 'One would have to make the *communicator* [communiquant], in the subtractive system, an original conceptual character . . . that establishes not creational [*créateurs*], not reactive, but *creative* [créatifs] becomings' (92). Like Deleuze and Guattari, he believes in life after death: 'To think is to cross the Acheron twice victorious: it is to visit the dead, or rather death, and above all manage to come back from it' (Meillassoux 93).

21. See especially K 14 note 5|92 note 5 and 40 note 13|93 note 13. Not all references are negative: K 89|48 and 75 note 16|95 note 16.

22. On the regression to the sense-bestowing acts of consciousness, see 'Expression and Meaning', the first of Husserl's six *Logical Investigations* (HUA 19:30–110|*Logical* I:181–233). Several years prior to the publication of *Kafka: Toward a Minor Literature*, Derrida expressly associates '*the reduction to meaning* [sens]' with phenomenologists (Hegel, Husserl and Heidegger) and 'the reduction *of* meaning [*sens*]' with contemporary French thought (*Marges* 161–2|*Margins* 134).

23. The sociolinguistic debate in which Deleuze and Guattari intervene with the major-minor distinction in the fourth plateau, '20 November 1923 – Postulates of Linguistics', ultimately concerns the capacity of a linguistic system to accommodate variation while remaining systematic. Both sides of the debate recognise this system and its variability as an inheritance of Saussure's distinction between *la langue* and *la parole*. See Labov, *Sociolinguistic Patterns* 186; Chomsky, *Aspects of the Theory of Syntax* 4; and Deleuze and Guattari, MP 117|92.

24. For more on this point, see my article, 'What Is Nonstyle in *What Is Philosophy?*'.

25. Not only do Deleuze and Guattari present the entire schizoanalytic project as 'a material psychiatry' (for instance, ACE 12|5); affects are – and bring the schizophrenic – 'closest to matter' (ACE 28|19 and 398|330). Contrary to those that take Deleuze and Guattari at their word, Peter Hallward is more astute: 'Rather than a philosopher of

nature, history or the world, rather than any sort of "fleshy material-ist", Deleuze is most appropriately read as a spiritual, redemptive or subtractive thinker, a thinker preoccupied with the mechanics of *dis*-embodiment and *de*-materialisation. Deleuze's philosophy is oriented by lines of flight that lead out of the world; though not other-worldly, it is *extra*-worldly' (Hallward 3). Hallward isn't wrong, to be sure, but he's only half right. The notion of style I'm mobilising here beyond the idea-matter divide to problematise the more common portrayal of Deleuze as a materialist would also problematise his portrayal as an idealist *rather than* a materialist. *Out of This World* demonstrates the extent to which one can indeed systematise Deleuze's work according to its idealist slant (see especially the reading of art in the fifth chapter), but Hallward reveals the limit of his reading rather than Deleuze's phi-losophy when he presumes, from the beginning, that one must choose between materialist and idealist tendencies. In this sense, Hallward's own idealist reading produces the political immaterialism of which he accuses Deleuze in conclusion. In order to draw still more brutal consequences, I'll return to Hallward's idealist reading in the context of Spinoza at the end of Chapter 5 below.

26. For instance, Martin Hägglund in chapter 1 – 'Memory: Proust' – of *Dying for Time* (especially 23–4). Hägglund too quickly assimilates Deleuze's reading of Proust to the orthodoxically teleological reading; he makes no reference to the violent and contingent encounter that, according to Proust according to Deleuze, begins thought that therefore might not have begun. Too quickly but not incorrectly because – as I have tried to show in every chapter so far – a *telos* (in thinking, in the third synthesis of time, in artistic signs, in the third genre of knowledge) will have oriented Deleuze's work despite its genetic violence and con-tingency. At which point the teleology becomes more teleological than Hägglund himself suggests insofar as the *telos* comes by overcoming even the absolutely contingent encounter meant precisely to counter all teleology.

27. See Buffon, 'Discours' 43–4|'Discourse' 285–6.

28. 'The best account I know of such rule-breaking poetic creativity is to be found in the work of Gilles Deleuze and in his concept of style' (Lecercle, 'Three Accounts of Literary Style' 156). See also chapter 6 of Jean-Jacques Lecercle's *Deleuze and Language*.

PART II

The Paradox of Spinoza

4

Spinoza, Socrates of Deleuze

El hecho es que cada escritor *crea* a sus precursores.

Borges (*Obras completas*
2:95|*Other Inquisitions* 108)

The Paradox

As a response to and a means of participating in a 1989 issue of *Lendemains* dedicated to his work, Deleuze places the variegated volume's entire enterprise under the auspices of an invocation of Spinoza. As if, according to Deleuze himself, both his work and work on him always also, whatever the subject or approach, worked on Spinoza. At the end of his brief but dense because consolidative contribution, 'Letter to Réda Bensmaïa on Spinoza', Deleuze reaches what he calls 'the paradox of Spinoza'.

> Thus, the paradox of Spinoza consists in being the most philosopher of the philosophers [*le plus philosophe des philosophes*], but at the same the philosopher that most addresses non-philosophers and most solicits an intense non-philosophical comprehension. (P 225|165)

This paradox, however, wouldn't exist without Deleuze. For Deleuze himself defines the sense of 'philosophical' and the sense of 'non-philosophical' in which the paradox consists. This redirection doesn't simply deny, avoid or resolve the paradox. On the contrary, the paradox only grows sharper, more paradoxical still, insofar as Deleuze draws the senses of 'philosophical' and 'non-philosophical' from the 'philosopher' to whom both most apply, namely, Spinoza. In this light, Spinoza isn't merely *the most* philosophical or *the least* philosophical; he is *more than* the most and *less than* the least.

By qualifying non-philosophical comprehension as 'intense', Deleuze relates non-philosophy to the sensible. Spinoza appeals to non-philosophers, more specifically, because he creates not only concepts but also affects and percepts. Yet, while Deleuze and Guattari attribute the creation of affects and percepts to the discipline of

147

art in *What Is Philosophy?*, Deleuze embraces all three – concept, affect and percept – as 'the philosophical trinity' two years earlier in his 'Letter to Réda Bensmaïa' (P 224|165). The discrepancy, of course, raises questions concerning philosophy's longstanding self-identification as the 'queen discipline' and its voracious effort to engulf even the non-philosophical. If philosophy creates concepts, if the concept constitutes one mode of thinking among others and thus – as Deleuze and Guattari insist – enjoys no privilege in *What Is Philosophy?*, does philosophy in Deleuze's letter to Bensmaïa take over the affects and percepts that belong to art and thus reclaim the disciplinary throne? Similarly, in a 1988 interview with Raymond Bellour and François Ewald for *Magazine littéraire*, Deleuze recognises percept, affect and concept as three inseparable powers or forces (*puissances*) that run 'from art to philosophy and vice versa', but he nevertheless calls the percept and the affect 'dimensions' of the concept (P 187|137). *Either* philosophy reigns regardless (a coup, if not a rightful monarchy) *or* philosophy is not philosophy without non-philosophy, without art, without interdisciplinarity. Deleuze's work often supports both readings, irreducible though they are, and I'll return to each on occasion in the remaining chapters of this book. For the moment, I stress only that the disciplinary distribution of *What Is Philosophy?* begins to clarify why the most philosophical is also non-philosophical: Spinoza creates concepts as well as affects and percepts, the creation of which pertains not to philosophy but to art.

To say Spinoza creates affects, however, doesn't do him justice. For Deleuze draws the very notion of affect from the scholia of the third part of the *Ethics*, 'Of the Origin and Nature of the Affects'.[1] Not simply *affects*, in other words, Spinoza creates *affect*. To be sure, Spinoza doesn't coin the term *affectus*, which has a dense philological history.[2] But affectability becomes both structurally and genetically so pervasive in the *Ethics* that in one way or another, on one level or another, it operates distinctions traditionally mobilised – before and after Spinoza – to circumscribe and coldly dismiss it: God and human and animal, infinite and finite, action and passion, adequacy and inadequacy, reason and emotion, knowledge and opinion, freedom and servitude, nature and society, mind and body, good and evil, virtue and vice, necessity and contingency, so on and so forth. When Deleuze seizes upon 'affect' in Spinoza, however, when he restores its ontological horizon and systematises its operation, the consequences are ambiguous. On the one hand, the term 'affect' can't be read anywhere in Deleuze without reference to Spinoza. Not even, for instance, in the decisive chapter 7 of *What Is Philosophy?* – 'Percept, Affect, and Concept' – where Deleuze and Guattari never refer to Spinoza by name. This isn't to deny certain ruptures and displacements, emphases and negligences, lapses and relapses, an array of betrayals operative in Deleuze's appropriation of Spinoza's affect. All of which will continue to inform the ambivalence established in Part I above. On the other hand, there's reason to suggest, preposterously, that 'affect' can no longer be read anywhere in Spinoza without reference to Deleuze. Not only because affect theorists tend to reach Spinoza through Deleuze bibliographically. Not even only conceptually. Deleuze made no small contribution to the very translation of *affectus* as 'affect' and thus, in a way, to the language and object of contemporary 'affect theory', which often claims a Spinozist heritage without recognising its filtration through Deleuze.[3]

A similar point holds at the other end of the paradox. To call Spinoza the most philosophical philosopher, namely, does him a similar injustice. Just as Spinoza in a sense creates *affect* and not *an* affect, he isn't *a* philosopher. Not even the purest. To speak of more or less pure philosophers still implicitly grants even the 'lesser' philosophers the status of 'philosopher' whereas, to believe *What Is Philosophy?*, Spinoza is the only philosopher to 'achieve' philosophy, the only philosopher to have ever really done philosophy, the only to have philosophised. Not only the purest, Spinoza is also the only.

In short, the double importance of Spinoza for Deleuze's understanding of both philosophy and non-philosophy or art, concept as well as percept and affect, can't be exaggerated, conflated or simplified. Accordingly, here in Chapter 4, I begin this second part by focusing upon the first Spinoza, the philosopher, in Deleuze in general. Chapter 5 returns to the second leg of the paradox, to affect, to non-philosophy. Chapter 6 concludes with 'Spinoza and the Three "Ethics"', with the final text of Deleuze's final book, not only because it constitutes Deleuze's most refined reading of Spinoza but also because, for the same reason, it takes the paradox to its greatest pitch with ambivalent consequences that Deleuze does not seem to have anticipated upon articulating it.

A Character Study

Although Deleuze calls Spinoza paradoxical because he seems both ultra- and non-philosophical, extra-philosophical, his philosophical prowess raises issues independently of the non-philosophical nature in relation to which it becomes paradoxical. I've assigned this chapter the task of appreciating the philosophical importance of Spinoza in Deleuze's work, but it's difficult – if not impossible – to situate Spinoza within Deleuze's philosophy. If only an example, according to Deleuze, Spinoza is the only example and thus the paradigm of philosophy: the only philosopher uncompromised by transcendence – Spinoza – would be the only philosopher worthy of the name. The only philosopher. Whatever debts Deleuze acknowledges (or hides) in relation to other philosophers, every other philosopher is in reality a 'philosopher' only so-called, only in quotation marks, only metaphorically if only Spinoza never compromises with transcendence. The entire history of philosophy emerges from and merges with one proper name: Spinoza, 'the prince', 'the Christ' of philosophers (QP 51|48, 62|60).

So, to situate Spinoza 'within' Deleuze and Guattari's philosophy, as far as possible, it would seem necessary to read at least *What Is Philosophy?* from the beginning and work toward Spinoza's transfiguration at the end of chapter 2, 'The Plane of Immanence', as a sort of summit. But I take 'Conceptual Characters', chapter 3, as my point of departure. This beginning might seem random, contingent, anachronistic, but the system itself justifies it. To be sure, when they shorthand philosophy as 'the creation of concepts',[4] Deleuze and Guattari tend to overshadow the role of conceptual characters, and commentators – critic, acolyte or peer – often follow suit. The very characterisation of 'conceptual characters' as *conceptual* already seems to subordinate character to concept. By contrast, Deleuze and Guattari don't speak of 'characteristic' or 'characterful' concepts; whereas concepts are simply 'concepts', they mark characters as 'conceptual' characters. Nevertheless, concepts and characters remain equally indispensable to philosophy. To all philosophy. Creating concepts, tracing a plane of immanence and inventing conceptual characters together form what Deleuze and Guattari call 'the philosophical trinity' (QP 78|77). The three activities differ in nature, but they're inseparable and 'strictly simultaneous' (QP 79|78). Each activity both presupposes and regulates the others, adapts and adapts to them such that, without one, there's none. Which is to say, even if philosophy in a strict sense begins with the creation of a concept (QP 44|40), no philosophy begins without the invention of a conceptual character. Always more than a creation of concepts, then, Deleuze and Guattari also could have abbreviated the definition of philosophy as the invention of characters.

150

Consequently, Deleuze himself can't dispense with conceptual characters. This also holds for *What Is Philosophy?* Strictly speaking, one might think Deleuze is no longer 'doing' philosophy in *What Is Philosophy?* I myself have emphasised the unique place of this book in Deleuze's oeuvre: 'what was it', he and Guattari ask in the opening lines of the 'Introduction', 'that I did my whole life?' *Ce que j'ai fait*, what I did, as if to say, I'm done doing the philosophy I did. It's time I define it. But doing and defining don't mutually exclude each other. On the contrary, Deleuze and Guattari still have to create a concept when they define philosophy as the creation of concepts systematically in *What Is Philosophy?* But not just any concept. In contrast to Deleuze's first concept, for instance, in contrast to the concept of difference Deleuze creates in *Difference and Repetition*, in *What Is Philosophy?* he and Guattari create 'the concept of concept' (QP 25|19). And, like any other concept, they need a character to operate it.

Though they offer numerous examples, from Plato's Socrates to Pascal's gambler and Kierkegaard's knight of faith, Deleuze and Guattari never name their own character(s). Which shouldn't dissuade us from searching. At least one conceptual character is always there, always at work, even if at times only implicitly. Even if, at times, the reader must reconstitute it. Deleuze and Guattari say so themselves, and what they say could be said of their own work and of *What Is Philosophy?* in particular: 'The conceptual character might appear for itself [*pour lui-même*] rather rarely, or by allusion. Nevertheless, it is there and, even when unnamed, subterranean, should always be reconstituted by the reader' (QP 65|63). Always also includes now: if Deleuze and Guattari continue to do philosophy when they define it, then we should reconstitute the conceptual character that they never name *pour lui-même*. And who would – who could – operate the concept of concept if not the prince and Christ of philosophers?

My opening gambit thus casts Spinoza as the conceptual character of *What Is Philosophy?* Not *a* but *the* conceptual character. Deleuze and Guattari make clear that there's no exhaustive cast of characters in any one work or in general. 'The list of conceptual characters is never closed' (QP 10|5; see also QP 72|70). One character can recur in several philosophies, and one philosophy can recur to several characters. Nevertheless, to the extent that only Spinoza has done philosophy as Deleuze and Guattari define it, in *What Is Philosophy?*, any other character plays at best a supporting role.

For the same reason, Spinoza wouldn't be one conceptual character in one philosophy among others. If, in *What Is Philosophy?*, Deleuze and Guattari create the concept of concept, the creation of which defines philosophy as a whole, the character operating it operates the whole of philosophy. In which case, more than a conceptual character, Spinoza becomes the conceptual archetype. I use this term knowing full well that, for Deleuze and Guattari, 'the archetype proceeds by assimilation, homogenization, thematics' (K 13|7). Some even credit Deleuze as the first to elaborate 'the requirements for the elimination of an immutable world of transcendent archetypes' (DeLanda 82–3). I nevertheless insist because, as the conceptual character of *What Is Philosophy?*, Spinoza also becomes the conceptual character of every work beyond it, which is to say, not only every other book in Deleuze's corpus but also even every book in the philosophical corpus in general. Whether it speaks of Spinoza or not. Even if a work ostensibly has its character already, that character too would token the Spinozist archetype. Spinoza thus anachronises the history of philosophy; he operates even every philosophy that preceded the historical personage named 'Baruch Spinoza'. Even Socrates, for instance.[5]

Clearly, 'Spinoza' is no longer 'Spinoza'. Not simply. No conceptual character is entirely unrelated to its namesake, to be sure, but it always has a unique existence in the philosophy that invents it. Which is why, early in the chapter on conceptual characters, Deleuze and Guattari specify that conceptual characters remain irreducible to their historical, mythological and colloquial namesakes (QP 67|65). Just as Plato's Socrates differs from the historical Socrates, Nietzsche's Zarathustra from the mythological Zarathustra, Descartes' idiot from the everyday idiot, 'Spinoza' and 'Spinoza' become homonyms. But, then, how can I confidently distinguish between one Spinoza and the other, between the author of the *Ethics* and the character of *What Is Philosophy?* Because the conceptual character is indispensable, we must reconstitute it in Deleuze and Guattari's philosophy, but what authorises me to call Spinoza a 'character', systematic modifications of the term notwithstanding, when to all appearances Deleuze and Guattari present their remarks on Spinoza as a reading of the seventeenth-century philosopher that lived and breathed, read and wrote, ground lenses and provoked spiders to fight in an attic by the Quiet Ferry Quay in The Hague?[6]

To loosen one Spinoza from the other, to whatever extent possible, calls simultaneously for two strategies. Although distinct, they remain inseparable because each necessitates the other.

1) Return to Spinoza's text to show, *first*, that Deleuze and Guattari's reading is, if never outright wrong, at least equivocal and more importantly, *second*, that their equivocal reading originates in demands generated by their idiosyncratic conception of philosophy. This strategy has clear limits. It ultimately presupposes or at least suggests that intentions – in this case not only Spinoza's but also Deleuze and Guattari's – are univocal, accessible and authoritative. More tempting, on the contrary, would be to assert that all philosophers read all others as characters in their own philosophy. This general characterisation goes beyond all of Deleuze and Guattari's formulations but isn't incompatible with any of them. Yet, however legitimate on one ground or another, it wouldn't step any closer to the specificity of the character named 'Spinoza'. On the contrary, it risks a dramatic solipsism that only makes the task of accounting for the Spinozist archetype more difficult and more urgent still.

2) Return to Deleuze's earlier texts to show that his reading of Spinoza wavers, evolves, leaps and forgets. Although it would indeed serve to resituate the many commentaries that read Deleuze's relation to Spinoza monochromatically, this strategy doesn't pedantically signal 'evolutions' or 'contradictions' in Deleuze's reading of Spinoza. More simply, that Spinoza wasn't always the prince and Christ of philosophers for Deleuze, that early and unsettled critiques of Spinoza would even otherwise preclude his later coronation and transfiguration, indicates that 'Spinoza' takes on a unique role in *What Is Philosophy?* This second strategy proves more modest because it doesn't directly rely upon Spinoza's intention as the univocal touchstone, but it too reaches a limit at the other extreme: taken seriously, it would suspend all reference to Spinoza's work. If 'Spinoza' the character isn't simply 'Spinoza' the philosopher, the homonymy that separates them also demands constant engagement with both.

To implement and implicate these two strategies in what follows, I'll undertake a double genealogy of sorts: on the one hand, the evolution of 'immanence' in the history of philosophy according to Deleuze; on the other, the evolution of Deleuze's narrative concerning the evolution of immanence in the history of philosophy. Deleuze presents at least three variants, three versions, three stories of philosophy's movement toward immanence, which is to say, toward the only ontology worth its name:

1. the first in *Spinoza and the Problem of Expression* (chapter 11, 'Immanence and the Historical Elements of Expression', SPE 153–69|169–86);
2. the second in *Difference and Repetition* (chapter 1, 'Difference in Itself', §3, DR 52–61|36–42);
3. the third in *What Is Philosophy?* (Example III in chapter 2, 'The Plane of Immanence', QP 48–52|44–9).

I'll address each of these accounts in the three sections that follow. While some names disappear and others replace them from one account to another, Deleuze recasts many of the same characters to plot milestones on philosophy's path toward immanence. But the recurring names don't always recur in the same order. The most volatile, the most peregrine, the most momentous is 'Spinoza'.

Cause and Attribution

According to *Spinoza and the Problem of Expression*, immanence in a strict sense irrupts for the first time in Spinoza's *Ethics*. But this irruption takes place within a certain history. Although Spinoza himself makes no direct reference to it, Deleuze places immanence within the tradition of the univocity of being. 'Immanence', says Deleuze, 'is the new figure that the theory of univocity takes in Spinoza' (SPE 150|166; see also 58|67). Univocity, for its part, opposes equivocity, analogy and eminence.[7] Although each opponent has unique traits and problems, Deleuze sometimes invokes all three without distinction and sometimes represents all three with reference to only one because, significant exceptions notwithstanding, they all turn upon the ontological abyss between being and beings or, in the more strictly theological tradition, between God and creatures. God 'is', and a creature 'is', but a creature *is not* in the same sense God *is*, so I can't say both 'are' without speaking equivocally (God's being doesn't have the same sense as a creature's), analogically (a creature's being is at most analogous to God's) or eminently (God fully possesses the being that creatures possess to an infinitely lesser degree). Without denying all difference between God and creatures, between being and beings, univocity by contrast attributes to one what it also attributes to the other in the same sense.

The specifically immanent form univocity takes in Spinoza, Deleuze says, has two aspects: univocity of *cause* and univocity of *attributes*. 'The Spinozist concept of immanence', he assures us, 'has no other sense' (SPE 150|165). The sense of immanence, in other words, the sameness of the sense in which being *is* and beings *are*, the only sense 'immanence' has upon irrupting in both Spinoza's system and in the history of philosophy, unfolds as a function of causation and attribution. Cause and attribute, then, comprise the first and most basic sense of the immanence that Deleuze celebrates in Spinoza's philosophy, that he mobilises in his own philosophy under a number of aliases (rhizome, plane of composition, body without organs and so on) and that he will rebuild as the engine driving the entire history of philosophy. Since *Spinoza and the Problem of Expression* isn't Deleuze's last word on immanence, however, I'll discuss both aspects relatively quickly.

Univocity of cause. The ontological argument traditionally posits God as *causa sui*, as a cause of himself, but in the same stroke must more or less implicitly distinguish one causality from another: the causality with which God causes his own existence and the causality with which God causes creatures or, in turn, one creature causes another in the world. Even Descartes dogmatically inherits this scholastic (and more specifically Thomist) heritage.[8] Spinoza, by contrast, univocalises causality when he proclaims that 'God must be called the cause of all things [*omnium rerum causa*] in the same sense [*sensu*] in which he is called the cause of himself [*causa sui*]' (*Ethics* IP25S). No longer two separate senses related only by analogy, 'efficient cause' causes in the same sense as 'self-cause' (SPE 149|164–5).

Univocity of attributes. Even if Deleuze summarily lists 'univocity of attributes' and 'immanence' as two 'great theories' of the *Ethics* in *Spinoza: Practical Philosophy* (SPP 41|28), as if they were distinct theories, he does so only after having made clear, years earlier in *Spinoza and the Problem of Expression*, that univocity becomes immanence in Spinoza by way of attributes. In general terms, Spinoza's system consists in substance, attributes and modes. There's only one substance, God or Nature (*Ethics* IP10S), and each attribute expresses an essence of this one substance. While Spinoza's substance has infinite attributes, the human being knows only two: thought and corporality (IP11). Modes, in turn, are individual things; they modify and to that extent express the attributes that express a substantial essence in turn (IP25C). There's no need to dwell upon Deleuze's 'paradox of expression' (SPE 162|179). This very schematic exposition, upon which I'll expand in the chapters that follow, already suffices to grasp the univocity that hinges upon attributes. 'Attributes, according to Spinoza, are unique forms of being, which

155

do not change their nature when changing their "subject," that is to say, when they are predicated of infinite being and finite beings, of substance and of modes, of God and of creatures' (SPE 40|49). I speak of the same attributes, which is to say, I speak univocally, whether I speak of substance or of mode, of God or of creature, in terms of thought or corporality. I am immanent to God, then, because my body expresses the same corporal attribute, my mind the same pensive attribute, that expresses the corporal and pensive essences of God. As the final form of univocity, 'immanence' means nothing else.

Indifference

From Plato and Plotinus to Aquinas and Duns Scotus, sometimes linearly and frontally and sometimes episodically and obliquely, Deleuze situates a number of names on the path toward the imma- nent form Spinoza finally gives univocity, but he goes no further than Spinoza in *Spinoza and the Problem of Expression*. Nor does he determine the nature of this end. Perhaps Spinoza's immanence provides the highest, the purest form of univocity and the story simply ends with him. Perhaps Spinoza completes philosophy. Which would authorise a leap from 1968 to 1991, from *Spinoza and the Problem of Expression* to *What Is Philosophy?*, from Deleuze's *thèse complémentaire* to the crowning work in which, indeed, he and Guattari affirm that Spinoza achieved, completed or culminated, *a achevé* philosophy (QP 51|48). Deleuze himself doesn't hesitate to take this leap. When the English translator of *Spinoza et le problème de l'expression* asks him about Spinoza's place in his development, Deleuze self-identifies as a 'Spinozist' because only Spinoza achieves absolute immanence. Then he adds: 'In the book I'm writing at the moment, *What Is Philosophy?*, I try to return to this problem of absolute immanence, and to say why Spinoza is for me the "prince" of philosophers' (*Expressionism* 11). *What Is Philosophy?* would thus seem to elaborate *Spinoza and the Problem of Expression* without rupture or detour.

But Deleuze ultimately crowns Spinoza in *What Is Philosophy?* only by forgetting, suppressing or in any case neglecting Spinoza's place in *Difference and Repetition*, a book published contemporane- ously with *Spinoza and the Problem of Expression* but in which, unlike the latter, Deleuze claims 'to do' his own philosophy.[9] There, in what I've isolated as the second of Deleuze's three historical accounts of univocal being, Spinoza is neither prince nor Christ. He's neither the beginning nor the end of philosophy. He's a necessary but insufficient step toward absolute immanence, a passage, a passing moment.

'The history of philosophy determines three principal moments in the elaboration of the univocity of being' (DR 57|39). In the first moment, Duns Scotus formulates the demand for univocity but ultimately fails to satisfy it because his fidelity to 'creationism' also demands that God transcend what he creates.[10] In the third, the final, Nietzsche affirms absolute univocity by way of the eternal return, which Deleuze reprises and reconfigures in different problematics throughout *Difference and Repetition* (the third synthesis of time in chapter 2, the faculty of thinking in chapter 3, the ideal synthesis in chapter 4). As the surmountable second and thus insurmountably secondary moment, forever accessory and subsidiary, Spinoza abandons the creationist demand that limited Duns Scotus and posits God as the 'immanent cause' of all things (*Ethics* IP18), but his system remains substantially limited, which is to say, minimally transcendent. He who discovers immanence and introduces it into the history of philosophy, according to this Deleuze, also betrays it. So often neglected (by Deleuze himself first of all),[11] one brief line in *Difference and Repetition* resituates every analysis in *Spinoza and Problem of Expression* and questions in advance every acclamation in *What Is Philosophy?*: 'An indifference between substance and modes nevertheless subsists: the Spinozist substance appears independent of modes, and modes depend upon the substance but as something else' (DR 59|40).

Paul Patton mistranslates this *indifférence* between substance and mode as 'difference'. On the one hand, the slip is substantial since the end of philosophy and Spinoza's contribution to it unfold in the difference between *difference* and *indifference*. On the other, it's also understandable. Even programmatic. Perhaps it's no slip at all or perhaps, indeed, Deleuze himself slips here since Spinoza, for his part, explicitly denies the 'indifference' of substance. Spinoza relates the indifference of a God allegedly 'indifferent to all things [*ad omnia indifferentem*]' to free will, to a capacity to refrain from creating, in short, to an illusion (*Ethics* IP17S). Spinoza's God is by contrast never indifferent because all things, all modes, all creatures follow from his nature necessarily. Which doesn't preclude, however, a difference between 'indifference' and 'indifference'. A difference, that is, between the indifference Spinoza denies and the indifference of which Deleuze accuses Spinoza. According to two of the most basic definitions of Spinoza's system, *substance* 'is in itself and is conceived through itself', while *mode* 'is in another through which it is also conceived' (IDef3 and 5). Substance subsists of itself, in other words, while a mode is and is conceived – to the extent that it is – only in substance. Substance is thus by definition ontologically and conceptually independent of the modes that ontologically and conceptually depend upon it. Substance is thus *indifferent* to modes in terms of essence, existence and analysis. Even if the unique substance that Spinoza also calls 'God' causes all things immanently (IP18), even if modes are nothing but attributes of the substance expressed 'in a certain and determinate way' (IP25C), even if God is not 'free' to cause or to refrain from causing (IP32C1), even if I exhaust all possible caveats, nothing diminishes substance's independence from and therefore indifference toward its own modes. Deleuze never denies that, even for Spinoza at his most immanent, substance differs from mode (being from beings, God from creatures, *Natura naturans* from *Natura naturata*); where one is indifferent to the other, however, there can be no immanence. One could multiply reasons against collapsing this substantial indifference or independence into transcendence, but it isn't immanence either. Not absolutely. Not according to Deleuze.

The consequences depend upon the context.

In *Difference and Repetition*, the divine substance's indifference, independence or quasi-transcendence renders Spinoza's system unserviceable for the philosophy Deleuze intends to do. Unserviceable, more specifically, for the first concept he attempts to create, namely, the concept of difference. Deleuze sets out to create a concept of difference because until then, on his account, philosophy only ever disposed of a simply conceptual difference. 'It was perhaps the mistake [*le tort*] of the philosophy of difference, from Aristotle to Hegel and passing through Leibniz, to have confounded the concept of difference with a simply conceptual difference' (DR 41|27). While 'conceptual difference' conceives difference as the difference between two self-identical entities and therefore grounds it on a prior identity, a proper concept of difference grasps difference in its originality, positivity and productivity. By making infinitely diverse modes immanent to substance, Spinoza introduces difference into being and thus strides toward a proper concept of difference (SPE 32|39); nevertheless, because the divine substance always remains prior to and independent of the modes immanent to it, any idea of difference in Spinoza's system is secondary still and once again.

It would be necessary for substance itself to be said *of* modes, and only *of* modes. Such a condition can only be fulfilled at the price of a more general categorical reversal, according to which being is said of becoming, identity of the different, the one of the multiple, etc. (DR 59|40)

This 'more general categorical reversal' is first of all the reversal of Platonism that, for Deleuze in *Difference and Repetition*, still defines the task of contemporary philosophy (DR 82|59). Only Nietzsche achieves it. Which not only means, his own critiques of Platonism notwithstanding, Spinoza's thought remains substantially classical, antiquated and backward. In the same revolutionary vortex that reverses Platonism, Nietzsche also reverses Spinozism.

That identity is not first, that it exists as a principle, but a second principle, as a principle that has *become*, that it turns upon the Different, such is the nature of a Copernican revolution that opens difference to the possibility of its proper concept, instead of maintaining it under the domination of a concept in general already posited as identical. With the eternal return, Nietzsche meant nothing else. (DR 59|40)

If Nietzsche opens the possibility of conceptualising difference, no one before him achieves a proper concept of difference or, therefore, the immanence with which it remains systematically solidary in and after *Difference and Repetition*. At this point, one couldn't even say Nietzsche 'achieves' the immanence that irrupts in Spinoza's *Ethics* since the step from Spinoza to Nietzsche isn't linear; a veritable revolution should make the passage irrevocable and irreversible.

In *What Is Philosophy?*, the stakes run higher still. No longer creating this or that concept like, say, the concept of difference created in *Difference and Repetition*, Deleuze and Guattari now create the very concept of concept the creation of which defines philosophy in general. And to the extent that philosophy is immanent or not at all, to the extent that philosophy is absolutely immanent or philosophy is religion,[12] they stake the very existence of philosophy in Spinoza. In Spinoza and not Nietzsche. Spinoza alone, they now allege, perhaps never compromised with transcendence. More fundamentally still, he alone will have made possible the impossible thought of immanence as such, what Deleuze and Guattari articulate definitively as THE plane of immanence (QP 61–2|59–60). As a result, if another reading is possible according to which, still according to Deleuze, Spinoza did indeed compromise with transcendence, then is there, has there been, can there be philosophy at all?

Coronation, Transfiguration

These questions haunt every page of *What Is Philosophy?* but never surface as such. Far from it, Deleuze and Guattari hardly hesitate to culminate and thereby save philosophy in fact and in principle with Spinoza, the prince, the Christ of philosophers. In view of Deleuze's earlier critique of Spinoza, however, this culmination doesn't occur without a seismic shift – Nietzsche's fall, Spinoza's rise – in Deleuze's varying accounts of philosophy's movement toward pure immanence. I'll map the hypocentre of this seism in Deleuze's work as precisely as possible, since the cartography proves revealing for the conceptual characterisation of Spinoza at stake in this chapter.

En route to redeem Spinoza, Deleuze takes a decisive step in the opening of 'Spinoza and Us', a text first presented at a conference commemorating the three-hundredth anniversary of Spinoza's death in 1977, first published in 1978 and finally reprinted as the last chapter of *Spinoza: Practical Philosophy* in 1981. Deleuze first pronounces the formulation 'plane of immanence' in this context but, while the term comes at the beginning of the text, Deleuze doesn't draw the notion from the beginning of Spinoza's system. The plane doesn't correspond to the first principle of *Ethics*. The first principle, rather, proclaims a single substance for all attributes. In 'Spinoza and Us', then, Deleuze doesn't approach Spinoza as a philosopher generally approaches the philosophy of another. He doesn't approach Spinoza like Spinoza, for instance, approaches Descartes in *Descartes' 'Principles of Philosophy'*. He doesn't begin with the first principle. Taking 'Spinoza and Us' to mean 'us in the middle of Spinoza', *au milieu de Spinoza*, Deleuze grasps Spinoza where the third, fourth and especially fifth principles of Spinoza's system are already active: Nature is itself an individual with infinite variations (that is, modes or modifications). At which point, Deleuze says in preparation of the formulation that will determine how he comes to conceive philosophy as a whole, substance no longer comes first, independently, *indifferent* to its modes. It becomes, rather, 'a *common plane of immanence* where all bodies, all souls, all individuals are' (SPP 161|122). 'Where' and not exactly 'on which', as Robert Hurley renders Deleuze's *où* into English, and certainly not on which all individuals are 'situated'. Although understandable, these mistranslations suggest there is first a plane and then individuals placed upon it. Individuals are, rather, only insofar as they are 'variations' of Nature, the single substance, the plane of immanence that is nothing but these variations. Only thus can Deleuze call the plane of immanence 'fully' immanent: *pleinement plan d'immanence* (SPP 161|122).

Deleuze never addresses or redresses his earlier critique, over which he passes here in silence. By taking Spinoza *au milieu*, Deleuze literally leaps over the indifference of Spinoza's substance legible in the early definitions of the *Ethics* (IDef3 and 5), which led Deleuze to secondarise Spinoza in the history of philosophy as univocity a decade earlier. Unburdened by indifferent beginnings, Spinoza now becomes the very measure of immanence. In the same text, Deleuze grants Goethe and Hegel immanent moments, for instance, but they aren't *vraiment* Spinozists. Among the true Spinozists, Deleuze ranks Hölderlin, Kleist and Nietzsche (SPP 169|128–9). For what concerns the evolution of Spinoza according to Deleuze, the moment is extraordinary. Anyone that truly (*vraiment*) constructs a plane of immanence now does so in the name of Spinoza. Far from 'a Nietzschefication of Spinoza' (Schaefer 10), Nietzsche – he who alone achieves univocity according to a younger Deleuze – becomes a Spinozist. Deleuze doesn't yet crown or transfigure Spinoza as uniquely or finally as in *What Is Philosophy?*, but levelling Spinoza and Nietzsche steps decisively in that direction. Whereas Spinoza's univocity was infinitely second to Nietzsche in *Difference and Repetition*, where Spinoza's system was ultimately anathema to the creation of a proper concept of difference, a decade later in *Spinoza: Practical Philosophy* Deleuze puts Spinoza and Nietzsche, if not on the same plane, at least on the same type of plane: planes of immanence.

Nietzsche doesn't remain there for long. In fact, two years earlier (in *Rhizome*) and two years later (in the reprisal of *Rhizome* as the 'Introduction' to *A Thousand Plateaus*), Deleuze and Guattari give reason to doubt Nietzsche's status as a true Spinozist. Indeed, Deleuze places Nietzsche where Spinoza once stood: a second and thus merely secondary moment on the path toward the absolute immanence that he and Guattari now call 'rhizome' or 'plateau'.[13] Rhizomatic writing, they claim, constitutes the third in a series of three types of books. Though they don't present it (and I haven't counted it) as such, this scriptural typology once again recounts the history of philosophy as immanence also told in *Spinoza and the Problem of Expression*, *Difference and Repetition* and *What Is Philosophy?* Classical but still dominant in linguistics, psychoanalysis and structuralism, the first book Deleuze and Guattari call the root-book (*le livre-racine*). It begins with the unity of a subject and/or object and, on its basis, branches out to ever greater terrain. The second book, the modern, they call the radicle-system (*le système-radicelle*). Radicle writing aborts the initial unity that the classical 'root-book' bases upon the subject or object and thus goes further, but it still falls short of rhizomatic writing since it presupposes another unity hidden in a 'supplementary dimension' (MP 12|6). Here, with Guattari in this second book, Deleuze turns on Nietzsche: 'Nietzsche's aphorisms break the linear unity of knowledge only by referring to the cyclical unity of the eternal return' (MP 12|6). Deleuze and Guattari don't elaborate but, offering Nietzsche as an example of radicle writing (even only one example among others), the brief sentence revises both the history and the system of *Difference and Repetition*. In doing so, moreover, Deleuze reprises the very formulation with which he defines transcendence in *Spinoza: Practical Philosophy*, where Nietzsche still ranks as a 'true' Spinozist, to criticise Nietzsche with Guattari in *A Thousand Plateaus*: 'a supplementary dimension' (SPP 169|128).

While far from linear, exhaustive or irreversible, a certain sequence thus takes shape in Nietzsche and Spinoza's struggle for the immanent crown in Deleuze's work:

- In 1968, in *Difference and Repetition*, Nietzsche reigns alone and thus over Spinoza.
- In 1981 (1978), in *Spinoza: Practical Philosophy* ('Spinoza and Us') Nietzsche shares the throne with Spinoza.
- In 1980 (1976), in *A Thousand Plateaus* (*Rhizome*), Nietzsche restores transcendence and loses his place upon the throne of immanence.

This basic progression no doubt calls for refinement, enlargement, complication and qualification. At the end of the 'Introduction' to *A Thousand Plateaus* (in which Nietzsche falls from immanence), for instance, Deleuze and Guattari parenthetically return to Nietzsche's notion of aphorism (the very form of his fall) in order to promote the rhizome-book (which his aphorisms never achieve) as a way of seeing things *au milieu*: '(Nietzsche said in the same way that an aphorism had to be "ruminated," and a plateau is never separable from the cows that populate it and that are also the clouds of the sky)' (MP 34|23).[14] Nietzsche will also continue to enjoy a lingering centrality in Deleuze's subsequent works. In *What Is Philosophy?*, Deleuze and Guattari even credit him with defining the task of philosophy as the creation of concepts (QP 11|5). With reason:

What dawns on philosophers last of all: they must no longer merely let themselves be given concepts, no longer just clean [*reinigen*] and clarify [*aufhellen*] them, but first of all must *make* [*machen*] them, *create* [*schaffen*] them, present them and persuade in their favour. (Nietzsche KSA 11: 34[195]|*Late Notebooks* 34[195]; see also 34[88], 34[92], 34[131], etc.)

Nevertheless, they never return Nietzsche to the immanent summit of either the history or the system of philosophy.

One would attempt in vain to save Nietzsche by claiming, for instance, that he succumbs to transcendence only at times or in part while on the whole remaining rhizomatic, immanent, univocal. First, because a year earlier in *Spinoza: Practical Philosophy* Deleuze ranks Nietzsche among the 'true' Spinozists precisely in distinction from the occasional or partial Spinozists like Goethe and Hegel who remain faithful to immanence only at times and in certain regards. Second, more decisively, because Deleuze and Guattari accuse Nietzsche of recourse to a 'supplementary dimension' in the eternal return, that is, precisely that which Deleuze mobilised in *Difference and Repetition* to position Nietzsche – beyond Spinoza – as the most and thus the only univocal philosopher. Indeed, one can measure the heights from which Nietzsche falls by recalling that the eternal return constitutes the culminating synthesis not only of *Difference and Repetition* (121–3|90–1) but also, complications and redistributions notwithstanding, of *Logic of Sense* (77–8|60–2) and of *Anti-Oedipus* (28|19 and 400|331). What Deleuze once interpreted as the only possible immanence – the eternal return – he now accuses of transcendence.

Perhaps, more generally, one might respond that the '*stratographic time*' of philosophy that Deleuze and Guattari distinguish from the chronological history of a 'before' and an 'after' would moot in advance every genealogy of the type I'm reconstructing (QP 60|58). Rather than a linear progression of one philosopher after another, all philosophical material coexists and redistributes, restratifies and recompounds, according to a particular concept a particular philosopher needs to create at a particular time. The history I tell, as a result, depends upon and thus varies according to the concept I create. While Nietzsche reigns one day, Spinoza might reign the next without regicide. This response would hold if at stake weren't precisely THE plane of immanence, 'the pedestal [*socle*] of all planes', that makes possible the stratographic time of philosophy in the first place (QP 61|59). Deleuze and Guattari coronate Spinoza as the Christ of philosophers precisely because only he achieves this plane, *the* plane, the plane of planes.

And he achieves it only in *What Is Philosophy?*

This last claim seems preposterous and overconfident. While Deleuze himself never makes any such claim and would no doubt deny it, I base it in part on Deleuze's own comment regarding the importance of *Spinoza and the Problem of Expression*. I've already cited other parts of the same comment.

> I consider this one of the most original aspects of my book. That is: the hope of making substance turn on finite modes, or at least of seeing in substance *a plane of immanence* in which finite modes operate, already appears in this book. [. . .] In the book I'm writing at the moment, *What is Philosophy?*, I try to return to this problem of absolute immanence, and to say why Spinoza is for me the 'prince' of philosophers. (quoted in *Expressionism* 11)

Here, more explicitly than elsewhere, Deleuze becomes one more commentator on his own work and not necessarily the most authoritative or astute. His commentary leaves something to be desired in at least two ways.

First, Deleuze retrojects his late reading of Spinoza onto his early work. In *Spinoza and the Problem of Expression* Deleuze already hoped, he says, to make substance 'turn upon finite modes', but the coetaneous *Difference and Repetition* ends with the claim that Spinozism lacks precisely this substance-mode relation. Because modes turn upon a substance indifferent to and independent of them, Spinoza doesn't reach absolute immanence or univocity. Which is to say, at that moment in Deleuze's work, Spinoza doesn't reach Nietzsche: 'For univocity to become an object of pure affirmation, Spinozism needed only [*il manquait seulement au spinozisme*] to make substance turn upon modes, *that is to say, to realise univocity as repetition in the eternal return*' (DR 388|304, Deleuze's emphases). This substantial 'independence' or 'indifference' that constitutes Spinozism's lack or failure, its *manque*, stays legible throughout *Spinoza and the Problem of Expression*, even if Deleuze never regards it there as the critical limit of Spinoza's immanence.[15] If Deleuze makes substance turn upon finite modes, in short, he does so not *in the name* but rather *at the expense* of Spinoza.

Second, more critically, even if substance constituted a plane of immanence, as Deleuze retrospectively hoped, it wouldn't be enough to crown Spinoza. Which Deleuze seems to realise shortly afterwards when, in 'Example III' in *What Is Philosophy?*, he and Guattari more rigorously distinguish *pure immanence* from *immanence to*.

Immanence is only immanent to itself, and henceforth it seizes everything, absorbs All-One [*Tout-Un*], and lets nothing subsist to which it could be immanent. In any case, each time one interprets immanence as immanence *to* Something, one can be sure that this Something reintroduces the transcendent. (QP 49|45)

One shouldn't gloss over 'Example III', as philosophers are wont to do, simply because it's an example. It concerns the very history of philosophy as immanence, the third version of which I've been preparing for some time now. Like those in *Spinoza and the Problem of Expression* and *Difference and Repetition*, this version also recounts the past of philosophy as a movement toward absolute immanence, but it now attributes past failures to a mistaken determination of *immanence* as immanence *to*. Rather than affirming immanence in its own right, past philosophy attributes immanence to something else. Not every philosopher, of course, submits immanence to the same thing. The various periods in the history of philosophy correspond to variations in the object of the preposition *to*: to the One (Plato and Neo-Platonism), to God (Christian 'philosophy'), to subjectivity (Descartes, Kant and Husserl).

Spinoza would provide yet another example of a failed or impure immanence if, as Deleuze still hoped presumably only a short time before writing this passage in *What Is Philosophy?*, modes were immanent *to* substance. Here, however, Deleuze subtly but decisively reimagines the substance-mode relation. Substance no longer names a plane of immanence *to which* modes would be immanent. Now, rather, substance and modes constitute 'concepts' on a plane that they both presuppose. Only here and thus does Spinoza receive his crown:

The one who knew full well [*pleinement*] that immanence was only immanent to itself . . . was Spinoza. Thus, he is the prince of philosophers. [. . .] It is not immanence that relates to the Spinozist substance and modes; it is the opposite; the Spinozist concepts of substance and modes relate to the plane of immanence as their presupposition. (QP 51–2|48)

Deleuze's rereading of Spinoza isn't unjustified. At least in part, for instance, I could underwrite it with recourse to causality. God is a 'free cause', says Spinoza, but God isn't 'free' to cause or not to cause (*Ethics* IP17C2–S). For Spinoza, 'free' only means that nothing beyond God contributes to the causation of the effect, but what follows from God still follows with a necessity that God himself can't dodge, detain or temper. God performs *no miracles*, gives *no gifts*, keeps *no secrets*. To use a distinction from *Descartes' 'Principles of*

Philosophy', God has no 'extraordinary' powers (I:333). In light of which one might legitimately suspect causality to be either the death of God or more divine than divinity itself. One thing, however, remains clear: if God causes by nature, if infinite creatures follow from God's nature necessarily, then God wouldn't be God without the creatures he causes. Creatures or modes are in this sense analytic to the very idea of God or Substance, which is to say (in spite and in light of the early definitions in the *Ethics*), substance cannot be or be conceived without its modes. In which case modes would no longer be immanent *to* an independent or indifferent substance. Now, rather, modes and substance would be two 'concepts' the relation between which presupposes immanence.

It's far from obvious, however, that Spinoza knew this. Let alone as *pleinement* as Deleuze and Guattari say. One can leap over but never erase the substantial indifference legible in the third definition of the first book of the *Ethics*: 'By substance I understand what is in itself and is conceived through itself' (ID3). A mode remains immanent to, by definition, a substance indifferent to it. For a younger Deleuze, this organised both the history of philosophy and his own philosophy at its most original moment.

'Spinoza', as a result, begins to equivocate. While there are ample passages with which to underwrite the claim, Deleuze's memory of his work perhaps oversimplifies when, in 1988, he says that everything tended toward 'the great Spinoza-Nietzsche identity' (P 185|135). Not only because it forgets the struggle between Spinoza and Nietzsche for the univocal summit of philosophy I've outlined here. More radically because one cannot even take a Spinoza-Spinoza identity for granted. There are, in sum, at least two Spinozas for one Deleuze: the absolutely immanent Spinoza of *What Is Philosophy?* and the *not quite* but therefore *absolutely not* immanent Spinoza of *Difference and Repetition*. If one Spinoza shows 'the possibility of the impossible' in the sense that he alone shows that it is indeed possible to think the impossible thought of pure immanence (QP 62|60), the other Spinoza might show 'the possibility of the impossible' in a very different sense: the possibility that the thought of pure immanence remains impossible.

Spinoza and Spinoza

Genealogical perspectives – one concerning the history of philosophy as immanence, another concerning evolutions in Deleuze's account of the history of philosophy as immanence – have so far borne most of the weight in my argument that Deleuze casts Spinoza as a conceptual character in *What Is Philosophy?* Despite any insights they contain, however, shifts in Deleuze's interpretation of Spinoza would amount to mere footnotes about one interpreter's caprice, abuse or evolution if left unsynchronised with a more systematic perspective. If not coordinated, that is, with what makes Deleuze's shifting interpretation of Spinoza (or Nietzsche) possible and even necessary.

Deleuze himself never reflects upon the vagaries of his own interpretations of Spinozism. He proselytises for Spinoza in *What Is Philosophy?* without a second thought for his enduring critique in *Difference and Repetition. A fortiori* he never considers how the two apparently incompatible interpretations are possible even though they bear upon the possible impossibility of philosophy as he and Guattari define it. Had he asked, in the final analysis he would have had to alloy the purity of immanence with the transcendence it opposes. Or so I'll argue in closing: Spinoza isn't Spinoza, that is, the absolutely immanent Spinoza isn't absolutely immanent, not because he does or does not compromise with transcendence, but because immanence always already compromises 'itself'. There is no absolution. Immanence compromises with transcendence *before* there is immanence or transcendence. Deleuze isn't entirely naive in this regard. While I draw this compromise from his work, I also mobilise it against the work from which I draw it insofar as a number of lucid observations never dissuade Deleuze from describing, demanding and praising an immanence the absolute purity of which he invents a character to achieve. So, to conclude this chapter on the place of Spinoza 'in' Deleuze's philosophy, I'll use a few of Deleuze's own observations to shape and sharpen the terms of this originary compromise. Although the compromise or contamination is legible elsewhere, I'll limit myself to three texts I've already broached.

1) *Plane.* In a sense, the very formulation 'plane of immanence' testifies to an originary compromise of the immanence it names. In the same stroke in which Deleuze introduces immanence as a plane in 'Spinoza and Us', thus in his work and even in philosophy in general, he also qualifies it. 'There are two very opposed conceptions of the word "plane" or of the idea of plane, even if these two conceptions mix together, and [even] if we pass from one to the other insensibly' (SPP 168|128). Deleuze's warning bears upon more than a merely semantic or grammatical confusion. His point isn't simply that we must work vigilantly to keep two meanings of the word 'plane' apart.

We don't pass from one 'plane' to another because of any error or fault if, as Deleuze says, the two conceptions of plane – as immanence and as transcendence – themselves mix together. Which is why, for our part, we pass 'insensibly' from the plane of immanence to the plane of transcendence.

In *Spinoza: Practical Philosophy*, Hurley's translation of *plan* as 'plane' whenever it refers to a *plan d'immanence* and 'plan' whenever it refers to *plan de transcendance* thus makes an impossible decision.[16] To be sure, a plane of transcendence predetermines or orients the 'development' of an individual, as when 'God' has a plan for me or when 'Nature' guides the evolution of a species, which is why Deleuze calls the development of forms and the formation of subjects 'the essential character of this first sort of plane' (SPP 168|128). The translation of *plan* as 'plan' would in this case seem justified. If the planes also mix, however, if we move between planes insensibly, then a transcendent 'plan' always contaminates the immanent 'plane' and vice versa. The translation of *plan* hides this co-contamination of planes and thus the irreducible equivocity of the word *plan*.

For the same reason, the task becomes thinking *le plan* before it translates into 'plane' or 'plan' not only in English but also in French itself, before it divides into immanence or transcendence, before it forces a decision between 'affect' on a plane of immanence or 'essence' according to a plan of transcendence. Deleuze, however, broaches the contamination of planes only to dismiss it. 'Even if' these two conceptions mix, he says, 'even if' we pass from one to the other insensibly, they remain 'very opposed'. While Deleuze isn't naive enough to ignore it, by presenting the contamination of *plans* as an inconsequential caveat, he suppresses any need to ask why or how such contamination is possible in the first place.

2) *Rhizome*. In the 'Introduction' to *A Thousand Plateaus*, Deleuze and Guattari recast the opposition between 'immanence' and 'transcendence' as an opposition between 'rhizome' and 'arborescence'. While the new terms introduce new connotations and respond to new problematics in new contexts, the distinction between 'rhizome' and 'arborescence' – like the distinction between 'immanence' and 'transcendence' – must be constantly cultivated and tended. Unlike the apparently passing caveat in 'Spinoza and Us', the rhizome's eventual contamination becomes a refrain in its own right in *A Thousand Plateaus*:

'Every rhizome includes lines of segmentarity according to which it is stratified, territorialized, organized, signified, attributed, etc., but also lines of deterritorialization through which it ceaselessly flees' (MP 16|9).

'There exist tree or root structures in the rhizomes, but inversely a tree branch or a root division can begin to bourgeon into a rhizome' (MP 23|15).

'There are knots [*nœuds*] of arborescence in the rhizome, rhizomatic outgrowths [*poussées*] in roots' (MP 30|20).

Later, in the tenth plateau, we learn that the Nietzsche Deleuze and Guattari accuse of failing to write rhizomatically in the 'Introduction' only fails because failures 'form an integral part of the plane' (MP 328–9|269). Consequently, how can Deleuze and Guattari so quickly, calmly and finally relegate Nietzsche's writing to the second sort ('the radicle-system') upon introducing the rhizome? Inversely and more generally, how can they ever isolate a purely 'rhizomatic' writing? Does the very distinction between 'arborescent' and 'rhizomatic' not reach its limit in their constant contamination? Deleuze and Guattari's distinction between two types of failure – a failure because the plane is infinite and therefore unmanageable; a failure in which *'an other plane'* (of transcendence) 'returns in force' (MP 316|259) – makes no difference in this regard. Precisely because I can't plan or organise the plane from a position of transcendence without losing immanence or from a position of immanence without restoring transcendence, because I can't totalise and thereby totally supervise it, I cannot prevent some form of organisation and therefore transcendence from taking root in and sprouting from it.

One might respond, as Deleuze and Guattari at times say in analogous contexts, that one can think and demand a pure rhizome in principle even if, in fact, no rhizome is ever pure. The rhizome remains pure in principle even if never pure in fact. The loss of fact might already worry some Deleuzians, but it doesn't go far enough. Insofar as a rhizome might always lapse into the arborescence that *tout rhizome* bears, insofar as the possibility of lapsing into the arborescent is therefore ineradicable, arborescence also forms part of the very concept of rhizome. Even in principle. Terms like 'lapse' and 'failure' no longer accurately describe the rhizome's relation to arborescence because not even the purest rhizome is ever totally independent of arborescence into which, therefore, it never simply 'falls'. If thought isn't arborescent, as Deleuze and Guattari proclaim (MP 24|15), the rhizome is nevertheless never thinkable without a strain of arborescence. No writer or writing can ever entirely seed the arborescence that thus makes the rhizome both what it is (rhizomatic) and what it isn't (arborescent).

Nevertheless, rather than rethink their purist lexicon in terms of the contamination that they themselves recognise as an ingrained possibility, Deleuze and Guattari once again double down on purity. The caveat of contamination serves only to refine and preserve the purity. The occasional recognition that there is no purity and the insistence upon it warp their discourse in a number of diagnosable ways: so-called rhizomatic writing becomes *melancholic* since Deleuze and Guattari lament the 'loss' of the rhizome (MP 28|18); *reactionary* since every rhizome constantly flees an arborescence already rooted within it (MP 16|9); *paranoiac* since the rhizome writer feels perpetually persecuted by the transcendent or arborescent mode of writing into which his or her writing risks relapsing (MP 16|9, 22|14, 26|16–17 and so on).

Melancholic, reactionary, paranoiac. I could have chosen other terms, to be sure, but I use these because Deleuze and Guattari expressly oppose them to the rhizome and immanent thinking in general. Appreciating the polemic risked by these diagnoses would require a patient reading of at least both volumes of *Capitalism and Schizophrenia*, but such a reading would ultimately only confirm my general point here by populating its scope with the many contexts, problems and questions of Deleuze and Guattari's multifarious interventions: the rhizome is contaminated even when – especially when – it's pure. If binary logic is indeed 'the spiritual [or mental: *spirituelle*] reality of the root-tree' (MP 11|5), then Deleuze and Guattari's own text would offer radical grounds in which to stake the claim that, by opposing opposition in general, the rhizome proves more arborescent than arborescence itself. Despite what Deleuze and Guattari seem to think (MP 31|20), no multiplication of binaries will ever eradicate arborescence from the rhizome. Rather, one must rethink both the rhizomatic and the arborescent on the basis of a mutual contamination that precedes them both.

3) *Illusion*. In *What Is Philosophy?*, Deleuze and Guattari finally seem to take the contamination into rigorous account. Even though

they continue to insist upon pure and absolute immanence over against transcendence that ruins it, immanence no longer simply opposes transcendence. At least once, the model is other: immanence itself produces transcendence as a transcendental illusion.

In one form or another, by one name or another, transcendental illusion remains one of Deleuze's most lasting and most often under-problematised concerns. He recurs to it not only in his early book on Kant (1963), as one would expect, but also already in his even earlier work on Hume (1953).[17] He reflects upon its most systematic consequences in *Difference and Repetition*, however, where he broaches it as an alternative to the dogmatic concept of 'error' (DR 195|150). Since the tradition of philosophy tends to determine all the 'misadventures' of thought in terms of error, Deleuze reads error as 'the only "negative" of thought' (DR 193|148), and it thus becomes coextensive and contemporaneous with dogma itself. As an alternative to error, consequently, Deleuze credits transcendental illusion with the potential to reverse the entire dogmatic image of thought. To understand how Deleuze expands the illusion beyond its transcendental horizon, which for Deleuze still belongs to the dogmatic image of thought, one must first understand how the illusion operates according to Kant.

The understanding unifies the sensible manifold through concepts, according to Kant, and reason unifies the concepts of the understanding in turn through ideas in its effort to give experience the greatest possible unity. Yet, reason doesn't generate the ideas through which it unifies the otherwise vagrant operations of the understanding. Rather, reason merely extends the concepts of the understanding beyond their application to objects of experience, at which point 'concepts' of understanding become 'ideas' of reason (*Critique* A408–9|B435–6). Now, while the ideas of reason – the soul, the world and God – don't apply to any object encountered in experience, ideas still resemble the concepts from which they derive and thus, like concepts, seem to apply to objects. What should remain merely subjective principles for the unity of experience nevertheless, Kant says, have the appearance entirely (*gänzlich*) of objective principles (A297|B353). Whence the illusion – for every human, even the wisest, even for Kant – of insight into the soul, the world and God as they are in themselves.

This is why, to Deleuze, 'Kant seemed armed . . . for reversing the Image of thought'. Namely, '[h]e substituted the concept of illusion for the concept of error: internal illusions, interior to reason, instead of errors coming from the outside that would be only the effect of a causality of the body' (DR 178|136). Kant only 'seemed armed', however, because he never capitalises upon his discovery. Not solely because he rehabilitates the ideas of reason: on the speculative plane, the ideas of reason retain a regulatory or guiding function within the subjective conditions of experience as long as they remain subordinated to the understanding (*Critique* A329|B385); on the moral plane, the critical distinction between appearance and thing in itself prevents speculation from disproving what the idea might represent and what the practical use of reason can therefore recover without contradiction (Bxxx). Kant never manages to reverse the dogmatic image of thought above all because he never moves beyond its first postulate.[18] Even the most problematic idea never problematises the regime of representation that, for Deleuze, ruins the chances for a philosophy of difference or, in later terms, of immanence. In the first section of the first book of the transcendental dialectic, which he presents as a provisional introduction and in which he justifies his recourse to the word idea (*Idee*), Kant closes with a recapitulation of the progression (*Stufenleiter*) of his terms, and the first, the most general, the *genus* is '**representation** in general (*repraesentatio*)' (A320|B376).

Deleuze's deployment of transcendental illusion is, consequently, more and less Kantian than that of Kant. *Less* because, in *Difference and Repetition*, representation itself becomes 'the site of transcendental illusion' (DR 341|265). *More* because representation thereby expands the mechanism of transcendental illusion beyond the ideas to which Kant himself limits it. Not only the soul, not only the world, not only God, the illusion now engulfs identity, resemblance and the other components of representation. Including subjectivity. Whereas 'transcendental' refers to the conditions of possibility for subjective experience, Deleuze and Guattari situate all subjective philosophies – they refer to Kant by name (QP 49|46) – among those that make immanence an immanence *to*, in this case, *to* a subjective field. The very transcendentality of transcendental philosophy, in other words, is itself part of an even greater illusion generated by immanence. Illusion thus becomes, although Deleuze and Guattari never use this formulation, extra-transcendental.

Why should this matter?

On the one hand, the expansion of 'transcendental' illusion allows Deleuze and Guattari to resolve a problem that, I've argued, always haunts their recourse to immanence. As an illusion internal to immanence, transcendence is no longer an error, a lapse or a failure; it no longer threatens immanence from the outside because immanence itself secretes it. In one and the same stroke, Deleuze and Guattari not only manage to subordinate transcendence to immanence and dispose of all opposition to immanence; more importantly, they offer an account as to why transcendence has reigned for so long in western philosophy. Why, that is, perhaps only one philosopher has never compromised with transcendence.

On the other hand, the *internalisation* of transcendence comes at a cost. One might appeal to the status of transcendence as an illusion, but the mere appearance of transcendence suffices to alloy every thought of pure immanence. In which case, in reality, one can eradicate transcendence less than ever. Immanence must cease to be what it is to be what it is because what it is now includes what it isn't: transcendence. Agamben rightly recognises that the illusion of transcendence internal to immanence constitutes 'something like a limit point', but he doesn't seem to appreciate the consequences of this limit point insofar as the hypothesis guiding his whole analysis relates immanence – and the concept of 'life' it implies – to 'the subject of the coming philosophy' (Agamben 228, 238). If transcendence now appears analytic to the very concept of immanence, if immanence plays with transcendence even at its purest, then immanence can't be thought without transcendence.

So, Deleuze might take the illusion further than Kant, but he proves naiver in one respect. While transcendental illusion constitutes the heart of Kant's critique of reason, Deleuze never critiques immanence. As a result, wherever Deleuze himself confronts the problem of illusion in his own philosophy, not only but especially with Guattari in *What Is Philosophy?*, his comments conform to one of three types of statements. Only the confrontation between a tenacious desire for immanence and its constant frustration can explain the somnambulistic hospitality to these mutually exclusive statements.

(a) *The illusion is inevitable, but the attending error is not.* Although knowledge is no longer decisive, although I'm deluded even when I know what I see or conceive is an illusion, Kant reserves the possibility of resisting the error that falling for an illusion would entail. Even if we're never entirely rid of the illusion (*den Schein . . . niemals vollig los werden*), even if the illusion still and always teases (*zwackt*) and mocks (*äfft*) us, 'after much effort' – Kant promises – the wisest human being 'may guard himself from error [*den Irrtum verhüten*]' (*Critique* A339lB397). Deleuze is less modest. In *Difference and Repetition*, when a proper concept of difference inevitably produces the illusion of identity, Deleuze proclaims it does so 'without ever falling into the attending error [*l'erreur attenante*]' (DR 165|126). Years later in *What Is Philosophy?*, Deleuze places the same confidence in Spinoza. The Christ of philosophers inspires 'the least illusions', which is to say the illusion is inevitable, but he never renders (*ne donne pas*) or surrenders to (*ne se donne pas au*) the transcendent (QP 62|60). He never falls for the illusion that his immanence always produces.

(b) *The illusion and the error are both inevitable.* The best and the worst planes, Deleuze and Guattari say, have something in common, and their commonality, in reality, should at least temper any criterion by which planes rank as 'better' or 'worse': 'They have in common the fact that they restore some transcendence and some illusion (they cannot stop themselves from doing so)' (QP 61|59). For a philosophy whose very status as philosophy hinges upon the purity of immanence, this aside is remarkable. The best and the worst, the most immanent and the least, all planes alike cannot stop themselves from restoring not only 'some illusion' (*de l'illusion*) but also the attending error: 'some transcendence' (*de la transcendence*). Whence Deleuze and Guattari's constant war cry. Every plane must 'relentlessly combat' (QP 61|59) illusion and transcendence because no plane can avoid generating some illusion and some transcendence. Immanence struggles relentlessly, *avec acharnement*, because it also struggles *against itself* in struggling *against transcendence*.

If this holds even for the best planes, does it also hold for Spinoza? To insist, one could return to Deleuze's earlier critique of Spinoza in *Difference and Repetition* for support, but he and Guattari leave a vestige in *What Is Philosophy?* when, at the very moment they praise Spinoza's refusal to surrender to transcendence, they say THE plane is 'the purest [*le plus pur*]', which isn't to say – not simply – pure (QP 62|60).

(c) *Neither the illusion nor the error is inevitable.* In chapter 3, on 'Conceptual Characters', Deleuze and Guattari stress that no list can exhaust the possible characteristics of conceptual characters. Which doesn't prevent them from enumerating five characteristic genres. One of which, drawing upon philosophy's longstanding relation to justice and judgment, they call 'juridical characteristics'. Yet, among infinite possible characteristics, the juridical is perhaps the most curious. Deleuze and Guattari immediately undermine it with reference to the possibility of an absolutely 'innocent' character that would upend the entire juridical process – judge, prosecutor, defendant and all. And they describe this innocent character as 'a Spinoza that allowed no illusion of transcendence to subsist' (QP 74|72). *A* Spinoza, of course, isn't *the* Spinoza. The indefinite article suggests that any character that leaves not even the illusion of transcendence becomes a Spinoza. A Spinoza would operate as the conceptual character, in other words, not only everywhere Deleuze and Guattari proclaim absolute innocence against psychoanalysis's guilt-ridden approach. In *Anti-Oedipus* and *Proust and Signs*, for instance. A Spinoza would also operate as the conceptual character everywhere Deleuze and Deleuze and Guattari proclaim a plane of absolute immanence on which alone such innocence would be possible. Which is to say, innocence is not one characteristic and Spinoza not one conceptual character among others; a Spinoza becomes the conceptual archetype of philosophy as Deleuze and Guattari define it.

Incidentally, in short, Deleuze and Guattari here confirm the characterisation of Spinoza I've been describing from the beginning. Conjugated here with Deleuze and Guattari's other propositions concerning illusion and error, however, one begins to suspect that 'a Spinoza' with no illusion of transcendence perhaps names the greatest illusion of all: the illusion that all illusions can be destroyed.

The prince of philosophers, the Christ, he who inspired the least illusions and allowed none, he who could not avoid producing some transcendence and chased it away everywhere, he who only prepared Nietzsche's eternal return and ultimately overthrew it: the characterisation of Spinoza, in short, is an epiphenomenon, a symptom, a sign of a deeper problem. One and the same philosopher, one and the same philosophy, can be read as both absolutely immanent *and* infinitely less than immanent, both *absolutely* and *absolutely not* immanent, both immanent and transcendent, only because the mixture of immanence and transcendence precedes immanence, transcendence and their opposition. Which is to say, immanence is never immanent, never pure, never absolute.

And yet, despite this critical consequence, I'm not simply criticising Deleuze or his Spinozas. Unlike Badiou, who deserves credit for invoking univocity in the reception of Deleuze's work, I avoid calling Deleuze's Spinoza – either Spinoza – 'an unrecognizable creature' (*Clameur* 8|*Clamor* 1).[19] Perhaps readers like Badiou struggle to recognise Deleuze's Spinoza, rightly or wrongly, because they look for a philosopher, a historical author, rather than a conceptual character operating the concept of concept on THE plane of immanence. Even if and precisely because philosophy itself depends upon this personage, I've domesticated my entire intervention by framing it as a conceptual characterology. Whatever else I've done, I've also affirmed Deleuze and Guattari's machine by commandeering one of its gears.

Notes

1. And that of 'percept' from the third genre of knowledge in Part V. For this distinction and the reason for which I focus primarily on affect, see especially Chapter 6 below.
2. For a brief discussion of *affectus*, its cognates and its grammatical and conceptual variants from Cicero to Spinoza, see Russ Leo, 'Affective Physics: *Affectus* in Spinoza's *Ethics*' (38 ff.). Also relevant in this regard are Joughin's decisions in his translation of *Spinoza et le problème de l'expression* (see *Expressionism* 413–14 note b).
3. In their French translations of the *Ethica*, Émile Saisset (1842), J. G. Prat (1860) and Henri de Boulainvilliers (1907) all render *affectus* as *passion*. The translation has precedent and justification. The Latin title of Descartes' *Les Passions de l'Ame* is *Passions, sive Affectus Animae*: 'passions' *sive* (that is to say, in other words, what amounts to the same thing) 'affects' of the soul. Throughout the text, the Latin uses both *passion* and *affectus* to translate what is only *passion* in the French (articles 17, 21 and 25), and sometimes the French *passion* is even translated solely as *affectus* (article 68). Spinoza himself would seem to authorise this translation indirectly when, in the brief preface to the third part of the *Ethics*, he critiques Descartes' treatment of the 'affects' he himself is about to treat. Indeed, among the little he owned in life was the Latin edition of Descartes' *Opera Philosophica* (Elzevir 1650), in which he would have read *affectus* as a synonym for *passion*. But, of course, the translation of *affectus* as *passion* obscures the fact that an 'affect', crucial for Spinoza, can be *either* an action *or* a passion (*Ethics* IIIDef3). In 1906 and 1908, respectively, Charles Appuhn and Raoul Lantzenberg render *affectus* as *affection*. Perhaps better than *passion*, this translation nevertheless obscures the distinction, decisive for Deleuze, between *affectus* ('affect') and *affectio* ('affection').

André Guérinot gives *sentiments* ('feelings' or 'emotions') in his 1930 translation, and Roland Caillois follows suit in 1954. In *Spinoza and the Problem of Expression*, Deleuze uses Guérinot's translation, but he already intimates a dissatisfaction with his rendering of *affectus*. When Deleuze first broaches the notion, he gives 'affects' (in quotations marks) but, as if unsure of his own rigour, quickly returns to Guérinot's 'sentiments' and glosses both with the Latin: 'des « affects » ou sentiments (*affectus*)' (SPE 199|220). After this initial formulation, he refers to *affectus* as 'affect' only three more times, each instance chaperoned by Guérinot's *sentiment* (SPE 199 note 10|383 note 10, 200|220 and 220 note 17|386 note 17), before ultimately yielding to *sentiment* without further question. By the time of *Spinoza: Practical Philosophy* (1981), however, he has standardised his translation of *affectus* as *affect* even though, at the time, there was no extant translation to support it. On 20 February 1981, complaining of the frequent translation of *affectus* as *sentiment* in a session of his seminar on Spinoza, Deleuze insists: 'it is better, it seems to me, to translate *affectus* as "affect" because the word exists in French' (session six, first recording, 38'10"–16"). Since then, Bernard Pautrat (1988) and Robert Misrahi (1993) have standardised the translation of *affectus* as *l'affect*.

In what's largely taken for the standard translation in English, the *Collected Works of Spinoza* with which I'll work throughout what follows, Edwin Curley gives 'affect' (1985). This translation, however, has never been and is still not generally accepted. R. H. M. Elwes (1887), Samuel Shirley (1982) and very recently Michael Silverthorne and Matthew J. Kisner (2018) all translate *affectus* as 'emotion'.

4. For the first time in *What Is Philosophy?* on page 8|2 (see also QP 10–11|5) but not for the first time in general. By the time Deleuze and Guattari ask *what philosophy is* on the first page of *What Is Philosophy?*, they 'already had the answer' (QP 8|2). See, for instance, the 1968 interview 'On Nietzsche and the Image of Thought' (ID 196 |141), which dates from the same year Deleuze first 'does' his 'own' philosophy in *Difference and Repetition*.

5. This apparent anachronism would find strategic support in the '*strato-graphic time*' of philosophy that, over against its linear history, Deleuze and Guattari characterise as 'a grandiose time of coexistence' (QP 60–1|58–9).

6. On Spinoza's arachnomachias, see Steven Nadler's *Spinoza: A Life* (289). Deleuze and Guattari refer to this curious pastime in *What Is Philosophy?* and in so doing, insofar as the anecdote exemplifies a generic trait of conceptual characters ('existential' traits), already characterise Spinoza in a strong sense (QP 74–5|72–3). On exactly how these spider fights exemplify Spinoza's system, see SPP 20 note 9|12 note 9 and 165|125. See also CS (13 January 1981, session five, second recording, 7'35"). For the anecdotal method more generally, see LS series eighteen. In the course of explaining the negativity of evil in a letter to Willem van Blijenbergh, when Spinoza speaks of the 'pleasure' and 'admiration' we take in 'warring bees' (I:358), one can't help but suspect that spiders weren't the only victims.

7. Deleuze recognises that Spinoza never broaches the univocity of being and makes a case for his familiarity with the tradition (SPE 57 note 28|359–60 note 28), but his argument doesn't depend upon any

biographical or bibliographical confirmation. He emphasises: '*Spinoza's philosophy remains in part unintelligible if not seen as a constant struggle against the three notions of equivocity, eminence, and analogy*' (SPE 40|48–9; see also 38 note 8|356 note 8 and 149|165). Although I won't stress it here, Deleuze makes an important genealogical caveat that has the potential to upset the univocity of the tradition of univocity: univocity originates in the tradition of emanation in which also originate equivocity, eminence and analogy (see SPE, chapter 11, especially §3).

8. See Descartes' response to the first set of objections to the *Meditations* (*Œuvres* VII:107–11, IX:86–8|*Writings* II:78–80) and Deleuze's commentary thereon (SPE 147|162). See also chapter 2 of *Metaphysical Thoughts* (the appendix to *Descartes' 'Principles of Philosophy'*), where an expository, that is, not overtly critical Spinoza asserts on Cartesian principles that '*creatures are in God eminently*' (I:303).

9. I say the books were published and not written contemporaneously because, according to François Dosse (*Biographie* 177|*Intersecting* 143), Deleuze had almost finished his complementary thesis by the late 1950s.

10. The basic schema is consistent with *Spinoza and the Problem of Expression* (see SPE 40|48–9 and 52–8|61–7).

11. In his history of *French Rationalism from Cavaillès to Deleuze*, Knox Peden concentrates most of his argument concerning Deleuze as the culminating Spinozist in *Difference and Repetition*. In the process, he cites Deleuze's critique of Spinoza (Peden 216) and even adopts it as an epigraph for chapter 6, he makes sporadic references to the climactic importance of Nietzsche in *Difference and Repetition* (Peden 202 and 223), but – particularly remarkable in a genealogy of Deleuze's Spinozism (211) – he never cites Deleuze's own account of the history of univocity in which Spinoza places second. Peden isn't alone in this regard. In 'The Vertigo of Immanence: Deleuze's Spinozism', Miguel de Beistegui reads chapter 11 of *Spinoza and the Problem of Expression* as a sort of 'synthetic account of immanence in the history of philosophy leading up to Spinoza', but he never addresses Spinoza's secondary place or Nietzsche's primary place in the history of immanence according to *Difference and Repetition*, which he himself calls the 'more systematic thesis' and places alongside *Spinoza and the Problem of Expression* (Beistegui 91). More sensitive, Foucault recognises the limit Deleuze attributes to Duns Scotus and Spinoza but suggests that, rather than Nietzsche, Deleuze himself culminates the progression toward univocity by determining the eternal return in terms of difference, which Foucault calls 'the great signified' (Foucault 907). Foucault could not have predicted, of course, that Deleuze would abandon both Nietzsche and the eternal return for reasons these comments are preparing.

12. 'There is religion each time there is transcendence' (QP 47|43). Years earlier: 'I call theological plane all organization that comes from above and that relates to a transcendence, even hidden' (SPP 168|128). I'll return to this second plane below.

13. One should be attentive to but not misled by the novel terms. Deleuze and Guattari relate the 'rhizome' to immanence (MP 30–1|20) and even call the plateaus comprising a rhizome a 'plane of immanence' (MP 32|22). (Otherwise a careful translator, what Massumi translates as a 'plane of consistency' here is, in French, *un plan d'immanence*.) Confirming both the continuity of their work and the importance of 'Spinoza and Us', Deleuze and Guattari add the passage containing the formulation – 'plane of immanence' – to *Rhizome* upon reworking it for *Thousand Plateaus*. For the page to which they would soon add the formulation, see R 63. See also the two 'Memories of a Spinozist' in plateau ten where all these terms circulate.

14. As if a palinode, this parenthetical remark was added to the 'Introduction' in 1980. Compare MP 34|23 and R 66.

15. For instance, see Deleuze's attempt to retain the superiority of the immanent cause while keeping it distinct from eminent causality (SPE 157|173 and 169|186).

16. See *Spinoza: Practical Philosophy* 122 note. Massumi shows more care in his translation of *Mille plateaux* but still attempts to decide between 'plane' and 'plan' (see *Thousand* xvii).

17. To name a few prominent instances, see ES 7|25, 75|75, 85 ff.|82 ff.; PCK 38|25; B 10|20–1. On illusion in Hume, in particular, see also the late preface to the American edition of *Empiricism and Subjectivity* (DRF 341|364); the 1972 text entitled 'Hume', originally published in François Châtelet's *Histoire de la philosophie* (ID 231|165); and the 1957–1958 'Course on Hume' (L 139|137, 141|139, 166|164, 168|166). These references would ultimately confirm that contemplation operates the greatest and most incorrigible illusion in Hume and, perhaps, in general (see Chapter 2 above).

18. For Deleuze's summary of the eight postulates comprising the image of thought, see DR 216–17|167. Although he names representation as the fourth postulate (just prior to error as the fifth), it already operates 'in the element' of the first, that is, common sense (DR 171|131). On the problem of representation for a philosophy of difference, see Chapter 1 above.

19. Badiou isn't alone in this regard. Reading Deleuze's philosophy as a synthesis of Heidegger and Spinoza, as either 'a rationalist Heideggerianism' or 'an existentialist Spinoza', Peden similarly claims Deleuze renders both 'unrecognizable' (196–7).

5

Affectus Becoming *l'Affect*

O body swayed to music, O brightening glance,
How can we know the dancer from the dance?

Yeats, 'Among School Children'

Part II hinges upon what Deleuze calls 'the paradox of Spinoza' (P 225|165). The most philosophical philosopher – Spinoza – is also the least. While the paradox bears upon Spinoza, it is unintelligible *as* a paradox without Deleuze because Deleuze himself determines the senses of 'philosophy' and 'non-philosophy' that describe Spinoza superlatively and simultaneously. In the last chapter, I approached the first leg of the paradox, arguing that Deleuze invents Spinoza as a conceptual character to operate the immanence with which he defines philosophy. Here, in Chapter 5, I turn to the second leg. Not only the most, Spinoza is also the least philosophical philosopher because his work isn't limited to conceptual understanding. It also solicits, Deleuze says, an affective understanding that appeals to non-philosophers in general and to artists in particular. If the same could be said of every philosopher, if all philosophy incidentally but inevitably has affective effects, all philosophers are not equally paradoxical. Spinoza is the most paradoxical because, beyond this or that and even the most intense individual affect, Deleuze draws the very notion of affect from Spinoza. To clarify and to sharpen the paradox in what follows, accordingly, I first approach the body according to Spinoza in order, in turn, to specify what Deleuze omits and emphasises in Spinoza for his own theory of affect and how, finally, this active inheritance *intensifies* the ascetic tradition in more than one sense.

Existential Choreography

If affect according to Deleuze cannot be understood without understanding affect according to Spinoza, affect according to Spinoza cannot be understood without understanding the body and the body, in turn, not without movement.

There's only one substance, which Spinoza calls 'Nature' or 'God'. Infinite attributes comprise the substance but, as finite beings, we know only two: thought and corporality. It would be necessary to linger indefinitely on Spinoza's determination of corporality as a divine attribute (*Ethics* IP15S), but only one consequence motivates me here. If corporality constitutes an attribute of Nature, of God, of the sole substance, then there's no substantial difference between individual bodies or what Spinoza calls 'modes'. Human, animal, vegetal, mineral, everybody as a body – every body – modifies the same attribute (corporality) of the same substance (Nature). One couldn't properly speak of a body 'embodying' substance since every body is, insofar as it is, the substance it modifies. So, if all bodies are equally bodily, all the same bodily substance, how does one body differ from another?

In the first lemma of the second part of the *Ethics*, Spinoza writes: '*Bodies are distinguished from one another by reason of motion and rest, speed and slowness, and not by reason of substance.*' Any given body consists in simpler bodies that, like all bodies, either move or rest. A body remains the same body, a body endures, as long as its component bodies maintain a fixed proportion of movement and rest. Component bodies can be exchanged (IIL4), some might accelerate and others decelerate (IIL5), their sizes might vary (IIL6), but the composite body remains the same body if the overall proportion of motion and rest remains constant. A body differs from another neither substantially nor ontologically (pleonastic adverbs here); one body is, one body is one, one body is the body it is and not another because the bodies that compose it maintain a unique and constant proportion of movement and rest.

In the final analysis, this constitutive relation between body and movement should make us hesitate to speak of 'bodies in movement', if this formulation supposes 'bodies' that, already constituted, subsequently enter into movement. At stake are not bodies in movement but rather movements in the body or, more accurately still, movements *qua* body. Spinoza thus motivates a distinction between *movement* and *movement*: the movement that a constituted body undertakes on the one hand and, on the other, the movement that constitutes the body before it undertakes a movement. No body can move without another movement, a prior movement, a movement before it moves that constitutes it as a body that can move. For which reason, even if one movement doesn't necessarily precede the other chronologically, it would be necessary to speak of *pre-, proto-* or even *im-mobile movement*. Before moving, without moving, I still move. For I am, if and whatever I am, insofar as I am movement.

On the basis of this distinction between movement and movement, between constitutive movement and constituted movement, between the movement that constitutes the body and the movement the constituted body undertakes, I could go on generating paradoxical formulations like 'immobile movement' or idiomatic economies like 'still movement', but at some point I'd have to recall that, for Spinoza, corporal constitution doesn't consist in pure movement. Rather, the body consists in a proportion of movement and rest. At which point I'd have to widen the term 'movement' to refer to both movement and rest or, to avoid confusion, look for another term that better embraces both.

One possible term – not the only – might be dance.

To elaborate this sense of 'dance', one Spinozist is perhaps as indispensable as Spinoza himself. In both 'Spinoza and Us' (SPP 163|123) and 'Spinoza and the Three "Ethics"' (CC 176|142), Deleuze uses the word *rhythm* to refer to the relation between movement and rest that constitutes the Spinozist body. The word is opportune. For what relates rest and movement, speed and slowness, if not a rhythm? And what relates body and rhythm if not a dance? 'Rhythm alone', says Aristotle in the *Poetics*, 'is the means in the dancer's imitations' (II:1447a26–7).

By naming the kinetic composition of bodies 'rhythm', Deleuze also necessarily broadens the word's horizon. At the limit, as the movements and rests of some bodies compose with those of others to form ever greater bodies, Nature as a whole becomes a 'universal rhythm' (CC 177|142). Deleuze doesn't limit this rhythmic expanse to Spinoza. The unity of Francis Bacon's oeuvre, the coexistence of three periods running from the body's contraction and isolation (*systole*) to its dissipation into cosmic forces (*diastole*), Deleuze also calls 'rhythm'. Rhythm, in this case, describes the cosmic forces that traverse Bacon's body and, by exceeding any given sense, relate every sense to every other in an originary unity of the senses, which constitutes the whole *Logic of Sensation*. 'This power is Rhythm, deeper than vision, audition, etc.' (FB 46|42; see also 37–8|33). Sensation or affect, accordingly, names the body in excess of itself as it attempts to accommodate the rhythm of the cosmos or – returning to Spinozist terms – Nature. Whatever justification he might have for speaking of 'rhythm' in Spinoza or in Bacon, one could make a method of confronting the same term in different contexts as a means to smoke Deleuze out of his analyses.

While one might expect the universality of rhythm to universalise dance in turn, Deleuze seems to limit the dance by referring to it as one corporal composition among others. Dance, in other words, is only an example. When I dance with another, the rhythms of my body combine with those of my partner in order to form a more complex body that occupies a determined level on the scale that begins with the simplest bodies (not to say simple bodies) and continues through more composite bodies up toward the one body composed of all bodies, the bodily substance, Nature or God.[1] Deleuze writes: 'If I learn to swim, or to dance, my movements and my rests, my speeds and my slownesses must have a rhythm in common with those of the ocean, or of the partner, according to a more or less durable adjustment' (CC 176–7|142). It might be worth accepting Deleuze's invitation to think a dance between two partners as a corporal composition, to be sure, but the example remains a rather limited idea of dance, even in Spinozist terms, since there's a dance more fundamental than what takes place between two human partners. Deleuze isn't unaware. A decade before 'Spinoza and the Three "Ethics"', in the first 'Memories of a Spinozist' in the tenth of *A Thousand Plateaus* ('Becoming-Intense, Becoming-Animal, Becoming-Imperceptible'), Deleuze and Guattari speak of a plane of immanence where, differentiated by speed and slowness rather than by form, elements and materials 'dance' (MP 312|255). If every body consists because it consists in a rhythm of movement and rest, if bodily rhythm means dance, then dance can no longer be held in any region of Nature. Dance now exemplifies nothing except, perhaps, a greater dance. No longer limited to the dance I do with more or less elegance when the music starts, no longer limited to my dance with a partner, no longer limited, this connatural dance describes Nature itself and circumscribes its regions. If rhythms of movement and rest constitute every body, then every body – from the simplest in Nature to Nature as a whole – every body dances. Every leaf, every tree, every forest; every person, every society, every international; every body dances in being whatever body it is and might become. This dance, indistinguishable from the dancer, one could call – without any simple metaphor – an existential choreography.

Because the movements and rests that define my body aren't the movements I undertake, Spinoza comes to a reasonable but nonetheless remarkable conclusion: 'no reason compels me to maintain that the Body does not die unless it is changed into a corpse' (*Ethics* IVP39S). Regardless of the outer signs by which you think me alive or dead, I die when – and only when – my body stops dancing. I dance to death, until another dance no longer mine begins, until another dance begins that I no longer am. So, the end of my dance is not the end of dance. Ultimately, there's *only* dance because there's *no* decomposition: 'For, from the point of view of nature or God, there are always relations that compose, and *there is nothing other than relations that compose* according to eternal laws' (Deleuze, SPP 51|36). Every body is a more or less subtle step in the greater dance called Nature or God.

This existential choreography, however, sets the stage for a silent discord between Deleuze and Spinoza, a counterstep or asynchrony, with respect to the affectability of the body in its corporal dance. I call the discord 'silent' because Deleuze himself never mentions it, even though – and perhaps precisely because – he writes voluminously and 'most seriously' on Spinoza.[2] For which reason, perhaps, commentators who come to Spinoza and to affect according to Spinoza by way of Deleuze regularly overlook or ignore this discord. The muted nature of the discord, however, doesn't preclude obstreperous consequences for the history of philosophy and the places of Spinoza, Deleuze and affect theory within it.

The Antinomy of Affect

One might think that, for Spinoza, the substantial equality of all bodies would preclude any privilege of one over another. How to privilege, say, the human body if all bodies are equally bodily? Indeed, Spinoza denounces anthropocentrism throughout the *Ethics* and does so, each time, with the weight of Nature as whole. He not only denies that nature caters to the human, for instance, that 'God has made all things for man, and man that he might worship God' (*Ethics*, I, Appendix, p. 440). Mobilising a logic analogous to the transcendental illusions that would tease and mock Kant a century later, he demonstrates the reason for which this idea is inevitable. Spinoza traces the illusion of all *universals* (Being, Thing, Something) and all *transcendentals* (Man, Horse, Dog) to the body itself: 'each will form universal images of things according to the disposition of his body' (IIP40S; see also IP8S2). Nevertheless, precocious and enduring though these critiques of anthropomorphism and anthropocentrism remain, Spinoza never revokes all human privilege. Ultimately, on the contrary, the Spinozist critique of the human only prepares another privilege at once greater and more modest.

Spinoza launches the entire discussion of kinetic corporality in the second part of the *Ethics* under the auspices of human excellence. 'And so', he says, 'to determine what is the difference between the human Mind and the others, and how it surpasses them, it is necessary for us, as we have said, to know the nature of its object, that is, of the human Body' (IIP13S). Spinoza speaks of determining how the human mind surpasses others but not how other minds surpass the human. This asymmetry isn't a casual omission or oversight. The word translated as 'the others' and pronominalised as 'them' is *reliquis*: remnant, remainder or residue (Lewis and Short 1559), that which is left like a relic, the word in this case means all the minds remaining once we subtract the human mind. Spinoza thus professes a faith before arguing a point. That he hasn't yet demonstrated or in any way deduced the essence of the human mind at this moment in the geometric order of the *Ethics* doesn't prevent him from taking for granted that the human mind – whatever it will be – surpasses 'the others'. Indeed, that Spinoza cannot and need not 'explain this here' (IIP13S), that he limits himself to the general principle that would ground any estimation of excellence, in a sense makes the apparently passing reference to human excellence appear more dogmatic still. The entire excursion into the body in a discussion 'Of the Mind' (Part II), a certain interruption of the geometric order that – however justified – calls for new axioms, becomes a testament to Spinoza's faith in a so far unspecified 'humanity'. Whatever other minds prove to be, rest assured, they are inferior.

Instead of getting lost in the axioms, lemmas and postulates that follow, I'll limit myself to a brief rehearsal of the affective principle that animates the discussion and would ground the Spinozist privilege of the specifically human mind. For Spinoza, namely, a mind's perspicacity – human or otherwise – is a function of the body's affectability, that is, its ability both to affect and to be affected. The more a body can affect and be affected, the more the mind can perceive and eventually understand:

> I say this in general, that in proportion as a Body is more capable than others of doing many things at once, or being acted on in many ways at once, so its Mind is more capable than others of perceiving many things at once. And in proportion as the actions of a body depend more on itself alone, and as other bodies concur with it less in acting, so its mind is more capable of understanding distinctly. (*Ethics* IIP13S)

The mind's perspicacity depends upon the body's affectability, and the body's affective capacity, in turn, depends upon the body's composition, that is, upon the movements and rests of the simpler bodies that compose it. Upon its dance in the existential sense I outlined earlier. A complex body can sustain greater changes in its component bodies without losing the general proportion of rest and movement, which is to say, it can interact with many external bodies without losing its existential rhythm or locomotive proportion in the interaction. Whence human excellence. The human mind surpasses others insofar as the human body enjoys greater affectability; its many bodies, its many movements and rests, give it more experiential latitude that guarantees at least the possibility – congenital illusions notwithstanding – of an ideal excellence. I'll cite only a few of the postulates with which Spinoza's concludes his discussion of the body.

> I. The human Body is composed of a great many individuals of different natures, each of which is highly composite. [. . .]
> III. The individuals composing the human Body, and consequently, the human Body itself, are affected by external bodies in many ways. [. . .]
> VI. The human Body can move and dispose external bodies in a great many ways.

Ending his digression on the body in the part of the *Ethics* dedicated to the mind, resuming his geometric order, the next proposition relates the human body's affectability to the human mind's perspicacity: '*The human Mind is capable of perceiving a great many things, and is the more capable, the more its body*' – Spinoza also capitalises the human Body here (*Corpus*) – '*can be disposed in a great many ways*' (IIP14).

Affect theorists who claim sensitivity to questions of body and affect in Spinoza regularly overlook or ignore this anthropocentrism (for example, Schaefer 12). Coming to terms with it, however, one might think the privilege rather modest for a number of reasons.

Since every mode modifies attributes that express the same divine substance, first, no two bodies and no two minds – human or otherwise – differ substantially in the whole of nature. This, however, ultimately only ratifies and intensifies the privilege because not even a substantial homogeneity deprives the human of it. The human excels without ever stepping forward.

Second, one might temper the privilege by recalling that humans know only thought and corporality, that is, only two of the infinite attributes that express the divine substance. Even within the attributes of which we know, moreover, Spinoza places essential limits on our capacities. We have only a confused and inadequate knowledge of individual thoughts and bodies – including our own (*Ethics* IIP24–31). Yet again, not despite but precisely because of these limitations, few anthropocentrisms or anthropologies appear more audacious, tenacious or ambitious. Not even our *infinite* ignorance concerning both infinite other attributes and the infinite things that modify them shakes Spinoza's faith in human excellence, which thus exceeds the infinite twice over. That the privilege bears only upon thought and corporality only suggests we humans don't know how privileged we truly are.

Finally, one might venture that, far from privileging the human, Spinoza humbles the human by situating it on a larger spectrum of corporeal compositions running from the simplest bodies to composite bodies, from composite bodies to bodies composed of composite bodies, and so on to Nature as a whole. There are no doubt bodies of both lesser and greater composition, and a more complex body might incorporate humans as one of its many components. A more complex body, moreover, means a more complex mind. So, one might insist on this human situation in order to moderate Spinoza's reference to human excellence. If, however, one takes both the situation and the excellence seriously, the excellence intensifies because it excels from a situated place on the spectrum of corporal composition. The human mind surpasses not only the rest, *reliquis*, but also its own.

Spinoza, of course, isn't the first or last philosopher to privilege the human. One would need time but no great ingenuity to show that philosophy, in fact or in principle, never unfolds without this problematic privilege. Although Derrida doesn't include him in his discussion, Spinoza's treatise obeys the double sense of 'end' he taps in 'The Ends of Man': the 'end' of man as the termination or death of man for the sake of man as a higher 'end', goal or *telos*.[3] Only the terms and scope of the *Ethics* innovate in this regard. I nevertheless linger on the privilege's form and platform in the *Ethics* because it economically illuminates a certain discrepancy between Spinoza and Deleuze with respect to affect. While Spinoza first broaches affect in the *Ethics* – and, for many affect theorists, in the history of ideas[4] – under the auspices of simultaneously finding and founding the human's superiority, Deleuzian affect would seem to outmode all human privilege. Rather than a principle for weighing human excellence, Deleuze defines affect with Guattari in *What Is Philosophy?* as the 'becoming nonhuman of the human' (QP 169|169, 173|173 and 184|183). The foundation of human excellence for Spinoza – affect – makes the human become other, other than human, nonhuman for Deleuze.

This tension becomes so great, indeed, it merits formulation as an antinomy. Kant, the terminological precedent here, reserves the name 'antinomy' (*Antinomie*) for the dialectic of reason when it bears upon the world. While reason also leads to the illusion of insight into the self (paralogisms) and God (the ideal of pure reason), the antinomies have a privileged status because the opposing but equally valid claims about the world – its beginning and end, its simplicity and composition, the freedom for which it does and does not allow, its contingency and necessity – reveal the dialectic of reason in general. *This* dialectic, in other words, reveals the very *dialecticity* of reason and, in so doing, invites the scrutiny that Kant will ultimately call the *Critique of Pure Reason*. This use of reason is the 'most remarkable', Kant says, because 'it works the most strongly of all to awaken philosophy from its dogmatic slumber, and to prompt it toward the difficult business of the critique of reason itself' (*Prolegomena* 4:338; see also §52b and §56).

When it bears upon affect, however, the antinomy differs in at least two related respects. First, although 'unavoidable [*unvermeidlich*] and neverending [*niemals ein Ende nehmende*]' (*Prolegomena* 4:339), Kant ultimately solves or, more accurately, dissolves the antinomies of reason. Of course, he doesn't decide in favour of either thesis or antithesis in any of an unchecked reason's dialectics. Rather, he provokes and exacerbates the conflict so as to investigate whether the object of controversy – in the case of antinomies: the world – is not a 'mere mirage [*Blendwerk*]' (*Critique* A423|B451). The antinomy, in other words, will have been no real antinomy. Second, Kant dissolves all four antinomies by redistributing appearances and the thing in itself. Nature as appearance permits no uncaused cause, for instance, but nothing forbids attributing freedom to the noumenal thing in itself about which we can know nothing. In the process, Kant relegates sensibility to nature, to necessity, to the phenomenal realm that on its own – without reference to the thing in itself or its freedom – bears no contradiction (e.g., *Prolegomena* 4:345–6).

As the name indicates, an 'antinomy' is a conflict (*anti-*) between two laws or principles (*-nomos*). The conflict, in this case, rises between what I'll call – provisionally – the 'Spinozist' law and the 'Deleuzian' law. Of course, neither Spinoza nor Deleuze thematise this antinomy, and it isn't limited to Spinoza or Deleuze, but it occurs with particular force where they cross. Once formalised, in any case, the Spinozist tenor of Deleuzian affect can no longer simply be taken for granted. Not even when Deleuze himself proclaims it.

According to the Spinozist law, an affect cannot affect the nature of the affected. In Spinozist terms, that is, an affect cannot affect the relation between movements and rests that composes me. If an affect affected my nature, my corporal and therefore mental constitution, my dance, I'd no longer be the individual I was prior to the affect. The affect will not have affected 'me' because 'I' thereby become other than what I was: another body, another mind, another individual. There can be local changes, there even must be local changes, but an affect that affects my general proportion of motion and rest isn't an affect. It's death itself: 'I understand the Body to die when its parts are so disposed that they acquire a different proportion of motion and rest to one another' (*Ethics* IVP39S). For which reason, upon describing the superior affectability of highly composite bodies in the scholium to lemma 7 of the second part of the *Ethics*, Spinoza stipulates – twice – that no changes whatsoever occur in the nature of the affected. The fact that Spinoza observes the law I name after him in subordinate clauses doesn't detract from its importance; on the contrary, the law is so basic it needs no postulate of its own, no demonstration, no proposition. My emphases:

> By this, then, we see how a composite Individual can be affected in many ways, *and still preserve its nature*. [. . .] For since each part of it is composed of a number of bodies, each part will therefore (by L7) be able, *without any change of its nature*, to move now more slowly, now more quickly, and consequently communicate its motion more quickly and more slowly to the others.

Even if the human's highly composite and therefore highly affect-able nature is paradigmatic in this regard, this 'Spinozist' law doesn't apply only to humans. All bodies have a limit of affectability beyond which they would cease to preserve their nature and, hence, cease to affect or be affected. Without this limit, indeed, one would have no grounds for speaking of a specifically human body or mind, let alone for ranking it above or below the others. Deleuze can proclaim that 'there is no essence of man' in Spinoza (CS, 9 December 1980, session two, first recording, 11'40") only by displacing the idea of 'essence' in such a way that permits him to neglect the *unsubstantiated* but *subsisting* privilege that the human's complex nature guarantees.[5]

According to the Deleuzian law, an affect must affect the very nature of the affected. If not, if the affect doesn't affect the affected profoundly, if the affected remains essentially the same before and after the affect, 'without any change of its nature' as Spinoza says, then the affect ultimately will have affected nothing. The affect itself will have been nothing. The only affect that can't be discarded as secondary or accidental, the only irreducible affect, the only affect would be an affect that affects essentially. Any affect that doesn't affect my essence doesn't deserve the name 'affect'; in truth, it deserves no name whatsoever because it makes no difference. It would 'affect' only in quotation marks – metaphorically, analogically, equivocally – because it falls insurmountably short of the affect that, rather than disappearing beneath the impassive essence of this or that being, reshapes it. I've called this law 'Deleuzian', at least provisionally, because Deleuze seems to observe it when he defines affect as the 'becoming nonhuman of the human'. Affect cannot ground or consolidate my privilege as a human if, indeed, it makes me become other than human.[6]

Accordingly, one might think that Derrida too precipitously interjects 'anthropomorphically' into Deleuze and Guattari's becoming-animal: 'it's a question of the becoming-anthropomorphically-animal of man and not a question of the animal or the beast, if one may say, themselves' ('Transcendental "Stupidity"' 39). Derrida's comment interrupts a quotation from the tenth plateau of *A Thousand Plateaus* (MP 317|260), which Derrida cites because it contains the only use in the book of the French idiom *bêtise* at stake in his article and in the larger seminar – *La bête et le souverain* – from which he extracts it. While the passage thus serves as the entrance for Derrida's entire discussion of *A Thousand Plateaus*, while he even recognises 'affect' and 'plane' as the central concepts of Deleuze and Guattari's analysis and strategy ('Transcendental "Stupidity"' 39), Derrida never refers to Spinoza in his discussion of a subsection nevertheless titled 'Memories of a Spinozist'. Had he invoked what Spinoza says of human affectability alongside Deleuze and Guattari, he might have had reason to hesitate before attributing anthropomorphism to the affect that, rather than consolidating human excellence, makes the human become other.[7]

Reason to hesitate but not to renege.

At the limit, on the contrary, Derrida's interjection perhaps doesn't go far enough. The very fact that Deleuze and Guattari recurrently define 'becoming' in human terms – even if only to make the human become other – might attest to a residual privilege. The 'residual' status would detract nothing from its scope since, in this case, the human would retain its privilege even when it becomes other. If Deleuze and Guattari define becoming precisely, *précisément*, as the becoming-nonhuman of the human (QP 169|169), if the human thus defines becoming or, at least, if becoming can't be defined without the human (becoming nonhuman), the human remains the remote measure not only of all things but even of its own alterity.[8]

Betrayal

The 'Spinozist' law forbids an affect to affect the essence of the affected; the 'Deleuzian' law requires an affect to affect the essence of the affected. Affect *must* and *must not* affect essentially, which is to say, affect must not be affect to be affect. A Spinozist affect is not yet an affect in the Deleuzian jurisdiction, just as a Deleuzian affect is no longer an affect in the Spinozist jurisdiction. Because both laws prove both indispensable and irreducible, one can't observe either without breaking the other.

Admittedly, affect according to Deleuze is subtler than what my rigid formulation of the 'Deleuzian' law suggests. In a discussion of the difference between 'becoming' in philosophy as the discipline that creates concepts and 'becoming' in art as the discipline that creates affects, Deleuze and Guattari write: 'Sensible becoming is the act by which something or someone ceaselessly becomes-other (while continuing to be what they are)' (QP 178|177). Deleuze and Guattari seem to recognise a variant of the Spinozist law here: if I become other while continuing to be what I am, then I become non-human, I become animal for instance, without ceasing to be human. Presumably without even ceasing to be the human I am. The parentheses with which Deleuze and Guattari surround this caveat are both telling and deceptive. Telling because they attempt to suspend, mute, contain or restrain the Spinozist law; deceptive because the point isn't minor. Deleuze and Guattari confirm that one 'becomes' without ceasing 'to be' every time they insist – and they often insist – that *becoming* isn't *transformation*. Captain Ahab 'becomes' whale without becoming a whale. Nor do I imitate, resemble, sympathise or identify with the other I become (QP 173–4|173, MP 315–16|258), but I stress that becoming is not transformation because, even when commentators cite the distinction, they struggle not to collapse it.[9]

There would seem to be no simple choice between 'Deleuze' and

'Spinoza' in this regard. Affect according to Deleuze seems to incorporate the whole antinomy I previously divided into Deleuzian and Spinozist laws. In so doing, it forces a series of questions that otherwise might have remained more or less implicit. How is it possible to become without coming to be, without transforming, without dying? Without ending one dance and beginning another? How can one become other while being the same? How can one become other while being the same without thereby homogenising, parenthesising or excluding the alterity alleged in becoming-other? Without thereby altering the sameness alleged in being the same? How can and why does *affect* force becoming and preserve being?

Deleuze unapologetically describes his own thought as 'metaphysics' but, if classical metaphysics unfolds in the division between being and becoming, the question of affect no longer fits entirely within the space of metaphysics. For the same reason, can one still ask what affect 'is'? The very form of the question (*what is . . .*) wouldn't be entirely legitimate insofar as it already simplifies affect by resubmitting it to 'being' at the expense of 'becoming' and thereby breaking the antinomy and resubmitting it to metaphysics. Nevertheless, the laws according to which one might rule the question illegitimate become clearest precisely by posing it. While Deleuze long sought to replace *what is . . . ?* with other questions,[10] in other words, no question better evidences the way in which 'affect', for Deleuze, might antedate and antiquate the distinction between being and becoming.

Both nevertheless and therefore, then, what is affect? Impossible to say without saying what affect isn't: 'affects are no longer feelings or affections' (QP 163–4|164); '[a]ffect exceeds affections' (QP 173|173). Deleuze derives the distinction between *affect* and *affection* from Spinoza, but Spinoza himself distinguishes between three degrees of affectability.

There is, for Spinoza, a single substance, 'God' *sive* 'Nature', which consists in infinite attributes. Individual things are spatiotemporal modifications of these attributes and, accordingly, Spinoza most often calls them 'modes'. But he also calls them *affections*. 'By mode I understand the affections of a substance [*substantiæ affectiones*]' (*Ethics* ID5; see also IP15 and IP25C). Corporality, for instance, is one of infinite attributes of the one and only substance, and every individual body is therefore an 'affection' of corporality. The first, the earliest, the most primordial affectability therefore isn't this or that 'affection' that my body suffers; 'affection' in this case first names the determination of Nature's infinite corporality as a particular body that, once constituted and therefore only in turn, can affect and be affected in the more familiar sense with which affect theory tends to begin (Massumi, for instance, *Politics* ix, 4, 48, 91 and so on). Before it *has* affections, my body *is* an affection that therefore, in panorama, would merit the name *pre-affective affection*.

Yet, if I left this always prior affection situated as the first in a series of affectabilities that culminate in affect proper, I'd eclipse its real scope. Whenever Deleuze himself speaks of these three degrees or species of affection, for instance, he doesn't draw attention to the fact that the first 'affection' isn't limited to bodies (for instance, SPE 199|219–20 and SPP 66|48). Not only of corporality, 'affection' describes *every* modification of *every* attribute. Which not only means this primordial 'affection' determines mind and body equally, the only two attributes that it is both our privilege and our limit as humans to know. Not only of thought, not only of corporality, but also of the infinite attributes we don't know, every mode is an affection. There is perhaps no greater 'affection' in the history of philosophy: it now names the genesis of every thing we know, can know, will ever and will never know. Affection operates the ontological difference between being (substance) and beings (modes) that don't open even to us, to the human being, whose mind supposedly surpasses that of every other.

While the first 'affection', then, modifies the universal attribute of corporality – for instance – into a particular body, the second (*affectio*) names the effect one body has upon another or, more precisely, the effect the movements and rests of the bodies composing one body have upon those composing another. If the first are *pre-affective affections*, for the same reason, the second are *affections of affections*.[11] Only after these two levels of affectability, *as* and *of* a body, does the third affectability – affect in a strict sense (*affectus*) – appear in Spinoza's system. 'By affect I understand affections of the Body by which the Body's power of acting is increased or diminished, aided or restrained, and at the same time, the ideas of these affections' (*Ethics*, IIIDef3). An external body affects mine and, as a result, my power of acting (affecting) is either increased or diminished. An affect, strictly speaking, is both the physiological affection and the idea that results. The idea of an affection that increases my power to act gives me *joy*, and what diminishes my power to act makes me *sad* (IIIP11S). *Desire*, in turn, drives me to pursue joy and to avoid or destroy all agents of sadness (IIIP9S). Joy, sadness and desire constitute the three 'primary' affects on which, from bondage to freedom, every step in the *Ethics* depends: 'apart from these three I do not acknowledge any other primary affect. For I shall show in what follows that the rest arise from these three' (IIIP11S).

So, when Deleuze and Guattari announce that affect 'exceeds' affection, they hang the discipline of art – as the creation of affects – upon the distinction between affection (*affectio*) and affect (*affectus*). Despite the declarative presentation of it in *What Is Philosophy?*, however, the distinction can't simply be taken for granted. Spinoza himself doesn't dwell or insist upon the distinction between *affectio* and *affectus* or even always employ the terms consistently. When Spinoza speaks of the body being '*affected by an affect*' (*Ethics* IIP17), for instance, Edwin Curley notes that we should probably read 'affection' instead of 'affect', especially since the Dutch translation of the *Ethics*, as if confirming the slip, gives 'mode' here (I:464 note 43). Other passages are also relevant in this regard (IIP18, for instance, and IIIP14). Rather than edit Spinoza and reread affect as affection (or mode), of course, a subtler approach would ask what such a 'slip' might symptomise concerning the hermetic rigour of the distinction between affection and affect.

Deleuze, however, chooses another path. In *Spinoza: Practical Philosophy*, he concentrates above all on the increase and decrease in power in order to harden the distinction between affection and affect. Elsewhere so important, power as such doesn't interest Deleuze here. The passage, rather, is decisive.[12]

> *Affectio* refers to a state of an affected body and implies the presence of an affecting body, while *affectus* refers to the passage from one state to another, account taken of the correlative variation of affecting bodies. (SPP 67|49)

A given affection determines my state, say, state A. Another body affects me, increases or diminishes my power to act, and now I find myself in state B. In a strict sense, on the Deleuzian reading, affect is neither state A nor state B but rather the passage from A to B, passage A-B, the becoming B of A that reduces to neither state A nor state B. It's this interstate that Deleuze and Guattari adopt and adapt as the 'becoming' that operates affect in *What Is Philosophy?*

I say adopt *and adapt* because here, at the heart of his inheritance, Deleuze betrays Spinoza. Assuming the specificity of affect indeed passes between states, affect for Spinoza takes place between two states or 'affections' lived by a single individual. Whether two affections of an animal or the individual *par excellence*, the Spinozist affect always pertains to one body. As the augmentation or diminishment of a body's power to act, affect has a mono-corporeal horizon that imposes an essential limit upon all becoming. Even if we still don't know 'what the Body can do' (*Ethics* IIIP2S), an affirmation made duly famous by Deleuze's admiration and insistence,[13] we know that a body can do no more than its constitutive movements and rests permit. Of course, as a reader of Spinoza, Deleuze knows this. 'With a maximum threshold and a minimum threshold', he says, 'the capacity for affects is a frequent notion in Spinoza' (SPP 163|124; see also MP 314|256–7). An affect beyond the body's 'maximum threshold' could only decompose the proportion of movements and rests that constitute it, ending its existential dance. What Deleuze calls the 'maximum threshold' of affect thus reformulates the Spinozist law: what affects cannot affect essentially.

This might seem obvious. Even if it doesn't originate there, an affect always pertains to one body. You don't experience my joy even if you occasion it, even if you too are joyful, even if my joy occasions yours or your joy mine. But Deleuze silently trespasses precisely this individual limit in his appropriation of *affectus*. Not that he posits some sort of telepathy through which the other's affect would become immediately accessible to me. Affect remains a passage between two states, between two affections, just as it is for Spinoza, but Deleuze's affect doesn't pass between two states of an individual body the nature of which, according to Spinoza, remains unaffected (its maximum threshold). It now takes place, rather, between at least two heterogeneous bodies. In the most prominent case of *What Is Philosophy?*, between the human and the nonhuman: 'Affect is not the passage from one lived state to another, but rather the becoming nonhuman of the human' (QP 173|173).

Once again, at least not – or perhaps especially not – for what concerns affect, Deleuze isn't simply a Spinozist. From one becoming to the other, from *affectus* to *l'affect*, from Deleuze's first few and tentative translations of *affectus* as *l'affect* in *Spinoza and the Problem of Expression* (where he largely and ultimately favours *sentiment*, that is, 'feeling') to the defining role he and Guattari give affect within the artistic discipline in *What Is Philosophy?*, the path is neither simply continuous nor absolutely broken. For more reasons than I'll develop or even suggest, Deleuze's displacement of the inner and individual limit of becoming makes him both more and less Spinozist than Spinoza. He betrays Spinoza, both exposits and crosses, and this betrayal marks a mobile and porous border between Deleuze the commentator, historian or professor and Deleuze the thinker and creator. The creation in this case, however, doesn't concern the creation of affects, which would make Deleuze an artist; rather, the stakes bear upon the very idea of affect and, thus, upon *the creation of art* as *the creation of affects*. In a sense, as *What Is Philosophy?* defines it, art takes place in the space opened by Deleuze's betrayal of Spinoza's affect.

On the one hand, no Spinozist could be more loyal. Far from simply countering or critiquing Spinoza, Deleuze delimits affect and extends it where Spinoza himself never dared. Beyond the human and beyond the animal, between them, Deleuze and Guattari describe becoming as a 'zone of indetermination' or 'indiscernibility' (QP 174|173, 183|182). This zone, moreover, would only be possible on a plane of immanence that, according to Deleuze, irrupts in the history of philosophy for the first time in the *Ethics*. Between two beings, between *any* two beings, affect is possible only if there's no ontological hierarchy to prevent certain beings from relating or to dictate their relation in advance. It makes little difference that Deleuze and Guattari reserve the term *plane of immanence* for philosophy and *plane of composition* for art. The terms are solidary, if not perfectly synonymous. Only when no higher or hidden unity on a transcendent plane guides the composition of bodies in advance can composition develop in its own right, without guarantee, to no end. Any composition that composes without losing its compositeness to a totality that precedes and/or absorbs it, in other words, takes place on a plane of immanence or not at all. This applies to artistic composition or to the composition of bodies in the Spinozist system. Which is why, in the text in which Deleuze first coins the formulation 'plane of immanence' and thus long before he attributes the plane of immanence to philosophy and the plane of composition to art, he also refers to the plane of immanence as 'a plane of composition' (SPP 169|128). Hence, when Deleuze and Guattari give the plane of composition its greatest scope, they refer to it as 'a plane of composition *of Being*' (QP 190|189, my emphasis). Albeit aesthetically, not conceptually, art operates at the same ontological and univocal level as philosophy.

On the other hand, by removing affect from its corporal solipsism, Deleuze also removes it from the Spinozist horizon. Passages from the commentator and the creator jar when juxtaposed:

> 'Affectio refers to a state of an affected body . . . , while *affectus* refers to the passage from one state to another' (SPP 67|49).

> 'Affect is not the passage from one lived state to another, but rather the becoming nonhuman of the human' (QP 173|173).

No longer the passage from one lived state to another, which is the very definition of *affectus* according to Spinoza according to Deleuze, *affect* is now the passage from one to an other, the becoming other of the affected, the becoming nonhuman of the human. The passage between lived states for Spinoza passes between heterogeneities for Deleuze and Guattari. This is perhaps why, at the most original moment of Deleuze's longstanding engagement with the specifically Spinozist problem of affect, at the moment he ceases to comment upon *affectus* in the *Ethics* and deploys *l'affect* for his own theory with Guattari in chapter 7 of *What Is Philosophy?*, the name 'Spinoza' disappears.[14]

The same betrayal clarifies how I can become while neither ceasing to be nor subordinating becoming to my being. Becoming isn't simply transformation because affect, for Deleuze, is the passage *between* (at least) two individuals, two bodies, two heterogeneities that therefore reduces to neither of the two. The result is a double exteriorisation of affect through the creation of a 'zone' in which, without simply fusing or transforming, affecting and affected become indiscernible: 'unity or reversibility of what feels [*du sentant*] and what is felt [*du senti*]' (QP 179|179).[15] Hence, the affect would never take place without me, without my body, without my body's affection, but it exceeds the latter and remains independent of it. That I become does not require I cease to be. My dance need not end.

Immaterial Material

Deleuze doesn't thereby resolve the antinomy of affect, however, so much as expand the jurisdiction of the law I named after him. The expansion is double:

– *being becomes irrelevant*. If becoming takes place *between* at least two bodies of which one is my own, then my 'own' becoming becomes indifferent to me, to my being, to what I continue to be. Becoming only becomes when being is displaced, bracketed if not removed, put in parentheses: 'Sensible becoming is the act by which something or someone ceaselessly becomes-other (while continuing to be what they are)' (cited above). Otherwise, I and my continued being risk being not only irrelevant, not only even insufficient, but also inhibitive. In *Kafka* and in *Francis Bacon*, in literature and in painting, with and without Guattari, Deleuze argues in the same vein that becoming-animal has essential limits, that it remains too 'terri-torialized' or too 'figurative', that it ultimately gives way to a deeper becoming-imperceptible (K 27–8|14–15 and 67|37, FB 33|27). The point hardens: becoming only truly becomes becoming, only truly becomes, when the beings in which it originates (the states, the affec-tions, human or animal) disappear. Only when any remaining being ceases to obscure becoming does becoming-other, becoming-animal, truly become by becoming becoming-imperceptible.

– *becoming becomes being.* As a becoming that takes place between heterogeneous bodies to which it remains irreducible, affect gains an autonomy that philosophy never willingly or wittingly grants it. The ascetic tradition regularly presupposes that a determined being (for instance a human being) precedes the sensations that it has. Which, for a sensible being, would seem the only logical possibility: I have *to be*, I have to be a *being*, before I can be affected. Even when empiricism is most empirical, for instance, even when Hume determines personal identity as a fictional effect of a certain *feeling* through what he calls 'contemplation', he retrojects someone prior to the uncanny feeling to whom he might attribute the feeling. He even gives this pre-personal person a name, the first name, the name of the person who would name everything else: 'Adam'.[16] As a result, sensation – even the most originary and productive – becomes sec-ondary, accidental, subordinated to the being that has it and, more generally, to the being that it doesn't have ('becoming' in the Platonic or pre-Deleuzian sense). In truth, sensation becomes secondary twice: secondary to the body that is itself, already or in the end, secondary to the mind, to the spirit, to the soul. But Deleuze and Guattari break from the tradition by holding that sensation, affect, becoming enjoys an autonomy that no longer depends upon any being that pre-exists it. Even if affect derives from affections, it remains independent of them. The formulation with which Deleuze and Guattari mark this autonomy is lapidary: 'a being of sensation' (QP 164|164). Not *the sensation of a being*, understood either as the sensation received from a being that affects me or the sensation belonging to a being to which it is secondary, but rather *a being of sensation*. Sensation *is* the being.

This autonomy of affect, then, goes well beyond the independence from intention and meaning for which, for instance, Ruth Leys cri-tiques it. Which isn't to say her critique doesn't hold more generally.

If one extends her terms to their broadest possible sense, when Leys argues that the definition and valorisation of affect in opposition and detriment to intention and meaning ultimately submits to 'a classical dualism of mind and body' (Leys 455), she broaches – without recognising it as such – the general risk run by affect theory at every turn: a more or less sterile reversal of Platonism.

Heidegger imposes himself here, not only because he warns of the surreptitious inefficacy of a 'reversal' or 'inversion' that leaves the oppositional structure intact, but also because he locates Nietzsche's reversal of Platonism in bodily becoming.[17] The apparent opposition between being and becoming, Heidegger says, structures philosophy since the Greeks. Hegel takes a decisive step toward the end of metaphysics by sublating this opposition and thereby in a sense preserving becoming. Yet, because he does so supersensuously, by raising becoming into being via the absolute Idea, he takes only a first step toward the end. Only Nietzsche takes the *final final* step by permanentising becoming itself into being. This path alone, for Heidegger, constitutes the proper or authentic fulfilment of metaphysics (*das eigentliche Vollendung*) because only thus does the sensuous truly 'usurp' the supersensuous that Hegel's sublation keeps intact. In 'The Eternal Recurrence of the Same and the Will to Power', a lecture written (but never delivered) in 1939 to conclude the three seminars he had delivered on Nietzsche in the preceding years,[18] Heidegger writes: 'Nietzsche, inverting Platonism, transposes Becoming to the "vital" sphere [*das »Lebendige«*], as the chaos that "bodies forth" [*das »leibende« Chaos*]. That inversion, extinguishing as it does the opposition of Being and Becoming, constitutes the fulfillment proper' (GA 6.2:12|*Nietzsche* III:172).

If affect theory still invests in the opposition between mind and body, if the affective turn merely turns Platonism on its head, if it valorises the body or the sensuous over any variant of the intelligible or supersensuous (being, mind, meaning, consciousness, intention), then it hovers in Nietzsche's twilight. Philosophy outlives itself, over a century after its end, as affect theory. Amplified and aggravated, all the consequences that Heidegger draws from Nietzsche's fundamental metaphysical position would transpose onto the affective turn (meaninglessness, nihilism, abandonment and so on). Leys, to her credit, carefully brackets Deleuze before elaborating her critique of his legacy: 'Probably the most influential figure in the rise of the new affect theory is Deleuze, but it is invariably an open question as to the accuracy with which one or another affect theory represents his views. I shall leave this question to the side' (Leys 441 note 20). What, then, of Deleuze? Does he re-extinguish the opposition between being and becoming by making becoming a being of sensation? Does his conception of art as the creation of affects linger at the end of philosophy? Deleuze often says the end of philosophy never concerned him (e.g., P 122|88), but his insouciance might turn into a liability in the end.

A generous response might insist that, though the sensuous seems 'to usurp' the supersensuous, Deleuze resists the Heideggerian schema at every turn. He doesn't debase the supersensuous into the sensuous (like Heidegger's Nietzsche) because the superiority of the supersensible revalorises, autonomises, ontologises the sensible as 'a being of sensation'. Nor, however, does he simply raise the sensuous to the supersensuous (like Heidegger's Hegel) because affect is always an effect of the bodies, the affections, the lived experience from which it remains distinct. Even as a 'pure concept', Deleuze insists, sensation remains 'strictly inseparable from the passage from one concrete to another [*d'un concret à un autre*]' (DRF 339–40|363). In the *Logic of Sense*, Deleuze credits the Stoics with 'the first great reversal of Platonism', not because they reset the sensuous above the supersensuous, but rather because they forge a notion of the incorporeal that – unlike Plato's immutable Idea – results from the interaction of bodies (LS 16–17|7).[19] This 'reversal', accordingly, doesn't readily conform to the Heideggerian schema.

A more critical response, however, might stress that Deleuze speaks of sensation, the tradition of the supersensuous, but both sensation and the supersensuous reduce the body. Deleuze ontologises *affect*, after all, only by bracketing the *affections* upon which it depends. Which isn't to say Deleuze naively relapses into the tradition over which he seems to leap. The consequences are far more brutal because, if indeed both Deleuze and the tradition disembody, they don't disembody the same body.

The ascetic tradition reduces the body *because* the body is reducible. A 'living tomb', Plato says even in his most sensual dialogue (*Phaedrus* 250c). If philosophers consider the body nothing, though grounds for doing so might vary, then they lose nothing upon losing it. On the contrary, they gain everything. Plato is only one of the first references in this sense. Others are dearer to affect theory. Even after positing corporality as a divine attribute (IP14C2–IP15S), even after opening the substantial perspective from which the mind *is* the body (IIP7S), even after positing that the mind is nothing but the idea of the body (IIP13), even Spinoza reaches the freedom toward which the *Ethics* progresses from the beginning only upon broaching 'the Mind's duration [*Mentis durationem*] without relation to the Body's existence [*Corporis existentiam*]' (VP20S, translation modified). In fact, the mind doesn't wait for humans to reach or fail to reach freedom to claim its privilege. Deleuze himself recognises a threefold structural 'privilege' of the attribute of thought: although there are infinite attributes, (1) only thought – divine thought, if not human – has an idea of the other attributes; (2) only thought has an idea of itself, that is, of the attribute it is; (3) only thought has an idea of the divine substance in which all attributes meet (SPP 92|89; see also SPE chapter VII). Even when Spinoza appears to privilege the body over the mind insofar as it orients inquiries into the mind whose object it is (*Ethics* IIP13S, IIIP2S and so on), the corporal privilege is only provisional because it ultimately aims at extending the mental: 'it is a matter of acquiring a knowledge of the powers of the body *in order*' – my stress – 'to discover in parallel fashion powers of the mind that escape consciousness' (SPP 94|90). Deleuze can deny idealism here but, ultimately, this asymmetry between mind and body allows the mind to survive the body; it even allows the body to survive itself in the mind, in the ideality of an idea, in incorporeality. No immanence separates Spinoza from Plato in this regard.

Deleuze and Guattari reduce the body *even though* the body is irreducible. The becoming-whale of Ahab takes place in neither Ahab's body nor the whale's but, because it takes place between them, it would never take place without them. In fact, Deleuze and Guattari stipulate at least three bodies: the two (or more) bodies caught in the becoming and the materiality of the artwork that creatively incarnates the becoming. Melville's words and syntax create the affect passing between the bodies of Ahab and the whale, but the affect isn't the materiality of Melville's style either, Deleuze and Guattari say, 'at least in principle' (QP 166|166).[20] In light of which the bodily reduction at work in Deleuze's notion of affect sets a new precedent. Not despite or in addition to but precisely because of the radicality of their rupture, Deleuze and Guattari become *more traditional than the tradition itself*. Their reduction reduces more and makes a greater sacrifice than anything the tradition offers. Perhaps they alone reduce anything at all. If indeed the body is or will have been nothing to a philosopher, the philosopher reduces nothing upon reducing it. To reduce the reducible reduces nothing; only the irreducible is really reducible, and only Deleuze and Guattari reduce it.

More brutally still: precisely because the body remains irreducible, because the Sensation (*la Sensation*) is 'in the body' (FB 40|35), because one grasps the event only via its inscription 'in the flesh' (LS 188|161), because '[a]ffects always presuppose affections from which they derive' (CC 174|140), because the affect must be wrested from affections (QP 167|167), all the more so because the material plane rises and reinvades the sensation (QP 166|166), Deleuze and Guattari never reduce the irreducible body once and for all. Affect suppresses the body – every-body – time and again, again and again, *ad infinitum.* In light of which labels like 'materialist' and 'idealist' no longer suffice. It isn't even enough, for instance, to say Deleuze is *less* materialist than the *most* idealist philosopher or vice versa. *Neither* the materialist *nor* the idealist reading of Deleuze is *either* incorrect *or* correct because only an account of *both* the antagonism *and* the inseparability of *both* matter *and* idea – both *affection* and *affect* – can make the brutality of Deleuze's immaterial materialism felt.[21]

Notes

1. On this corporal scale, see Spinoza, *Ethics* IIL7S: 'the whole of nature is one Individual, whose parts, i.e., all bodies, vary in infinite ways, without any change of the whole Individual'.
2. 'It was on Spinoza that I worked most seriously according to the norms of the history of philosophy, but it was he who had the greatest effect on me as a gust of air that pushes you from behind each time you read him' (D 22|15).
3. See Derrida, *Marges* 129–64 (especially 144–7)|*Margins* 109–36 (especially 121–3).
4. Spinoza is the only 'formidable philosophical precursor' that Massumi names for 'the project of thinking affect' (*Parables* 28).
5. In *Descartes' 'Principles of Philosophy'* (or, more precisely, in the 'Appendix Containing Metaphysical Thoughts'), Spinoza critiques classifications of genus and species as a 'being of reason' and, thus, any specious understanding of man as a being of reason (I:300–1). Beings of reason are ultimately modes of thinking; they facilitate mental operations like memory and thus remain practically legitimate but, because they have no object in reality, they become problematic when taken for truth. Spinoza critiques beings of reason, accordingly, not merely for generating an illusory 'human essence' but rather, more precisely, for failing to explain it.
6. All five antinomies with which Ronald de Sousa introduces emotion

as a philosophical hub in the opening chapter of *The Rationality of Emotion*, along with their axiological 'analogue' he calls 'ambivalence' (de Sousa 17), fall under the jurisdiction of only one law in the antinomy I've outlined here, namely, the Spinozist. In chapter 2, de Sousa sketches the maladaptation of emotion to past models of personhood, not to liberate emotion from personhood, but rather to improve the adaptation, and every subsequent chapter solidifies the gesture in one way or another. Rather than the limits within which he situates emotion, however, it would be tempting to stress the proliferation of antinomies that arise even on only one side of the more general antinomy of affect, but de Sousa – like Kant – never seems to doubt their resolvability (de Sousa 9 and 328).

7. At least three more reasons would add to this hesitation. I relegate them to an endnote because they anticipate analyses from subsequent sections of this chapter. That these points appear to contradict each other only indicates the difficulty of grasping exactly what Deleuze and Guattari mean by 'affect'.

1. Affects involve animals at least as much as humans. They 'grip every animal in a becoming no less powerful than that of the human being with the animal' (MP 295|241). Derrida cites this passage ('Transcendental Stupidity' 38), but it doesn't seem to stop him from seeing Deleuze and Guattari's becoming as strictly anthropomorphic.

2. The animal itself isn't in question in the becoming but, then, neither is the human. Affect takes place *between* the human and the animal, between little Hans and the horse, to both of which it therefore remains irreducible: 'Is there a still unknown assemblage [*agencement*] that would be neither that of Hans nor that of the horse but, rather, that of the becoming-horse of Hans?' (MP 315|258).

3. Deleuze and Guattari distinguish becoming from all anthropomorphic projection: 'it is not a question of imitating the horse, of "playing" horse, of identifying with it, or even feeling sentiments of pity or sympathy' (MP 315|258).

For the corresponding passage of the seminar from which Derrida compiles his text on Deleuze, see *La bête* 195 ff.|*Beast* 141 ff.

8. One could confirm Deleuze's lingering humanism through his various calls, with and without Guattari, for a new human. If the dissolved self common to *Difference and Repetition* (4|xxi), *Logic of Sense* (166|141, 249|213) and *Anti-Oedipus* (438|362), for instance, marks the end of the 'human' as we know it (as it knows itself), all three books nevertheless end the human for the sake of another: *Difference and Repetition*, for a 'man without name' (DR 121|90); *Logic of Sense*, for 'the free man' (LS 179|152); *Anti-Oedipus*, for 'men of desire' (AŒ 158|131). Deleuze, too, thus conforms to the long list of philosophers who implicitly subscribe to the double 'end' of man.

These passages alone suffice to reveal the remarkable negligence conditioning appeals to Deleuze for support in a 'posthuman' discourse. Rosi Braidotti's *The Posthuman* is exemplary in this regard twice over. She not only takes Spinoza's monistic premises concerning a single substance as 'the building blocks' for a posthuman theory that 'carefully avoids anthropocentrism' (Braidotti 56), thus missing the fundamental anthropocentrism that Spinoza substantiates; she also calls the subjective and epistemic transformations that accompany posthuman theory 'becomings' (becoming-animal, becoming-earth, becoming-machine) with explicit reference to Deleuze and Guattari (Braidotti 66). She claims to remain 'very independent' of Deleuze and Guattari – without ever elaborating their theory of becoming, the necessity of her recourse to it or her independence from it – but her 'independence' never questions the generally posthuman and specifically post-anthropocentric posture of becoming according to Deleuze and Guattari.

9. Schaefer's approach is emblematic in this regard not only because he takes responsibility for 'the evolution of affect theory' but also and more particularly because his critique of Deleuze hinges upon a critique of becoming: 'I argue that a theory of affect *and power* can't work if affect is defined as *becoming*' (Schaefer 2). When he in turn argues that affect must be understood in terms of 'becoming and being' (Schaefer 2), however, he doesn't seem to realise that, if I continue to be what I am when I become, becoming never simply opposes being. See also Schaefer 13 and 28–9.

10. See the opening lines of 'The Method of Dramatization', a 1968 synthesis of his research presented to the *Société française de philosophie* shortly before his defence of *Difference and Repetition*: 'It is not certain that the question *what is?* is a good question for discovering essence or the Idea. It might be that questions of the type: *who?, how many?, how?, where?, when?* are better – both for discovering essence and for determining something more important concerning the Idea' (ID 131|94). See also Ferdinand Alquié's response in the discussion following Deleuze's presentation (ID 147–50|105–7).

11. Though not the former, Deleuze uses the latter formulation in SPE 199|219.

12. Compare the second session of Deleuze's *Cours sur Spinoza* (9 December 1980, especially the first recording, 35' ff.).

13. See first of all *Spinoza and the Problem of Expression*, chapter 14, 'What Can a Body Do?' (SPE 197–213|217–34).

14. Deleuze and Guattari refer to Spinoza's distinction between *affectio* and *affectus* only in passing in chapter 6, 'Prospects and Concepts' (QP 154|154), but it is legible throughout chapter 7 and the book at large.

15. See also QP 174|173. Other emphases would require dwelling upon the literal but oblique reference to *Matter and Memory* in which (especially

in chapter 1) Bergson uses the formulation 'zone of indetermination' to describe a cerebral mediation that delays the inevitable reaction to sensory stimuli, which gains the organism time to call upon memories and choose the best course of action.

16. See Chapter 2 above.

17. On the reversal of Platonism: 'To overturn Platonism thus means to reverse the standard relation: what languishes [*steht*] below in Platonism, as it were, and would be measured against the supersensuous, must now be put on top; by way of reversal, the supersensuous must now be placed in its service. When the inversion is fully executed [*Vollzug*], the sensuous becomes being proper [*eigentlich Seienden*], i.e., the true, i.e., truth. The true is the sensuous [*das Sinnliche*]' (Heidegger, GA 6.1:156|*Nietzsche* I:154).

On the limit of the reversal of Platonism: 'What is needed is neither the abolition of the sensuous nor abolition of the nonsensuous. On the contrary, what must be cast aside is the misinterpretation, the deprecation, of the sensuous [*des Sinnlichen*], as well as the extravagant elevation of the supersensuous [*des Übersinnlichen*]. A path must be cleared for a new interpretation of the sensuous on the basis of a new hierarchy [*Rangordnung*] of the sensuous and nonsensuous. The new hierarchy does not simply wish to reverse matters within the old structural order [*alten Ordnungsschemas*], now reverencing [*hochschätzen*] the sensuous and scorning [*geringschätzen*] the nonsensuous. It does not wish to put what was at the very bottom on the very top. A new hierarchy and new valuation mean that the ordering *structure* [*Ordnungs*schema] changes. To that extent, overturning [*Umdrehung*] Platonism must become a twisting free [*Herausdrehung*] of it' (Heidegger, GA 6.1:212–13|*Nietzsche* I:209–10, translation slightly modified).

Which is not say that Nietzsche 'overturns' without ever 'twisting free' of Platonism (see Heidegger, GA 6.1:202–4|*Nietzsche* I:200–1) or, in turn, that Heidegger frees his own thought of all naivety when it comes to affect. For instance, see my reserves concerning Heidegger's concept of anxiety in Chapters 1 and 3 above.

18. See Heidegger, GA 6.1:594 note; for an English translation, see *Nietzsche* III:ix–x.

19. I'll address affect in *Logic of Sense* in my conclusion below.

20. Here, I return to the more brutal consequences of the immaterialist streak I broached as a question of style in the last section of Chapter 3 above.

21. Donovan Schaefer critiques Deleuze's affect for lacking concreteness (Schaefer 4 *et passim*); Eugenie Brinkema critiques Deleuze's affect for 'holding tight' to the body (Brinkema 24–5). While Marc B. N. Hansen argues that Deleuze abandons the body ('Affect as Medium, or the "Digital-facial-image"'), Richard Rushton argues that Deleuze liberates

affect ('Response to Marc B. N. Hansen'). Peter Hallward focuses upon Deleuze's idealism, Darren Ambrose upon his materialism. Slavoj Žizek thematises the incompatibility of Deleuze's materialism and his idealism (Žižek 19), while Brian Massumi slips insensibly from 'irreducibly bodily' affects to affects irreducible to the body (*Parables* 28 and 35). The point in all these pairings isn't to intervene on one side or the other in favour of embodiment or disembodiment, idealism or materialism, their conflict or their unity. None is outright wrong, and each has its strength, but they all revolve around a common oversight. Anyone who focuses upon Deleuze's materialism, anyone who focuses upon Deleuze's idealism, anyone who recognises his materialism and his idealism but separates or unites them, everyone misses the endless *brutality* of their interaction.

6

Deleuze and the First 'Ethics'

If, however, you still ask what can move you to perform the act I call virtuous rather than the other, I reply that I cannot know what way, of the infinitely many there are, God uses to determine you to such works.

Spinoza, Letter to Willem van Blijenbergh
13 March 1665 (I:389–90)

Although in *What Is Philosophy?* Deleuze sets out to clarify why, for him, Spinoza is the prince of philosophers, *What Is Philosophy?* isn't his final word on Spinoza. Here in Chapter 6, however, I conclude with 'Spinoza and the Three "Ethics"', the last text of his last book,[1] not simply for the sake of exhaustion, a principle to which I neither have claimed nor could. The culminating text is indispensable here, rather, because it hardens the paradox structuring the latter part of this book: the most philosophical philosopher, Spinoza, is also the least and even not philosophical at all. Ostensibly, in Deleuze's earlier accounts, nothing in principle prevents Spinoza from holding both titles. On the contrary, the disciplinary difference between the philosophical 'concept' and the non-philosophical 'affect' would seem to displace any conflict before it could arise. Both, moreover, presuppose the immanence that, for Deleuze and Guattari, Spinoza alone achieves. In 'Spinoza and the Three "Ethics"', however, affect and concept do indeed conflict, although 'conflict' is only part of the story. As the first 'Ethics', affect both grounds and hobbles the progress of Spinoza's system toward its philosophical achievement in the third. Which isn't to say Deleuze is wrong. On the contrary, one could perhaps say of Deleuze with respect to the paradox of Spinoza what Bataille says of Hegel with respect to sacrifice: he didn't know how right he was (Bataille, *Œuvres* XII:32).

One More Hitch

When he returns to the *Ethics* after *What Is Philosophy?* in 'Spinoza and the Three "Ethics"', once again – at least apparently – explicating

Spinoza's system rather than creating his own, Deleuze redistributes basic elements he and Guattari borrowed in *What Is Philosophy?*

> The *Ethics* presents three elements, which are not only contents but also forms of expression: Signs or affects; Notions or concepts; Essences or percepts. They correspond to the three genres of knowledge, which are also modes of existence and expression. (CC 172|138)

Affect, concept and percept: rather than the disciplines of philosophy (as the creation of concepts) and art (as the creation of percepts and affects), these three elements, along with the genres of knowledge and modes of expression that correspond to them, now constitute the three 'Ethics' of 'Spinoza and the Three "Ethics"'.[2]

The first Ethics unfolds in the scholia and bears upon affections and affects that, despite their hermetic distinction in *What Is Philosophy?*, Deleuze groups together here. Deleuze already associates scholium and affect in *Spinoza and the Problem of Expression* and never ceases to insist that Spinoza writes the scholia in a style, a tone, even a language (all Deleuze's terms) that differ from that of the rest of the *Ethics*.[3] Less demonstrative, less 'geometric', the style of composition suits the genre of knowledge it describes. Deleuze associates affect and affection with 'signs' because they pertain to an external body's effect upon my own. A body affects me and yields an image or idea that indicates the nature of my body and the body that affects it. Spinoza insists that any affection indicates the nature of my body more than that of the body that affects it (*Ethics* IIP16C2), but no sign – no affect or affection, no impression, no image or idea – ever yields an adequate idea of my body (IIP27), my mind (IIP29) or *a fortiori* the body that affects it (IIP25). Less still the idea of the body – the 'mind' – that affects my own. Hence, sensible signs pertain only to the first level of knowledge, which Spinoza calls 'knowledge from random experience [*cognitionem ab experientiâ vagâ*]', 'opinion', 'imagination' (IIP40S2).[4] First in this instance means lowest. Based on everyday encounters over which we have little control, if any, and therefore never systematically accessible or reliable, *experientiâ vagâ* would be more economically and literally translated as *vague experience* (Bernard Pautrat gives *expérience vague* in his French translation) since the word 'vague' embraces not only the sense of 'random' or 'wandering' or 'vagabond' but also 'unclear', 'opaque' or – in Spinozist terms – 'inadequate'. The first genre of knowledge nevertheless constitutes a genre of knowledge because a sign can be correct, as when I read certain signs in a reliable book (Spinoza's example), but it's never entirely adequate because this knowledge isn't based on any conception or perception of the cause of what I thereby come to know. For the same reason, however, the first genre not only proves inadequate; it also causes falsity. It is *the* cause of falsity, more accurately, *'the* only *cause of falsity'* (IIP41, my reemphasis). The point will be decisive for everything that follows.

The second Ethics unfolds under the other headings of the *Ethics*: definitions, axioms, demonstrations, corollaries. Properly 'geometric', it covers the majority of the *Ethics* at large and has for its object what Spinoza calls 'common notions' or what Deleuze calls 'concepts'. Through the latter, I no longer grasp a body according to signs produced in the vague affections of daily experience but, rather, according to the movements and rests that constitute it. Notions common to all bodies, indeed, motion and rest constitute the first axiom of Spinoza's excursion into the physiology of bodies in the second part of the *Ethics*: 'All bodies either move or are at rest.' Once again, style and genre correspond. Notwithstanding certain syncopations, the style of the second *Ethics* can be properly geometric, demonstrative, linear and ultimately unified because it no longer treats the obscure domain of signs. This second genre of knowledge is the first, in truth, since it's the first of the three that, for Spinoza, is necessarily true (IIP41). Because common notions provide the basic building blocks of all reasoning, he calls this second genre 'reason' (IIP40S2; see also IIP40S1).

The third Ethics takes place only in Part V and, even then, only in part. If the first *Ethics* isn't yet geometric, the third is no longer geometric because, while it unfolds under the same headings (demonstrations, corollaries and so on), it isn't entirely demonstrative, deductive or even discursive. It no longer grasps the body through affect or concept, sign or common notion, imagination or reason, but rather through what Spinoza calls 'intuitive knowledge [*scientiam intuitivam*]' (IIP40S2) or what Deleuze calls 'percept', evidently on the basis of the etymology of 'intuition', confirmed by the 'eyes of the mind' in the *Ethics* (V23S) and the *Theological-Political Treatise* (II:260), and in participial analogy with 'affect'. The 'object' is neither the obscure effect of a foreign body on my own in random encounters nor the constitutive movements and rests common to all bodies; intuition or percept contemplates the essence of a body in conjunction with the divine attribute of corporality it modifies. Not vague effects on a body (a sign), not even the essence of bodies in general (a common notion), at stake is 'the very essence of any singular thing [*ipsâ essentiâ rei cujuscunque singularis*]' (*Ethics* VP36S), which is why Deleuze speaks somewhat counter-intuitively of 'Essence' and 'Singularity' interchangeably. Style and genre also correspond here in the third and ultimate knowledge because, just as essence moves between a singular body and God or Nature at 'infinite speeds' that defy the patient steps of deduction and even 'all orders of discursiveness' (Deleuze, CC 185|149), the third *Ethics* unfolds through hiatuses, ellipses and contractions.

The percept circumscribes the most significant topological redistribution from *What Is Philosophy?* to 'Spinoza and the Three "Ethics"'. In Deleuze's appropriation of Spinoza's terms in *What Is Philosophy?*, art names the discipline that creates 'sensations', which is to say, 'percepts' and 'affects'. In Deleuze's exposition of Spinoza's system in 'Spinoza and the Three "Ethics"', the percept names the third genre of knowledge, the noblest, the contemplation of body and mind and Nature at infinite speeds. Even if it doesn't bear the name 'percept', however, the third knowledge isn't absent from *What Is Philosophy?* On the contrary, there is philosophy only if there is percept. In *What Is Philosophy?* Deleuze and Guattari call Spinoza 'the prince of philosophers', credit him with completing or achieving (*achever*) philosophy, only and precisely through what Deleuze calls the percept in 'Spinoza and the Three "Ethics"'. Spinoza, they say, 'made the movement of the infinite and gave thought infinite speeds in the third genre of knowledge, in the last book of the *Ethics*' (QP 51|48). The interdisciplinary task in this instance would be to relate Spinoza's infinite philosophical speeds to the artistic percept. The result would inevitably reiterate the 'paradox' around which the latter half of this book revolves: the most philosophical philosopher – Spinoza – is also not philosophical at all.

The cryptic comments in *What Is Philosophy?*, however, take for granted the third genre of knowledge they celebrate. Spinoza made the infinite movement and achieved philosophy, past tense, period. Citing only the result, Deleuze and Guattari praise Spinoza from a structural perspective that hides a genetic problem with which Deleuze struggled for nearly three decades. How did Spinoza – how does any Spinozist – reach the third genre, the percept, the third *Ethics*? The three genres of knowledge aren't simply contemporaneous, although Deleuze at times presents them as such and although Spinoza himself presents each as an epistemic genre (*genus*). Even if the movement is never unilateral or irreversible, never continuous or complete, even if percept already transluminates the first *Ethics* and affect still haunts the third (CC 183|148 and 187|151), the three *Ethics* constitute a chain running from the first genre of knowledge to the third, from sign to essence, from affect to percept.[5] They are contemporaneous only after they are sequential. If Spinoza wears the crown in *What Is Philosophy?*, 'Spinoza and the Three "Ethics"' chronicles his ascent. In the same stroke, it gives full scope to Deleuze's insistence, easily mistaken for a scholastic technicality, that Spinoza doesn't start with the idea of the most perfect being – of God – but must reach it as quickly as possible.[6] For if Spinoza completes philosophy, if he's the only philosopher because the only truly philosophical philosopher in the history of philosophy, then philosophy itself depends upon this genetic chain.

And thus upon affect first of all.

On the one hand, as far as possible, both affect and affection must be overcome. In *What Is Philosophy?*, there's no hierarchy between affect and percept in art or, more generally, between art as the creation of affects and percepts and philosophy as the creation of concepts. No hierarchy, in short, between affects, percepts and concepts. They are distinct but equal, that is, equally pensive: they all constitute forms of thinking. Arguably, for that reason, only in *What Is Philosophy?* does 'affect' come into its own: not enchained and certainly not the weakest link leading to a finality meant to leave it behind, affect co-operates the discipline of art and enjoys an irreducibility guaranteed by and constitutive of disciplinarity. Even if, as I argue in Chapter 5, the onto-autonomy of affect poses other problems in turn. 'Spinoza and the Three "Ethics"' incidentally gives reason for focusing on *What Is Philosophy?* as Deleuze's definitive statement on affect. Affect, concept and percept no longer think equally; affects constitute the lowest level of knowledge and, of the three, only they produce not only inadequate but also even false ideas. If affects constitute a primordial form of thinking in *What Is Philosophy?*, they hardly think at all in the 'Three "Ethics"'. Thinking begins rigorously, adequately, truly only after affects in the second and third genres of knowledge. Deleuze, of course, is aware: 'It thus seems that, if signs-affects intervene in the *Ethics*, it is only to be severely critiqued, denounced' (CC 179|144).

On the other hand, the chain will have been a chain only by way of affect. The enchainment of the chain, in other words, necessitates affect. On these grounds, Deleuze denies that Spinoza simply critiques or denounces signs or affects in the *Ethics*.

It thus seems that, if signs-affects intervene in the *Ethics*, it is only to be severely critiqued, denounced. [. . .] But when one asks *how* we manage to form a concept, or how we regress from effects to causes, it is indeed necessary for certain signs at least to serve as a trampoline and for certain affects to give us the necessary momentum (book V). (CC 179|144)

Catherine Malabou thus dismisses Deleuze too quickly when, in her attempt to recuperate a symbolic space in Spinoza through a certain necessity of 'signs', she accuses Deleuze of simply rejecting signs for their inadequacy.[7] The distinction between adequacy and inadequacy no longer suffices to describe or circumscribe the first necessity of affect that Deleuze pronounces here. The passage through concepts is also necessary, to be sure, but it would be a mistake to think that the adequacy of concepts makes them more necessary than affects. Genetically, the concept's adequacy only intensifies affect's necessity. For the concept and its adequacy depend upon affect insofar as the distinction between adequacy and inadequacy only becomes possible from the perspective of concepts that one only reaches by way of affect. Concept and percept *and* adequacy and inadequacy lie at the genetic mercy of affect.

The stakes are familiar. As I show in Chapter 1, Deleuze calls sensibility the 'royal faculty' in *Difference and Repetition* (DR 198|152) on the same genetic grounds: like affect in the three 'Ethics', sensibility constitutes the first link in the facultative 'chain' upon which all philosophy hinges. Although Deleuze formulates affect's privilege as the genetic origin twenty-six years later in the 'Three "Ethics"' more modestly, the platform remains the same. At least two points, however, temper Deleuze's recuperation of affect in advance.

First, the value of affect as a 'trampoline' would lie exclusively elsewhere, any and everywhere else, in concepts and percepts. Affect would ultimately have no value of or on its own. This alone essentially displaces, if not entirely discredits, Deleuze's revaluation of affect. Affect's worth resides only in the time it takes to reach concepts and percepts. Without a genetic lag between affect and concept, if there were already concepts or percepts by the time there's affect, if the three *Ethics* coincided as Deleuze suggests whenever he adopts a structural perspective, then affects would be less than worthless; they seduce, distract, obstruct. *Either* affect has value *or* the three elements compound simultaneously. Yet, even if the chain takes time to connect and validates affect as a trampoline, affect's temporal value is also only temporary; it will have had no value because, in the end, its value emanates from the later stages to which it leads. The debased basis for percepts, affects are no longer the autonomous being they were in *What Is Philosophy?* The Spinozist has at least this much in common with the Platonist: the only reliable affect effaces itself.

Second, the fundamental position of affect jeopardises the entire chain and thus the very systematicity of the system. If the percept properly achieves or completes philosophy, if philosophy becomes philosophy (and Spinoza the prince and Christ of philosophy) only in the third *Ethics*, then philosophy depends upon the security of every link in the chain, to be sure, but it depends first and most of all upon the chain's first link, the first *Ethics*, affect. As the foremost link, there's affect before there's a chain and thus before there's philosophy. No one is born a Spinozist. There will be philosophy, if at all, only if affect cooperates and bends to the *telos* of percepts. Such that *any* problem of affect, any ambivalence, becomes *the* problem of philosophy. Not a *philosophical* problem. This problem isn't *in* philosophy, whether one conceives the problem – like the tradition – as something that one could solve at a later date with greater rigour and reflection or – like Deleuze – as an irresolvable impetus to think. The problem of affect, rather, constitutes the only problem that problematises philosophy as a whole. Both more and less valuable than the concept and percept it precedes, in a word, affect is *invaluable*.

Deleuze doesn't use the word 'chain' to describe the movement from affect to percept in 'Spinoza and the Three "Ethics"'. Yet, because they link together, he does use the word several times to describe the movement between the three genres of knowledge at the beginning of the eighth session of his *Cours sur Spinoza* (3 February 1981). I insist upon the word not only because the imagery underscores the relation of Spinoza's epistemological 'chain' to the facultative 'chain' in *Difference and Repetition*. I insist upon the word above all because affect constitutes what, with at least two senses in mind, I call the sensible hitch: the first sense refers to the act of or mechanism for fastening, especially to a motive power; the second – and in this case simultaneous – sense refers to hobbling or a sudden halt, a difficulty, a usually unforeseen obstacle. As the first link in the chain that binds the three *Ethics*, the other links depend upon affect. Affect forms only part of the chain and, once constituted, will have been the least important part but, until then, it remains the only part upon which the entire chain hinges. The two senses of 'hitch' are thus inseparable. Indeed, affect is problematic because it's the first and, for a time, only link in the chain. And the problem of affect is amplified *ad infinitum* because the chain, of which affect constitutes the first and at first only link, should lead to the unique and infinite substance, to God, to Nature.

I've said nothing simply against Deleuze. He recognises the difficulties that affect poses for the passage from the first to the later genres of knowledge. But what's difficult isn't impossible. Deleuze never seems to doubt the possibility of moving from the obscurity of signs to the ever purer and more rarefied light of concepts and percepts. His recognition of affect as a problematic origin on the one hand and, on the other, his faith that one will reach the end ambivalate his entire discourse on Spinoza's system.

A Bizarre Sign

How elastic is Deleuze's trampoline? Perhaps nothing signals the stakes more clearly than the determination of all affects and affections as a sign. For all signs are equivocal and, as such, preclude univocity. 'Spinoza and the Three "Ethics"' might mislead in this respect since Deleuze describes equivocity when speaking of hermeneutical or interpretive signs, one of several types, and attributes it to all signs alike somewhat in passing and as only one characteristic among others.

> The characteristics common to all these signs are associability, variability, and equivocity or analogy. [. . .] With respect to interpretations, they are fundamentally equivocal according to the variable association operating between something given [*un donné*] and something that is not given. (CC 174|140)

To read only this late text, then, one would never know that Deleuze first establishes the Spinozist fulfilment of univocal being – immanence – in a more fulsome opposition to equivocity.[8] I recall this more general context, although Deleuze doesn't mention it, because it brings to light the gravity of the more or less implicit charges against the sign and the affect solidary with it, that is, against the 'sign-affect'.

According to Deleuze's most consistent and condensed formulation of univocity, everything said of being (God, substance, so on) is said of beings (creatures, modes, so on) in the same sense. If, for instance, God's goodness transcended the faculties with which I comprehend it and the language in which I express it, if God were so good that my own goodness couldn't compare, then I would have to speak of 'goodness' in at least two senses, the human and the divine, mine in analogy with God's. The abyss between God's goodness and my own equivocates the word 'good'. When I advocate univocity, by contrast, and say 'I am good' and 'God is good', two distinct senses don't bifurcate the 'good' because, albeit far from equally good, God and I are nevertheless 'good' in the same sense.[9]

Consequently, to call any class of sign-affect equivocal already says a great deal. And yet, it doesn't say enough. One body affects another. The affection signals the nature of the affecting and the affected bodies but never yields an adequate idea of either. Without an adequate idea of the cause, I can't stop myself from imagining it and projecting my imaginations upon the real cause. At the limit, I imagine a final and uncaused cause by enlarging or aggrandising what I think affects me to the point that I no longer speak of the sensible, I begin to speak of the supersensible, and I can't speak of the sensible and the supersensible in the same sense. I equivocate.

> The last scalar signs, finally, are imaginary effects: our sensations and perceptions make us think of supersensible beings that would be their final cause, and inversely we imagine [*nous nous figurons*] these beings in the immeasurably enlarged image of what affects us (God as infinite sun, or again as Prince or Legislator). These are *hermeneutical or interpretive* signs. (CC 173–4|140)

By the standards of his own interpretation, Deleuze doesn't go far enough when he calls these signs-affects 'fundamentally equivocal'. More than an instance of equivocity, this class of sign-affect constitutes the very foundation of equivocity in Spinoza's system as Deleuze himself describes it.

One easily understands why Deleuze would reserve the label 'hermeneutical' and 'interpretive' for such extreme signs-affects. Not one interpretation among others, they bear upon or, more precisely, generate the very realm of the supersensible. Nevertheless, because no sign-affect gives an adequate idea of its cause, every sign-affect demands interpretation. All signs equivocate, in other words, and one enters the world of univocity only by leaving the world of signs.[10] All signs. Which is why negative formulations quickly overtake Deleuze's recuperation of the signs-affects to which – this is one example – we're initially 'condemned' (CC 180|145).

The stakes of interpretation would nevertheless remain relatively

DELEUZE AND THE PROBLEM OF AFFECT

negligible if there weren't only affects initially or if, as Malabou seems to think, signs were eventually 'sublated' without remainder in higher genres of knowledge.[11] For a time only affects, only signs, only interpretations are guaranteed. As a result, equivocity must platform univocity. The Spinozist must find a means for *surpassing* the sign *within* it.

He calls it *joy*.

Everything hinges upon this one class of signs. For Spinoza, 'joy' names any affect that increases my power to act, 'sadness' any affect that decreases it (*Ethics*, IIIP11S). Since the mind is nothing but the idea of the body (IIP13), any increase in my power to act increases my power to think. Deleuze argues that, since more joy thus entails more thought, enough joy should make possible my passage from sign to common notion, that is, from the first genre of knowledge to the next and eventually to the third, to the percept, to the infinite speeds of Essence and Singularity that achieve this philosophical movement. Affects don't cease to be the lowest level of knowledge, but one affect in particular constitutes an insurmountable step. Which is no doubt why, already in *Spinoza and the Problem of Expression*, Deleuze goes so far as to call the sense of joy (or its direction – *sens* – since after all a progression is at stake) 'the properly ethical sense' (SPE 251|272). The *Ethics* would lose its sense and sense of direction without joy as both its premise and its promise.

Rather 'bizarre signs', Deleuze says (CS, session seven, first recording, 11'48"). As a passion, joy belongs to the world of signs and thus remains equivocal but, at the same time, it makes possible a departure from the world of signs. Although joy itself yields no adequate ideas, it capacitates me for common notions and adequacy in general. Joy is *exceptionally* equivocal in this sense. It not only equivocates like any other sign. It not only opens equivocity itself because its inadequacy still allows for fabricating divergent registers (the human or sensible and the divine or supersensible), rupturing univocity by bifurcating the sense of words like 'good', 'just' or 'understanding'. Joy also constitutes both an exception to and aggravation of the equivocity it opens because, as the portal to univocity, joy equivocates the very categories of equivocity and univocity. They no longer simply oppose from the genetic point of view since *this* sign, this *equivocity*, this affect also signals the possibility of univocity. Joy demarcates the unsung frontier of univocity and equivocity and as such, beyond anything Deleuze himself says, the site of their traffic, their porosity, their contamination and thus the possible impossibility of everything that pivots upon their purity. Which is to say everything.

The Phenomenologist and the Pantheist

The truth 'requires no sign', Spinoza famously says in the *Emendation* (I:18). But the truth requires no sign because, following Deleuze, it requires a sign that already effaced itself. Joy *designates* truth.

Without detracting from the originality of its deployment in Spinoza's system or Deleuze's genetic interpretation of it, the sign called 'joy' isn't nearly as bizarre as Deleuze seems to think. At least not for the reason he thinks. A sign that reduces itself, a self-abasing sign, signals philosophy's most classical and persistent dream of immediate presence. Be it to the Good, to God, to an object or to myself, presence commands philosophy. Since the sign functions in absence (of the referent, of course, but also of those that emit and receive the sign), it always constitutes first and foremost an obstacle – perhaps the first and foremost obstacle – to presence and thus to philosophy. Caught between the unyielding desire for proximity and the begrudging necessity of mediation, the philosopher doesn't accept the inevitable passage through the sign as an indication that pure presence isn't possible, that a certain distance always conditions presence, but rather seeks signs that debase or destroy themselves in the very act of signifying.

The Spinozist is no exception. What the tradition from the Greeks to Heidegger calls presence, Deleuze calls 'absolute speed', the newest name for philosophy's long pursuit of pure presence. Accordingly, a prior and more profound continuity with the tradition conditions all novelty of the kinetic, kinaesthetic or cinematic approach Deleuze mobilises to break with it. The absolute speed at which the percept moves, the third genre of knowledge according to Deleuze, achieves nothing other than the absolute presence of mode to substance or vice versa, of substance to substance, of mode to mode as immanent effects of substance.

> But essences are pure figures of light: they are themselves "contempla-tions," that is to say, they contemplate as much as they are contemplated in a unity of God, subject, or object (*percept*). Common notions refer to relations of movement and rest that constitute relative speeds; essences, by contrast, are absolute speeds [. . .] absolute speed is the way in which an essence overflies [*survole*] its affects and affections (speed of power) in eternity. (CC 184|148–9)

At absolute speed, there'd be no delay or distance and thus no signs to mediate or to interpret. A sign is mediate, mediation and thus impedance. Yet, since we don't begin at absolute speed, since we're obliged to pass through signs in the affect in order to reach the absence of signs in the percept, since we suffer significant inertia, the Spinozist searches for a self-abasing sign. Optimistic, he calls it joy. As an increase in my power to act and think that trampolines me toward intuiting my singular existence as an immanent effect of God, joy would ultimately enjoy unadulterated self-presence.

Whence the proximity between Deleuze and philosophers whose projects seem to have little in common with his own or even oppose it. This proximity suggests once again that Spinoza isn't the absolutely unique philosopher Deleuze portrays him to be. This time, however, not because he too 'fails' to reach univocity or immanence, as I argue through Deleuze in Chapter 4 above, but rather because of the immanence he would achieve. Rather than culminating the history of philosophy, in this light, Spinoza takes his place within it.

Alongside Husserl, for example.

If every philosopher as a philosopher must eventually negotiate the superfluity of the sign with a necessary passage through it, any could serve as an example here, but I haven't chosen Husserl arbitrarily. An abyss separates Husserl from Spinoza on precisely Deleuze's account. In the history of philosophy as a lineage of more and less successful instaurations of immanence, Deleuze classifies Husserl as a subjectivist philosopher.[12] The decisive distinction falls between immanence *to* and *pure* immanence. Subjectivist philosophers lay a plane of immanence, like all philosophers, but they never reach *pure* immanence because they make the world and everything in it immanent *to* subjectivity. Of course, Husserl distinguishes phenomenological subjectivity from subjectivity in the more traditional sense. Rather than a thing in the world, the ego in phenomenology constitutes the world itself. It thus has no simple exterior. By contrast, by taking the ego as a mere residuum that survives the radical doubt methodologically cast upon everything else, Descartes ultimately limits the transcendental ego to an empirical psyche. He replaces 'egological immanence', Husserl says, with 'psychological immanence' (Husserl, *Crisis* 83|81). Though not the only, Husserl's reference to 'immanence' is propitious here. If the dividing line falls between *immanence* and immanence *to*, then the distinction between 'psychological immanence' and 'egological immanence', so decisive not only for Husserl's critique of Descartes but also for his understanding of the modern history of philosophy leading up to its culmination in phenomenology, remains both relative and porous.

Like every other philosopher, Husserl falls infinitely short of Spinoza, the prince, the Christ of philosophers who alone managed to make immanence pure and absolute by freeing it from, in this instance, transcendental subjectivity.

And yet, like a Spinozist, the phenomenologist privileges self-erasing signs. In phenomenology, this self-erasure takes the form of what Derrida famously calls phonocentrism. When I speak a word, the word's sonorous body seems to dissipate immediately, as soon as I say it, and thereby leave me with nothing but the ideal sense that the word expresses. Because the 'pure diaphaneity' of the spoken word seems (but, of course, only seems) to allow me to forego all passage through the opaque and alienating externality of the world, my voice seems to allow me to produce meaning while at the same time remaining entirely present to myself and the meaning I produce. 'My words are "living"', Derrida writes, 'because they seem not to leave me, not to fall beyond me, beyond my breath, in a visible distancing [*éloignement*], not to cease to belong to me, to be at my disposition' (*La voix* 90/*Voice* 65). I master my meaning, my meaning is mine, because the words I speak never escape me. Despite what one might think, my immediate presence to spoken meaning doesn't limit its scope or horizon. On the contrary, the ethereal element of the voice also seems to suit it to the ideality of meaning. Were I to entrust meaning to any external body that, like writing, exists and persists independently in the external world, not only would my access to it become mediated and therefore uncertain. Not only would I lose control as soon as I exert it. I would limit the reach of whatever meaning I express by binding it to a spatiotemporally finite body.

For the same reason, more significantly for my purposes here, Derrida describes the auto-reduction of the vocal sign as an auto-affection. When I speak, I seem to hear and understand myself without the intervention of any body, so he calls this auto-affection *pure*. Because every other form of auto-affection either passes through an irreducible and foreign exteriority – even when I affect myself with my own body – or relinquishes its universality, he also calls this auto-affection *unique*. *Absolument unique*, Derrida insists more than once (93/67, 94/68, 95/69).

But there's reason to question this absolute uniqueness.

Where the philosopher aims for pure auto-affection sealed from all foreignness or alienation, an auto-affection with neither need nor room for signs, at least two general paths open, neither of which is entirely unique: *the phenomenologist* reduces all spatiality, all exteriority, to the point that neither the world nor anything in it could affect him or her except him- or herself by way of his or her ephemeral voice; *the pantheist* totalises, interiorises, incorporates everything into a single substance that, because nothing escapes it, 'suffers' nothing because it 'suffers' only itself. Any affection would be pure auto-affection for the pantheist for whom there's no exterior, no non-proper, no transcendence. A strange ultimatum: either the voice or anything. Yet, for the phenomenologist and the pantheist, for the subjective and the divine, auto-affection idealises the same self-presence. Even if self-presence distinguishes modern philosophy, its roots reach back to philosophy's 'first and definitive unfolding' through the Greek experience of being as *phusis*, emerging and abiding sway, presencing in a primordial sense (Heidegger, GA 40: 15|*Introduction* 15). With or without the world, immanence *to* or *pure* immanence, Husserl's transcendental subject and Spinoza's God differ only regionally in this respect.[13]

Divine auto-affection thus constitutes the horizon for every mode aspiring to the third genre of knowledge. More precisely, if I reach what Spinoza calls 'intuition', Deleuze 'percept', and manage to contemplate the singularity of my essence through God as its immanent cause, my contemplation of myself is in reality God's contemplation of himself, and my intellectual 'love' of God is in reality nothing but God's love of himself (*Ethics* VP36). Careful to point out that the concept originates long after Spinoza's time, Deleuze himself relates this at once egoless and narcissistic love to auto-affection.[14] And yet, although an implacable animosity toward the idea of the self motivates his first interventions into the history of philosophy and hardens as his writings progress (my point in Chapter 2 above), Deleuze doesn't thematise or *a fortiori* problematise the self-presence that this auto-affection operates.

I confronted the pantheist with the phenomenologist to show that a self-reducing sign in philosophy – joy or otherwise – isn't as bizarre as Deleuze seems to think. I invoked Husserl in particular because Deleuze opposes him to Spinoza just before crowning Spinoza in Example III of *What Is Philosophy?*, and everything separating Spinoza and Husserl – centuries, concepts, strategies, immanence both pure and to – only sediments their common ground. However privileged, nevertheless, Husserl provides only one example of the general tension between an allergy to the sign and resignation to the necessity of at least provisional recourse to it. As the predicament of philosophy itself, I could have invoked a number of other names to the same end.

Including Deleuze.

When Deleuze first attempts to do philosophy in *Difference and Repetition*, before Spinoza comes to reign in his work, the philosopher first grasps difference in itself only by sensing it, and sensibility first grasps difference as a 'sign'. Yet, because the sign also tends to cancel that which it signals, because the sign of difference in itself only signals and therefore isn't difference in itself, both sign and sensibility are ultimately reduced on a path toward thinking. I discuss this iteration of the sensible hitch at length in Chapter 1; I won't reiterate it here. I invoke it in this context only to stress that thinking is thus a thinking without signs. Insofar as the sensible sign leads to thinking, once again, the sign should even lead to its own reduction.

It would be no exaggeration to say, aberrances notwithstanding, that presence never ceases to horizon Deleuze's philosophy in general. Nor to say that it horizons Deleuze's philosophy in particular. Deleuze remains not only *metaphysical* generally speaking, in other words, but even *particularly* metaphysical in a sense he never endorsed. Far from challenging the axiom of presence, Deleuze generalises it to an unprecedented degree. Still in *Difference and Repetition*, for instance, Deleuze defines univocity in terms of being's 'simple presence' and 'absolute proximity' to all beings alike (DR 54–5|37). On the one hand, this ontology could drown out Heidegger's question of being, which privileges one being in particular for its essential nearness to being even after he abandons the word 'ontology' for its ontic baggage.[15] On the other hand, Deleuze generates the rupture and novelty of univocity only by ubiquitising an unwritten axiom of proximity. No being reigns – this is why Deleuze speaks of 'anarchy' (DR 55|37) – because all beings are 'simply' and 'absolutely' present to being. In which case absolute presence would be the source of both *anarchy* and the *archē* it allegedly annihilates.

Decades later in *What Is Philosophy?*, in the philosophical system wherein Spinoza finally comes to reign, the design remains fundamentally the same: the 'absolute speed' that describes Part V of Spinoza's *Ethics* – percept, Essence, Singularity, third genre of knowledge – describes the concept's 'co-presence' to its components.

'Traversing them according to an order without distance, the concept is in a state of *overflight* [survol] in relation to its components. It is immediately	'He who fully knew that immanence was immanent only to itself and thus that it was a plane traversed by movements of the infinite

221

co-present without any distance to all its components or variations [. . .] The concept is defined by *the inseparability of a finite number of heterogeneous components traversed by a point of absolute overflight at infinite speed*' (QP 26|20–1).

. . . was Spinoza. Thus, he is the prince of philosophers. Perhaps the only [*le seul*] never to have compromised with transcendence, to have chased it away everywhere. He made the movement of the infinite and gave thought infinite speeds in the third genre of knowledge, in the last book of the *Ethics*' (QP 51|48).

Even if a generous reader denies Deleuze nothing (difference, intuition or percept, absolute and infinite speed, univocity, immanence, Nietzsche, Spinoza), he will not have stepped beyond philosophy's most classical ambit and ambition. At least not where he thinks he or Spinoza has.

On the contrary, he burrows more deeply still. More deeply because more naively. In 'Spinoza and the Three "Ethics"', Deleuze concentrates 'metaphysics' in only one class of signs. Because affects and affections yield inadequate ideas of their causes, 'hermeneutic' or 'interpretive' signs are those that lead us to imagine ultimate causes as supersensible beings or, as Deleuze calls them, 'metaphysical idols' (CC 174|140). But metaphysics isn't so quickly or easily circumscribed. A more general, more fundamental metaphysics informs the desire to escape signs, which is to say, to escape metaphysics. Precisely because Deleuze implies that Spinoza leaves metaphysics behind in the world of signs, he hits the metaphysical ground of presence harder still upon relapsing. If, of course, one could still speak of 'relapsing', 'collapsing' or any sort of 'lapse' into what one never simply leaves behind.

Select and Organise

To say the least, metaphysics doesn't end where Deleuze suggests. Nevertheless, even when the relegation of metaphysics to – in this case – a particular class of signs heightens expectations of vigilance, to cry 'metaphysics' elsewhere doesn't suffice.

First, the metaphysical axiom of presence never results simply from error or oversight. In phenomenology or pantheism, in any case, the necessity is evident: by intuition or speed, apodicticity or a third knowledge, only presence – to myself or my mental processes, to an object, to Nature, Substance or God – could generate rigorously 'scientific' or 'adequate' knowledge. Presence to conditions knowledge of.

Second, even if immanence remains 'metaphysical' in a sense Deleuze never intended, even if immanence proves an even *more* and perhaps the *most* extreme manifestation of presence to date, what adulterates the purity of the pantheist's auto-affection? In the vein I've opened here, more specifically, why will the sign never entirely reduce itself or thus fulfil its self-effacing purpose? Why always one more interpretation? In the 'Three "Ethics"', Deleuze recalls that first order affects never simply disappear but, obviously, hindering differs from lingering. To say that affects don't disappear, in the end, might complicate the trajectory but only reveals an unshakable confidence in the eventuality of the concept and the percept. Before affects never disappear, then, a more fundamental question might ask why the concept and the percept might never appear, why affects might eclipse the latter *Ethics*, why they might bar the passage – the only passage – to the subsequent genres of knowledge that depend upon them as a 'trampoline'. Why, in short, might the third genre of knowledge, the percept that presents me to Nature and Nature to itself, remain at an insurmountable distance?

Because joy increases my power to act, to think, and thereby conditions my passage to the next genre of knowledge, because sadness inhibits my progress, Deleuze insists on *selecting* affects and *organising* encounters that produce them. This is 'the very condition' for moving from affect and the first *Ethics* to percept and the third.

> It is in the random encounter between bodies that we can select the idea of certain bodies that suit ours and that give us joy, that is to say, augment our power. [. . .] There is therefore a *selection* of passional affects and of ideas on which they depend, which must isolate [*dégager*] joys, vectorial signs of augmentation of power, and repel sadnesses, signs of diminishment: this selection of affects is the very condition for leaving the first genre of knowledge and reaching the concept by acquiring sufficient power. (CC 179|144)

Neither in this passage nor elsewhere in the 'Three "Ethics"' does Deleuze use the word 'organise' when speaking of random encounters, but it staples his other writings on Spinoza,[16] and it remains audible here in the call to isolate joys and repel sadnesses. An itinerary begins to take shape. I suffer affects randomly in the everyday life Spinoza describes as 'vague experience'. Of these affects, most are sadnesses, since in infinite nature many more bodies harm than nourish my body, but at least a few will likely be joys. A few will augment my power. I must *select* these joys and, henceforth, attempt to *organise* encounters with more of the same class. If I experience enough joys, if I augment my power enough, I come into ever greater possession of my own powers of thought and action and depend less and less on 'random' or 'vague' encounters with external objects. I slowly begin to conceive the laws that all things obey – my mind and body included – and thus leave the world of equivocal signs for the world of univocal expression. No longer interpreting what vagrant affects and affections only vaguely signal (first genre of knowledge), I now adequately conceive what bodies have in common (second genre) and, little by little, begin to perceive or intuit every mode as an expression of God's divine attributes (third genre).

Accordingly, if indeed affect threatens to break the chain leading toward the third *Ethics*, toward the percept and the third genre of knowledge, toward my intuition of nature that is in reality *both* my intuition of myself *and* nature's intuition of itself through my intuition of myself, then it does so in these processes of selection and organisation. I'll address each in turn.

Selection. I suggested above that Deleuze gives his most definitive account of affect with Guattari in *What Is Philosophy?* because he frees it there from any epistemic progression in which it constitutes the first and lowest step. *What Is Philosophy?*, however, operates on the assumption that all affect in a strict sense is positive, creative and pensive. Deleuze's writings on Spinoza – and 'Spinoza and the Three "Ethics"' as the most formulaic – reveal or recall that not all affect is indiscriminately desirable (in either the loose sense or the strictly Spinozist sense of 'desire'). There is joy *and* sadness and *both* are fundamental affects: one increases my power, the other diminishes it. In light of which, chapter 7 of *What Is Philosophy?* suddenly seems rather insensitive. Affect opposes not only affection but also affect.

Although the category 'affect' contains opposing affects and although the entire ethical enterprise consists in analysing and moderating the affects, if not eradicating them,[17] it's not clear that either Spinoza or Spinozist ever take a radical ambivalence into account as an essential possibility. After positing joy (*puissances augmentatives*) and sadness (*servitudes diminutives*) as two species of 'vectorial signs of affect' ('vector' referring to whether an affect directs power up or downward), Deleuze hesitates to grant ambivalence the status of a third species. He labels four species of signs pertaining to affection but two *or three* pertaining to affect in a strict sense.

> There are still two sorts of vectorial signs of affect, depending on whether the vector is of augmentation or diminishment, of increase or decrease, joy or sadness. These two species of signs would be called augmentative powers and diminutive servitudes. One *could* add a third species, ambiguous or fluctuating signs, when an affection augments and diminishes our power at the same time, or affects us with joy and sadness at the same time. There are therefore six signs, *or seven*, that ceaselessly combine. (CC 174|140, my emphases)

One might easily surmise why Deleuze hesitates to accept a sign that wavers between joy and sadness. The passage from affect to concept (to philosophy, freedom and immortality in turn) hangs upon the possibility of selecting joy and thus both theoretically and practically isolating it from sadness. Everything, in other words, depends upon a certain univalence. Ambivalence must be unoriginal, a mere mixture of pre-existing joy and pre-existing sadness that therefore doesn't qualify as a species of sign in its own right. If joy were always possibly impure, then the 'trampoline' could never support a leap – a sort of *saut* or *bond* (CS, 3 February 1981, session eight, second recording, 34'02") – from the first genre of knowledge to the second, from affect to concept, from sign to common notion and on to intuition. To be sure, Deleuze often insists on the difficulty of finding and accumulating joys in a world where incomparably more bodies decompose my corporal composition than compose with it, but he never seems to doubt the possibility of accumulating enough joy, enough increase in power, to pass to the second genre of knowledge. Which means, like Spinoza before him, he never doubts the possibility of distinguishing joy from sadness.

Which is to say, more generally and more precisely, neither Deleuze nor Spinoza thematise or *a fortiori* problematise the presence and even the self-presence – the metaphysics – that alone could decide between joy and sadness. To be sure, there is no Spinozist 'subject', only modes of a unique substance, and Spinoza's alternative to the Cartesian subject fascinates Deleuze. His 1980–1 seminar on Spinoza hinges upon individuation in Spinoza's model, and he makes a point of arguing that, in a world of signs where I initially know myself only through affection, no *cogito* is possible (CS, 3 February 1981, session eight, first recording, 2'10"). Deleuze's confidence here isn't entirely justified since, as I argue at the outset of Chapter 1, a *sentio* could replace the *cogito* without displacing Descartes' fulcrum or disrupting the deduction he bases upon it. Yet, even granting the discrepancy between Spinozist *affectio* and Cartesian *cogito*, the possibility of an affect – of knowing or recognising it as such, of experiencing it as the affect it is, as a joy or as a sadness and never undecidably both – still shares a basis with the *cogito* in self-transparency and -immediacy. Even if my sadness never yields an adequate idea of the object that occasions it, I have enough clarity to know that and when – if not why – I'm sad; inversely, my joy can't springboard me toward the second genre of knowledge if my mind or body doesn't know, with unspoken but absolute certainty, that I experience joy when I experience it.

Consequently, I must know joy before it empowers me to know anything else, before I know the object that occasions it, before I know my own mind and body, before I know anything and even if I know nothing else. Although joy divides from sadness within the first genre of knowledge that, as the sole source of falsity, can prove worse than ignorance, knowledge of this distinction precedes all three genres of knowledge and conditions them before the genesis even begins with the first genre of knowledge. To know my sadness or my joy, I'm transparent to myself *before* I'm either obscure (first genre) or transparent (third) to myself. Affect and affection always yield an inadequate idea of the body affecting me, of my own body and of my mind, but they always yield a proto-adequate idea of themselves as my affective reality. Despite all grounds and technicalities through which Deleuze carefully distinguishes Spinoza and Descartes throughout his writings, Spinoza remains fundamentally Cartesian in this respect. In a sense, the Spinozist proves more Cartesian than Descartes by supposing a certain self-certainty even where no *cogito* seems possible.

To question this certainty as it quietly but surely guides Spinoza's system and Deleuze's genetic reading of it is therefore to question joy first and above all, its purity, its monovalence. The problem I've been calling 'ambivalence' throughout this book reaches one of its clearest and most consequential expressions in this context. If ambivalence should prove irreducible and therefore original (or even pre-original if, indeed, it precedes the first genre of knowledge), if the fundamental affects 'joy' and 'sadness' should prove abstracted from a prior and more profound ambivalence, then no sign could signal the way out of the first genre of knowledge in which we begin and to which we're thus irredeemably 'condemned'. Which is perhaps why one would struggle to find any real ambivalence in Spinoza, Deleuze or even philosophy as such.

The greatest ambivalence in the *Ethics*, Spinoza calls 'vacillation of mind' (*animi fluctuatio*). This vacillation or fluctuation is often accidental. If I hate something because it affects me with sadness, for instance, but imagine it to be similar to something else that affects me with equal or greater joy (or vice versa), then I both love and hate the object (IIIP17). In fact, though Spinoza doesn't say so, I love and hate both objects in the simile. Now, Spinoza doesn't explain how an object that affects me with sadness might resemble another that affects me with joy without, however, making me joyful like the object it resembles, which is why the ambivalence remains entirely accidental. The joy caused by the object I hate remains contingent upon an imagined association with another object from which it borrows the affect that it doesn't cause of its own accord. In the scholium of the same proposition, however, Spinoza describes a more radical and actually more common ambivalence: 'vacillations of mind for the most part arise from an object which is the efficient cause of each affect' (IIIP17S), that is, of both joy and sadness, of ambivalence, *animi fluctuatio*. But the whole argument relies upon the composite nature of my body and not that of the affect that therefore remains simple. Because the highly complex human body comprises 'a great many individuals of different natures' (IIIP17S), the privilege that founds Spinoza's lingering humanism (as I argue in Chapter 5 above), one and the same object might affect one and the same body with both joy and sadness because it affects some components with joy and others with sadness. As long as the ambivalence compartmentalises, as long as an object affects the same individual only insofar as it affects *different* parts of different *natures*, the ambivalence isn't radical or irreducible. I vacillate, as if of two minds, but my vacillation arises from independent affects that analysis can always isolate, reorganise, cultivate or avoid. Which is why, in short, Spinoza doesn't recognise any ambivalence among the primary affects (IIIP11S).

After Spinoza and before Deleuze, it would be tempting to intercalate psychoanalysis in the search for a system more sensitive to ambivalence. The death drive, after all, seems to outmode *conatus* and, as one might expect, Freud gives ambivalence a structuring role in both psyche and society.[18] Drawing parallels between taboo and obsessional neuroses in the second chapter of *Totem and Taboo* ('Taboo and Emotional Ambivalence'), for instance, Freud describes the fixation (*Fixierung*) of a psychological constellation in which

227

coexist an instinct (in this case – not one among others for Freud – a boy's desire to touch his genitalia or 'primitive' man's desire to touch a taboo object) and its prohibition (initially enforced externally by the parents or by the community but eventually internalised). This conflicted attitude toward a single act bearing upon the same object, Freud says, constitutes *Ambivalenz* in the proper sense. The ambivalence – the tension between desire and repulsion – grows until forced to find another discharge. The result is the neurosis in the study of which psychoanalysis originates as a discipline. Which is to say, the very field of psychoanalysis opens in the discrepancy between the irreducible valences of a fundamental ambivalence that, far from an incidental vacillation of mind, motivates the whole genetico-genital narrative that Freud's later works refine and deepen but never abandon.

And yet, insist as he might on its proper sense, Freud never clearly diagnoses any real ambivalence. For the same reason as Spinoza.

> The conflict [*Gegensatz*] between these two currents cannot be promptly settled [*nicht ausgleichbar*] because – there is no other way of putting it – they are localized [*lokalisiert*] in the subject's mind [*Seelenleben*] in such a manner that they cannot come up against each other [*zusammenstoßen*]. The prohibition is noisily conscious, while the persistent desire to touch is unconscious and the subject knows nothing of it. If it were not for this psychological factor, an ambivalence like this could neither last so long nor lead to such consequences. (Freud, GW IX:40|*Totem* 29–30)

Like Spinoza's composite body, everything hinges upon a complex topology rather than a complex affect: the desire to touch lies in the unconscious (more specifically, to use Freud's later terminology, in the *id*), while the internalised prohibition to touch lies in consciousness (in the *superego*). For Freud, only this local insulation can account for the sustainability and the consequentiality of ambivalence. The mutually exclusive impulse and repulsion, desire and prohibition, never cancel each other out because they never come into contact or collide (*zusammenstoßen*).

How ambivalent is the psychoanalytically proper sense of 'ambivalence' if an uncrossable border separates the two valences, the two 'feelings' or 'emotions', that therefore remain perfectly identifiable and univalent each in itself? No accumulation of unambivalent emotions will ever yield ambivalence. Do the emotions in Freud's case, despite his assumption that they do, even bear upon the same act or object? As long as the desire to touch and the prohibition to touch never come into contact themselves, touching for consciousness – whatever it is – *is not* whatever *it is* for the unconscious. But, then, how could it be otherwise? Ambivalence toward the same act from the same psychic space wouldn't yield so readily to an analysis of the psyche, to psycho-analysis, to any analysis whatsoever – even schizo-analysis – insofar as it seeks to loosen its object back into its fundamental elements. Although in prior works he already establishes that the unconscious cares nothing for logical consistency,[19] Freud remains bound to an Aristotelian principle of noncontradiction when he assumes here that a congenital ambivalence, a positive valence and a negative in the same locale, would self-destruct. Any ambivalence that keeps its name resists philosophical analysis and psychoanalysis on the same irreducibly synthetic grounds.

What makes ambivalence possible, for Freud, thus makes it derivative. Toward the end of *Totem and Taboo*, he returns to ambivalence in the proper sense (*im eigentlichen Sinne*), recognises it as the source of many social institutions and even admits his ignorance concerning its origin. Which doesn't prevent him from speculating on two possibilities. According to one radical possibility, he says, ambivalence constitutes a fundamental phenomenon of our emotional life (*ein fundamentales Phänomen unseres Gefühlsleben*). In which case the psychoanalyst would have to rethink ambivalence before its division into individual emotions and even before the development of the psyche into regions. Indeed, the very topography of the psyche, along with the discipline that analyses it, would respond to the ambivalence that thus structures it. According to the other possibility, which Freud seems to endorse, ambivalence isn't original at all: 'originally foreign [*fremd*] to our emotional life, it was acquired by humanity through the father-complex' (GW IX:189|*Totem* 157, translation modified). Deleuze and Guattari's critique of the psychoanalyst's despotic reduction of all psychic life to the paternal pattern applies here more than ever. Indeed, one could say of ambivalence what Deleuze and Guattari say of desire in *Anti-Oedipus*: Freud uncovers it as such (*tout court*) only to resubmit it immediately to the Oedipus complex.

By a happy coincidence, perhaps, Deleuze and Guattari describe Freud's nearly simultaneous discovery and re-covering of libido as a 'very complex ambivalence' (AŒ 362|301). Even if Deleuze and Guattari's critique of Freud could support an account of ambivalence, however, Deleuze himself comes no closer to taking a constitutive ambivalence into account. At least not where it counts in his reading of Spinoza. In the 'Three "Ethics"', for instance, Deleuze seems to attribute the difficulty of selecting joy explicitly to a certain ambivalence: 'This selection is very hard, very difficult. This is because joys and sadnesses, increases and decreases, clarifications and obscurations, are often ambiguous, partial, changing, mixed together' (CC 180|145). Yet, rather than exploring this mixture as an essential or original possibility, Deleuze quickly turns to denounce the priestly cult of sadness, which already presupposes the resolution or at least resolvability of the 'ambiguity' he just invoked. One can discard the priest of sadness only insofar as sadness can be isolated from the joy one selects. Ambivalence happens, it's even widespread, but it's never original enough to make Deleuze doubt the possibility of joy in its purity or, in tandem, the passage to the concept upon which his denunciation of priests and sadness in this instance depends.

In the eighth session of his *Cours* on Spinoza (3 February 1981), Deleuze articulates more clearly still why this ambivalence will never essentially trouble him. Not only, once again, does he admit a certain ambivalence. He goes so far as to say that the two 'lines' of joy and sadness are never pure.[20] But he speaks of an impure *line*, rather than impure *joy* or *sadness*, because the impurity intervenes only after an unadulterated starting point; sadness contaminates an earlier and in itself pure joy and vice versa. A hateful object makes me sad, for instance, then I imagine it destroyed and rejoice: joy intervenes after the initial sadness that in itself remains unequivocally and transparently sad. So, even if Deleuze admits there's no pure line of joy or sadness, even if my joy always eventually mixes with sadness, joy in itself remains unambivalent.

Beyond Spinoza, beyond Freud, beyond Deleuze, to say joy itself is never pure isn't simply to condemn all creatures to pure sadness, which would avoid confrontation with originary ambivalence as much as the insistence upon pure joy. That there's no pure joy also means there's no pure sadness. In this sense, little separates Deleuze from the priests against whom he proselytises. Both preach unambivalence; both are puritans. That the Deleuzian or Spinozist will nevertheless take me for a priest, a reactionary cultivator of sadness, only confirms that profound ambivalence has no place within the system it secretly governs. The ambivalence doesn't combine two previously independent affects, doesn't wait in line to overtake a previously pure point of joy or sadness and doesn't compartmentalise the conflicting feelings into various regions of the body or the psyche. A more profound ambivalence resists all analysis geometric, schizo-, psycho- or otherwise. For all the efforts to drive an essential wedge between them, why do joy and sadness both qualify as *affects*? What is affect if it motivates *both* regression *and* progress or *both* desire *and* repulsion, generates *both* ground *and* illusion, constitutes both *hitch* and *hitch*? What is affect *before* it divides into joy and sadness? Before I can select joy or sadness?

Deleuze himself inadvertently authorises this series of questions through a double recourse to the idea of selection. On the one hand, he prescribes a certain 'selection' of affects.[21] We must 'select' joys, pursue and accumulate them, while avoiding and destroying sadnesses in the blind but telic effort to reach the second and third genres of knowledge in the latter *Ethics*. On the other hand, Deleuze mobilises the same word – citing Spinoza and others like Berkeley and Hume – to define and denounce abstraction: the process by which, what is in reality one, I separate in thought by 'selecting' only a part (CS, session eight, 3 February 1981, third recording, 10'00"). Are Deleuze's two uses of selection rigorously separable? If the word 'selection' is in this sense symptomatic, if 'selection' and 'selection' are not casual homonyms, then joy and sadness suddenly appear to be abstractions of a more general and primordial ambivalence. Before the Spinozist critique of abstract ideas can take root, before sad passions generate my illusions and superstitions, before the accumulation of joys empowers common notions to oppose them, the first abstract ideas might be joy and sadness themselves. If the first genre of knowledge is the only source of falsity because my affect – especially my sadness – yields only inadequate knowledge of a cause and thus leaves room for idle and idolatrous speculations about the supersensible, the prior illusion concerns the isolatable affects called 'joy' and 'sadness'. The illusion of *an* affect takes surreptitious hold before *any* affect engenders illusions of universals, gods or man. From this more primordial perspective, the common notion affirmed and the universal denounced would differ only as two abstract classes of illusion.

Organisation. Even supposing that joy can be unambivalently isolated and selected, abstracted, how do I organise joyful encounters? Ideally only joyful but realistically, since far more things in nature decompose my body than compose with it, only primarily joyful. Even tempered, however, one problem with this organisation appears immediately.

According to Deleuze himself in works like *Difference and Repetition* and *Proust and Signs*, the 'encounter' is necessary, it ruptures the dogmatic image of thought according to which a transcendent Idea determines and thus defuses thinking in advance, the encounter is an encounter precisely and only because it is not selected, not organised, not in any way anticipated or guided. Thinking affirms the encounter, to be sure, but it has no force or authority without this violence by Deleuze's own account. Indeed, he even accuses Socrates, spokesman for the dogmatic image of thought that Proust combats, of the very thing that he prescribes in his reading of Spinoza and does so with the same word: 'In Socrates, intelligence precedes the encounters, invokes them, and *organizes* them' (PS 123|101, my italics). Similarly, if I truly open to encounters, then I must also open to the essential possibility of encountering sadness. After I select joy and attempt to organise an encounter with it, indeed, the only rigorous encounter possible would perhaps be an encounter with the sadness I no longer expect. Which is not to endorse sadness but, rather, merely to say that organisation runs counter to the very nature of the encounter. In truth, one hardly needs Socrates, Spinoza, Proust or Deleuze to draw this lesson: to organise an encounter is already to lose it.[22]

Of course, although the word itself – a veritable term for Deleuze – invites the confrontation, the Spinozist 'encounter' isn't the Proustian 'encounter'. When Deleuze broaches Spinoza's 'fortuitous encounters' in *Spinoza and the Problem of Expression*, a formulation he borrows directly from Spinoza's *Ethics* (*fortuitus occursus* [IIP29S]), he specifies that there's nothing 'contingent' about it (Deleuze, SPE 217|238). The encounter appears or feels fortuitus only for a mode that vaguely suffers the necessity with which everything follows from the absolute nature of God. Which, however, only sharpens the problem of organisation. How do I organise anything at all when, Spinoza is notoriously clear in this regard, free will is an illusion? If I must organise encounters with joy and repress sadness, therefore or nevertheless, this *devoir* remains suspended between two very different readings. Both, however, anachronise the entire system's genesis.

At times, Deleuze describes what happens as a function of the affective mechanics over which we have no control. The illusion of free will, according to Spinoza, arises because I'm conscious of my action but not what causes it (*Ethics* I, Appendix, p. 440 and IIP48). Were I to gain consciousness of my action's cause, I'd realise that affect operates everything I do or, rather, everything I mistakenly think I do. Joy increases my power, sadness decreases it, and I act according to the desire to seek what brings me joy and avoid or destroy what causes me sadness. What some consider inexpressibly individual – affect – precludes 'individuality' in the loose sense. Joy and sadness determine the desire that determines my actions, and this basic machinery allows Spinoza to treat the affects – both passions and actions – '*as if it were a Question of lines, planes, and bodies*' (*Ethics*, III, preface).

On this mechanical or geometric reading, Deleuze's terms are convenient at best and misleading at worst whenever they lead me to think I organise. No one chooses to pursue joy. The world nevertheless contains more sadness than joy because, while everyone strives for joy (and therefore for knowledge), nature comprises more bodies that conflict than compose with my own, with my proportion of movements and rests, and the immediacy of local joys eclipses what Freud will call the 'reality principle' centuries later. As a result, I reach higher levels of knowledge, if I do, only through *felicitous* encounters over which 'I' have no control.

Deleuze inclines in this direction, for instance, when he attributes the effort to select and organise joyful encounters *not* to the individual but to *reason* (SPP 123|55). He doesn't seem to mind drawing upon reason to reach the second genre of knowledge even though, strictly speaking, reason *is* the second genre of knowledge. In other words, only reason explains the genesis of reason, which therefore becomes autogenesis. In the more intimate setting of a classroom, Deleuze admits this rational anachronism without naming it as such: 'the first effort of reason before there's even any reason'.[23] But he doesn't dwell on the paradoxical consequences: if affect intertwines with reason from the beginning, if reason already operates through or on affects or vice versa, not only do both affect and reason demand redefinition and redistribution, which Spinoza both *necessitates* by treating affects rationally and *precludes* by placing reason proper beyond the affects in the second genre of knowledge. Reason before the second genre of knowledge, reason before reason, a prerational reason reduces affect before it ever operates and, hence, without ever operating; affect becomes more rational than reason because it extends rationality where reason doesn't yet operate; reason rules even in its absence or, inversely, affect governs nothing even when there's nothing else; 'reason' opposes 'reason', 'affect' 'affect', so on so forth.

At other times, Deleuze describes the organisation of joyful encounters as if it required considerable effort on our part. For instance: 'This selection is very hard, very difficult' (CC 180|145). This approach predominates in his *Cours* on Spinoza where, for the same reason perhaps no coincidence, Deleuze reduces the fundamental affects of the *Ethics* to joy and sadness.[24] In his most visibly peda-gogical engagement with Spinoza, in other words, the schizoanalyst and libidinal metaphysician ignores desire, that is, the fundamental affect that determines me to pursue joy and evade sadness and, without an awareness of which, I think myself free. Without desire, without desire as a fundamental affect, nothing would drive me; free would mean unresponsive, indifferent, effectively unaffected by affect. Desire constitutes the engine of Spinoza's affective mechanics and, at the limit, makes any idea of individual effort irrelevant. Such that the freedom to organise my encounters would be possible, however 'difficult', only if desire were not fundamental. Only if, perhaps, one silently reintroduced a non-Spinozist notion of free will into the system that denies it. That Deleuze recognises the pivotal role of desire in *Spinoza and the Problem of Expression* (SPE 210 ff.|231 ff.), for instance, only emphasises the symptomatic oversight in his *Cours*. The desire for joy grows so strong that, paradoxically, Deleuze ceases to desire it.

Even if a generous reading granted the difficulty – thus the capabil-ity and the possibility – of actively organising encounters, what status would this organisational activity have? Only the later stages of the system allow this question, however, precisely because it presupposes that this organisation constitutes an activity. Whence the second anachronism: organising encounters requires action before I possess my own power to act, that is, the very activity this organisation must cultivate and deliver. Prior and conducive to 'action' in the strict sense, I'll close with two comments about this equally *proactive* and *inactive* activity.

First, one might cite certain passages from Deleuze to argue that one begins with a minimal activity that, with enough effort and luck, might provide both the seed and the means necessary to cultivate it into an ever greater and more active activity. In *Spinoza and the Problem of Expression*, for instance, Deleuze stresses that our passiv-ity, our capacity for suffering, our impotence (*impuissance*) is in reality *'the lowest degree of our power to act'* (SPE 204|224). There'd be no leap to activity but, rather, only a gradual movement toward greater degrees of the activity that one always minimally enjoys. Yet, to con-ceive passivity as a degree of activity might displace but doesn't resolve the very old – and very problematic – distinction between activity and passivity on which the system still runs. Indeed, the displacement only intensifies the opposition by doubling down on one of its terms. Far from eradicating passivity, determining passivity as a degradation of activity only interiorises the opposition, divides action from itself and makes it minimally inactive, ineffective, impotent and thus all the less reliable on my path to freedom. Which is why neither an expansion nor a degradation of action, which ultimately amount to the same, will ever overcome the preposterousness of the proactive activity upon which Deleuze's genetic reading of the Spinozist system depends.[25]

Second, an affect can be either a passion or an action. Spinoza defines affect as a bodily affection that increases or decreases the body's power to act, together with the idea of that affection. If the affect comes from without, from an external source of which I'll never have adequate knowledge, the affect is a passion, but the affect I cause myself is action. When I cause the affect affecting me, when I auto-affect, I act.

> By affect I understand affections of the Body by which the Body's power of acting is increased or diminished, aided or restrained, and at the same time the ideas of these affections.
> *Therefore, if we can be the adequate cause of any of these affections, I understand by the Affect an action; otherwise, a passion.* (*Ethics* IIID3)

An unprecedented redistribution, affect now operates unopposed. If suffering, ignorance and evil are still a function of affect in Spinoza's system, they no longer exhaust affect. All action, knowledge and good also depend upon affect. Not that, for instance, I mobilise concepts of the understanding to synthesise the sensible data of an affection worth little – if anything – on its own. More profoundly, if I – this I also holds for God – only know what I alone cause and if this action also constitutes an affect, then affect opens the entire epistemic horizon. Which is why Deleuze eventually corrects his unqualified association of affects with signs and the first genre of knowledge at the outset of the 'Three "Ethics"' (CC 179|144). Action-affects operate all adequate knowledge and, therefore, still operate in both the second and the third genres of knowledge, in concepts and in percepts, in common notions and in intuition. Regardless of whether or the extent to which passion-affects – 'signs' – have been left behind. In short, the oppositions between adequacy and inadequacy, between sign and expression, between univocity and equivocity, passion and action no longer suffice to describe affect. Their circumscription and description, on the contrary, depends upon affect. Hence, even though Spinoza seeks remedies (*remedia*) for the affects (*Ethics* VP20S), the Spinozist never simply aims to overcome affect. We humans, excellent but still finite modes of body and thought, can only hope to moderate passions, to enact or activate them as far as possible, to replace them with actions, which is to say, to replace one affect with another. This, indeed, is the programme of the first twenty propositions of *Ethics* V. But even the divine and passionless substance would continue to affect and be affected, if only by itself in eternal auto-affection.

And yet, these revolutionary redistributions within affect undermine none of the genetic problems I've outlined on the basis of the sign-affect solidarity in the first genre of knowledge. On the contrary, the affective redistribution of passion and action only intensifies the systemic ambivalence. For now *affects* (passions) both anchor and hinder the passage to *affects* (actions). No longer a stark opposition between affection and affect as in *What Is Philosophy?* – problematic in its own right – the antagonistic valences now divide between *affect* and *affect*.

Whether I organise the encounter or the encounter occurs with a necessity before which I can do nothing, in short, the result remains the same. A free man who '*thinks of nothing less than of death*' (*Ethics* IVP67), for the same reason, thinks of nothing other than death. What rigorously happens in a world where – by me, by another or by the other that I am – every encounter is organised?

Notes

1. 'The Exhausted', originally published as the afterword to a volume of works by Beckett in French (Minuit, 1992), is incorporated as the final text of the English translation, desensitising anglophone readers to the climactic status of 'Spinoza and the "Three" Ethics'. See 202 note 1 of the English translation of *Critique et clinique*.
2. While Deleuze holds that there are multiple *Ethics* from the very beginning and consistently, only relatively late does he count three:
   (i) the appendix to *Spinoza and the Problem of Expression* (1968), 'Formal Study of the Plan of the *Ethics* and the Role of the Scholia in Its Realization', the subtitle of which is 'The Two *Ethics*' (the scholia and everything else);
   (ii) *Spinoza: Practical Philosophy* (1981), where Deleuze continues to count only two *Ethics* (SPP 41–2|29–30, 148|112, 155 note 13|118 note 13, 170–2|129–30), although he already has the lexicon to describe the characteristics of what he will soon grant the status of an entirely other *Ethics*, the third and highest, Book V;
   (iii) the brief 'Letter to Réda Bensmaïa, on Spinoza' (1989), where

236

there are now three *Ethics*, which Deleuze presents schematically and tersely (PP 223–5|164–6);

(iv) 'Spinoza and the "Three" Ethics' (1993) where, finally, the trinity of the *Ethics* becomes the organising principle of Deleuze's entire reading. Given the reprisal of developments in Deleuze's 1980–1981 *Cours sur Spinoza* (especially sessions seven and eight), Deleuze might have written or at least prepared 'Spinoza and the Three "Ethics"' much earlier. An earlier redaction would only accentuate the text's culminating status at the end of Deleuze's oeuvre.

3. On affect and scholia, see SPE 320–1|348–9; on the style of the scholia, see SPE 317|344 and CC 181|146.

4. Spinoza presents knowledge 'from singular things which have been represented to us through the senses' and knowledge 'from signs' separately (IIP40S2), but Deleuze isn't unjustified in his attempt to solder them at least insofar as they both constitute what Spinoza calls knowledge of the first kind.

5. For Deleuze's earlier attempts to make the movement between the genres of knowledge, see the penultimate chapter of SPE ('Toward the Third Genre'), SPP 154–7|117–20, and sessions seven and eight of his *Cours sur Spinoza* (27 January and 3 February 1981). Whatever factors remain constant throughout Deleuze's longstanding engagement with the problem of genesis in Spinoza, the very existence of 'Spinoza and the Three "Ethics"' suggests a certain dissatisfaction with earlier texts.

6. In support of which, stressing the temporality of each, Deleuze tends to cite any or all of the following passages from Spinoza's *Emendation of the Intellect*:

> If, by chance, someone should ask why I did [not] *immediately, before anything else*, display the truths of Nature in that order – for does not the truth make itself manifest? – I reply to him [. . .] and at the same time I warn him not to try to reject these things as false because of Paradoxes that occur here and there; he should first deign to consider the order in which we prove them, and then he will become certain that we have reached the truth; and this was the reason why I have put these things first. (I:21–2)

> So in the beginning we must take the greatest care that we arrive at knowledge of such a Being *as quickly as possible*. (I:23)

> But we shall not need to fear any such deception, if we proceed as far as we can in a manner that is not abstract, and begin *as soon as possible* from the first elements, i.e., from the source and origin of Nature. (I:33)

> As for order, to unite and order all our perceptions, it is required, and reason demands, that we ask, *as soon as possible*, whether there is a certain being, and at the same time, what sort of being it is, which is the cause of all things, so that its objective essence may also be the cause of all our ideas, and then our mind will (as we have said) reproduce Nature as much as possible. (I:41)

Most commentators tend to think this origin elsewhere constitutes only a provisional hitch that a more mature Spinoza will overcome in the *Ethics*. In this regard, Deleuze refers on multiple occasions to Alexandre Koyré's annotation of his French translation of the *Emendation*, with which, incidentally, the English translator Curley agrees (see Spinoza, *Collected Works*, I:21 note 35). But Deleuze insists: 'far from correcting this point, the *Ethics* rigorously maintains it' (SPE 122 note 24|370 note 24); 'that one cannot begin with [*partir de*] the idea of God, that one cannot from the beginning install oneself in God, is a constant of Spinozism' (SPE 122|136–7). See also SPP 111–12|84, 146–7|111–12, along with the first session of CS (2 December 1980). This initial exile renders uncircumventable the problem of genesis – the genesis of genesis, rather, the genesis of the idea of God as the genesis of all ideas – that I'll prolong indefinitely in this chapter.

7. In 'Before and Above: Spinoza and Symbolic Necessity', Malabou's critique of Deleuze's contempt for the inadequacy of signs is no doubt legitimate. In fact, Deleuze suppresses the sign even more problematically than Malabou suggests because she doesn't trace the systematic relation of sign to affect, which opens the suppression to another host of problems. Malabou's originality lies in arguing for the necessity of signs on the basis of the divine substance itself, but she can claim to discover the necessity of signs more generally – sacred or profane – only by neglecting Deleuze's earlier articulation of it. Her discovery ultimately authorises her call for a '*new reading of the hierarchy between the three kinds of knowledge in Spinoza*' according to which the three forms of knowledge would be 'intermingled rather than rigidly hierarchized and, in a certain sense, exclusive from one another' (Malabou 105). Regardless of whether or the extent to which Spinoza's text authorises this epistemic redistribution, is this not precisely what Deleuze prepares throughout his early work and finally formalises – not to say achieves – in the last paragraph of 'Spinoza and the Three "Ethics"'?

> The *Ethics* of definitions, axioms and postulates, demonstrations and corollaries, is a river-book that runs its course. But the *Ethics* of the scholia is a subterranean book of fire. The *Ethics* of book V is an aerial book of light that proceeds by flashes. A logic of the sign, a logic of the concept, a logic of essence: Shadow, Color, Light. Each of the three *Ethics* coexists with the others and continues in the others, despite its differences in nature. It is one and the same world. Each holds out bridges to cross the vacuum [*vide*] that separates them. (CC 187|151)

8. On immanence as the final form of univocity, see Chapter 4 above.
9. Deleuze makes recourse to this classical and convenient example (SPE 38|46), but one must recall that, for Spinoza, one can't call God either good or evil without anthropomorphism. Nor do I strive for good; the

good is good because I strive for it, and I strive for it because it increases my power to act. See the Appendix to Part I of the *Ethics* and IIIP10S.

10. See CS, session seven (27 January 1981), where Deleuze elaborates Spinoza's theory of signs. A week later, in the first part of session eight (4'41"), Deleuze also speaks of univocity as *le but* and *l'idéal*.

11. See Malabou 92. Deleuze disagrees: 'inadequate ideas and passional affects, that is to say signs, nevertheless will not disappear' (CC 179|144).

12. See Example III of *What Is Philosophy?* (QP 48–52|44–9). On Deleuze's shifting accounts of the history of philosophy, see Chapter 4 above.

13. When Knox Peden situates Deleuze's reading of Spinoza – 'the vitalist Spinoza', 'the Spinoza of affect', 'the dominant Spinoza in the humanities today' – both at and as the end of his study of the antagonism between Spinozism and phenomenology in twentieth-century French philosophy because, he argues, Deleuze's metaphysics synthesises the two movements (*Spinoza Contra Phenomenology* 9 and 197), he suggests both too much and too little. *Too much* because Deleuze unambiguously subordinates phenomenology to Spinoza since, while Husserl only ever managed immanence *to* (consciousness), only Spinoza ever managed an immanence immanent to itself. *Too little* because, for all their chronological and conceptual differences, Spinoza and Husserl take two paths toward the same pure auto-affection. Peden eclipses both perspectives in the first instance because, not without justification, he approaches Deleuze's engagement with phenomenology exclusively by way of Heidegger.

14. CS, session thirteen (24 March 1981), second recording, 23'01". See also SPP 69|51 and (although the formulation 'auto-affection' doesn't literally occur there) SPE 82–3|93–4 and 276|297. In his seminar, Deleuze only vaguely remarks that the concept of auto-affection originates with later German philosophers. See §34 of Heidegger's *Kant and the Problem of Metaphysics* (GA 3).

15. 'The human being' – to quote only one of many similar affirmations in Heidegger's 'Letter on Humanism' – 'is the neighbor of being' (GA 9:342|*Pathmarks* 261). For Heidegger's abandonment of the word 'ontology', see GA 40:44|*Introduction* 45–6.

16. SPE 239–40|261, 241|262, 252|274, 259|280; CS, session eight (3 February 1981), second recording, 21'18"; SPP 34|23, 77|82, 123|55, 136|103, 157|119. In *Spinoza and the Problem of Expression* (SPE 314|340), Deleuze bases the organisation of encounters on *Ethics* IVP19–45.

17. '*But no one, to my knowledge, has determined the nature and powers of the Affects, nor what, on the other hand, the Mind can do to moderate them*' (*Ethics*, III, preface). This agenda explains why, although affect theorists hail Spinoza as the source of affect theory, others characterise

him as an advocate for 'release from the "bondage" of passions' in line with a Stoic tradition (Hägglund, *This Life* 46). This characterisation easily slips into caricature, since to 'moderate' is not to 'eliminate' (*This Life* 47), but the more general and interesting question concerns how Spinoza both grounds affect theory and continues the ascetic tradition.

18. For Spinoza, given that everything strives to persevere in its being (*Ethics* IIIP6), suicide can only result from 'external causes' that run contrary to one's nature (IVP18S; see also I:322). In *Beyond the Pleasure Principle* (GW XIII:41|39), inversely, in view of the conservative nature of the instincts and death as the original state, Freud – on the cusp of articulating the death instinct – argues that all self-preservation serves only to secure for the organism its own path toward death (*eigenen Todesweg*). Accordingly, the death drive doesn't simply oppose *conatus*, although Freud himself presents it as a *Gegensatz*. Deleuze attempts to give *conatus* and the death drive a more symmetric reconciliation in *Difference and Repetition* (333|259). He and Guattari then reprise and redistribute some of these terms in their attempt 'to schizophrenize' death in *Anti-Oedipus* (397 ff.|329 ff.). Later, in *A Thousand Plateaus*, they mobilise the Spinozist body directly against Freud and psychoanalysis in the name of children. See MP 313|256 (via movement) and 314–15|257–8 (via affect). On death in Deleuze more generally, see Chapter 3 above.

19. For instance, see the kettle logic at work in his pivotal dream about Irma's injection in *The Interpretation of Dreams* (especially GW II/III:123–5|143–4).

20. CS, session eight, first recording, 31'36". Deleuze already invokes the image of the line to evoke ambivalence in *Spinoza and the Problem of Expression* and grounds it in Spinoza's vacillations of the mind (SPE 222|243).

21. This idea of an affirmative selection exceeds the immediately Spinozist context. What I'll call the problem of *predilection* also applies, for instance, to Deleuze's reading of the eternal return in *Nietzsche and Philosophy* (chapter 2, section fourteen) and *Difference and Repetition* (2|xx, 13|6, 60|41 and so on). One would also have to factor in the preconscious 'selection' by which, according to the first chapter of Bergson's *Matter and Memory*, my body itself already 'selects' the images that I'm capable of perceiving.

22. The problem of organisation resurfaces in *Proust and Signs* when, after scolding Socrates, Deleuze turns to describe the Proustian approach to encounters: 'One must have a gift [or be skilled: *être doué*] for signs, open to their encounter, open to their violence' (PS 123|101). *Either* the encounter is not a rigorous encounter because my gift or skill or opening anticipates and thus defuses them in advance, *or* the encounter remains rigorous and my gift or skill or opening does nothing to

make me any more hospitable than anyone else to the violence of the encounter. One could say the same of the 'art of encounter' in *Logic of Sense* (LS 298|258). None of this usually dissuades commentators from pursuing joy with Deleuze (Heaney 389–90, 393, 395).

23. CS, session eight (3 February 1981), second recording, 3'40". See also session three (16 December 1980), second recording, 46'55".

24. On the omission of desire as a fundamental affect, see CS, session six (20 January 1981), second recording, 24'50" and third recording, 2'40". On our efforts to organise encounters with joy, see session eight. While it would ultimately only redouble the effort, a more exhaustive account would require confronting Deleuze's reconception of effort in the *Logic of Sensation*, not as an extraordinary enterprise beyond my body's capacities and bearing upon a distinct object, but rather as the body's attempt to escape the ego and its organisation as an organism by way of a 'spasm' (FB 23–4|15–16 and 51|49).

25. The same holds for Deleuze's displacement of the passive-active divide into an active-reactive opposition in *Nietzsche and Philosophy*. See NP, chapter 2. Brian Massumi follows this path when, concerning affect, he denies a 'state of freedom' but affirms a more modest 'degree of freedom' (*Politics* 105).

Conclusion: The Body without Affects

Wenn man die N ü t z l i c h k e i t von irgend welchem physiologischen Organ (oder auch einer Rechts-Institution, einer gesellschaftlichen Sitte, eines politischen Brauchs, einer Form in den Künsten oder im religiösen Cultus) noch so gut begriffen hat, so hat man damit noch nichts in Betreff seiner Entstehung begriffen . . .

Nietzsche, *Zur Genealogie der Moral* (KSA 5:314|51)

tout organe est un parasite . . .

Artaud, Draft for *Le Théâtre de la cruauté*,
18 November 1947 (167)

Closing Negotiations

Not only pure, irreducible, hyperbolic and systemic but also profound, congenital, absolute, invaluable, contaminative . . . A conventional conclusion would replace each comma with an explanation of the adjectives they separate so as to recapitulate the ambivalence upon which, in its most general formulation, this book focuses. *Pure* because, rather than this or that object, the ambivalence bears upon sensibility itself. *Irreducible* because the positive valence and the negative share a ground that renders them indivisible. *Hyperbolic* because it intensifies the ascetic tradition broadly understood. *Systemic* because, rather than the mixed sentiments of an individual named 'Deleuze', ambivalence operates the system itself.

This consolidation would serve a purpose, to be sure, but it could never conclude. Not because it would remain too abstract, cryptic or formulaic without the driving arguments that produce this list of adjectives. Not even because the list itself remains unfinished. Even and especially the most exhaustive recapitulation won't suffice because, rather, a certain aporia inhibits all conclusions from closing what they conclude. On the one hand, since pure recapitulation would be at worst superfluous and at best convenient, a conclusion must add something to the argument and analyses it concludes. On the other hand, a conclusion that adds something new fails to conclude since whatever it adds inevitably calls for another conclusion in turn. No conclusion concludes without prolonging what it concludes and, to that extent, repelling the vanishing point of conclusion. A conclusion remains reclusive and inconclusive by its very existence and thus always demands another conclusion to conclude *ad infinitum*. Rather than conclude, consequently, every conclusion negotiates.

To negotiate a conclusion here, I'll read one more text or, rather, one more series of texts. The 'schizophrenic series', namely, from *Logic of Sense* to *Capitalism and Schizophrenia*. ('Schizophrenic series' wears quotation marks because, for reasons that precisely affect will expose, the schizophrenic threatens the very seriality of all series.) In so doing, in principle, I add nothing to the preceding chapters because, I'll argue, the 'same' ambivalence operative throughout Deleuze's work also operates in the schizophrenic series. I merely cement the ambivalence with one more instance that, moreover, I situated in passing in earlier chapters.

At the same time, however, the schizophrenic instance discloses the ambivalence in a unique light. I stress in my Introduction that the systematicity of ambivalence doesn't require recourse to every work. In Deleuze or elsewhere, on the contrary, no accumulation of readings will ever present 'systematicity' in itself. As a result, I choose strategic coordinates. Structurally but far from exclusively, I often privilege *Difference and Repetition* and *What Is Philosophy?*, the first work in which Deleuze does philosophy and the work in which he defines the philosophy he did, because they effectively frame Deleuze's oeuvre and thus provide expedient landmarks for mapping his ambivalence. In the same sense, my focus upon schizophrenic ambivalence here in conclusion is also strategic. Between the *Logic of Sense* and *Anti-Oedipus*, with more or less nuance, commentators generally accept a turn or even a rupture in Deleuze's philosophy catalysed, for better or for worse, by his encounter with Guattari. While it would be naive to ignore or deny any sort of shift, which Deleuze himself admits, neither turn nor rupture precludes continuity. On the contrary, the perhaps greatest discontinuity in Deleuze's oeuvre creates conditions for taking measure of an even greater continuity in his ambivalent treatment of affect and embodiment. If it continues across works otherwise separated by an abyss, in other words, then there is perhaps no more conclusive confirmation of a systemic ambivalence.

Conjurer l'affect

All too easily could one *both* under- *and* over-estimate the schizo-phrenic in Deleuze's work.

Underestimate because schizophrenia already characterises 'the highest power of thinking' in *Difference and Repetition* (DR 82|58). Even when Deleuze refuses to oppose the dogmatic image of thought with a schizophrenic image of thought (DR 192|148), the very refusal bespeaks the importance of the schizophrenic for the project as a whole. To speak of a 'thought' of schizophrenia or even schizophrenic 'thinking', indeed, would do injustice to schizophrenia because schizophrenia, in this instance, merges with thought itself. Accordingly, even though Deleuze only references schizophrenia a handful of times in *Difference and Repetition*, it plays a constitutive role in all the major components of his first philosophy. If the same being is finally said of all beings according to the univocity of being, for instance, the schizophrenic speaks. If empirical sensibility reaches its transcendent exercise, the schizophrenic feels. If time fractures the I and dissolves the self, the schizophrenic exists.

Overestimate as well, however, because Deleuze lists the schizo-phrenic as a conceptual character at the other end of his oeuvre in *What Is Philosophy?* (QP 72|70). Even if conceptual characters are indispensable to philosophy and even if the schizophrenic is already – implicitly – the conceptual character of *Difference and Repetition*, the schizophrenic is only one conceptual character among many and countless more to come. 'The list of conceptual characters is never closed' (QP 10|5).

Rushing to either extreme at either end of Deleuze's oeuvre, however, risks overlooking a whole adventure of affect that plays out in the meantime, in the middle, from the *Logic of Sense* to the two volumes of *Capitalism and Schizophrenia*. Deleuze's own reflections on his progression from *Difference and Repetition* to the *Logic of Sense* are telling in this regard. In his preface to the Italian translation of *Logique du sens*, Deleuze claims to go further in the *Logic of Sense* than in *Difference and Repetition* because, while the concepts are the same (multiplicity, singularity, event, so on), they unfold on the surface and seem to dispense with the ancient topology of (Platonic) heights and (Pre-Socratic) depths.

> Even if, for my part, the history of philosophy no longer satisfied me, my book *Difference and Repetition* nevertheless still aspired toward a sort of

classical height and even toward an archaic depth. [. . .] In the *Logic of Sense*, the novelty for me consisted in learning something about surfaces. (DRF 59|65)

Insofar as all logic of sense keeps to the surface, as Deleuze holds in the *Logic of Sense* (LS 114|93), the logic doesn't simply place the depths above the heights because at the limit, at the surface, *'there is no longer either depth or heights'* (LS 155|130). Nevertheless, while the logic of sense keeps to the surface, the *Logic of Sense* does not. The superficial metaphysics of the *Logic of Sense* still begins in the depths, and nothing guarantees arrival at the surface once and for all or even at all. The depths are the realm of bodies and affect, and a profound ambivalence surges since, once again, an affective genesis effectively threatens and promises philosophy – here – of surfaces. In this respect, *Logic of Sense* remains systemically consistent with the works that both precede and follow it.

Deleuze calls the progression from the depths to the surface the 'dynamic genesis'. When he finally broaches this genesis in its own right in series twenty-seven (finally, in its own right, because it remains operative long before this relatively late series), he commandeers fundamental tenets of Melanie Klein's psychogenetic narrative. In the earliest stage of psychic development, dominated by what Klein calls the 'paranoid-schizoid position', the infant doesn't relate to objects in their entirety. On the one hand because the infantile ego is weak, unorganised, unintegrated, and on the other because its oral-sadistic tendencies shred objects into bits, the infant 'introjects' only parts of objects into its ego and 'projects' only parts of its ego into external objects.[1] While some of these 'part-objects' or 'partial objects' are good (the bountiful breast first of all), others are bad (the withholding breast), and the developing psyche becomes the frontline of a struggle between good objects and bad. Because the ego splits as a defence mechanism that disperses threats posed by bad partial objects, Klein describes this position as 'schizoid', but this description risks confusion for two related reasons.

First, this position grounds any future schizophrenic disorders, which thus anachronistically lend their name to their source.[2] Consequently, Klein often parries misguided accusations that she regards 'all infants as psychotic' (III:1). For Klein, in fact, the contrary is true. The schizoid position, second, constitutes part of 'normal' psychic development. A sort of psychic autoimmunity, however, the at once 'schizoid' and 'normal' defence of splitting also weakens the infant's already weak ego, and splitting too long or too frequently heightens the risk of hardening what should be a temporary schism into a permanent abyss and, in the same stroke, the normal position into a clinical condition (III:8–10).

Many factors condition this possible fixation or regression, and the schizophrenic disorder itself takes many forms, but the pathology always concerns an inability to unify the ego. Although in *Anti-Oedipus* Deleuze and Guattari will critique Klein's reparative narrative ordaining part to wholeness (AŒ 54–5|44–5), a point to which I'll eventually return, in *Logic of Sense* Deleuze accepts the wholesome horizon, even insists upon it, and only takes issue with how the infantile psyche totalises and to what end. This totalisation, in short, constitutes the first of three stages in the dynamic genesis that ultimately leads to the metaphysical surface on which Deleuze rests the logic of sense. Not, however, without a profound and congenital ambivalence that unfolds on two tiers.

1. *Intracorporeal ambivalence.* The first tier Deleuze recognises and even names as such: 'ambivalence' (LS 108|88, 113|92, 226|194). To anticipate its contrast with the second, this first ambivalence remains entirely within the corporeal depths, that is, without reference to the incorporeal surface. More precisely, it corresponds to two corporeal configurations. The first concerns the body fragmented by and into partial objects (*le corps morcelé*). Because the Deleuze of *Logic of Sense* holds that all partial objects are in principle bad (LS 219|188), at a distance in this regard from not only Klein's axiology but also and more remarkably his own in *Anti-Oedipus* (to which I'll return below), he associates the fragmented body with pure persecution and therefore suffering, passion and passivity. The developing psyche overcomes this passivity, it transforms painful passion into triumphant action, by totalising its partial objects, and this totality leads to later stages of psychogenesis. Yet, whereas Klein totalises her partial objects by introjecting a whole object upon which the ego models its own integration (Klein III:3), Deleuze holds that all introjection fragments and thus corrupts the object it introjects. Without recourse to a whole object, accordingly, he invokes another model. This other model of totalisation constitutes a second body or a second aspect of the body that Deleuze calls variously 'a glorious body', 'an organism without parts' and 'the superior body'. More notoriously, he calls it 'the body without organs'.

> What the schizoid position opposes to the bad partial objects introjected and projected, toxic and excremental, oral and anal, is not a good object, even partial, but rather an organism without parts, a body without organs, without mouth and without anus, having renounced all introjection and projection, and complete at this price. (LS 219–20|188)

Whence Deleuze's 'ambivalence': on the one hand, the fragmented body, partial objects without organisation or integration, pure passion and suffering; on the other, the 'whole' or 'complete' body without organs, totalisation, activation of passion and the end of the psyche's initial suffering.

Enigmatically, the positive valence of the body without organs reaches its highest and clearest expression not when Deleuze opposes it to the fragmented body, however passive and persecutory, but rather when he contrasts the pioneer of depths to the carpenter of surfaces, the schizophrenic poet to the superficial poet, Antonin Artaud to Lewis Carroll. When Deleuze broaches the schizophrenic body without organs for the first time in the *Logic of Sense*, for the first time in his oeuvre in general, he does so in terms of language, and the dynamic genesis is so far only implicit. The basic axiom organising the *Logic of Sense* posits that 'sense' both differentiates and unites words and things. On which I won't say more because, in 'the language of schizophrenia' (which, Deleuze eventually recognises, is not a 'language' in any sense),[3] sense fails and words collapse into things the materiality of which persecutes the body directly. A 'pure affect-language', Deleuze says (LS 107|88).

> For the schizophrenic, then, the issue is less recuperating sense than destroying the word, dispelling affect [*conjurer l'affect*] or transforming the painful passion of the body into triumphant action, obedience into commandment, still in this depth beneath the split surface. (LS 108|88)

When Mark Lester translates *conjurer l'affect* as 'conjuring up the affect', he inadvertently marks how unexpected this moment might seem. Unthinkable that Deleuze, pillar of affect theory, should speak of *dispelling affect*. And yet, in French, *conjurer* doesn't mean 'to conjure' or 'to summon' but rather 'to dispel' or, as Daniel Smith translates it in a related context in *Francis Bacon*, 'to avoid' (FB 54|53). Like English, the French word also has religious and magical connotations but, even then, it doesn't mean 'to call forth' but rather 'to divert' or 'deflect' (Littré: *détourner*). The literal translation of *conjurer* as 'conjure up', in short, desensitises readers to the suffering and thus the originary ambivalence that the schizophrenic strives to overcome by transforming passion into action. This transformation, more specifically, transforms the fragmented body of language into a body without organs, and the latter's impassive activity ultimately grounds the anomalous comparison with which Deleuze closes his discussion of the 'The Schizophrenic and the Little Girl' in series fourteen. Although Deleuze eventually associates the first three chapters of *Alice in Wonderland* with 'the schizoid element of depth' (LS 273|234), *all* of Carroll does not compare with *any* of Artaud.

> For all of Carroll, we [*nous*] would not give one page of Antonin Artaud; Artaud alone has been absolute depth in literature, and he alone discovered a vital body and the prodigious language of this body by way of suffering, as he says. He explored the infra-sense, today still unknown. But Carroll remains the master or carpenter of surfaces that one believed to be so well known that one did not explore them, [surfaces] to which nevertheless the whole logic of sense keeps [*se tient*]. (LS 114|93)

Once the focus shifts to the unconscious and its components in *Anti-Oedipus*, one might expect a comparison of this sort. Over against Carroll, 'the coward of belles-lettres' who neurotically recodifies schizophrenic decodifications, Artaud duly becomes the very 'accomplishment' – *l'accomplissement*: the fulfilment, the achievement, the end – 'of literature' (ACE 163|135). But how does Deleuze reach this estimation within the horizon of the *Logic of Sense*? The necessary references are of limited help here.[4] If indeed the whole logic of sense keeps to the surface, then Deleuze's valorisation of Artaud's corporeal page over Carroll's superficial oeuvre has no rigorous place in the *Logic of Sense*. Unless, however, the valences of the two ambivalent poles – fragmented organs versus body without organs – open onto an axiology that swallows the entire horizon of sense, series and surface.

Accordingly, if the positive valence doesn't divide from the negative as clearly as Deleuze presumes, action from passion, the fragmented body from the whole body without organs, then the consequences of this radical and insurmountable ambivalence go far beyond the *Logic of Sense*. To be sure, Deleuze himself readily recognises that the body without organs is 'necessarily corrupted'. But he entrusts the purity of the body without organs to the difference between *corrupted* and *corrupt*. 'The fluid', which for Deleuze operates the unity of the body without organs, 'is necessarily corrupted, but not by itself, only by the other pole from which it is inseparable' (LS 108–9|89). The other pole is passion. Action is corrupted by passion

248

because, if it were corrupt in itself, action would include elements of passivity in its very constitution, and it would cease to be entirely active. Action would be 'action' only so to speak. As long as something else overtakes action and corrupts it, by contrast, action might in fact be corrupted, but it remains pure and positive in itself and in principle. Yet, Deleuze doesn't seem to realise the aporia. Even the purest action would prove incapable of at least one act: it could never be the agent of its own corruption. Corrupted by the other pole, not only does action suffer; it suffers passion itself. In which case, inversely, passion not only acts; it acts upon action itself. Even at its purest, action remains minimally passionate just as, inversely, the purest passion is never purely passionate. If action suffers without simply becoming passion (because it suffers passion) and passion acts without simply becoming action (because it acts upon action), the very opposition of action and passion points to a more originary ambivalence that divides action from itself before dividing action from passion and vice versa. Rigorously irreducible and insuperable, undiagnosable and incurable, indiscernible and indiscriminate, this more originary ambivalence offers no pure valence in which to take comfort. Needless to say, corruption never registers as an activity or passivity in Deleuze's action-passion ambivalence.

2. *Extracorporeal ambivalence*. While the first ambivalence or first tier of ambivalence divides body from body, the passive and fragmented body from the active and full body without organs, the second pertains to the body's fundamental role in the larger context of the dynamic genesis that culminates in the constitution of the metaphysical surface. From series twenty-seven to twenty-nine, Deleuze posits three stages in all. The initial ambivalence, the intracorporeal, unfolds only in the first phase.

– First Phase (§27). Partial objects persecute. Body without organs totalises partial objects and thereby integrates ego. Ego strengthens, relates to whole objects. Beyond bodily 'depths', projection of whole object into 'heights'. Remorse for damage done to parts of whole object in self-defence. Schizoid position becomes depressive position.
– Second Phase (§28). Heights open perspective from which body becomes surface. Demarcation of partial zones upon surface of body around orifices (oral, anal, so on). Genital zone constellates all partial zones into a single surface. Depressive position becomes sexual position. Oedipus complex begins.
– Third Phase (§29). Castration anxiety disintegrates Oedipus complex. Desexualisation. Disinvested libido (sublimation) reinvests in thinking

(symbolisation). Physical surface becomes metaphysical surface. Impassive and impassible, beyond action and passion, beyond the body and its mixtures. Pure thought. The logic of sense unfolds.

I won't engage or even list Deleuze's revisions of Klein or Freud or, for that matter, Klein's revisions of Freud. I've telegraphed these three psychogenetic stages only to situate the body and affect, actions and passions, within the larger undertaking of the *Logic of Sense*. Whatever the novelty with respect to its terms, stages and end, the ambivalent place of affect is far from new. In a word, it constitutes another hitch.

On the one hand, everything depends upon affect. Just as sensibility inaugurates the facultative chain that ends in thinking in the first book in which Deleuze does philosophy (*Difference and Repetition*), just as affects springboard the movement toward percepts in the last text of Deleuze's last book ('Spinoza and the Three "Ethics"'), just as I argue in Chapters 1 and 6 above, so too the affective depths constitute the first indispensable step toward the apathetic surface of 'pure thought' in *Logic of Sense* (LS 243|208). The first and the most indispensable because, even if every step is indispensable, only upon the *first* step does *every* step depend. Following *Difference and Repetition*, moreover, in *Logic of Sense* Deleuze continues to critique 'common sense' for organising the faculties around the supposed identities of a unified subject and a unified object that reduce the singularity of each faculty (LS 95–6|77–8), but even the most paradoxically exercised sensibility, once again, leads to its own repression when it leads to an impassible surface.

On the other hand, affect threatens the entire genetic progression it inaugurates. 'Nothing more fragile', Deleuze says for the first of many times, 'than the surface' (LS 101|82). Nothing is more fragile because, he goes on to specify, the schizophrenic body threatens not simply to resurface but, rather, to rip the surface itself (LS 106|86 *et passim*), to engulf all sense (LS 111|91 *et passim*), to block all series (LS 111|91 *et passim*). Which is why, when he finally reaches his surface and despite his anomalous admiration for every page of Artaud, Deleuze still refers to the corporeal depths as an 'enemy' (LS 239|205). Can the purely cerebral surface ever be entirely 'impassive' if, even when allegedly beyond all bodily actions and passions, it remains vulnerable to affectability itself? Since the corporeal effectuates the incorporeal, the threat proves unavoidable; since the incorporeal represses the corporeal without eradicating it, the threat proves enduring.

Deleuze returns to the fragility of his enterprise obsessively throughout *Logic of Sense* with various attempts to reinforce and reassure the surface.[5] Until finally, at the beginning of the last series and thus even after all his specifications and qualifications, he invokes the threat one last and conclusive time from a holistic perspective on the entire trajectory just traversed. Separating physical depth from metaphysical surface as 'two extremes', he calls their confusion – the relapse into corporeal depths – 'the greatest danger' and, inversely, the constitution of the metaphysical surface 'the greatest chance' (LS 279|239). Perhaps too eagerly, however, too optimistically, in any case certainly too simply. For if everything begins in bodily depth, if the metaphysical surface results from the physical depths and even if cause (corporeal affects) and effect (impassible incorporeals) differ in nature, then the greatest threat is also the greatest chance. Even greater than the greatest chance because the first and, at first, the only chance for the greatest chance as Deleuze understands it.

At which point, the concept of 'fragility' invoked so often in *Logic of Sense* ceases to suffice. The concept harbours a surreptitious security insofar as it describes something that already exists. In other words, it implicitly assumes not only the possibility but also, however fleeting and precarious, the existence of that to which it applies. Fragility, in this case, presupposes that one *can* and already *has* reached the metaphysical surface – pure and impassible thought – that only therefore risks breaking, relapsing, collapsing into the depths. Fragility, then, struggles to describe the risk when the risk also constitutes the chance and thereby weighs upon the very existence of what might not and never exist. None of Deleuze's many references to fragility take this possible impossibility into account. The possibility, that is, not only that the depths might swallow the surface, but also that the depths swallow the surface before it surfaces, in which case there would be nothing either 'fragile' or 'secure'. This more primordial risk proves absolutely uninsurable, and it both undermines and intensifies not only the *Logic of Sense*, not only the other avatars of the same genetic threat throughout Deleuze's work, but also every transcendental discourse on fragility, vulnerability, precarity and the like.

Pre-Primary Emotion

Deleuze famously credits Guattari with helping him break with psychoanalysis. If indeed *Anti-Oedipus* constitutes 'a rupture'

(P 197|144), the rupture registers most clearly in the work's opposition to numerous elements mobilised in the dynamic genesis of *Logic of Sense* only three years earlier: not only Oedipus, of course, but also the whole accompanying conceptual complex (guilt, castration, phallus and so on). The rupture, however, isn't clean. Not only because *Anti-Oedipus* never entirely eradicates concepts like castration and not only, inversely, because earlier works already anticipate certain ruptures.[6] More importantly, any rupture separating *Logic of Sense* and *Anti-Oedipus* – along with debates to which it leads in the secondary criticism[7] – also serves to manifest an even greater continuity. The greatest rupture provides the greatest opportunity to glimpse, namely, the ambivalence that traverses both books and thus Deleuze's thought at large.

The greatest rupture and the greater continuity, all things considered, register on the body without organs. Although the body without organs already fascinates Deleuze in the *Logic of Sense*, he still views it as at best a prelude and at worst an enemy to his superficial metaphysics in *Logic of Sense*. The body without organs develops in its own right, accordingly, only when the metaphysical surface no longer orients the inquiry, only when the schizophrenic body becomes the object of inquiry, only in and after *Anti-Oedipus*. 'I have changed', Deleuze announces at a conference shortly after *Anti-Oedipus* appears. 'The surface-depth opposition no longer concerns me. What interests me now are the relations between a full body, a body without organs, and running flows [*des flux qui coulent*]' (ID 364|261). These relations, more precisely, break down into three syntheses. Each synthesises according to a law that distinguishes it from the other two, and together they form the theory of the unconscious in *Anti-Oedipus*. Deleuze and Guattari dedicate the first three sections of the first chapter to each synthesis, respectively, but they spend the entire book refining, resetting and redeploying them. Schematic and emphatic so as to come more quickly to the third, where affect culminates the entire process but ambivalence still underpins it, my treatment here will no doubt leave much to be desired.

The first synthesis synthesises by 'connection' or 'conjunction' (AŒ 13|5). It describes the interaction of partial objects, more specifically, by way of flows (*flux*) and cuts (*coupures*). Each partial object emits a flow that another cuts. The synthesis between any two partial objects is never closed or static, however, because the partial object that cuts one flow also emits a flow cut by another partial object in turn. The mouth that cuts the milk emitted from the breast in a nursing machine, examples from the first page of *Anti-Oedipus*, might also emit a flow in an anorexic machine.

The second synthesis synthesises partial objects by 'disjunction' or 'inscription'. When partial objects connect in the first synthesis, if only minimally and even if dynamically, they inevitably organise the body. Defined in opposition to all organisation rather than to any organs *per se*, as a result, the body without organs suffers. 'The desiring machines' – the part-objects, the organ-machines – 'make us an organism, but at the heart of this production, in its very production, the body suffers from being organized thus' (AŒ 16|8). (Pivotal to both the function and the malfunction of the machine, I'll return to this suffering more than once in what follows. For the moment, so as to continue the process, I only note this early entrance of affect discreetly.) This suffering triggers a double reaction from the body without organs. First, it repels or neutralises partial objects in what Deleuze and Guattari call, commandeering the psychoanalytic concept, 'primary [*originaire*] repression' (AŒ 17|9). But they call the conflict between partial objects and the body without organs 'apparent' because, second, the body without organs appropriates the partial objects so thoroughly that it seems to become their cause or, rather, their 'quasi-cause' (AŒ 18|10).[8] When the 'repulsion machine' thus gives way to an 'attraction machine', the topography becomes difficult to navigate. Deleuze and Guattari describe the body without organs variously as a surface *upon* which partial objects distribute (AŒ 17|9), a network that spreads *between* partial objects (AŒ 20|12) and a whole *beside* the partial objects it trails (AŒ 53–4|42, 393|326). Every description, however, ultimately describes a 'disjunctive' synthesis because the body without organs synthesises the partial objects, not by totalising them into a prior or a higher whole, but rather by affirming their difference to and distance from each other.[9]

The third synthesis, finally, synthesises by 'consumption' or 'consummation'. Even after repression gives way to attraction in the second synthesis, the opposition between partial objects and the body without organs persists (AŒ 19|11, 25|17). Partial objects resurge, they regroup and reorganise, but the return of the repressed doesn't return the repression. Rather, the ongoing conflict leads to a third synthesis at once *consumptive* because it feeds off leftovers (*restes*) from the second synthesis and *consummate* because it weds the previous syntheses in a final synthesis of syntheses. The tendency to organise and the tendency to repress all organisation, the force of repulsion and the force of attraction, the remaining *tensions* between partial objects and the body without organs, in short, create *intensities* that Deleuze and Guattari call 'affect' (AŒ 27|18–19, 104|84) of or as a subject they call 'nomadic' (AŒ 24 ff.|16 ff. and 36|26).[10] For Freud, strictly speaking, "there are no unconscious affects [*Affekte*]" (GW 10:277|'Unconscious' 178); for Deleuze and Guattari, by contrast, affect consummates the unconscious. This consummatory position, however, isn't entirely positive. By neglecting this precise place and technical role of affect in *Anti-Oedipus*, commentators commonly forfeit the tools necessary to appreciate – wherever their sympathies lie – both the consummate value of affect in the unconscious machine and its intractable threat to jam the machine beyond repair.[11] Although inseparable, I'll address each in turn.

From a functional perspective, the ambivalence in *Logic of Sense* appears to dissipate in *Anti-Oedipus*, and Deleuze seems to sing affect a palinode. When partial objects persecute the body in *Logic of Sense*, the body without organs responds with a gesture of totalisation meant, in Deleuze's words, to dispel affect (*conjurer l'affect*), and every subsequent stage in Deleuze's psychogenetic narrative heightens this fundamental neutralisation of affect until – hitches notwithstanding – finally reaching the impassive surface of 'pure thought'. In *Anti-Oedipus*, the conflict still produces misery as well as glory, pain as well as pleasure, but Deleuze and Guattari no longer drive affect out or away. They no longer speak of ambivalence. Now, rather, they insist: intensities are 'all positive' (AŒ 27|19).

Not only does positivity prevail. Affect even consummates the unconscious syntheses, the libidinal metaphysics, the entire schizoanalytical project. According to Deleuze and Guattari's fundamental principle, the unconscious invests the social realm immediately. Immediately means, above all, without mediation through the family. Despite early plans and prophecies to study jurisprudence, as an adult Freud had 'no more than the average interest in politics and modes of government' (Jones 5). Deleuze and Guattari constantly criticise Freud for either ignoring socio-political factors in his case studies or interpreting them as displacements of more fundamental familial relations. If desire invests the social immediately, however, then my delusions about God (Schreber) and my dreams about wolves (Pankejeff) no longer represent my unconscious relation to either or both of my parents in part or as wholes. No longer limited to family members, the partial elements of my unconscious invest all

254

strata of all societies from all eras and all areas, from all parties of all wars and all conflicts both revolutionary and reactionary, from all tribes and all races, from all animals, from all of what Deleuze and Guattari call, in sum, 'universal history' (AŒ 30|21). Since affect operates these historical investments in the third synthesis of the unconscious, not only does every affect break the Oedipal axis. Affect also operates the socio-politicisation of the unconscious that transforms psychoanalysis into schizoanalysis.[12]

From a still more sensitive perspective, however, the unconscious doesn't produce intensities without a sensible hitch in the chain of syntheses. The third synthesis of the unconscious produces what Deleuze and Guattari call 'a truly primary emotion' (AŒ 27|18) but, as I noted above in passing, it isn't the first affectivity in *Anti-Oedipus*. Not if, before it 'attracts' and 'appropriates' them, the body without organs 'repels' and 'represses' partial objects because they afflict it by organising it. Since it therefore suffers before *either* repelling *or* attracting the partial objects that affect it, and since the tensions between these forces of repulsion and attraction produce what Deleuze and Guattari call 'primary emotion' in a third synthesis that therefore presupposes the first two, logically if not chronologically (AŒ 395|327), the body without organs suffers partial objects as a *pre-primary emotion* or *affect*. So, for all the reasons Eric Alliez draws from both Deleuze and Artaud, the body without organs no doubt 'hurts the philosopher' (Alliez 93), but it hurts in the *transitive* only after it hurts in the *intransitive* sense.

This earlier early affect reintroduces a certain ambivalence into the unconscious machinations the very processes of which, in the third and consummate synthesis, would otherwise affirm affect without reserve. If the body without organs neutralises partial objects in order to neutralise its suffering, if this double neutralisation is the first force in the tensions that constitute intensity or affect in a strict sense, then 'primary emotion' presupposes not only a more primordial affect, a pre-primary emotion, but also and more importantly a prior effort to neutralise affectivity. Although it operates different machinery to different ends in a different topology, differences to which I'll eventually return, the effort to neutralise affectivity through the body without organs in *Anti-Oedipus* remains legible as the struggle between partial objects and the body without organs to which, in *Logic of Sense*, Deleuze himself refers as 'ambivalence'. In which case Deleuze and Guattari's unconscious never affirms affect in a strict sense without already having dispelled or at least sought to dispel affect more broadly. Formulated more forcefully, the very affirmation of affect reduces it. To 0. In both *Anti-Oedipus* (AŒ 27|19) and *A Thousand Plateaus* (MP 189|153), to be sure, Deleuze and Guattari insist that there's nothing negative in their formulation of the body without organs as 'intensity = 0'. But 0 isn't positive either and, for even the strangest subject, there would be affectively no difference between zero intensity and absolute distension. Deleuze and Guattari suggest as much when they refer to the body without organs as the threshold of the liveable in *Anti-Oedipus* (AŒ 27|18, 103|84) and an inaccessible limit in *A Thousand Plateaus* (MP 186|150).

The pre-primary reduction harboured in primary emotion suffices to establish that intensity isn't initially or therefore ever purely positive in *Anti-Oedipus*, never entirely univalent and always minimally ambivalent, but the point isn't merely to articulate Deleuze and Guattari's understated complicity with the ascetic tradition that runs at least from Plato to the passionless surface of pure thought in the *Logic of Sense* (to the faculty of thinking in *Difference and Repetition*, to the percept in *Critical and Clinical* and so on). In seeking to end its suffering by repressing partial objects, by dispelling affect, by becoming *a body without affects*, the body without organs also introduces an element of 'anti-production' into the otherwise purely productive machinations of the unconscious. Which gives pause. If indeed 'everything is production' (AŒ 11|4), if Deleuze and Guattari introduce production into desire as one means with which to break the traditional basis of desire on lack since Plato (AŒ 31|22),[13] then why not denounce anti-production as an abomination? One would think – not without textual support – that the unconscious machine opposes all *non*-production and especially all *anti*-production, which suggests not only unproductivity but also sabotage. And yet, they introduce the body without organs in tandem with anti-production: 'The body without organs', they say, 'is of [i.e., of the order of] anti-production' (AŒ 16|8). I'll formalise the resulting undecidability as a means to focus the problem of affect and indicate its scope in conclusion.

On the one hand, anti-production keeps the machine running by refusing all organisation. Not only the organisation of partial objects in the first synthesis, it also refuses the still more insufferable organisation of the unconscious – and, indeed, the world – into an Oedipus complex. While Deleuze and Guattari oppose partial objects to the whole person and thus to parents, to Oedipus, Oedipus and partial objects cease to oppose each other from the therefore more general perspective of affect. Because both organise, the body suffers all the same, and any difference in nature or value between a *partial* organisation and an *Oedipal* organisation scales the same sensitivity. Concerned lest their introduction of the body without organs as a 'third term' be taken for a pro- or proto-Oedipal triangulation (partial object flow + partial object cut + body without organs),[14] Deleuze and Guattari insist that the body without organs as anti-production 'intervenes as such only to refuse all attempt at triangulation implying a parental structure' (AŒ 23|15). More than a morphological continuity, there is thus a conceptual solidarity between the two *anti-* of anti-*production* and anti-*Oedipus*, which not only explains how Deleuze and Guattari can but also why they must introduce anti-production into their unconscious machinery. Anti-production, in short, no longer opposes production because, whether micro-organisations of partial objects or the global imperialism of the Oedipus complex, anti-production disorganises all the organisations that would prevent the unconscious machinations from continuing to function. Deleuze and Guattari even submit that desiring machines only work insofar as they are dysfunctional (AŒ 16|8), going so far as to proportion the machine's functionality to its dysfunctionality (AŒ 182|151), because production produces nothing without anti-production.

On the other hand, anti-production strains the machine to the point of breaking. Deleuze and Guattari implicitly distinguish between a *functional malfunction* and a *dysfunctional malfunction* because the malfunction can itself malfunction and, rather than resetting the machine and lubricating the gears, jam the entire process. It is impossible, of course, to exhaust the wealth of tensions and nuances in *Anti-Oedipus* but, whenever commentators celebrate the body without organs or even – like the more cautious Deleuze and Guattari of *A Thousand of Plateaus* (MP 198–200|160–1) – stress the catastrophic risks involved in becoming a body without organs, they neglect one passage first of all: 'It is only' – *seulement*, Deleuze and Guattari say and I stress, *only* – 'in relation to the body without organs . . . that something is produced, counter-produced, that deviates or exasperates the entire production of which it is nevertheless a part' (AŒ 47|37–8). Insofar as the Oedipus complex remains the greatest deviation, the greatest exasperation, it follows that the body without organs – and only the body without organs – makes possible the Oedipus complex. The body without organs that suffers the Oedipus complex makes it possible; it suffers the Oedipus complex it alone makes possible. We learn why a hundred pages later: when the body without organs neutralises partial objects, when the machine idles, Oedipal forces take advantage of this sterility in order to project or, rather, to retroject whole objects onto the partial objects and thereby introduce parents, the whole family and thus the Oedipus complex into the deepest regions of the unconscious (ACE 146|120–1).

I could have called this dilemma by a number of different names, each with another advantage (double bind, predicament, aporia, collaboration), but I take my cue from Deleuze and Guattari's lexicon. Borrowing the mathematical term more than once in *Anti-Oedipus*, they refer to Oedipus as strictly 'undecidable' (ACE 99|81, 152|126, 156|129). They relate this undecidability to the fact that one cannot subscribe to Oedipus without at the same time fleeing Oedipus. Three years later, although they no longer use the term 'undecidable', they transform this principle into a strategy in their reading of Kafka who, they say, enlarges Oedipus with the aim of revealing 'a whole micropolitics of desire' (K 19|10), which subtends familial triangulations. In light of anti-production, however, the inverse also holds. The same anti-production that prevents Oedipal triangulations (by disorganising the machine) also prepares it (by idling the machine). One cannot de-Oedipalise without re-Oedipalising because, in other words, the anti-production that breaks triangulation also breaks ground for triangulation. The body without organs *grounds* the anti-Oedipal enterprise in the double sense of both making it possible and preventing it from taking off. No amount of resistance to the Oedipus complex with anti-production will destroy or eradicate it if resistance complies and collaborates on the same grounds on which it resists.

From here, at least two paths open or, rather, two directions on the same path.

The path forward follows Deleuze and Guattari as they multiply subtle, massive and sometimes conflicting arguments in the attempt to integrate anti-production into the process while, at the same time, insulating the process from the Oedipality that anti-production also conditions. Very schematically, Deleuze and Guattari wedge an interval between the libidinal regime of the unconscious and the social regime of world history that, nevertheless, they insist are one and the same. The libidinal *is* the social because it invests the social realm immediately. This principle, as I've already mentioned, operates the politicisation that transforms psychoanalysis into schizoanalysis; it plugs affect into all eras and areas of an orphan world. While the libidinal and the social do not differ in nature, however, they do differ in regime (A Œ 40|31), and this double gesture is pivotal. It creates space to manoeuvre: whenever they seek to challenge psychoanalytical familism by insisting upon the socio-politicality of the unconscious, Deleuze and Guattari stress the identity; whenever they seek to maintain the purity and innocence of the unconscious, its victimisation at the hands of an outside culprit (Oedipus and its psychoanalytic handlers), they stress the difference and place all abuse in the social realm.

Among the various elements splintered by the difference in regime between the unconscious and the social, the most important concerns the situation of the body without organs and the anti-production it introduces. In the social regime, the body without organs is an 'extrinsic condition' (A Œ 42|32). As such, it becomes mere anti-production; it halts flows without reconditioning, regenerating or reproducing others, and this sterility allows Oedipus to invade the deepest regions of the unconscious (A Œ 146|32). In the unconscious regime, however, the body without organs is an 'internal result' (A Œ 42|32). The threat that anti-production poses in the social regime seems to dissipate in the unconscious because there, one cog among many in greater machinations, anti-production integrates into productivity. As long as anti-production is a part of productive desire, as long as it also produces, it no longer leads to the sterile conditions of which Oedipus could take advantage.

And yet, even if I bracket Deleuze and Guattari's recourse to an opposition between the 'internal' and the 'extrinsic', which they themselves contest from the very beginning of *Anti-Oedipus* ('exterior and interior no longer mean anything' [A Œ 10|2]), the internalisation of anti-production into production in the unconscious regime raises at least two related series of questions that the first schizoanalysts never pose.

First, if production and anti-production no longer oppose, if the very productivity of production supposes anti-production, then what asymmetry authorises Deleuze and Guattari to retain only the name 'production' when they refer to the whole unconscious, for instance, as desiring production? Unless, of course, productivity remains 'the only authentic relation' (A Œ 33|24), and anti-production ceases to oppose production only because production relegates and regulates anti-production. But, then, is anti-production really anti-productive? Wouldn't the only 'authentic' anti-production sabotage rather than serve productivity? Given that they reserve 'authenticity' for pro-duction, Deleuze and Guattari would likely find this reformulation unpalatable, but they nevertheless move in this direction when, as if the only anti-production worthy of the name, they call Oedipus 'the great agent of anti-production in desire' (AŒ 69|56).

Second, if one accordingly insists upon anti-production as an anti-productivity that refuses to cooperate with productivity, then does any internalisation of anti-production into production ever really assure the productivity of production? On the contrary, wouldn't the incorporation of the body without organs into the process, anti-production into production, radicalise rather than eradicate the threat of an absolute malfunction? Left to its own devices, wouldn't the machine always jam irreparably and, in the same stroke, beckon to Oedipus? In which case (pre-primary) affect would unleash an irreversible process that prevents the machine from ever culminating, that is, from ever culminating in (primary) affect.

In a sense, the task and thus the very existence of schizoanalysis raise these questions. Most often, Deleuze and Guattari describe their task as janitorial: scour Oedipus from the unconscious so as to reveal its real investments (AŒ 92|74, 100|81, 120|98, 127–8|105, 136|112 and so on). This non-invasive procedure is entirely consist-ent with Deleuze and Guattari's claim, when they first introduce the body without organs in *Anti-Oedipus*, that the machine itself couples anti-production to production: 'The full body without organs is of anti-production, but it is another characteristic of the connective or productive synthesis to couple production to anti-production, to an element of anti-production' (AŒ 16|8). Late in the fourth and final chapter, however, the 'destructive' task gives way to a 'positive' task that only incidentally reveals something very different about the nature of the machine. Deleuze and Guattari explicitly recognise that Oedipal illusions could never take hold without support from the unconscious itself, and they attribute this collaboration once again to the body without organs, to anti-production, to the repression of partial objects that I've stressed as the anesthetisation of a pre-primary affect. The conversion of anti-production into production that they previously *describe* as a characteristic of the unconscious machine's automated functioning, however, they now *prescribe* as a task for schizoanalysis:

undo the blockage or jamming [*coincidence*] on which repression prop-erly speaking rests, transform the apparent opposition of repulsion (body

without organs-partial object machines) into a condition of real functioning, ensure this functioning in the forms of attraction and the production
of intensities, then integrate the failures in the attractive functioning, as
well as envelope the degree zero in the intensities produced, and thereby
make the desiring machines relaunch [*repartir*]. (ACE 410|339)

The machine is manual. The schizoanalyst must unjam the machine
so that anti-production produces, *so that* repulsion attracts, *so that*
failure functions and the process proceeds, *so that* the machine produces affect in the third and consummative synthesis. The tendency
to reduce all affect precedes and prevents the tendency to produce
affects unless schizoanalysis intervenes – against the nature of the
machine in whose name it operates – to assure its conversion. To
telescope only one consequence: if the unconscious doesn't produce
a productive anti-production, if its malfunction doesn't function,
if in short the unconscious doesn't become what it is until schizoanalysis fulfils its positive task, then schizoanalysis avoids the accusations of illegitimacy that it levels at psychoanalysis, if at all, only
to the preposterous extent that it manufactures the unconscious
from which it draws the 'immanent' criteria with which it judges
legitimate and illegitimate uses of the unconscious (see ACE 92|74–5
et passim).

The path backward retraces all of Deleuze and Guattari's difficulties, not to their source in the body without organs (anti-production),
but to the source of the source in pre-primary affect and then on back
to *Logic of Sense*. I've reserved a fundamental difference between
Logic of Sense and *Anti-Oedipus* for this moment. In both works,
the body without organs responds to the persecution of the body by
partial objects, but a change in the nature of partial objects changes
the nature of the persecution profoundly from one enterprise to the
next. In *Logic of Sense*, the partiality of partial objects persecutes.
For Deleuze and for Klein, whose psychogenetic account informs
his own in this context, the ability to relate to 'a complete object'
constitutes progress in the psychic development of a child because
the infantile psyche uses the whole object as a model for integrating
its own ego. But Deleuze raises the stakes on Klein's wholesome *telos*
when he claims that all partial objects are 'bad' because 'only the
whole, the complete is good' (LS 218–19|187–8).[15] In *Anti-Oedipus*,
by contrast, partial objects are – I emphasise – '*essentially* fragmen-
tary and fragmented' (ACE 13|5), and with Guattari Deleuze now
critiques Klein for sacrificing the partiality of the partial object to a

whole, a 'mistake' he not only made but also exacerbated only a few years prior:

> she does not rid herself of the idea that schizo-paranoid objects refer to a whole, whether original in a primitive phase or to come in the later depressive position (the complete Object). Partial objects thus seem to her extracted from global persons; not only will they enter into totalities of integration concerning the ego, the object, and drives; they also already constitute the first type of object relation between the ego, the mother, and the father. Yet, it is there indeed that everything is decided in the final analysis. (ANŒ 54–5|44)

And yet, despite the decisive shift from the good whole to the essential fragment, where 'everything is decided', partial objects continue to persecute the body in *Anti-Oedipus*. No longer because they fragment, partial objects now persecute the body, as if despite themselves, because they organise: 'the body suffers from being organized thus' (cited above). In Husserl's method of eidetic variation, various iterations of a phenomenon – in the world or the world itself – serve to reveal an invariant structure, the phenomenon's essence, its *eidos*. From *Logic of Sense* to *Anti-Oedipus* a sort of aesthetic variation takes place in which variations in the source of suffering from fragmentation to organisation reveal an invariant through which the otherwise heterogeneous projects continue to communicate: the absence of affect. Every variation – every shift, rupture or revolution from *Logic of Sense* to *Anti-Oedipus* and beyond – only emphasises this invariant drive to disaffect. The body might organise, it might fragment, but it must desensitise.

In fact, in *Anti-Oedipus*, this ascetic drive even intensifies. In contrast to the incorporeal nature of the superficial metaphysics in *Logic of Sense*, the neutralisation of affect in the libidinal metaphysics of *Anti-Oedipus* takes place through the impassivity of a surface that remains corporeal. Accordingly, whereas the body without organs threatens to collapse the surface into the depths in *Logic of Sense*, in *Anti-Oedipus* it threatens to crush even the depths, even the unconscious, even the cuts and the flows. Even the world historical affect that, however 'primary', still comes too late (if at all).

Gilles Blanched

In a simultaneously vitriolic and flirtatious letter, Michel Cressole accuses Deleuze of profiting from the experiences and experimentations of others – schizophrenics, homosexuals, addicts – without ever risking an experience of his own. In his reply, Deleuze calls one sentence in particular from the penultimate paragraph of *Anti-Oedipus* his favourite: 'Someone asked us if we had ever seen a schizophrenic; no, no, we have never seen one' (AŒ 460|380; P 22|12; in Cressole 118). How is one to take this statement? What does it even state? Is it an affirmation or a confession? An observation or a principle? Will anyone ever see a schizophrenic and why does the visual register prevail? Who is the 'someone' that asked? In his 'Letter to a Harsh Critic', Deleuze argues that experiences are never reserved for this or that individual or group of individuals, closed off from the rest, because one can always reach by other means the same effect reached by, for instance, drug addicts: 'Why will I not speak of drugs without being drugged, if I speak as a little bird?' (P 22|11–12; in Cressole 117).

Deleuze and Guattari wrote *Anti-Oedipus* largely through correspondence. Guattari sent his texts to Deleuze and Deleuze, in turn, polished and underwrote them with a more rigorously philosophical discourse. They usually met only once a week to work on the manuscript together. In an interview he conducted for his biography of Deleuze and Guattari, François Dosse transcribes an exceptional anecdote explaining why the pair most often met in Paris at Deleuze's house rather than in La Borde at or near Guattari's experimental clinic. In the words of a witness: 'One day, Félix, Arlette Donati, Gilles, and I' (Alain Aptekman) 'were eating at Dhuizon' (a chateau near La Borde),

> and we got a call from La Borde saying that a guy had set fire to the chateau chapel and run off into the woods. Gilles blanched [*blêmit*], I froze, and Félix called for help to find the guy. At that point, Gilles said to me, 'How can you stand those schizos'? He couldn't bear the sight of crazy people. (Quoted in Dosse, *Biographie* 19|*Intersecting* 7–8)

While Diogenes Laertius recorded anecdotes to capture a philosopher's thought, Nietzsche made the vital aphorism a veritable method and Deleuze himself applied it, but it also applies to Deleuze: 'find vital Aphorisms that are also Anecdotes of thought' (LS 153|128). What might this anecdote suggest?

The critic – a harsh critic like Cressole – might take the anecdote to confirm Deleuze's practical detachment from the experiences he theorises. There would seem to be no better emblem of the schizoanalytical project than a 'schizo' fleeing his clinical confines and setting fire to the stronghold of the holy trinity that Deleuze and Guattari denounce as one more instantiation of Oedipal triangulation. In light of everything Deleuze and Guattari say in the opening pages of *Anti-Oedipus* about getting the schizophrenic off the analyst's divan and out into nature, even the flight into the woods becomes significant. And yet, Deleuze grows pale. He can't bear the sight – not even the thought – of 'those schizos'.

The schizoanalyst might retort that a schizophrenic isn't schizophrenic since Deleuze and Guattari distinguish the metaphysical schizophrenic from the clinical schizophrenic. They deny 'schizophrenia' in the metaphysical sense any restricted referent, even deny schizophrenia itself any specificity at all, because it refers more generally to 'the universe of productive and reproductive desiring machines' (ACE 13|5). No one has ever seen *a* schizophrenic because schizophrenia refers to the unconscious process as a whole and, as a whole, the unconscious process involves the whole universe. So, the only schizophrenic anyone will ever actually see is 'the artificial schizophrenic that one sees in the mental institution [*l'hôpital*]' (ACE 13|5). Even when you see a schizophrenic, you don't see a schizophrenic, but the point's irrelevant.

Yet again, don't Deleuze and Guattari name the process 'schizophrenia' because it has an 'intimate relation' with the eponymous disorder (ACE 164|136)? In which case to see even an artificial schizophrenic would be to see something of even the most universal schizophrenia after all.

As the critic and the analyst continue to argue, a more sensitive approach might stress Deleuze. He blanches; he can't bear it. But what affects him? If the schizophrenic process culminates in the production of affect, if emotion is truly primary because it precedes not only the subject but also all delirium and all hallucination, if pure intensity burns the chapel and flees into the wilderness, then does anything affect Deleuze other than affect itself? In this case, perhaps, anecdote and aphorism would meet in pure ambivalence.

Notes

1. The infant's sadistic tendencies, according to Klein, correspond to its earliest anxieties concerning the already operative death drive, the trauma of birth and frustrated physical needs (Klein III:4-5). For the history of the complementary processes 'projection' and 'introjection' as Klein inherits them, see Freud's 1905 'Fragment of an Analysis of

a Case of Hysteria' and 1917 'Mourning and Melancholia', chapter 2 of S. Ferenczi's *Contributions to Psycho-Analysis* on 'Introjection and Transference' (originally published in 1909) and Karl Abraham's proposal of 'partial incorporation' in his 1924 'A Short Study of the Development of the Libido, Viewed in the Light of Mental Disorders' (for a schematic view, see Abraham 90|496).

2. Even before Klein renamed the 'paranoid position' the 'paranoid-schizoid position' in 1946 and systematised its use in 1952 (III:2 note 1), she had marked the source of schizophrenia in the infant's earliest psychogenetic stage. For instance, see I:263 and I:288, as well as *Psychoanalyse* 154–5|*Psychoanalysis* 204–5.

3. Compare LS 103|84 and 159|134, but see also 220|189.

4. In addition to following the intervening pages in detail, this passage would require recourse to Deleuze's conjugation of 'the critical' and 'the clinical' not only throughout *Logic of Sense* (LS 102|83, 113|92, 276–8|237–8), but also in other works ranging from *Coldness and Cruelty* (1967) to *Critical and Clinical* (1993).

5. LS 115|94, 151|125–6, 159|134, 165–6|140–1, 183–4|156–8, 196–7|167–8, 232|199, 236|202, 243–4|208–9, 285|244–5. I isolate only Deleuze's attempt to reinforce and reassure the surface by redoubling causality, *first* because this attempt is the most original and radical, *second* because it allows me to acknowledge the complexity of Deleuze's schema in more detail, and *third* – above all – because the assurance ultimately only exacerbates the risk. The corporeal produces the incorporeal, both the surface and the sense that rests upon it, but cause and effect differ in nature. Incorporeal effects, Deleuze says, relate to each other independently of their relation to their corporeal cause. Whence the central idea of 'double causality' (series fourteen *et passim*): the corporeal is the 'real' and 'material' cause of the incorporeal, but an incorporeal is the 'fictive' and 'quasi' cause of another incorporeal. In fact, although Deleuze names only two, four causalities operate the *Logic of Sense*: (*i*) corporeal to corporeal; (*ii*) corporeal to incorporeal; (*iii*) incorporeal to incorporeal; (*iv*) incorporeal to corporeal. Deleuze's 'double causality' refers only to (*ii*) and (*iii*), but (*iv*) grounds the idea of a 'static genesis' (series sixteen and seventeen). While the 'dynamic genesis' (series twenty-seven to twenty-nine) moves from corporeal to incorporeal, the static genesis moves from incorporeal back to corporeal.

One might think this proliferation of causalities lessens and even dissipates the bodily threat to Deleuze's superficial metaphysics. *Lessens* because incorporeal relations constitute a causal chain independent of the corporeal, and the corporeal threat thus seems only partial and therefore containable. *Dissipates* because the static genesis, no longer from body to sense but now from sense to body, seems to avoid the corporeal threat entirely. Deleuze himself calls sense 'safe' (it *se sauve*) when the causal relation takes into account the heterogeneity of cause and effect (LS 115|94).

Everything, however, depends upon the order. Deleuze might speak of 'coexistence' in the last series (LS 284|243 and 289|247), but the surface coexists with the depths only after the depths produce it. The static genesis presupposes the dynamic; it takes effect only 'in turn' and, even then, only 'as long as the surface holds' (LS 151|125). Sense *first* results from a 'measureless pulsation' (LS 150–1|124) and *then* individuates the material mass. To get 'there', Deleuze says with explicit reference to the object of the static genesis, 'it was necessary to pass through all the steps of the dynamic genesis' (LS 281|241). The sequence is crucial because it allows Deleuze to resolve the apparent contradiction according to which sense both results from and determines a bodily state of affairs (LS 116|95 and 149–51|124–6). More crucially still, however, the multiplication of causalities falls far short of insuring or reassuring the genetic threat of schizoid corporality. Indeed, it has the very opposite effect. Insofar as sense produces, determines or individuates my body from material pulsations, any relapse into the depths isn't simply a relapse into *my* body. It is not my mouth, my tongue, my teeth that hurt, all of which depend upon sense for their individuation. Because my body as I know it depends upon sense for its organisation into organs and systems, any schizophrenic relapse falls into the immeasurably deeper depth of a senseless and unlocalisable pain that, prior to all individuation, does not even qualify as a 'state of affairs'.

6. For instance, Deleuze and Guattari speak of 'an an-Oedipal castration [*une castration anœdipienne*]' (AŒ 91|74) and, more generally, present schizoanalysis itself as a reversal (*réversion*) internal to psychoanalysis (AŒ 100|82). Inversely, Deleuze excuses his 'naïve and guilty' relation to psychoanalysis in *Logic of Sense* with reference to an innocuous Oedipus unrecognisable in the Freudian tradition. 'I nevertheless attempted, very timidly, to make psychoanalysis *inoffensive* by presenting it as an art of surfaces, which deals with events as superficial entities (Oedipus is not mean; Oedipus has only good intentions . . .)' (DRF 60|65). On Oedipus's good intentions in *Logic of Sense*, see series twenty-nine. See also *Kafka* where, with Guattari, Deleuze in a way returns to 'the hypothesis of an innocence of the father' (K 18|9). One would also have to add the determination of Oedipus as a man 'without family' earlier still in *Difference and Repetition* (DR 121|90). More stylistically, Deleuze also claims, in explicitly anti-Oedipal terms, that he already began to treat writing as a 'flow' rather than a 'code' in *Difference and Repetition* and *Logic of Sense* (P 16|7).

7. While Slavoj Žižek outright rejects *Anti-Oedipus* in favour of 'Deleuze

proper' in *Logic of Sense* (Žižek 18), Daniel Smith is more sensitive to its continuity with *Logic of Sense*. Nevertheless, it isn't enough to say Deleuze 'dove into the depths' in *Anti-Oedipus*, even if one carefully recalls that 'the concept of depth' retains relevance only in relation to 'a theory of surfaces' (Smith, 'From the Surface' 146–7), because when Deleuze 'dives' he also sinks the surface. Rather than the depths from which it emerges, the body without organs now becomes the surface and, upon it, Deleuze and Guattari will register their entire theory of the unconscious in *Anti-Oedipus* (ACE 19|11). The new topography will prove crucial not because it renders the surface invulnerable, as one might expect in light of the constant threat posed by the depths in *Logic of Sense*, but rather because it also translates a certain asceticism from the 'surface' of *Logic of Sense* to the 'depths' of *Anti-Oedipus*.

8. On 'quasi-causality', see LS series fourteen; see also note 5 above. Literal evidence that, contrary to what Žižek seems to think (82), there is indeed a place – a decisive place – for quasi-causality in *Anti-Oedipus*. Rather than simply accusing Žižek of negligence in this regard, the more interesting question would concern the prior investments that necessitate his refusal to recognise quasi-causality in *Anti-Oedipus*.

9. For the clearest explanation of the disjunctive synthesis in *Anti-Oedipus*, see ACE 93|76. For the clearest explanation of the disjunctive synthesis in general, see LS 201–2|172–3. Kant, whom Deleuze and Guattari name in this connection, derives the three Ideas of reason from the logical function (the 'act of reason') in three classes of syllogism: categorical, hypothetical and disjunctive. The corresponding ideas based thereon are – respectively – the psychological, the cosmological, the theological (Kant, *Prolegomena* §43). While the displacement from a disjunctive *syllogism* in Kant to a disjunctive *synthesis* in Deleuze is decisive, one would be both tempted and obliged to track the relation of the disjunctive to the divine in Deleuze's work, as well.

10. Hence, it doesn't categorically follow, as Rei Terada argues in *Feeling in Theory*, that 'we would have no emotions if we *were* subjects' (Terada 4). Terada's argument is not so much flawed as circumscribed. If emotion pertains to a 'self-difference', then 'emotion would have to be nonsubjective' (3), to be sure, but this does not exclude the relation between emotion and another subjectivity – not an 'alternative to subjectivity' (8) but an alternative subjectivity – of the type operative in what Deleuze calls the 'nomadic subject' in *Anti-Oedipus*. Terada never really considers this other subject, even though Deleuze in general and *Anti-Oedipus* in particular lay cornerstones in *Feeling in Theory*.

11. Because it claims to subvert the traditional concept of literature and the models of interpretation corresponding to it, because it does so without a second thought for the possibility of any lingering complicity with the tradition, because it indicates the scope of the stakes of 'affect' by

applying it to texts and in contexts Deleuze himself didn't anticipate, Adam Joseph Shellhorse's recent *Anti-Literature: The Politics and Limits of Representation in Modern Brazil and Argentina* constitutes a particularly clear instance of this abstract faith in the 'revolutionary potential' of affect:

> In effect, anti-literature subverts the traditional idea of literature and the Latin American literary state model: it does not encode texts or cultures in essentialist framings but breaks down structures in their ideological moorings and, following Gilles Deleuze and Félix Guattari's thesis in *Anti-Oedipus* (1972), articulates flows of desire, affect, and perception as a revolutionary potential . . . (Shellhorse 23)

Is the risk of affect's reactionary potential not greatest when it haunts unwitting proclamations of its revolutionary potential? Deleuze and Guattari never waver: 'Even the most repressive and deadliest forms of social reproduction are produced by desire' (A Œ 38|29); 'even fascism is desire' (MP 203|165).

12. 'One has never done history as much as the schizo, and in the way that the schizo does it. The schizo consumes universal history all at once' (A Œ 30|21). Although Fredric Jameson traces his notion of schizophrenia to Jacques Lacan by way of Deleuze and Guattari in *Anti-Oedipus* (Jameson 420 note 12), Deleuze and Guattari's schizophrenic is – unlike Jameson's – far from satisfied with 'an eternal present' (Jameson 10). In the same vein, this intensive historicity answers accusations that affect risks a certain ahistoricality more effectively and comprehensively than the phenomenological conceptuality with which Brian Massumi responds in *Politics of Affect* (146–8). See also Lauren Berlant's claim, with reference to Deleuze and Massumi, that 'affect theory has no place in the work of literary, or any history' (Berlant 14). On Deleuze's recourse to phenomenology in the first synthesis of time in *Difference and Repetition* and the problems it entails for sensibility, see Chapter 2 above. On Deleuze and Guattari's principle of immediate investment in the social regime, see A Œ 39|30 *et passim*; on intensity as a critique of the Oedipal structure, see especially A Œ 29|20; on the intense sociopoliticisation of psychoanalysis, see A Œ 120|98.

13. *One* means because *another* might challenge the logic of lack by redetermining the temporality of desire: 'It is such an account that I seek to develop as the notion of *chronolibido*' (Hägglund, *Dying for Time* 3). Curiously, Martin Hägglund's introduction to the problem of desire begins with Plato but ends with Lacan, thus stopping short of any reference to Deleuze and Guattari's parallel project in *Anti-Oedipus*. On the one hand, one might symptomatise this avoidance. Especially since Proust, one of the three authors from whom Hägglund extrapolates the notion of chronolibido, is a central gear in Deleuze and

Guattari's libidinal machine. On the other, a chronolibidinal account would no doubt find much to criticise in a reading of Proust oriented toward an unknown homeland where 'there is no longer any time' (AŒ 85|69). Deleuze and Guattari themselves ultimately forfeit recourse to an implicit distinction between a *socio-molar* temporality and a *libido-molecular* temporality that might temper or reorient their claim to atemporality when they stress the identity of the libidinal and the social (AŒ 39|30 *et passim*).

14. A few years later in *Kafka*, however, Deleuze and Guattari hesitate less to speak of 'other, infinitely more active triangulations' from which familial triangulation borrows its force (K 20|11).

15. In response to W. R. D. Fairbairn's claim that only bad objects internalise, Klein asserts that only the introjection of a good and whole object can orient and unify the ego (Klein III:3, 6). The stakes are high: 'without the good object at least to some extent becoming part of the ego, life cannot continue' (III:265). For Deleuze, by contrast, the child can't introject 'good' objects to counter the bad insofar as all introjection fragments and all fragmentariness is bad. This discrepancy is decisive because, renouncing the introjection of a wholesome object, Deleuze's child introduces a body without organs to counter partial objects and to integrate the ego (LS 219–20|188–9).

Bibliography

Abraham, Karl. 'A Short Study of the Development of the Libido, Viewed in the Light of Mental Disorders'. In *Selected Papers of Karl Abraham*. Trans. Douglas Bryan and Alix Strachey. London: Hogarth Press, 1927, pp. 418–501.

Abraham, Karl. *Versuch einer Entwicklungsgeschichte der Libido auf Grund der Psychoanalyse seelischer Störungen*. Leipzig / Vienna / Zürich: Internationaler Psychoanalytischer Verlag, 1924.

Agamben, Giorgio. *Potentialities: Collected Essays in Philosophy*. Ed. and trans. Daniel Heller-Roazen. Stanford: Stanford University Press, 1999.

Alliez, Eric. 'The BwO Condition or, the Politics of Sensation'. In *Discern(e)ments: Deleuzian Aesthetics / Esthétiques deleuziennes*. Ed. Joost de Bloois, Sjef Houppermans and Frans-Willem Korsten. Amsterdam and New York: Rodopi, 2004, pp. 93–111.

Ambrose, Darren. 'Deleuze, Philosophy, and the Materiality of Painting'. *Symposium* 10:1 (2006): 191–211.

Aristotle. *Poetics*. Trans. I Bywater. In *The Complete Works of Aristotle*. Volume Two. Ed. Jonathan Barnes. Princeton: Princeton University Press, 1984, pp. 2316–40.

Artaud, Antonin. *Pour en finir avec le jugement de dieu,* suivi de *Le théâtre de la cruauté*. Ed. Évelyne Grossman. Paris: Gallimard, 2003.

Artaud, Antonin. *The Theatre and Its Double*. In *Collected Works*. Volume 4. Trans. Victor Corti. London: John Calder, 1974, pp. 1–110.

Artaud, Antonin. *Le théâtre et son double*. Paris: Gallimard, 1938.

Bacon, Francis and David Sylvester. *The Brutality of Fact. Interviews with Francis Bacon 1962–1979*. New York: Thames & Hudson, 1987.

Badiou, Alain. *Deleuze. 'La clameur de l'Être'*. Paris: Hachette, 1997.

Badiou, Alain. *Deleuze: Clamor of Being*. Trans. Louise Burchill. Minneapolis: University of Minnesota Press, 2000.

Bataille, Georges. 'Hegel, la mort et le sacrifice'. In *Œuvres complètes*. Volume XII. Paris: Gallimard, 1988, pp. 326–45.

Beistegui, Miguel de. 'The Vertigo of Immanence: Deleuze's Spinozism'. *Research in Phenomenology* 35 (2005): 77–100.

Bell, Jeffrey A. *Deleuze's Hume: Philosophy, Culture and the Scottish Enlightenment*. Edinburgh: Edinburgh University Press, 2009.

Bibliography

Bergson, Henri. *Bergson. Mémoire et vie.* Ed. Gilles Deleuze. Paris: Presses Universitaires de France, 1975.

Bergson, Henri. *L'Énergie spirituelle.* Ed. Frédéric Worms. Paris: Presses Universitaires de France, 2009.

Bergson, Henri. 'Life and Consciousness'. *Hibbert Journal* 10:24 (October 1911): 24–44.

Bergson, Henri. *Matière et mémoire. Essai sur la relation du corps à l'esprit.* Ed. Frédéric Worms. Paris: Presses Universitaires de France, 2012.

Bergson, Henri. *Matter and Memory.* Trans. Nancy Margaret Paul and W. Scott Palmer. New York: Zone Books, 1991.

Bergson, Henri. *Mind-Energy: Lectures and Essays.* Trans. H. Wildon Carr. New York: Henry Holt and Company, 1920.

Berlant, Lauren. *Cruel Optimism.* Durham, NC: Duke University Press, 2011.

Bertelson, Lone and Andrew Murphie. 'An Ethics of Everyday Infinities and Powers: Félix Guattari on Affect and the Refrain'. In *The Affect Theory Reader.* Ed. Melissa Gregg and Gregory J. Seigworth. Durham, NC: Duke University Press, 2010, pp. 138–57.

Bewes, Timothy. 'The Surge: Turning Away from Affect'. *Deleuze and Guattari Studies* 12:3 (2018): 313–35.

Blanchot, Maurice. *L'espace littéraire.* Paris: Gallimard, 1955.

Blanchot, Maurice. *The Space of Literature.* Trans. Ann Smock. Lincoln: University of Nebraska Press, 1989.

Boljkovac, Nadine. *Untimely Affects: Gilles Deleuze and an Ethics of Cinema.* Edinburgh: Edinburgh University Press, 2013.

Borges, Jorge Luis. *Otras inquisiciones.* In *Obras completas.* Volume 2. Ed. Sara Luisa del Carril. Buenos Aires: Emecé Editores, 2010, pp. 11–163.

Borges, Jorge Luis. *Other Inquisitions: 1937–1954.* Trans. Ruth L. C. Simms. Austin: University of Texas Press, 1995.

Braidotti, Rosi. *The Posthuman.* Cambridge: Polity, 2013.

Brinkema, Eugenie. *The Forms of Affect.* Durham, NC: Duke University Press, 2014.

Bryant, Levi. *Difference and Givenness: Deleuze's Transcendental Empiricism and the Ontology of Immanence.* Evanston: Northwestern University Press, 2008.

Buchanan, Ian. *Deleuze and Guattari's* Anti-Oedipus: *A Reader's Guide.* New York: Continuum, 2008.

Buffon, Georges-Louis Leclerc de. *Discours sur le style.* Ed. Félix Hemon. Paris: Librairie Ch. Delagrave, 1894.

Buffon, Georges-Louis Leclerc de. 'Discourse on Style'. In *The Writer's Art by Those Who Have Practiced It.* Ed. Rollo Walter Brown. Cambridge, MA: Harvard University Press, 1921, pp. 277–87.

Chomsky, Noam. *Aspects of the Theory of Syntax.* Cambridge, MA: MIT Press, 1965.

Bibliography

Clough, Patricia Ticineto. 'The Affective Turn: Political Economy, Biomedia, and Bodies'. In *The Affect Theory Reader*. Ed. Melissa Gregg and Gregory J. Seigworth. Durham, NC: Duke University Press, 2010, pp. 206–25.

Clough, Patricia Ticineto. 'Introduction'. In *The Affective Turn: Theorizing the Social*. Ed. Patricia Ticineto Clough and Jean Halley. Durham, NC: Duke University Press, 2007, pp. 1–33.

Copleston, Frederick. *History of Philosophy IV: Modern Philosophy from Descartes to Leibniz*. New York: Image Books, 1960.

Crépon, Marc. *The Thought of Death and the Memory of War*. Trans. Michael Loriaux. Minneapolis: University of Minnesota Press, 2013.

Crépon, Marc. *Vivre avec. La pensée de la mort et la mémoire des guerres*. Paris: Éditions Hermann, 2008.

Cressole, Michel. *Deleuze*. Paris: Éditions Universitaires, 1973.

Cross, D. J. S. 'Apocrypha: Derrida's Writing in *Anti-Oedipus*'. *CR: The New Centennial Review* 17:3 (2017): 177–97.

Cross, D. J. S. 'What Is Nonstyle in *What Is Philosophy?*' In *Deleuze and the Schizoanalysis of Literature*. Ed. Ian Buchanan, Tim Matts and Aidan Tynan. London and New York: Bloomsbury Academic, 2015, pp. 82–98.

Cummins, Harold and Charles Midlo. *Fingerprints, Palms and Soles: An Introduction to Dermatoglyphics*. New York: Dover, 1961.

de Sousa, Ronald. *The Rationality of Emotion*. Cambridge, MA: MIT Press, 1987.

DeLanda, Manuel. *Intensive Science and Virtual Philosophy*. London and New York: Bloomsbury Academic, 2002.

Deleuze, Gilles. *Bergsonism*. Trans. Hugh Tomlinson and Barbara Habberjam. New York: Zone Books, 1991.

Deleuze, Gilles. *Le bergsonisme*. Paris: Presses Universitaires de France, 1966.

Deleuze, Gilles. *Coldness and Cruelty*. Trans. Jean McNeil. In *Masochism*. New York: Zone Books, 1991, pp. 7–138.

Deleuze, Gilles. *Cours sur Spinoza*. Available online at *La voix de Deleuze*, <http://www2.univ-paris8.fr/deleuze>

Deleuze, Gilles. *Critique et clinique*. Paris: Minuit, 1993.

Deleuze, Gilles. *Desert Islands and Other Texts: 1953–1974*. Trans. Mike Taormina. Ed. David Lapoujade. New York: Semiotext(e), 2004.

Deleuze, Gilles. *Deux régimes de fou. Textes et entretiens 1975–1995*. Ed. David Lapoujade. Paris: Minuit, 2003.

Deleuze, Gilles. *Difference and Repetition*. Trans. Paul Patton. New York: Continuum, 1994.

Deleuze, Gilles. *Différence et répétition*. Paris: Presses Universitaires de France, 1968.

Deleuze, Gilles. *Empiricism and Subjectivity: An Essay on Hume's Theory of Human Nature*. Trans. Constantin V. Boundas. New York: Columbia University Press, 1991.

Bibliography

Deleuze, Gilles. *Empirisme et subjectivité. Essai sur la nature humaine selon Hume*. Paris: Presses Universitaires de France, 1953.

Deleuze, Gilles. 'L'épuisé'. In Samuel Beckett. Quad *et autres pièces pour la télévision*. Paris: Minuit, 1992, pp. 55–106.

Deleuze, Gilles. *Essays Critical and Clinical*. Trans. Daniel W. Smith and Michael A. Greco. Minneapolis: University of Minnesota Press, 1997.

Deleuze, Gilles. *Expressionism in Philosophy: Spinoza*. Trans. Martin Joughin. New York: Zone Books, 1992.

Deleuze, Gilles. *Francis Bacon. Logique de la sensation*. Paris: Seuil, 2002.

Deleuze, Gilles. *Francis Bacon: The Logic of Sensation*. Trans. Daniel W. Smith. New York: Continuum, 2003.

Deleuze, Gilles. *L'île déserte. Textes et entretiens 1953–1974*. Ed. David Lapoujade. Paris: Minuit, 2002.

Deleuze, Gilles. *Kant's Critical Philosophy*. Trans. Hugh Tomlinson and Barbara Habberjam. London: Athlone Press, 1984.

Deleuze, Gilles. *Letters and Other Texts*. Ed. David Lapoujade. Trans. Ames Hodges. New York: Semiotext(e), 2020.

Deleuze, Gilles. *Lettres et autres textes*. Ed. David Lapoujade. Paris: Minuit, 2015.

Deleuze, Gilles. *Logic of Sense*. Trans. Mark Lester. London: Athlone Press, 1990.

Deleuze, Gilles. *Logique du sens*. Paris: Minuit, 1969.

Deleuze, Gilles. *Negotiations: 1972–1990*. Trans. Martin Joughin. New York: Columbia University Press, 1995.

Deleuze, Gilles. *Nietzsche and Philosophy*. Trans. Hugh Tomlinson. New York: Continuum, 1986.

Deleuze, Gilles. *Nietzsche et la philosophie*. Paris: Presses Universitaires de France, 1962.

Deleuze, Gilles. *La philosophie critique de Kant*. Paris: Presses Universitaires de France, 1963.

Deleuze, Gilles. *Pourparlers. 1972–1990*. Paris: Minuit, 1990.

Deleuze, Gilles. *Présentation de Sacher-Masoch. Le froid et le cruel*. Paris: Minuit, 1967.

Deleuze, Gilles. *Proust and Signs*. Trans. Richard Howard. Minneapolis: University of Minnesota Press, 2000.

Deleuze, Gilles. *Proust et les signes*. Paris: Presses Universitaires de France, 1964.

Deleuze, Gilles. *Spinoza et le problème de l'expression*. Paris: Minuit, 1968.

Deleuze, Gilles. *Spinoza. Philosophie pratique*. Paris: Minuit, 1981.

Deleuze, Gilles. *Spinoza: Practical Philosophy*. Trans. Robert Hurley. San Francisco: City Lights Books, 1988.

Deleuze, Gilles. *Two Regimes of Madness: Texts and Interviews 1975–1995*. Trans. Ames Hodges and Mike Taormina. Ed. David Lapoujade. New York: Semiotext(e), 2007.

Bibliography

Deleuze, Gilles and Claire Parnet. *Dialogues*. Paris: Flammarion, 1996.

Deleuze, Gilles and Claire Parnet. *Dialogues II*. Trans. Hugh Tomlinson and Barbara Habberjam. New York: Columbia University Press, 2007.

Deleuze, Gilles and Félix Guattari. *Capitalism and Schizophrenia. Anti-Oedipus*. Trans. Robert Hurley, Mark Seem and Helen R. Lane. Minneapolis: University of Minnesota Press, 1983.

Deleuze, Gilles and Félix Guattari. *Capitalism and Schizophrenia 2: A Thousand Plateaus*. Trans. Brian Massumi. Minneapolis: University of Minneapolis Press, 1987.

Deleuze, Gilles and Félix Guattari. *Capitalisme et schizophrénie 1. L'Anti-Œdipe*. Paris: Minuit, 1972.

Deleuze, Gilles and Félix Guattari. *Capitalisme et schizophrénie 2. Mille plateaux*. Paris: Minuit, 1980.

Deleuze, Gilles and Félix Guattari. *Kafka. Pour une littérature mineure*. Paris: Minuit, 1975.

Deleuze, Gilles and Félix Guattari. *Kafka: Toward a Minor Literature*. Trans. Dana Polan. Minneapolis: University of Minnesota Press, 1986.

Deleuze, Gilles and Félix Guattari. *Qu'est-ce que la philosophie ?* Paris: Minuit, 1991.

Deleuze, Gilles and Félix Guattari. *Rhizome. Introduction*. Paris: Minuit, 1976.

Deleuze, Gilles and Félix Guattari. *What Is Philosophy?* Trans. Hugh Tomlinson and Graham Burchell. New York: Columbia University Press, 1994.

Derrida, Jacques. *The Beast and the Sovereign. Volume I*. Trans. Geoffrey Bennington. Chicago: Chicago University Press, 2009.

Derrida, Jacques. *Chaque fois unique, la fin du monde*. Ed. Pascale-Anne Brault and Michael Naas. Paris: Galilée, 2003.

Derrida, Jacques. *Marges de la philosophie*. Paris: Minuit, 1972.

Derrida, Jacques. *Margins of Philosophy*. Trans. Alan Bass. Chicago: Chicago University Press, 1982.

Derrida, Jacques. *Séminaire. La bête et le souverain*. Volume I (2001–2002). Paris: Galilée, 2008.

Derrida, Jacques. 'The Transcendental "Stupidity" ("Bêtise") of Man and the Becoming-Animal According to Deleuze'. In *Deleuze, Derrida, Psychoanalysis*. Ed. Gabriele Schwab. New York: Columbia University Press, 2007, pp. 35–60.

Derrida, Jacques. *Voice and Phenomenon: Introduction to the Problem of the Sign in Husserl's Phenomenology*. Trans. Leonard Lawlor. Evanston: Northwestern University Press, 2011.

Derrida, Jacques. *La voix et le phénomène. Introduction au problème du signe dans la phénoménologie de Husserl*. Paris: Presses Universitaires de France, 1967.

Bibliography

Derrida, Jacques. *The Work of Mourning*. Ed. Pascale-Anne Brault and Michael Naas. Chicago: University of Chicago Press, 2001.

Descartes, René. *Œuvres de Descartes*. 11 volumes. Ed. Charles Adam and Paul Tannery. Paris: Librairie Philosophique J. Vrin, 1996.

Descartes, René. *The Philosophical Writings of Descartes*. 3 volumes. Trans. John Cottingham, Robert Stoothoff, Dugald Murdoch and Anthony Kenny. Cambridge: Cambridge University Press, 1984/1985/1991.

Dickinson, Emily. *The Poems of Emily Dickinson*. Ed. R. W. Franklin. Cambridge, MA: Belknap Press, 1998.

Dobbin, Robert (ed. and trans.). *The Cynic Philosophers from Diogenes to Julian*. New York: Penguin Books, 2012.

Dosse, François. *Gilles Deleuze and Félix Guattari: Intersecting Lives*. Trans. Deborah Glassman. New York: Columbia University Press, 2010.

Dosse, François. *Gilles Deleuze et Félix Guattari. Biographie croisée*. Paris: La Découverte, 2007.

Fañanás, L., P. Moral and J. Bertranpetit. 'Quantitative Dermatoglyphics in Schizophrenia: Study of Family History Subgroups'. *Human Biology* 62:3 (1990): 421–7.

Ferenczi, Sándor. *Contributions to Psycho-Analysis*. Trans. Ernest Jones. Boston: The Gorham Press, 1916.

Ferenczi, Sándor. *Introjektion und Übertragung. Eine Psychoanalytische Studie*. Leipzig and Vienna: Franz Deuticke, 1910.

Figlerowicz, Marta. 'Affect Theory Dossier: An Introduction'. *Qui parle: Critical Humanities and Social Sciences* 20:2 (2012): 3–18.

Foucault, Michel. 'Theatrum Philosophicum'. *Critique* 282 (1970): 885–908.

Freud, Sigmund. 'Fragment of an Analysis of a Case of Hysteria'. In *The Standard Edition of the Complete Psychological Works of Sigmund Freud*. Volume VII. Trans. and Ed. James Strachey. London: Hogarth Press and the Institute of Psycho-analysis, 1957, pp. 1–122.

Freud, Sigmund. *Gesammelte Werke*. 18 volumes. Ed. Anna Freud et al. Frankfurt am Main: Fischer Taschenbuch Verlag, 1999.

Freud, Sigmund. *The Interpretation of Dreams*. Trans. and Ed. James Strachey. New York: Basic Books, 2010.

Freud, Sigmund. 'Mourning and Melancholia'. In *The Standard Edition of the Complete Psychological Works of Sigmund Freud*. Volume XIV. Trans. and Ed. James Strachey. London: Hogarth Press and the Institute of Psycho-analysis, 1957, pp. 237–58.

Freud, Sigmund. *Totem and Taboo*. In *The Standard Edition of the Complete Psychological Works of Sigmund Freud*. Volume XIII. Trans. and Ed. James Strachey. London: The Hogarth Press and the Institute of Psycho-analysis, 1955, pp. 1–162.

Freud, Sigmund. 'The Unconscious'. In *The Standard Edition of the Complete Psychological Works of Sigmund Freud*. Volume XIV. Trans.

and Ed. James Strachey. London: The Hogarth Press and the Institute of Psycho-analysis, 1957, pp. 159–215.

Gasché, Rodolphe. *Geophilosophy: On Gilles Deleuze and Félix Guattari's What Is Philosophy?* Evanston: Northwestern University Press, 2014.

Guattari, Félix. *Chaosophy: Texts and Interviews 1972–1977*. Ed. Sylvère Lotringer. Trans. David L. Sweet, Jarred Becker and Talyor Adkins. Los Angeles: Semiotext(e), 2009.

Hägglund, Martin. *Dying for Time: Proust, Woolf, Nabokov*. Cambridge, MA: Harvard University Press, 2012.

Hägglund, Martin. *This Life: Secular Faith and Spiritual Freedom*. New York: Pantheon Books, 2019.

Hallward, Peter. *Out of This World: Deleuze and the Philosophy of Creation*. London and New York: Verso, 2006.

Hansen, Mark B. N. 'Affect as Medium, or the "Digital-facial-image"'. *Journal of Visual Culture* 2:2 (2003): 205–28.

Hardt, Michael. 'Foreword: What Affects Are Good For'. In *The Affective Turn: Theorizing the Social*. Ed. Patricia Ticineto Clough and Jean Halley. Durham, NC: Duke University Press, 2007, pp. ix–xiii.

Heaney, Conor. 'Pursuing Joy with Deleuze: Transcendental Empiricism and Affirmative Naturalism as Worldly Practice'. *Deleuze and Guattari Studies* 12:3 (2018): 374–401.

Heidegger, Martin. *Being and Time*. Trans. Joan Stambaugh, rev. Dennis J. Schmidt. Albany: State University of New York Press, 2010.

Heidegger, Martin. *Beiträge zur Philosophie (Vom Ereignis)*. Gesamtausgabe 65. Ed. Friedrich-Wilhelm von Herrmann. Frankfurt am Main: Vittorio Klostermann, 1989.

Heidegger, Martin. *Contributions to Philosophy (of the Event)*. Trans. Richard Rojcewicz and Daniela Vallega-Neu. Bloomington and Indianapolis: Indiana University Press, 2012.

Heidegger, Martin. *Einführung in die Metaphysik*. Gesamtausgabe 40. Ed. Petra Jaeger. Frankfurt am Main: Vittorio Klostermann, 1983.

Heidegger, Martin. *Four Seminars*. Trans. Andrew Mitchell and François Raffoul. Bloomington and Indianapolis: Indiana University Press, 2003.

Heidegger, Martin. *Identität und Differenz*. Gesamtausgabe 11. Ed. Friedrich-Wilhelm von Herrmann. Frankfurt am Main: Vittorio Klostermann, 2006.

Heidegger, Martin. *Identity and Difference*. Trans. Joan Stambaugh. New York: Harper & Row, 1969.

Heidegger, Martin. *Introduction to Metaphysics*. Second Edition. Trans. Gregory Fried and Richard Polt. New Haven: Yale University Press, 2014.

Heidegger, Martin. *Kant and the Problem of Metaphysics*. Fifth Edition. Trans. Richard Taft. Bloomington and Indianapolis: Indiana University Press, 1997.

Heidegger, Martin. *Kant und das Problem der Metaphysik*. Gesamtausgabe

3. Ed. Friedrich-Wilhelm von Herrmann. Frankfurt am Main: Vittorio Klostermann, 2010.

Heidegger, Martin. *Nietzsche I*. Gesamtausgabe 6.1. Ed. Brigitte Schillbach. Frankfurt am Main: Vittorio Klostermann, 1996.

Heidegger, Martin. *Nietzsche II*. Gesamtausgabe 6.2. Ed. Brigitte Schillbach. Frankfurt am Main: Vittorio Klostermann, 1997.

Heidegger, Martin. *Nietzsche I–II: The Will to Power as Art* and *The Eternal Recurrence of the Same*. Trans. David Farrell Krell. New York: Harper & Row, 1984.

Heidegger, Martin. *Nietzsche III–VI: The Will to Power as Knowledge and as Metaphysics* and *Nihilism*. Ed. David Farrell Krell. Trans. Joan Stambaugh, David Farrell Krell and Frank A. Capuzzi. New York: Harper & Row, 1987.

Heidegger, Martin. *On* Time and Being. Ed. J. Glenn Gray and Joan Stambaugh. Trans. Joan Stambaugh. New York: Harper & Row, 1972.

Heidegger, Martin. *Pathmarks*. Ed. William McNeill. Cambridge: Cambridge University Press, 1998.

Heidegger, Martin. *The Question Concerning Technology and Other Essays*. Trans. William Lovitt. New York: Harper & Row, 1977.

Heidegger, Martin. *Sein und Zeit*. Tübingen: Max Niemeyer Verlag, 2006.

Heidegger, Martin. *Seminare*. Gesamtausgabe 15. Ed. Curd Ochwadt. Frankfurt am Main: Vittorio Klostermann, 1986.

Heidegger, Martin. *Vorträge und Aufsätze*. Gesamtausgabe 7. Ed. Friedrich-Wilhelm von Herrmann. Frankfurt am Main: Vittorio Klostermann, 2000.

Heidegger, Martin. *Was heißt Denken?* Gesamtausgabe 8. Ed. Paola-Ludovika Coriando. Frankfurt am Main: Vittorio Klostermann, 2002.

Heidegger, Martin. *Wegmarken*. Gesamtausgabe 9. Ed. Friedrich-Willhelm von Herrmann. Frankfurt am Main: Vittorio Klostermann, 2004.

Heidegger, Martin. *What Is Called Thinking?* Trans. Fred D. Wieck and J. Glenn Gray. New York: Harper & Row, 1968.

Heidegger, Martin. *Zur Sache des Denkens*. Gesamtausgabe 14. Ed. Friedrich-Willhelm von Herrmann. Frankfurt am Main: Vittorio Klostermann, 2007.

Housset, Emmanuel. *Husserl et l'énigme du monde*. Paris: Seuil, 2000.

Hughes, Joe. *Deleuze's* Difference and Repetition: *A Reader's Guide*. New York: Continuum, 2009.

Hume, David. *Dialogues concerning Natural Religion* and Other Writings. Ed. Dorothy Coleman. Cambridge: Cambridge University Press, 2007.

Hume, David. *An Enquiry Concerning Human Understanding*. In *Enquiries Concerning Human Understanding and Concerning the Principles of Morals*. Ed. L. A. Selby-Bigge, rev. P. H. Nidditch. Oxford: Oxford University Press, 1975, pp. 5–165.

Hume, David. *Essays Moral, Political, and Literary*. Ed. Eugene F. Miller. Indianapolis: Liberty Fund, 1994.

Bibliography

Hume, David. *The Natural History of Religion*. In *Writings on Religion*. Ed. Antony Flew. Chicago and La Salle: Open Court, 1992, pp. 105–82.

Hume, David. *A Treatise of Human Nature*. Ed. David Fate Norton and Mary J. Norton. Oxford: Oxford University Press, 2000.

Husserl, Edmund. *The Crisis of European Sciences and Transcendental Phenomenology: An Introduction to Phenomenological Philosophy*. Trans. David Carr. Evanston: Northwestern University Press, 1970.

Husserl, Edmund. *Ideas pertaining to a Pure Phenomenology and to a Phenomenological Philosophy. First Book: General Introduction to a Pure Phenomenology*. Trans. F. Kersten. The Hague: Martinus Nijhoff, 1982.

Husserl, Edmund. *Ideen zu einer reinen Phänomenologie und phänomenologischen Philosophie. Erstes Buch. Allgemeine Einführung in die reine Phänomenologie*. Husserliana III/1. Ed. Karl Schuhmann. The Haag: Martinus Nijhoff, 1976.

Husserl, Edmund. *Die Krisis der europäischen Wissenschaften und die transzendentale Phänomenologie. Eine Einleitung in die phänomenologische Philosophie*. Husserliana VI. Ed. Walter Biemel. The Hague: Martinus Nijhoff, 1954.

Husserl, Edmund. *Logical Investigations: Volume I*. Ed. Dermot Moran. Trans. J. N. Findlay. London and New York: Routledge, 1970.

Husserl, Edmund. *Logische Untersuchungen. Zweiter Bande: Untersuchungen zur Phänomenologie und Theorie der Erkenntnis*. Husserliana 19/1. Ed. Ursula Panzer. The Hague: Martinus Nijhoff, 1984.

Jameson, Fredric. *Postmodernism, or, the Cultural Logic of Late Capitalism*. Durham, NC: Duke University Press, 1991.

Johnson, David E. *Kant's Dog: On Borges, Philosophy, and the Time of Translation*. Albany: State University of New York Press, 2012.

Jones, Ernest. *The Life and Work of Sigmund Freud. Volume I: The Formative Years and the Great Discoveries 1856–1900*. New York: Basic Books, 1953.

Kafka, Franz. *The Diaries of Franz Kafka, 1910–1923*. Trans. Joseph Kresh. New York: Schocken, 1948.

Kafka, Franz. *Journal. Texte intégral 1910–1923*. Trans. Marthe Robert. Paris: Éditions Bernard Grasset, 1954.

Kafka, Franz. *Tagebücher 1910–1923*. Ed. Max Brod. Frankfurt am Main: Fischer Taschenbuch Verlag, 1973.

Kant, Immanuel. *Critique of Pure Reason*. Trans. and Ed. Paul Guyer and Allen W. Wood. Cambridge: Cambridge University Press, 1998.

Kant, Immanuel. *Prolegomena to any future metaphysics that will be able to come forward as a science*. Trans. Gary Hatfield. In *Theoretical Philosophy after 1781*. Ed. Henry Allison and Peter Heath. Cambridge: Cambridge University Press, 2002, pp. 29–169.

Kant, Immanuel. *Werkausgabe*. 12 volumes. Ed. Wilhelm Weischedel. Berlin: Suhrkamp, 1974/1977.

Bibliography

Klein, Melanie. *Envy and Gratitude and Other Works 1946–1963*. The Writings of Melanie Klein 3. New York: The Free Press, 1975.

Klein, Melanie. *Love, Guilt and Reparation and Other Works 1921–1945*. The Writings of Melanie Klein 1. New York: The Free Press, 1975.

Klein, Melanie. *Die Psychoanalyse des Kindes*. Vienna: Internationaler Psychoanalytischer Verlag, 1932.

Klein, Melanie. *The Psychoanalysis of Children*. Trans. Alix Strachey. New York: Grove Press, 1960.

Labov, William. *Sociolinguistic Patterns*. Philadelphia: University of Pennsylvania Press, 1972.

Lapoujade, David. *Aberrant Movements: The Philosophy of Gilles Deleuze*. Trans. Joshua David Jordan. South Pasadena: Semiotext(e), 2017.

Lapoujade, David. *Deleuze, les mouvements aberrants*. Paris: Minuit, 2014.

Lawlor, Leonard. *The Challenge of Bergsonism: Phenomenology, Ontology, Ethics*. New York: Continuum, 2003.

Lawlor, Leonard. *Derrida and Husserl: The Basic Problem of Phenomenology*. Bloomington and Indianapolis: Indiana University Press, 2002.

Lawlor, Leonard. 'A Nearly Total Affinity: The Deleuzian Virtual Image Versus the Derridean Trace'. *Angelaki* 5:2 (2000): 59–71.

Lawrence, D. H. 'Chaos in Poetry'. In *Selected Critical Writings*. Ed. Michael Herbert. Oxford and New York: Oxford University Press, 1998, pp. 234–42.

Lecercle, Jean Jacques. *Deleuze and Language*. New York: Palgrave Macmillan, 2002.

Lecercle, Jean Jacques. 'Three Accounts of Literary Style'. *CR: The New Centennial Review* 16:3 (Winter 2016): 151–71.

Leo, Russ. 'Affective Physics: *Affectus* in Spinoza's *Ethica*'. In *Passions and Subjectivity in Early Modern Culture*. Ed. Brian Cummings and Freya Sierhuis. New York: Routledge, 2013, pp. 33–49.

Lewis, Charlton T. and Charles Short. *A New Latin Dictionary*. New York: Harper & Brothers, 1891.

Leys, Ruth. 'The Turn to Affect: A Critique'. *Critical Inquiry* 37 (2011): 434–72.

Malabou, Catherine. 'Before and Above: Spinoza and Symbolic Necessity'. *Critical Inquiry* 43 (2016): 84–109.

Massumi, Brian. 'The Future Birth of the Affective Fact: The Political Ontology of Threat'. In *The Affective Turn: Theorizing the Social*. Ed. Patricia Ticineto Clough and Jean Halley. Durham, NC: Duke University Press, 2007, pp. 52–70.

Massumi, Brian. *Parables for the Virtual: Movement, Affect, Sensation*. Durham, NC: Duke University Press, 2002.

Massumi, Brian. *Politics of Affect*. Cambridge: Polity, 2015.

Meillassoux, Quentin. 'Soustraction et Contraction. À propos d'une remarque de Deleuze sur *Matière et mémoire*'. *Philosophie* 96 (2007): 67–93.

Bibliography

Nadler, Steven. *Spinoza: A Life*. Cambridge: Cambridge University Press, 1999.

Nietzsche, Friedrich. *The Birth of Tragedy and Other Writings*. Ed. Raymond Geuss and Ronald Speirs. Trans. Ronald Speirs. Cambridge: Cambridge University Press, 1999.

Nietzsche, Friedrich. *Kritische Studienausgabe*. 15 volumes. Ed. Giorgio Colli and Mazzino Montinari. Berlin: Walter de Gruyter & Co., 1988.

Nietzsche, Friedrich. *On the Genealogy of Morals*. Ed. Keith Ansell-Pearson. Trans. Carol Diethe. Cambridge: Cambridge University Press, 1997.

Nietzsche, Friedrich. *Twilight of the Idols*. In *Anti-Christ, Ecce Homo, Twilight of the Idols*. Ed. Aaron Ridley and Judith Norman. Trans. Judith Norman. Cambridge: Cambridge University Press, 2005.

Nietzsche, Friedrich. *Writings from the Late Notebooks*. Ed. Rüdiger Bittner. Trans. Kate Sturge. Cambridge: Cambridge University Press, 2003.

Nussbaum, Martha C. *The Fragility of Goodness: Luck and Ethics in Greek Tragedy and Philosophy*. Cambridge: Cambridge University Press, 2001.

O'Keefe, Brian. 'Deleuze on Habit'. *The Comparatist* 40 (2016): 71–93.

Peden, Knox. *Spinoza Contra Phenomenology: French Rationalism from Cavaillès to Deleuze*. Stanford: Stanford University Press, 2014.

Plato. *Apology*. In *Five Dialogues*. Trans. G. M. A. Grube, rev. John M. Cooper. Indianapolis: Hackett, 2002, pp. 21–44.

Plato. *Euthyphro*. In *Five Dialogues*. Trans. G. M. A. Grube, rev. John M. Cooper. Indianapolis: Hackett, 2002, pp. pp. 1–20.

Plato. *Phaedo*. In *Five Dialogues*. Trans. G. M. A. Grube, rev. John M. Cooper. Indianapolis: Hackett, 2002, pp. 93–154.

Plato. *Phaedrus*. In *Selected Dialogues of Plato*. Trans. Benjamin Jowett, rev. Hayden Pelliccia. New York: The Modern Library, 2001, pp. 111–99.

Plato. *Republic*. Trans. G. M. A. Grube, rev. C. D. C. Reeve. Indianapolis: Hackett, 1992.

Posteraro, Tano. 'Habits, Nothing But Habits: Biological Time in Deleuze'. *The Comparatist* 40 (2016): 94–110.

Protevi, John. 'Larval Subjects, Autonomous Systems and E. Coli Chemotaxis'. In *Deleuze and the Body*. Ed. Laura Guillaume and Joe Hughes. Edinburgh: Edinburgh University Press, 2011, pp. 29–52.

Proust, Marcel. *À la recherche du temps perdu* I. *Du côté de chez Swann*. Paris: Gallimard, 1954.

Proust, Marcel. *Swann's Way*. Trans. C. K. Scott Moncrieff and Terence Kilmartin. New York: Random House, 1981.

Rushton, Richard. 'Response to Mark B. N. Hansen's "Affect as Medium, or the 'Digital-facial-image'"'. *Journal of Visual Culture* 3:3 (2004): 353–7.

Saussure, Ferdinand de. *Cours de linguistique générale*. Ed. Charles Bally and Albert Séchehaye. Paris: Payot & Rivages, 2005.

Saussure, Ferdinand de. *Course in General Linguistics*. Ed. Charles Bally and Albert Séchehaye. Trans. Wade Baskin. New York, Toronto, London: McGraw Hill, 1966.

Schaefer, Donovan O. *The Evolution of Affect Theory: The Humanities, the Sciences, and the Study of Power*. Cambridge: Cambridge University Press, 2019.

Seigworth, Gregory J. and Melissa Gregg. 'An Inventory of Glimmers'. In *The Affect Theory Reader*. Ed. Melissa Gregg and Gregory J. Seigworth. Durham, NC: Duke University Press, 2010, pp. 1–25.

Shellhorse, Adam Joseph. *Anti-Literature: The Politics and Limits of Representation in Modern Brazil and Argentina*. Pittsburgh: University of Pittsburgh Press, 2017.

Smith, Daniel W. *Essays on Deleuze*. Edinburgh: Edinburgh University Press, 2012.

Smith, Daniel W. 'From the Surface to the Depths: On the Transition from *Logic of Sense* to *Anti-Oedipus*'. *Symposium: Canadian Journal of Continental Philosophy / Revue canadienne de philosophie continentale* 10:1 (2006): 135–53.

Spinoza, Baruch. *The Collected Works of Spinoza*. 2 volumes. Ed. and trans. Edwin Curley. Princeton: Princeton University Press, 1985 and 2016.

Spinoza, Baruch. *The Ethics*. Trans. R. H. M. Elwes. London: G. Bell and Sons, 1887.

Spinoza, Baruch. *Ethics*. In *Complete Works*. Trans. Samuel Shirley. Indianapolis: Hackett, 2002 [1982], pp. 213–382.

Spinoza, Baruch. *Ethics: Proved in Geometrical Order*. Trans Michael Silverthorne and Matthew J. Kisner. Ed. Matthew J. Kisner. Cambridge: Cambridge University Press, 2018.

Spinoza, Baruch. *Éthique*. Trans. Émile Saisset. Paris: Charpentier, 1842.

Spinoza, Baruch. *Éthique*. Trans. J. G. Prat. Paris: Decaux, 1860 (Hachette, 1880).

Spinoza, Baruch. *Éthique*. Trans. Henri de Boulainvilliers. Paris: Armand Colin, 1907.

Spinoza, Baruch. *Éthique*. Trans. Raoul Lantzenberg. Paris: Flammarion, 1908.

Spinoza, Baruch. *Éthique*. Trans. Charles Appuhn. Paris: Garnier Frères, 1913 [1906].

Spinoza, Baruch. *Éthique*. Trans. André Guérinot. Paris: Éditions d'art Édouard Pelletan, 1930.

Spinoza, Baruch. *Éthique*. Trans. Roland Caillois. Paris: Gallimard, 1954.

Spinoza, Baruch. *Éthique*. Trans. Bernard Pautrat. Paris: Seuil, 1988.

Spinoza, Baruch. *Éthique*. Trans. Robert Misrahi. Paris: Presses Universitaires de France, 1993.

Bibliography

Terada, Rei. *Feeling in Theory: Emotion after the 'Death of the Subject'*. Cambridge, MA: Harvard University Press, 2001.

Vernant, Jean-Pierre. *Les origines de la pensée grecque*. Paris: Presses Universitaires de France, 1969.

Vernant, Jean-Pierre. *The Origins of Greek Thought*. Ithaca: Cornell University Press, 1982.

Yeats, W. B. *The Collected Poems of W. B. Yeats*. Revised Second Edition. Ed. Richard J. Finneran. New York: Scribner Paperback Poetry, 1996.

Žižek, Slavoj. *Organs without Bodies: On Deleuze and Consequences*. London and New York: Routledge, 2012.

Index

Index

Index

corporality, 155–6, 181–4, 185, 187, 189, 192–3, 196, 200–1, 202n, 209, 225, 266
corruption, 246, 248–9
creation of concepts, 20, 24, 62n, 95–6, 135, 147–8, 150–2, 158–9, 162, 191, 208, 211
creationism, 157
  creature, 154–8, 166, 175, 178n, 214, 230
Crépon, Marc, 141n
Cressole, Michel, 2–3, 26n, 262–3
critical, ix, 13, 14–15, 27n, 33, 38, 45, 124, 164, 172, 175, 178n, 200, 265n
  critical theory, 109
culture, 7, 81, 82, 268n
Cummins, Harold, 1
Curley, Edwin, 177n, 194, 238n
custom, 75, 92

dance, 180, 182–4, 186, 189, 192, 195, 197
Dasein, 14, 33, 39, 49, 118–22
de Man, Paul, 16
de Sousa, Ronald, 26–7n, 202–3n
death, 33, 105, 107, 110–23, 130, 141n, 142n, 160, 166, 184, 187, 189, 236, 240n
  death drive, 117, 227, 240n, 264n
DeLanda, Manuel, 17, 65–6n, 87, 102n, 152
depths, 15, 95, 111, 244–52, 262, 266n, 267n
Derrida, Jacques, 16, 35, 62n, 63–4n, 90–1, 102n, 120, 141n, 142n, 187, 190, 202n, 203n, 219
Descartes, René, Cartesian, 11, 18, 22, 31–3, 44, 46, 50, 92, 115–16, 134, 152, 155, 160, 165, 176n, 178n, 202n, 218, 225–6
desire, 70, 164, 173, 193, 203n, 217, 222, 224, 228–9, 231–4, 241n, 252, 254, 256, 258, 259–60
  desiring machine, 141, 253, 257, 261, 264, 268n
dialectic, 44, 128, 172, 188
Dickinson, Emily, 121
Diogenes Laertius, 2, 263
disciplinarity, 10, 23, 57, 95–7, 100, 104, 105–6, 108, 122, 133, 135, 139, 147–8, 191, 194–5, 207–8, 210–11, 228–9

interdisciplinarity, 108–9, 148, 210
discussion, 36, 40, 117–18, 142n
dogma, 35, 37–8, 46, 48, 51, 56, 86, 93, 96–7, 100, 137, 155, 171, 185, 188
  dogmatic image of thought, 35, 37, 43, 49, 92, 93–4, 171–2, 231–2, 244
Donati, Arlette, 263
Dosse, François, 26n, 178n, 263
double bind, 258
doubt, 32, 55, 63n, 69, 74, 75, 78, 81, 86, 89, 91, 120, 129, 136, 161, 203n, 214, 218, 225, 230
doxa, 105, 107, 115–16, 140n
  heterodoxy, 111
  orthodoxy, 107, 140n, 143n
  paradox, 4, 6, 20, 24–5, 36, 40, 48, 55, 60, 62n, 85, 103n, 124, 140n, 141n, 147–50, 155, 180, 182, 207, 210, 233–4, 237n, 250
dramatisation, 134, 204n
dream, 25n, 32, 103n, 112–14, 132, 141n, 217, 240n, 254
dualism, 199
Duns Scotus, 156–7, 178n

effect, 9, 19, 48, 54, 73, 77, 81, 88, 93, 98–100, 128, 130, 136, 137, 165, 171, 180, 193, 198, 200, 202n, 208, 209, 212, 215, 217–18, 235, 245, 250–1, 263, 265–6n, 268n
ego, 22, 91, 115, 218, 220, 241n, 245–6, 249, 261–2, 269n
  egoism, 80
Elwes, R. H. M., 177n
emanation, 178n, 213, 58
eminence, 154, 178n, 179n
emotion, 5–7, 16, 26n, 70, 148, 176–7n, 202–3n, 227–9, 251, 255–6, 264, 267n
empiricism, 6, 18, 32, 34–43, 47, 54, 56, 58, 59, 62n, 63n, 64n, 69, 74, 75, 77, 87, 95–6, 103n, 198, 218, 244
encounter (*rencontre*), 25, 37–40, 43–5, 47, 49, 51–2, 54–6, 59, 76, 82, 92, 101n, 111, 137, 143n, 171, 208–9, 223–4, 231–4, 236, 239n, 240–1n, 243
enemy, 8, 106, 109, 117, 122, 250, 252

Index

287

Index

Index